Components of Technical Writing

Components of Technical Writing

Susan Feinberg
Illinois Institute of Technology

Holt, Rinehart and Winston, Inc.
New York   Chicago   San Francisco
Philadelphia   Montreal   Toronto
London   Sydney   Tokyo

Acquisitions Editor: *Charlyce Jones Owen*
Developmental Editor: *Lisa Moore*
Senior Project Editor: *Lester A. Sheinis*
Production Manager: *Annette Mayeski*
Design Supervisor: *Gloria Gentile*
Text Design: *Caliber Design Planning, Inc.*
Cover Design: *Adaptation of an illustration by Tom Voss, La Jolla, California*

AND GLADLY WOLDE HE LERNE, AND GLADLY TECHE
GEOFFREY CHAUCER

To my husband, Barry,
who encouraged me every step of the way

Library of Congress Cataloging-in-Publication Data

Feinberg, Susan.
  Components of technical writing/Susan Feinberg.
    p. cm.
  Bibliography: p.
  Includes index.
  1. Technical writing. I. Title.
T11.F45 1988
808'.0666021—dc19   87-27869
                                CIP
ISBN 0-03-071576-8

Printed in the United States of America

9 0 1 2   090   9 8 7 6 5 4 3 2 1

Holt, Rinehart and Winston, Inc.
The Dryden Press
Saunders College Publishing

Preface

For the Instructors

This book attempts to do three things: to teach, to provide examples, and to offer advice based on current research and experience in the field. The modular approach allows you the flexibility of designing the course to suit your approach and your students' needs. You are invited to present the modules in the order you prefer and customize the course every semester you teach it.

Of course, I have tried to adopt a sequential approach to technical writing that begins at the beginning, with the reader in a rhetorical situation. The first five modules establish the components of technical writing. Following them, you may choose to teach letters and memos before proposals and oral presentations and interviews before case and design reports. In fact, because the modules are self-contained units, an engineering instructor collaborating with an English instructor, for example, should feel comfortable about assigning Module 11 on laboratory reports out of sequence because each module establishes its own objectives.

The modules offer extensive coverage of report types, with a variety of formats and ample student and professional examples. The text illustrates—and the exercises reiterate—the emphasis on audience analysis, design, and readability.

Students enter technical writing classes with a myriad of experiences. I am assuming students have had a freshman writing course and that they have dealt with invention and rhetorical devices before this course in technical writing. The process approach to writing used in this text is an attempt to help students sequence the steps in writing, a sequence of steps that is an algorithm for the organization of the thought process.

Fortunately, we are all taking a serious approach to technical writing. Students have heard the clear message that communication is important in their career, especially in their technical career. In this text, you will find major issues in technical writing explored in depth: Reader's tasks, information-gathering techniques, collaboration, readability, visual design, document evaluation are a few of the topics. Never before have we been in a better position to demand professional communication from our students and inspire them to persevere from the rough draft through the revision to the finished document.

For the Students

This book is intended to accompany you to your desk or to the computer when you begin to draft your technical report, proposal, or product evaluation. All of us are becoming more practical in our need to acquire information, and the tone of this textbook is prescriptive; the book offers plenty of advice and examples for you to follow. But you will also have choices in composing and designing, choices that will allow you to invent and manipulate documents. To produce your documents, you are invited to draw on your previous learning and on your technical expertise.

The modular approach of this text will help you with your writing tasks. A module is similar to a minicourse that establishes a clear purpose in terms of accomplishable objectives. Each module, or minicourse, uses instructions, illustrations, models, a summary, and a checklist. In fact, you may digest a module at your own pace because each module establishes an overall goal, identifies tasks to accomplish that goal, and provides some exercises to test your mastery. The tasks of technical writing you are practicing now are the communication skills you will use to advance your professional career. First, however, you should have an overview of the contents of this book.

What Is in This Book?

The book has 14 modules, each of which is self-contained although loosely connected to the others because of recurring components. But the first five modules are a unit of information, chunks to be digested as the components of technical writing.

Module 1 prepares you to gather information and use it in the documents you write. Instruction, experience, and research inform everything we write.

Module 2 introduces the theory behind clear and effective technical communication. To be clear and concise, I have to introduce some terms that we can use consistently. These terms are not difficult, but they provide us with a vocabulary that will let us discuss the components of technical writing. The components of audience, purpose, and design are introduced in this module, and the discussion about gathering information is expanded.

Module 3 introduces the thought processes and organizational strategies that help you sequence the steps in the writing process. These strategies are options to help you make decisions about how to present the data for the best results in a given situation. In other words, they are the strategies for the familiar reports you will write on the job.

Module 4 offers advice on how to write clearly. A clear style is a major component in the overall effect a document has on the reader; this overall effect is called readability. For most readers, the problem is not only in the writing but in the editing as well. This module describes a process for writing and editing for readability.

In Module 5, I present the design and illustration components that must be the concerns of writers as well as designers. Typography, layout, and visual aids influence readability and the kinds of decisions readers will make about the documents. The discussion of typography and layout uses terminology such as typeface and leading that insists on the importance of design as a factor in readability.

Modules 6 through 11 are chunked into a unit—the components of technical reports. These modules are self-contained and deal specifically with the strategies in 10 types of technical documents. The designs for these documents are flexible and may be adapted to any type of report writing you have to do. I have clearly explained the components that go into these designs.

Module 6 explains description of a mechanism, place, and process; Module 7 explains instructions and how to evaluate them; Module 8 describes proposals and progress reports; Module 9 discusses evaluation/feasibility reports and the secondary material that accompanies formal reports and proposals; case/assessment and design reports are the document types in Module 10; and research, laboratory, and field reports complete the unit in Module 11.

The components of professional communication fill the last unit. These modules deal with the complexities of letters and memos in Module 12, including the important résumé and job application letter. Many people who write on the job often have to distribute trip notes and minutes or notes from a critical meeting; Module 13 describes the components for reporting this professional information. In Module 14, I discuss oral presentations and interviews because so many professionals have to present their information verbally to others. These modules may be more appropriately placed earlier in the course, and the modular approach allows the flexibility of reordering the tasks.

Finally, the appendix presents a handbook on grammar, government style, and documentation from *The Chicago Manual of Style*.

An Instructor's Manual to go with the text may be obtained through a local Holt representative or by writing to the English Editor, College Department, Holt, Rinehart and Winston, 111 Fifth Avenue, New York, NY 10003.

Acknowledgments

My emphasis in this book is on the three resources that have contributed to my knowledge of technical writing: teaching, experience, and research. But the real resources behind my knowledge are the people. In teaching, I thank my colleagues: Robert Albrecht, who encouraged me to write the book and painstakingly read the first draft; Robert Irving, whose knowledge of verbal communication aided me in Module 14; Henry Knepler, who set an intellectual atmosphere for publishing; Barbara Mirel, whose critique of the entire manuscript went above the call of collegiality; Cheryl Price, who contributed her expertise to the section on library resources; and Joseph Williams, who inspired and read the module on style. I also want to thank my students who motivated, praised, and then generously lent examples so that others could benefit from their wisdom.

For my experience, I thank the many people who invited me to consult, to train, and to write in the technical writing profession: Joe Sorce, Chuck Cranford, Marilene Walker, Robert Thayer, and David Stringham, who are exemplars for those dedicated people working for the government; Linda Orr and Jerry Pogemiller for their insight into the importance of technical communication; Candace Frawley, who suggested the module on meetings and minutes; Sumner Katz, for sharing his expertise on writing proposals; and Sandra and Sherwin Pakin, whose professional attitudes toward computer documentation and document design inspired me to practice what I preached.

Finally, I thank the Society for Technical Communication and its members, who funded my research and provided me with articles written by experts; and the National Endowment for the Humanities, who initiated my research into document design and readability.

I would also like to thank the following reviewers who offered me invaluable advice: Carol H. Adams, Delaware Technical and Community College; Larry R. Andrews, Kent State University; Virginia A. Book, University of Nebraska, Lincoln; Suchindran S. Chatterjee, Tennessee State University; Barbara J. Craig, Del Mar College; William E. Evans, Bell Laboratories; Joyce Hicks, Valparaiso University; John W. Johnston, Tyler Junior College; David Kann, California Polytechnic State University; Jack Klug, San Antonio College; Bill Mowatt, West Valley Community College; Rose Norman, The University of Alabama in Huntsville; Gary A. Olson, University of South Florida; and Mark E. Rollins, Ohio University.

I could not have accomplished my goal without the help of my children, Leah and Joel, who managed for themselves while "Mom finished the book."

SF

Contents

UNIT 3

The Components of Professional Communication   383

U N I T 1

The Components of Technical Writing

M O D U L E 1

An Introduction

About This Book

This book is the outgrowth of my research, teaching, and experience in the field of technical writing. Research into the writing needs of a sample of people from the industrial and governmental sectors provided an initial foundation for the structure of this book. Teaching this material to undergraduate, graduate, and postgraduate students provided a dynamic environment to test the material for ease of learning, acceptability, and applicability. My experience as a document designer and consultant allowed me to update continually the content and the methodology to meet the needs of those who write on the job.

Research

In the initial research, a sample of communicators from industry, government agencies, and academia responded to a two-part survey that asked them what they thought colleges should teach in technical communication classes.[1] The first questionnaire asked them to list the topics that should be covered in a technical communication class. More than half of the respondents listed the first five topics as follows, and the rest were listed by about one-third of the respondents:

Topic
audience
editing/revising
formats/designs
word processing/text editing
grammar/usage
style
project management/planning
layout/illustration
printing/typesetting
organization
interview techniques

The communicators listed 33 topics in all, and on the basis of similarity of topics they even organized the topics into teaching categories. The categories they generated appear in Figure 1.1. In essence, these communicators expressed the idea that, in their experience, this material is what they need to understand, and it is what students will need to understand when they have to write in their fields.

Category 1	Category 2	Category 3	Category 4	Category 5	Individual Item Categories 6–11
Audience	Formats/ designs	Schedules and budgets	Oral presentation	Ethics	6 Interviewing
Editing/ revising	Word processing/ text editing	Planning/ project management	Platform presentation	Legal aspects	7 Indexing
Grammar/ usage					8 Data base/ research
Style	Graphics	Interfacing with team members			9 AV displays
Tone	Headings/ captions				10 Documentation/ testing
Jargon	Layout/ illustration	Problem analysis			11 Elements of technical writing
Diction	Typesetting/ print				
Reader-based prose					
Purpose					
Clarity					
Readability					
Knowing content					
Logic/ organization					

FIGURE 1.1 Teaching categories designed by communicators
Source: S. Feinberg and J. Goldman, "Content for a Course in Technical Communication: Results of a Survey," *Technical Communication* (1985). Reprinted with permission of the Society for Technical Communication.

Teaching

The next contribution to the book came from teaching technical writing. It is important to understand how students can learn to write technical documents. When we write, we must know something about the content. But how do we write? What is our composing process? There is a variety of writing techniques.

Perhaps you write in stages, moving from a prewriting or planning stage to a writing stage and then to a postwriting or evaluating stage and back to the planning and rewriting stages. Or you may prefer writing first almost as a brainstorming technique; you write to think, moving back and forth continually between writing, thinking, planning, evaluating, and rewriting.

Although almost all writing is a cyclical, or recursive, process, the process-oriented strategy of composing is an attempt to sequence the steps in writing. One such sequence is presented in the model in Figure 1.2.[2] The model is presented in a linear sequence for clarity's sake, but the steps are recursive.

This model incorporates many of the topics listed by the communicators and answers the question, How do we write?

Experience

Finally, experience modified the research and also contributed to the content and approach of this book. As a designer of documents, I learned that topics such as project management, interfacing with team members, and ethical and legal aspects are important factors in technical writing. For example, project management and interfacing with team members are part of the constraints of scheduling, interviewing, and collaborating on documents. Ethics and legal aspects may also constitute constraints on writing a document. After the document is completed, writers often become speakers who make oral presentations and use audiovisual displays. For these reasons, this text adds two other communication tasks—oral presentation and interviewing.

Technical writing encompasses a wide range of writing and provides us with examples that include the following:

style manuals	ads
procedures	reports
instructions	questionnaires
summaries	evaluations
policy	trip notes
proposals	letters/memos
descriptions	

You will find these writing experiences in this text, and you will be asked to practice them either as a complete document or as part of an assignment.

From this research, teaching, and experience, the content and the methodology for this book evolved.

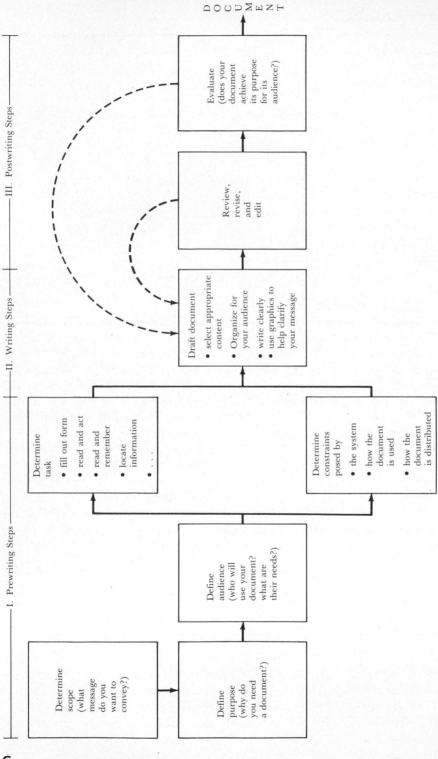

FIGURE 1.2 The process model of document design

Source: Dixie Goswami, Janice C. Redish, Daniel B. Felker, and Alan Siegal, *Writing in the Professions* (Washington, D.C.: American Institutes for Research, 1981). Copyright owned by the American Institutes for Research and the Document Design Center; and this material is used with permission.

About the Module Approach

A word about modules in general is appropriate here. A module is a self-contained unit that performs a specific task but supports the final product. The modules in this text perform specific tasks, tasks that support the major function of the text: writing clear, readable documents. Documents are the final product, and Modules 2, 3, 4, and 5 introduce the structural components used repeatedly to produce documents. They are building blocks for all documents. The remaining modules apply these components and augment them by illustrating their use. For this reason, you should study the first five modules as a unit and consult them frequently even when studying the rest of the modules. The remaining nine modules are self-contained so that you may take them up in any order relevant to the tasks you have to perform.

Each module has an overview of the components in that module, specific objectives, explanations and examples, and exercises. The modules help you write clear, readable documents.

Components for a Case

Most technical persons and managers have to write documents on the job. In fact, most people can tell you exactly what writing tasks they have to do most of the time. But these same people do not always consider the components of these writing tasks, components such as audience, purpose, design, or the role of revision. For example, Rick, a senior engineer with a company that manufactures business equipment, explains that his writing tasks fall most frequently into three categories: memos, letters, and reports.[3]

When Rick is asked to think about his writing process, he explains that his memos are informal because they are handwritten to other engineers in the company and are often followed by a verbal explanation. His letters are more formal because they communicate with suppliers, buyers, and a sales staff. These letters help Rick accomplish his job; he writes letters often, and frequently he writes five letters to complete a single project. Each letter accomplishes a different goal; Rick writes to

Letter 1: Request information about size, power requirements, work output, weight, price, and so on.
Letter 2: Request a unit to use as a test unit.
Letter 3: Suggest improvements to the unit on the basis of tests.
Letter 4: Respond to manufacturer's compromise on improvements.
Letter 5: Confirm acceptance of product.

Rick sends his most important writing to his superior. These are Rick's reports on the status of a design project, updates on negotiations with suppliers, explanations of test results, and proposals for acquiring new equipment. Essentially, these reports indicate that Rick is doing his job well. In explaining the importance of these reports, Rick summarizes the key components of technical writing: research the content, report information accurately, write clearly, and reach the audience you want to reach so that they arrive at your conclusion. "Sometimes," Rick adds, "you may have to reach the boss by reaching the conclusion the boss wants." The audience, the purpose, the content, the style—these are the components of technical writing.

How do you master these components? Some of the answers are complex; others are straightforward and practical. These modules provide a solution.

Notes

1. Susan Feinberg and Jerry Goldman, "Content for a Course in Technical Communication: Results of a Survey," *Technical Communication* 32:2 (1985): 21–25.
2. Dixie Goswami, Janice C. Redish, Daniel B. Felker, and Alan Siegal, *Writing in the Professions* (Washington, D.C.: American Institutes for Research, 1981): 142. Copyright owned by The American Institutes for Research and the Document Design Center, and this material is used with permission. The log and assignment in this book provided the model for the log and exercise in Module 1.
3. Keith Primdahl, "Case Study," Writing Workshop 425, Illinois Institute of Technology, 1986. This study provided the background material for the section on writing tasks.

Applying Your Knowledge

EXERCISE 1.1

In the example on page 7, Rick described his three major writing tasks: memos, letters, and reports. He was also aware of his readers; some were internal and others worked outside his company. A log of Rick's writing tasks appears in Figure 1.3. To appreciate the complexity of applying research and experience to the writing process, you should interview at least two people and ask them about the writing they do on the job.

Directions Interview two people from different occupations and work environments. For example, interview a state employee and a person working in a private firm. Or interview a person working in a not-for-profit organization and an employee of a large corporation. Go to the interview with specific objectives:

• Provide the writer with a log page and headings similar to the ones Rick used.
• Ask the writer to keep a log of the types of documents the writer produces in a workweek.
• Make arrangements to collect the completed log.
• Send a thank-you letter to the writer.

Writing Task	Audience	How Is the Document Drafted?	Is Revision Required?
Memos	Internal; usually other engineers	Handwritten, brief; often accompanied by a verbal explanation	Reread for accuracy; rarely revised
		Includes diagrams, blueprints, and so on	
Letters	External	Typed, block format	Revised for clarity, accuracy, spelling, and grammar
often bad news	Suppliers, sales reps	Often includes test data	
often persuasive	Suppliers, engineering staff		
Reports	Internal	Typed, block format	Revised for clarity, accuracy, spelling, and grammar
usually formal	Supervisor	Often includes test data, tables, graphs, schedules, and updates	Reviewed for compatibility of conclusions

FIGURE 1.3 Rick's log of writing tasks
Source: Adapted from Goswami et al., *Writing in the Professions* (Washington, D.C.: American Institutes for Research, 1981). Copyright owned by the American Institutes for Research and the Document Design Center, and this material is used with permission.

- After studying the log, prepare a report describing the writing tasks, the audience, and the drafting methods.

EXERCISE 1.2

Prepare a transparency of the writer's log, and present the information to the class.

MODULE 2

Audience, Purpose, Design: The Major Components

$\mathbf{T}$his module introduces you to three concepts underlying effective technical communication, concepts you must consider every time you write a technical document. These concepts are **audience, purpose,** and **design**. As you learn these concepts, you will begin to apply them to your writing.

Communicators in industry, government, and academia listed audience as the first topic in a course in technical communication. Knowing your audience and meeting their needs engage you in asking some questions about your readers before you begin to draft your document. These questions lead to the reasons why you are writing the document, the reasons that you articulate as the purpose for the document. And to make the purpose of the document clear to the reader, you will have to

- Gather your data.
- Select the content for your document.
- Organize the selected content.
- Write clearly.
- Plan layout and visuals.

In other words, you will have to design the document for the reader. It is difficult to indicate exactly where thinking and planning end and writing begins. The steps are recursive; that is, they require you to return to thinking and planning even after you have written. This process will involve you in a process-centered approach to writing that includes three parts:

- prewriting
- writing
- revising

Most writers agree that this three-part model is useful for discussion of the process, but in practice writers do not write in discrete stages. Writing is a generative process that moves cyclically through these parts.

     This module is only an introduction to the writing process and these important principles of technical writing. Your understanding of the process and principles will increase as each subsequent module builds on them.

Scope

In this module you will learn to

1. Apply three basic principles of technical writing.
2. Explain the difference in reader- versus writer-centered writing.
3. Determine the characteristics of your audience.
4. Write a clear purpose statement.
5. Gather information.
6. Consider factors that influence the design of a technical document.

Audience: Who Will Read Your Document?

Knowledge of the reader is so important that writers often use the formal term *audience* to refer to the types of readers who may be reading your documents. Is the reader a novice in the field, an expert, John Q. Public, a seventh-grader, a scientist, an insurance agent, an engineer, a clerk, a technician, an accountant? Or, are there two readers: the chief executive officer and the director of research for the laboratory? Briefly, to present technical information, you have to consider the background of the audience, their educational level, their experience, and their need to know certain kinds of information. In most cases, you will have to develop a design plan and a style to suit the background of your audience. How do you begin to analyze your audience?

Reader- Versus Writer-centered Writing

We often forget the reader when we begin to write because when we first learned to write in school, we were told to write about ourselves and what we knew. This emphasis on writing about ourselves often led to writing for ourselves as if we were the only readers of what we wrote. Of course, we were aware of writing for the teacher also. But somehow the teacher was an extension of ourselves, one who would try to understand our communication if we were sincere in our effort to express ourselves. This writer-centered writing makes the reader work hard to understand what we are trying to say.

Now, good technical writing insists that the writer work hard, and the burden of making the document comprehensible rests on the writer, not on the reader. All technical writing must be reader-oriented, not writer-oriented. The reader receives the writer's message without benefit of knowing the writer or the writer's ego. In fact, the writer of technical documents must understand the reader's background before beginning to write technical documents.

Can You Simplify the Analysis?

Sometimes we write for colleagues; other times we write for supervisors, clients, and members of the public who know less than we do about the subject. This means that our rhetorical stance—where we stand in relation to our audience—shifts depending on the audience. We may write the same information one way for our colleagues and another way for the public. Sometimes several readers with more than one background may be reading the same document, thus making it difficult to analyze our audience. Consider the organizational chart in Figure 2.1 and the backgrounds of the people in the various positions in the organization.

The chairperson and president communicate with each other, and both receive information from the vice president in charge of Administration and Purchasing. But it is obvious that the chairperson receives financial reports from the treasurer and comptroller, and the president oversees the operation of the technical division, receiving reports from the plant manager and the director of technical services. Whereas both the chairperson and the president are experts in their fields, because of their different backgrounds, you could not present technical information the same way for both readers. How do you handle this problem?

Let's take the simple solution first. Many technical writers simplify audience analysis by placing readers in three categories: the expert, the executive or general reader, and the technician.[1] Experts are readers with professional, technical, or scientific training and experience necessary to understand both detailed theory and technical terms. They are comfortable with the presentation of data in tables, charts, and graphs. However, in the workplace usually these experts are our colleagues; they work side by side with us, and we talk to them about our mutual work.

So, though we would be comfortable writing to these readers, we seldom have the need to write to them. Thus, in the workplace, we write to the other two categories of readers more frequently. The one exception when we do write for our own group of experts occurs in the writing we do for our professional journals, conferences, or seminars with our peers.

The executives or general readers are people reading outside their fields

Organization Chart

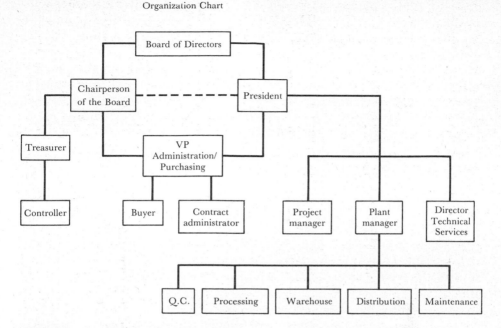

FIGURE 2.1 Organizational chart
Source: Sumner Katz, Contact International Corp. (Chicago, Ill.). Used with permission.

of specialization. These people will need definitions of specialized terms, as well as explanations by analogy or clearly labeled illustrations. The general reader reads to comprehend general scientific and technological concepts; the executive reads to make decisions for the company, to determine the significance of the work to the company, or to find out what action to take next or what to recommend.

The technicians may be readers who are first-time users of equipment and who need user-friendly documentation; or they may be experts in their craft, knowing how to install, repair, and operate various devices and systems. The experienced technicians may be more knowledgeable about technical terms than the general reader or the executive, but most technician-readers who are reading to acquire instructions to operate equipment or complete a task will benefit by an illustration or a diagram. All of us find ourselves in each one of these audiences: We are user-technicians when we learn the word processing system for the computer and general readers when we try to understand the big bang theory for the creation of the universe. We are executives when we decide what printer to purchase for the computer.

What Are Your Options When the Analysis Is Complex?

Although the categories of readers—expert, executive, general, technician— are convenient, they are not always practical. Complicating the question of audience is the reality of the workplace. Many writers write for the signature of directors above them. But the directors are not the primary audience because the document is going to leave the organization and go to a reader outside the company. Does the writer write to please the director or to inform the primary reader?

If you analyze the audience or audiences carefully, sometimes you will be able to please both the director and the reader without compromising the content or style of your document. To please the director, who is, after all, an agent of the company, you have to consider at least two factors:

- What are the stylistic idiosyncracies of the director or the company?
- What image does the company want to convey?
  —The company must provide accurate information.
  —The company must sell its product.
  —The company wants to promote its point of view.

Considering stylistic idiosyncracies, when you know that the director of the department dislikes the word *I* in a document because the Department of Strategic Planning doesn't represent a single opinion, then you can use the subject ("the department" or "the agency").

The company's image is important to the company and should be important to you. If you work for a telephone company, you are expected to sell the product. So, although the competition may have less expensive long-distance phone rates, your company offers more service. You are expected to promote the quality of the service as opposed to the expense of the long-distance rate.

To characterize your primary readers, you should consider their formal education, their experience, their reasons for reading or need to know the information, and their cultural backgrounds. To analyze the complex audience, before you begin to write, ask yourself some questions about your readers.

Some Questions You Should Ask Yourself to Help You Define Your Readers

1. How are the readers going to use the document? (Will they refer to it repeatedly as they would a reference manual? Will they read it once and take action?)
2. How much does the audience already know about the subject?
3. Is the reader external or internal to the organization? (If the reader is internal, are there idiosyncrasies to consider?)
4. Are there several audiences being addressed?
5. Does the educational background of the reader demand that you explain technical aspects?
6. Will the reader's age affect the reader's response (because of certain biases)?

7. How much does the reader usually read? (Should more graphics be used for this audience?)
8. Is the language new or familiar to the audience? (Consider native language, cultural differences, acronyms, or other shoptalk.)
9. What special needs or constraints do the readers have (physical handicaps, time constraints, prejudices)?
10. Will they need special equipment?

Looking at the example of the medical diary in Figure 2.2 (on p. 16), answer some of the questions about the reader/user of this diary. When you have considered the needs of your readers, you are ready to draft your document.

Purpose: What Will the Reader Learn?

Readers want to know why they should read a document, especially a technical one. They want to learn information, to act on information, to follow instructions, or to file information for future reference. To answer their question and focus their reading, you should usually state the *purpose* early in the document. Most of the time the writer has a task or an assignment, and the purpose statement presents the reason for writing the document. Sometimes the writer has a "hidden agenda," an unstated purpose that the writer hopes to accomplish either subtly or without the reader's actually knowing it. For example, in Module 1, Rick speaks of knowing the conclusion the boss wants him to reach. Rick may have the hidden purpose of wishing to please his boss, but the purpose Rick states in the document is

> In this report I compare the procedures for testing components and select the most efficient procedure.

Technical writing prides itself on being clear and accurate, but, like all writing, it is complex because it is a human activity.

The Clear Purpose Statement

A clear statement of what the writer proposes to write about, what the reader's task is, or what the document does is called the purpose statement. When the purpose statement is unclear or, worse, nonexistent, the document lacks focus. The reader does not know what the writer or the document is going to do. Remember that the document should be reader-centered, not writer-centered, and the purpose statement is an opportunity for the writer to explain the reason for the document. Such a statement may seem easy to construct, and it is, when the writer clearly knows what information the document

Patient Diary

How to Keep Your 24-Hour Diary:

A Holter electrocardiogram is a continuous tape recording of your heart's activity for periods up to 24 hours at a time. Your doctor ordered this test to determine exactly how your heart functions during your normal daily routine or prescribed activities.

Warning: *Do not* tamper with the recorder or disturb its action in any way. *Do not* pull the electrodes off or take a shower or bath or enter the water while wearing the unit.

Remember that your part of this procedure is important to ensure its success. Your doctor will interpret the results obtained from this recording according to your own medical history. During this recording, use your diary as follows:

1. Check the box corresponding to your activity and symptoms. If your activity or symptom is not listed, write your symptom or activity in the column under "other."
2. Record the time of day shown *on the recorder*. Remember to record A.M. or P.M., too.

Instructions: Fill in the following chart. Remember to record the time of day shown *on the recorder* (not the time on your watch or clock).

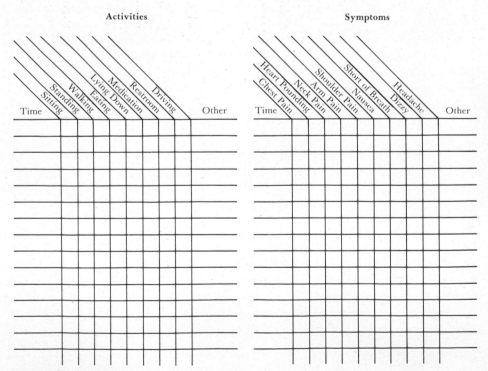

FIGURE 2.2 Patient's use of a diary

will present or what action the reader is being asked to take. Essentially, the purpose of the document may answer one or all three of these questions:

Is there a problem?
Why does the reader need a document?
How will this document assist the reader?

Although a clear purpose statement usually appears near the beginning of the document, it may be presented in several different ways. The examples illustrate purpose statements written from three different perspectives:

> *Example 1*
> This report presents the results of a study on the subject of xerography and describes the step-by-step instructions detailing a unique use for the Xerox 3107.
>
> *Example 2*
> In this booklet you will learn to use System/23.
>
> *Example 3*
> We wish to inform you of the procedures to follow for the Occupational Safety and Health Act (OSHA) inspection.

Example 2 uses the "you" scenario. The writer establishes a scenario or an outline with commentary for a sequence of events and speaks directly to the reader, addressing the reader as "you." Using the you scenario has advantages for both the reader and writer:

- You address the reader directly, involving the reader personally in the document.
- You explain to the reader the needs you are meeting.
- You help readers picture themselves in the situation.
- You explain the task to the reader, eliminating an explicit purpose statement. (For example: To lease space on government property, you should apply to the Region V Office of Government Property.)

The Precise Purpose Statement

When writing purpose statements, you must word the statement carefully. The investigator may have to test a piece of equipment, but the document presents the results of the test. As the writer, you would not say

> This document tests the respirometer.

but rather

> I tested the respirometer, and this report presents the results of the tests.

The writer may state the purpose in terms of what the writer will do, what the document will do, or what the reader will do.

(Writer will compare options against a single standard—cost.)

We present the results of our investigation comparing the cost-effectiveness of sending a computer terminal off-site for maintenance versus paying a systems engineer to repair the computer terminal on-site.

(Report presents the results of investigator's study.)
This report presents the results of a study to determine the cost-effectiveness of repairing a computer terminal on- and off-site.

(Reader will act on implicit purpose statement.)
In this practicum, you will learn to use the library resources.

(Writer explicitly wants to persuade the reader.)
Our purpose is to persuade headquarters that the PT 200 computer terminal is a more feasible choice for the Dallas office than the PST 100 terminal.

(Writer will evaluate and recommend.)
In this study we evaluate the PT 200 and PST 100 computer terminals and make a recommendation for the Dallas office.

(Report presents results of investigator's evaluation.)
This report explains why the PT 200 terminal is more appropriate than the PST 100 terminal for the Chicago office.

(Reader will act on implicit purpose statement.)
To apply for your tax return, enclose a self-addressed, stamped envelope with your tax form.

Questions to Ask Yourself About the Purpose of the Document

To arrive at a clear purpose statement, you might ask yourself the following questions:

1. Why does the reader need a document (to learn information, to act on information, to follow instructions, to use as a reference)?
2. Should I present the purpose in terms of what I (the writer) will do? (For example: I present the new design for your evaluation.)
3. Should I present the purpose in terms of what the document will do? For example: This report presents the results. . . . *or* This report explains why . . . is the best choice. [This style seems more objective to some readers.]
4. Should I present the purpose in terms of what the reader will do? For example: You will learn how to . . .

Design: Will You Present Information Clearly?

How can you present the information clearly so that your reader understands and learns quickly? First, you must, of course, gather the information and select the appropriate content. The remainder of this module helps you gather information and begin to design it. How you organize it, write it, and place it on the pages of the document are all components of design. Module 3 explains organization; Module 4 describes style; and Module 5 illustrates typography, layout, and visuals.

The appearance of the information on the page and the order in which the information appears—in the larger organization of the entire document and in the very sentences you write—are incorporated in the concept of design. But you must have the information to organize and design.

How Do You Gather Information?

When you gather your information, consider these resources:

* personal experience
* laboratory observation
* the library
* computerized information retrieval systems

Personal Experience and Related Resources

Frequently, you can collect information and material from people you know and situations in which you participate.

Interviewing

Interviewing and observing are ways of gathering information. Most experienced technical communication interviewers tell you to examine first everything that has been written or drawn on the subject. Then you can identify the information you need and select the person who is the best possible source for this information. If the project involves many people, you may wish to interview first the person with the overview of the project, perhaps the project manager or lead engineer.[2] During the interview you must be

* polite
* diplomatic
* persistent, continuously active in asking questions
* mentally ready to listen.

In technical communication, interviewing has become an important way to gather information. Modules 7 and 14 further explain interviewing.

Brainstorming

Critical reading and thinking influence the content and writing of your document. But you can't read everything and have every good idea. Brainstorming is a technique that influences critical thinking, provides information, and drives you back to more reading and forward to rewriting. After you or your group has defined the communication problem, you can gather in a group and generate ideas that are compiled without any judgments. One such technique is the **Nominal Group Technique**. It is a problem-solving or idea-generating method most effective when used with 8 to 10 participants and a facilitator.[3] The technique has five steps:

Nominal Group Technique
1. Facilitator presents problem statement.
2. Without discussion, each participant spends from 10 to 15 minutes writing ideas in response to problem statement.
3. Each person contributes one idea at a time in a round-robin, and the leader lists each on flip charts. No evaluation/judgment is given by the leader or a participant.
4. Each idea is discussed, some are combined, or new ideas are added.
5. Participants silently examine clarified items and are asked to vote on their top five ideas. The votes are tallied on the flip chart.

Surveys
Like the interview, surveys allow you to ask questions about people's needs and desires. These surveys are also called needs assessments and often take the form of a questionnaire the reader completes. By using a printed form to ask your questions, you can reach many more people with your survey. The introduction to this book describes two surveys. The first survey required 75 communicators to complete two questionnaires about technical communication. Figure 2.3 shows the instructions and the form for the questionnaire.

In the second survey, Rick, a senior engineer, completed a writer's log. This writer's log appears in the exercises in Module 1 and is in a form that you can distribute to other people who write on the job. From your surveys, you can examine your data and responses and draw conclusions.

Designing questionnaires is a specialized field that requires some knowledge. Modules 7 and 9 offer further advice on assessing needs and designing and evaluating questionnaires.

FIGURE 2.3 A questionnaire for communicators
Instructions for Completing the Form on Page 21
1. Place the first item in column 1.
2. If the second item is similar, place the second item in column 1. If unrelated, place the second item in column 2.
3. Continue to place each item in a column, using each item only once.
4. Create no more than eight columns.
5. Ask yourself, "Is this item related or similar to a previous item?" If so, place it in the same column as the related item; if not, create a new column up to a maximum of eight columns.

Example:	*Items*	*Column 1*	*Column 2*	*Column 3*
	1. Graphics	Graphics	Grammar	Interviewing
	2. Grammar		Usage	
	3. Usage			
	4. Interviewing			

Items	Column 1	Column 2	Column 3	Column 4	Column 5	Column 6	Column 7	Column 8
1. Style								
2. Graphics								
3. Word processing								
4. Grammar								
5. Audience								
6. Editing/revising								
7. Formats/designs								
8. Interviewing								
9. Planning/project management								
10. Knowing content								
11. Oral presentation								
12. Readability								
13. Layout/illustration								
14. Diction								
15. Tone								
16. Clarity								
17. Indexing								
18. Database/research								
19. Purpose								
20. Headings/captions								
21. Platform presentation								
22. Typesetting/printing								
23. Jargon								
24. AV displays								
25. Reader-based prose								
26. Documentation/testing								
27. Logic/organization								
28. Elements of technical writing								
29. Problem analysis								
30. Interfacing with team members								
31. Legal aspects								
32. Schedules & budgets								
33. Others								

FIGURE 2.3 (cont.)

21

Runway Road
R.R. #1 Box 347
Menominee, WI 60446
818/638-0136

January 4, 19XX

Dr. Pamela Debrowski
U.S. Water Quality Division
932 S. Randolph St.
Flint, MI 57234

Dear Dr. Debrowski:

As the supervisor of Blackhawk County, I have to report to the county Board of Directors. I have some questions about water quality. Your answers would help us plan our land use. Blackhawk County is studying the use of either the Eagle or Door River as a source of drinking water to relieve the depletion of wells. Our local water utilities have had some difficulties in treating sewage, and we have some concerns about landfill sites and the use of individual treatment systems as an alternative to septic systems.

1. What is the status of the federal goal for fishable, swimmable waters throughout the nation by 19XX? Are the following now in that condition: the Eagle River; the Door River; the Wisconsin, Illinois, and Michigan canals? Do the fishable, swimmable criteria apply to the entire length of such waterways or only to mixing zones three-quarters of a mile upstream and downstream of outfalls?

2. Is the Corps of Engineers currently involved in issuing permits for the discharge of foreign substances and pollutants into waterways? If so, what role does your division play in monitoring the discharge?

3. Please furnish a list of all pollutants and their current maximum limits, proposed standards, and so on, for drinking water and aquatic life. Are trihalomethanes also included in the standards? If not, we would appreciate reference material on this and other halogenated organics.

Thank you for providing us with this information.

Sincerely yours,

Frank Deeder
Supervisor, Blackhawk County

FIGURE 2.4 Letter of inquiry

Requests for Information

The letter of inquiry also allows you to ask questions, but these letters are tailored to the reader and request specific information. Unlike the written survey, the letter of inquiry is individualized and does not easily lend itself to gathering quantifiable data. The two most common letters of inquiry request information on a subject or ask an open-ended question to which the reader responds. Figure 2.4 illustrates a letter of inquiry that both asks an open-ended question and requests information.

Laboratory Observation

The laboratory can provide you with three sources of information:

- laboratory notes
- experimental data
- calculations

Your laboratory notes or notebooks record the methods you used to obtain results as well as sketches of the apparatus or product, a written description of the experiment or product, and the details of the daily events. From your notebooks you can organize your thinking and begin to focus your document.

To organize your thinking, you will find it a good idea to put your data into tables or graphs first. This compact, visual form will help you see implications and trends more vividly. But before you begin to write, the time to recheck your calculations is now. Nothing is more disheartening than to forecast a major breakthrough and discover you have made an error in your calculations.

The Library

The library is a resource that you should approach with a plan. You will need to spend a few hours acquainting yourself with this repository of information.[4]

1. Go to the reference desk or circulation desk and ask for a
   - *Guide to the library.* This guide will usually tell you whether your library uses the Library of Congress or Decimal Classification Numbers. With these letters and numbers you will then be able to find books shelved by subject. Figure 2.5 lists the Library of Congress and corresponding decimal classification numbers.

   - *Guide to the electronic card catalog, if available.* Many libraries now have information from their card catalog on a computer database. Figure 2.6 illustrates a guide to an electronic card catalog. With this database, you can search for books by author, title, or subject. The system will give you bibliographic, call number, and location information.

   - *Guide to an on-line search system for interlibrary loan, if available.* Libraries may also be members of a computerized circulation system providing

Library of Congress and Corresponding Decimal Classification Numbers

Subject	L.C.	Decimal	Subject	L.C.	Decimal
GENERAL WORKS	A	000	LAW	K	340
Encyclopedias	AE	030	EDUCATION	L	370
Periodicals	AP	050	History of	LA	370
Societies	AS	060	Theory and Practice	LB	371
Yearbooks	AY	040	Universities (U.S.)	LD	378
PHILOSOPHY	B	100	MUSIC	M	780
Logic	BC	160			
Metaphysics	BD	110	FINE ARTS	N	700
Psychology	BF	150	Architecture	NA	720
Ethics	BJ	170	Sculpture	NB	730
RELIGION	BL-BX	200	Graphic Arts	NC	740
			Painting	ND	750
HISTORY—			LANGUAGE	P	400
AUXILIARY SCI.	C	900	French	PC	440
Civilization	CB	901	Spanish	PC	460
Antiquities	CC	913	Italian	PE	450
Heraldry	CR	929	English	PE	420
Genealogy	CS	929	German	PF	430
Biography	CT	920	LITERATURE	P	800
HISTORY—			Classical	PA	870-880
OUTSIDE AMER.	D	900	General	PN	800-800
British	DA	942	French	PQ	840
French	DC	944	Italian	PQ	850
German	DD	943	Spanish	PQ	860
Classical	DE	913,930	English	PR	820
Greek	DF	938,949	American	PS	810
Italian	DG	937,945	German	PT	830
Russian	DK	947	SCIENCE	Q	500
Spanish	DP	946	Mathematics	QA	510
Asian	DS	950	Astronomy	QB	520
African	DT	960	Physics	QC	530
Oceanian	DU	990	Chemistry	QD	540
			Geology	QE	550
HISTORY—AMERICAN			Botany	QK	580
American—General	E	970	Zoology	QL	590
U.S.—General	E	973	Human Anatomy	QM	610
U.S.—Local	F	974-979	Physiology	QP	610
Outside the U.S.	F	980	Bacteriology	QR	610
GEOGRAPHY	G		MEDICINE	R	610
Physical Geography	GB	551			
Anthropology	GN	572	AGRICULTURE	S	630
Manners and Customs	GT	390	TECHNOLOGY	T	600
Sports and Games	GV	790	Chemical	TP	660
SOCIAL STUDIES	H	300	Photography	TR	770
Statistics	HA	310	Domestic Science	TX	640
Economics	HB-HJ	330	MILITARY SCIENCE	U	350
Labor	HD	331			
Commerce	HF	380	NAVAL SCIENCE	V	350
Finance	HG	332			
Sociology	HN-HX	300			
POLITICAL SCIENCE	J	320,350			
United States	JK	353			
Europe	JN	354			

FIGURE 2.5 Library of Congress and decimal classification systems

LUIS: LIBRARY USER INFORMATION SERVICE

   LUIS can be used to find BIBLIOGRAPHIC, CALL NUMBER, and
LOCATION information for materials held by Northwestern University
Libraries and by the Garrett/Seabury Library. (Use the card catalog
for materials not in the LUIS database.) CIRCULATION information is
currently available only for titles in the LUIS database which are located
in the main (except Transportation), music, and science engineering
libraries. Please inquire at service desk for circulation status of other
materials.

TYPES OF SEARCHES: COMMANDS:
- FOR INTRODUCTORY SCREEN FOR
                  TITLE SEARCHES: Type t
              AUTHOR SEARCHES: Type a
             SUBJECT SEARCHES: Type s
- FOR USERS ALREADY FAMILIAR WITH   Type t=, a=, s=, st=, or
  LUIS: sm=, followed by a SEARCH
  (To start a search from any screen) TERM (title, author, or sub-
                                    ject)

TO CORRECT A MISTAKE, type over the error or clear screen to start
over.
TYPE COMMAND AND PRESS ENTER
F1:Sav F2:NuSav F3:AscSnd F5:Recv F6:Send F8:DOS F9:Time F10:Parms
F12:Abort
  (to start a search from any screen)   followed by a SEARCH TERM
                                    (title, author, or subject)

TO CORRECT A MISTAKE, type over the error or clear screen to start
over.
TYPE COMMAND AND PRESS ENTER A.

TO SEARCH BY AUTHOR: EXAMPLES:
- TYPE a= followed by author's last   a = bellow
  name or portion of last name. Omit   a = shakespea
  accent marks.
- When last name is common, type com- a = johnson s
  plete last name followed by author's a = clarke a
  first initial.
- Authors may be organizations or   a = american hospital sup
  institutions.
- If correct form of name is not known,
  try alternate forms. Common variants a = de la mare a = calderon
  are these: de la
  —Use of prefix (varies by language). a = twain m
  —Pseudonyms (sometimes used).   a = organization a =
  —Variant spelling.   organisation

FIGURE 2.6 Electronic card catalog

IIT

LCS: A Brief Guide

LCS is an on-line circulation system providing access to over 25 academic libraries in Illinois. You can search the holdings of the Paul V. Galvin Library by following these instructions.

1. Initiating a Search

If You Know	Type This Command	Followed by These Letters		Remember To:	Examples:
Author and title	ATS/	4 letters (author's last name)	5 Letters* (first word of title)	Press return key	*The Immense Journey* by L. Eiseley ats/ eiseimmen
Title	TLS/	4 letters* (first word)	5 letters* (second word)	Press return key	*The Immense Journey* tls/ immejourn
Author	AUT/	6 letters (last name)	3 letters (first name)	Press return key	Loren Eiseley aut/Eiselelor
Call number of specific item	DSC/	Complete call number of a specific item		Press return key	dsc/573E36
Call number in specific area	SPS/	Call number (whole or part)		Press return key	sps/573E

FIGURE 2.7 Guide to an on-line search system

access to holdings in other libraries in the state or the region. Figure 2.7 illustrates a guide to an on-line search system. Using this search system, you can locate books in other libraries. But sometimes the electronic databases do not list all the material available, and it is important to use the card catalog.

2. Learn to use the card catalog. You can search for material in the card catalog by author, title, or subject. The information on the card tells you some details about the material. Figure 2.8 provides you with an illustration of a card as well as an explanation of the information on the card.

3. Ask professional librarians to explain some of the library's references and research resources.

Catalogs and Union Lists

Books in Print—complete guide to books printed in America

Cumulative Books Index—guide to books printed in English anywhere in the world

Scientific and Technical Books in Print

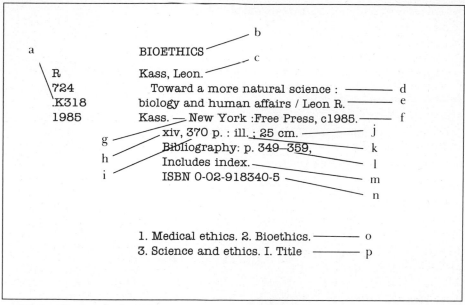

a. Dewey Decimal classification
number
b. subject entry
c. author
d. title
e. publisher
f. year
g. place of publication
h. introductory pages

i. text
j. size
k. illustrated
l. pages for bibliography
m. index notes
n. International Standard Book
Number
o. subject tracings (keywords)
p. access points (search by title)

FIGURE 2.8 Information from the card catalog

National Union Catalog
Guide to Microforms in Print

Selected Handbooks for Specialized Fields
Handbook of American Natural History
Handbook of Basic Economic Statistics
Handbook of Chemistry and Physics
Handbook of Latin American Studies
Handbook of Private Schools
Editor and Publisher Market Guide
Sources of Business Information
Information Sources in Biotechnology

Business and Industry Guides
Conan's Sources of Business Information
Daniell's Business Reference Sources

Business and Industry Guides *(continued)*
Moody's Investor's Service
Standard & Poor's Register of Corporations, Directors, and Executives
ValueLine
Thomas' Register of American Manufacturers

Specialized Dictionaries
Chambers Dictionary of Science and Technology
Dictionary of Technical Terms
A Dictionary of Scientific Units
The Penguin Dictionary of Science

Encyclopedias—General and Specialized
Encyclopedia Americana
Encyclopaedia Britannica
Collier's Encyclopedia
Cowles Encyclopedia of Science
Harper Encyclopedia of Science
McGraw-Hill Encyclopedia of Science and Technology
Van Nostrand's Scientific Encyclopedia

Bibliographies for Reference Books
American Reference Books Annual
A Guide to Reference Books—Eugene P. Sheehy
Walford's Guide to Reference Materials (entries dealing with science and
     technology)

Reviews
Book Review Digest
Book Review Index
Microform Review
Index to Scientific Reviews
Technical Book Review Index

Periodical Indexes (for information on magazines and journals)
Ayer Directory: Newspapers, Magazines, and Trade Publications
Chemical Abstracts Service Source Index (CASSI)
Ulrich's International Periodicals Directory

General Magazine Indexes
Reader's Guide to Periodical Literature
Magazine Index

Professional Journals—Indexes
Accountant's Index
Applied Science and Technology Index
Bibliography and Index of Geology
Biological and Agricultural Index
Business Index
Business Periodicals Index

Cumulative Index to Nursing Literature
Current Index to Journals in Education
Engineering Index
General Science Index
Humanities Index
Index Medicus and *Abridged Index Medicus*
Index of Economic Journals
Index of Legal Periodicals
Natural History Index-Guide
Predicasts F & S Index
Pandex Current Index to Scientific and Technical Literature
Science Citation Index (reference sources cited in footnotes and bibliographies)
Social Sciences Index

Professional Journals—Abstracting (journals that serve the same purpose as indexes but give a summary of each article)
Abstracts and References on Electrical Safety
Agricultural and Horticultural Engineering Abstracts
Animal Breeding Abstracts
Chemical Abstracts Service Source Index (CASSI)
Economic Abstracts
Electronics Abstracts
Forestry Abstracts
Geological Abstracts
Geoscience Abstracts
*Library of Congress Guide to the World's Abstracting and Indexing Services in Science
    and Technology*
Mechanical Engineering Abstracts
Metals Abstracts
Nutrition Abstracts and Reviews
Owen and Hanchey's Abstracts and Indexes in Science and Technology
Psychology Abstracts
Science Abstracts: Computer and Control
Social Science Abstracts
Sociological Abstracts
Wildlife Abstracts

Indexes of Government Publications
Andriot Guide to U.S. Government Publications (short guide)
Congressional Information Service
Cumulative Subject Index to the Monthly Catalog of U.S. Government Publications
Energy Research Abstracts
Government Reports Announcements and Index
Index to the U.S. Government Periodicals
Monthly Catalog of United States Government Publications
Selected U.S. Government Publications (A monthly supplement to the *Monthly
    Catalog*)

Guides to Using Government Publications
Government Publications and Their Use—L. F. Shmeckebier and R. B. Eastin
Subject Guide to Major United States Government Publications—Ellen Jackson
Introduction to United States Government Publications—Joe Morehead

Fact Books and Specialized Sources
American Statistics Index
Council on Planning Librarians
ERIC
Rand Abstracts
Statistical Abstract of the United States (a yearbook for important statistics published by U.S. Bureau of the Census)
World Almanac and *Book of Facts*

Selected Atlases
Atlas of the Cereal-Growing Areas in Europe
Goode's World Atlas
The Rand McNally Commercial Atlas and Marketing Guide

Newspaper Indexes
Christian Science Monitor
New York Times Index
Times of London
Wall Street Journal Index

Computerized Databases
BRS Information Retrieval Services
Computerized Information Service
Dialog Information Retrieval Services
LEXIS—law
OCLC—interlibrary loan
Vutext—newspapers
Westlaw—law

The completed Checklist for Research shows the possible resources for a specific topic.

Checklist for Research Consultation

Topic: "The ethics of bioengineering." This topic is not specific enough. You should be able to state a well-defined research topic in a complete sentence. A more precise topic might be this: "What are the ethics of bioengineering in research in universities and businesses? How much research is done? What types of research are done? What is the ethical reaction of people to this research?"

Card Catalog: Check the Library of Congress Subject Headings books for these terms used for subject headings:

       Bioengineering   Human Engineering
       Bioethics   Human Genetics—Moral and
       Bioethics—Bibliography   Religious Aspects
       Biomedical Engineering   Human Genetics—Social Aspects

Handbooks, Manuals, and Guides
      Information Sources in Biotechnology, 2d ed. (New York: Stockton Press,
          1986).
Dictionaries and Directories
      Encyclopedia of Bioethics
Encyclopedias
      McGraw-Hill Encyclopedia of Science and Technology
Bibliographies
      Bibliography of Bioethics
      Bibliography of the Philosophy of Technology
Indexes and Abstracts
      Reader's Guide to Periodical Literature (very general articles on the ethics
          of bioengineering).
      Index Medicus (articles that are medically oriented).
         Use the term *bioethics* when checking the indexes.
      Philosopher's Index (articles of a more philosophical and value-oriented
          approach)
         Use the terms *biology* and *genetics*.
      Public Affairs Information Service Bulletin (Articles are oriented toward
          public policy.)
         Use the terms *biotechnology* and *genetic research*.
These indexes will lead you to a variety of journals. Journals such as
      Annals of Biomedical Engineering incorporating
      Journal of Bioengineering
      Annual Review of Biophysics and Bioengineering
      Applied Biochemistry and Bioengineering
      Biotechnology and Bioengineering
are only a few of the journals you will discover in the course of checking
for journal articles.
Government Publications, Technical Reports, and Proceedings
      Monthly Catalog—Check the headings under "Genetic Engineering." In
         1981 the Library of Congress published a bibliography entitled
         "Biotechnology."
      National Technical Information Service—Check the heading "Bioengineer-
         ing" for research reports.
Statistics
      American Statistics Index—Check the headings "Biomedical Engineering"
         and "Genetics."
Dissertations—These resources tend to be so specific in researching a topic
    that it is best to leave this search to the researcher.
Others—One resource such as the card catalog will lead to other sources,

such as handbooks and directories. The research process tends to build on itself.

After using some of these references in the library and gathering information, you will certainly need to cite some of your sources. If you quote material, use data, paraphrase ideas, or copy visuals, you must cite your sources. Style guides provide you with the models to document your sources. You should examine the style guides in your field to see how authors document their text. In general, citations include

For a Book	**For an Article**
author's name	author's name
book title	title of article
volume number	name of periodical
edition, if reprinted	volume number
city of publication	date
publisher's name	pages
date of publication	

Appendix A illustrates the proper format for documentation as established in *The Chicago Manual of Style*, one of the most popular general style guides. The following list will help you find some style guides for citations in special fields.

Style Guides—General Formats

American National Standards Institute. *American National Standard for Bibliographic References*, 1977.

Modern Language Association. *MLA Handbook*, 1984 (for the humanities).

Trelease, Sam F. *How to Write Scientific and Technical Papers*. Cambridge, Mass.: MIT Press, 1969.

Turabian, Kate L. A. *A Manual for Writers of Term Papers, Theses, and Dissertations*. 5th ed. Chicago, Ill.: The University of Chicago Press, 1987.

University of Chicago Press. *The Chicago Manual of Style*, 13th ed., 1982.

U.S. Government Printing Office. *GPO Style Manual*, rev. ed., 1984.

Style Guides—Formats for Specialized Fields

American Bankers Association. *Publication Style Manual for Authors and Editors*, 1986.

American Chemical Society. *Handbook for Authors of Papers in the Journals of the American Chemical Society*, 1978.

American Institute of Physics. *Style Manual*, 1978.

American Mathematical Society. *Manual for Authors of Mathematical Papers*, 1980.

American Medical Association. *Stylebook/Editorial Manual*, 1976.

American Psychological Association. *Publication Manual of the American Psychological Association*, 1983.

Council of Biology Editors. *CBE Style Manual*, 1978.

Engineers Joint Council. *Recommended Practice for Style of References in Engineering Publications*, 1977.

U.S. Geological Survey. *Suggestions to Authors of Reports of the U.S. Geological Survey*, 1978.

Computerized Information Retrieval Systems

Supplementing the library and the electronic card catalog searches are the databases accessed through computers or terminals. These databases are collections of documents, abstracts, patents, and statistics archived in an electronic form. Figure 2.9 shows a partial list of databases you can access through an information retrieval system.

Databases are helping us manage the information explosion by allowing us to search for information at electronic speeds. Computerized information retrieval systems can save you days or even weeks of traditional library search time. With access to a computerized database, you can search for and retrieve information in seconds. This explanation introduces you to the general concept and power of information retrieval systems but does not attempt to instruct you in using the specifics of any one system. The manuals accompanying the systems will instruct you in the use of the systems.

Using DIALOG as a model of a database supplier, once it is connected, you type your user's number and password into the computer. You then

Databases
Chemical Industry Notes
Chemical Regs and Guidelines System
Chemlaw
Chemname
Chemsearch
Chemsis
Chemzero
Child Abuse and Neglect
Chronolog Newsletter
CIS
Claims/Citation
Claims/Class
Claims/Compound Registry
Claims/Uniterm
Claims/U.S. Patents
Claims/U.S. Pat ABS Weekly
Coffeeline
Commerce Business Daily
Compendex
Comprehensive Dissertation Index
Conference Papers Index
Congressional Record Abstracts
Criminal Justice Periodicals Index
CRIS/USDA
D and B—Dun's Market Identifiers

FIGURE 2.9 Partial list of databases

```
B 195
        11jan87 19:41:15 User100973
   $0.96    0.032 Hrs File1
   $0.25  Dialnet
   $1.21  Estimated cost this file
   $1.21  Estimated total session cost   0.031 Hrs.

File 195:Commerce Business Daily - 861001-870109
```

FIGURE 2.10 Cost of using a database

enter the name of the database you wish to search. The system responds with the cost of using this database and the total cost of the session to this point, as illustrated in Figure 2.10.

Then, by typing commands and keyword terms on the terminal keyboard and transmitting them to the computer, you enter into a dialogue with the retrieval system. If you assume that a term is searchable in the database, then you type the command to select the term. You can even select several terms related to each other and combine them by using <**AND, OR, NOT**>. For example, if you want information on writing manuals for the government, and you type the command **SS MANUALS**, the system will respond with all the manuals listed in its database, a total of 331 manuals. If you want only those manuals related to writing, then you would use the logical operator **AND** to relate MANUALS to WRITING.

     ?SS MANUALS AND WRITING

SS is the command to DIALOG to search for manuals dealing with writing. DIALOG responds with the fact that there are 28 listings on MANUALS AND WRITING. The system responds with the number of citations for that set of terms, as displayed in Figure 2.11.

As you can see, using two terms and a logical operator has focused the search on just 28 of the 331 records. You could narrow the search even further by using logical operators and more search or key words, but this may not be necessary for your needs.

After you look at the number of citations, you can have the system display the records on your computer or terminal screen by using the TYPE

```
                    Set   Items   Description
                    ---   -----   -----------
              ?SS MANU7ALSUALS
                    S1      331   MANUALS
              ?SS MANUALS AND WRITING
                    S2      331   MANUALS
                    S3     2862   WRITING
                    S4       28   MANUALS AND WRITING
```

FIGURE 2.11 Citations from the database

command and the number of the set you wish to display. For example, in the next illustration, Figure 2.12, the system responds to the command

> ?TYPE 4/6/1-28

The TYPE command tells DIALOG to list on your computer or terminal screen the records indicated in the sequence of numbers

```
?TYPE 4/6/1-28

 4/6/1
1629198
   OPEN-END TITLE I AND II A-E SERVICES

 4/6/2
1626909
   MARINE MAGNETOMETER SYSTEM

 4/6/3
1625951
   SPACE STATION WORK PACKAGE 1 (WP01)

 4/6/4
1624977
   UNDERSEA WARFARE OPERATING GUIDELINES DEVELOPMENT

 4/6/5
1624477
   DIGITAL  EQUIPMENT CORPORATION (DEC) PERIPHERALS AND DIAGNOSTIC PROGRAMS
OR EQUAL NASA/GSFC

 4/6/6
1624465
   DATA SYSTEM,
```

FIGURE 2.12 List of titles from the database

4/6/1-28

The number 4 stands for the set you want to review; the number 6 stands for the format in which you want the records to appear (6 = short title; 5 = full record). The last two numbers request the number of records you wish to review, in this case all 28 records.

If you want a paper or "hard" copy of the citation printed and mailed to you from the system's office, you can type a PRINT command instead of TYPE and the printout is mailed to you, usually the same or next day. You may want this service when there is a large amount of material to be printed and you don't want to remain connected to the database any longer.

If you have a printer attached to your terminal, you can have your printer print the information from the screen by using the TYPE command. When you type

　　?TYPE 4/5/18

your printer will print the complete record number 18 from set number 4, as illustrated in Figure 2.13.

Finally, when you have all the information you need from the database, you must LOGOFF the system to stop the accounting record. The LOGOFF command also shows estimated cost for the search, as it does in Figure 2.14.

In summary, when you begin to gather information for the content of your document, you will want to consider personal experience, laboratory observations, the library, and computerized information retrieval.

```
 4/5/18
1590714
   COMPUTER   ASSISTED   INSTRUCTIONAL   SYSTEM  M67004-87-R-0047.   Closes
12-29-86.  Contract  Specialist:  Walt  Fisher  (Code  908),  912/439-6745.
Contracting Officer: D Sanford Wills (Code 908). IAW statement o0 work. All
offerors    must    satisfactorily   perform   an   operational   capability
demonstration/live  demonstration  test  at  the Marine Corps Communications
Electronics  School  (MCCES),  29  Palms,  CA,  10  days  after  receipt  of
proposals  to  be considered for award. The computer assisted instructional
system  shall  be  used to design and develop training courses and to train
students.  Total  requirements  consist  of  providing  all required system
hardware  and  software  including  installation, maintenance, training and
training  materials,  systems  manuals  and  documentation.  Indefinite qty
contract  shall  result.  Contract  life  one  year from acceptance of last
ordered  system/equipment.  Delivery  orders  shall require initial 120-day
delivery  of  systems,  90-day  delivery  for additional system hardware or
software.  Request  for  sol  must be in writing, Attn: Code 905-E, Saundra
Beaver.  All  responsible  sources  may  submit  an  offer  which  will  be
considered. (311)
   SPONSOR:  Contracts  Div,  PO Drawer 43018, Marine Corps Logistics Base,
Albany, GA 31704-5000
   SUBFILE: PSU (U.S. GOVERNMENT PROCUREMENTS, SUPPLIES)
   SECTION  HEADING:  70  General Purpose ADP Equipment Software, Supplies
and Support Eq.
   CBD DATE: NOVEMBER 13, 1986            ISSUE: PSA-9215
```

FIGURE 2.13 Abstract from a database record

How Do You Draft the Document?

After you have gathered your information, what will you include in the document? In other words, how do you select the content, organize it, write it, and lay it out with graphics? The answer, of course, cycles back to the three concepts: audience, purpose, and design. Drafting a document is like throwing a pot on a potter's wheel. Figure 2.15 (p. 39) illustrates this cyclic process of shaping communication.

Computer Technologies Help

The computer technologies available today are transforming the three parts of the writing process to

- prewriting
- writing
- revising and shaping.[5]

In the prewriting stage, you can alter prescribed structures, change headings, consider type size and style, and research computer graphic capabilities. In the writing stage, even with the computer technology, it is best to focus on content and organization, leaving design to the third stage. In revising, you can automatically

- Move and replace sections of text.
- Redefine pages.
- Create indexes and a table of contents.

```
?LOFFGOFF HOLD
        11jan87 19:55:05 User100973
    $12.47    0.231 Hrs File195
            $0.00   6 Types in Format   5
            $0.00  50 Types in Format   6
    $0.00  56 Types
    $1.84  Dialnet
    $14.31  Estimated cost this file
    $15.52  Estimated total session cost   0.262 Hrs.
Logoff: level 11.8.13  B  19:55:05


DIALNET: call cleared by request
```

FIGURE 2.14 Ending a database search

In shaping, you can select these:

- page size
- headers and footers
- type font
- page numbering
- boxed items
- justified or ragged margins

But whether you use computer technology or typewriters, you will have to design your document. Module 3 on organization explores two essential elements of document design: selecting information and organizing information.

Finally, the design of a document depends on the audience and the purpose of the document. The order, style, layout, type, and visuals assist the reader in understanding the document.

A Team Effort

When the communication project is large, a team may produce the final product. Collaborating on these large projects requires project planning, outlining, and writing.[6] A manager selects a team (preferably a technical expert, an instructional designer, a writer), and the team

Collects information.
Outlines the content and the order.
Establishes format, size, and graphics.
Schedules writing and editing.
Produces the document.

Whether you write individually or collaboratively, the document you design should meet your reader's needs and fulfill the purpose of the document.

Summary

Audience, purpose, and design are concepts that influence all technical communication. An audience analysis includes cultural background, educational level, experience, and need to know information. The writing must be reader-oriented, but the readers may be quite diverse. To simplify audience analysis, many writers place readers in three categories: expert, executive or general reader, technician. When the writing is for the signature of another person, the writer may have to please two entirely different readers.

The purpose of a document is stated early because readers want to know why they should read the document. Sometimes a writer can have a *hidden agenda*, an unstated purpose for the document. But most documents state what the writer proposes to do, what the reader's task is, or what the document does. When the writer speaks directly to the reader and places the reader in the situation involving a sequence of events, the writer is using the *you scenario*, an effective way to communicate with the reader.

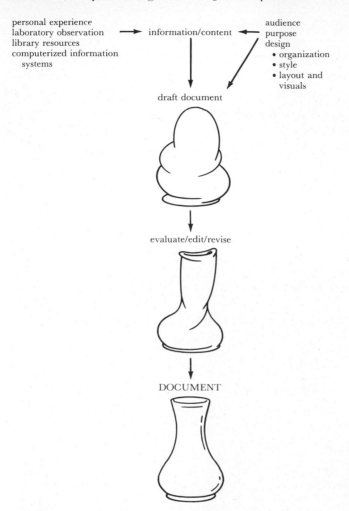

personal experience
laboratory observation → information/content ← audience
library resources   purpose
computerized information   design
systems   • organization
                             • style
                             • layout and
                               visuals

draft document

evaluate/edit/revise

DOCUMENT

FIGURE 2.15 Shaping the document

Design helps the writer present the information clearly and efficiently. After gathering information from personal experience (interviewing, brainstorming, surveys, letters of inquiry), laboratory notes and data, library resources, and computerized databases, writers use design to organize the document and shape it. Computer technology provides many design options, including automatic remove and replace features and typography choices, as well as computer graphics and page headers/footers. Design must be considered at the time the document is drafted because that is the time the document begins to take shape. When the communication project is large, a team may produce the document. A technical expert, a writer, and a designer should collaborate from the beginning of a large project to produce the final document.

Checklist for Audience, Purpose, and Design

These three concepts are important for every stage of the writing process and for the final product. Check those items that apply to the document you are drafting.

TO CONSIDER YOUR AUDIENCE, DID YOU

1. Analyze the reader's

_____ cultural background?

_____ education?

_____ experience?

_____ reason for reading or need to know?

_____ special constraints such as foreign language, handicap?

_____ position in relation to you, such as your supervisor?

_____ 2. Plan to write for several audiences?

3. Categorize the reader as

_____ expert?

_____ technician?

_____ executive/general?

_____ 4. Use a reader-oriented style, such as a *you scenario*?

TO STATE THE PURPOSE CLEARLY, ARE YOU

_____ 1. Explaining your reason for writing the document?

_____ 2. Telling your readers what the document will do for them?

_____ 3. Describing the document's communication purpose?

TO DESIGN THE DOCUMENT, HAVE YOU

1. Gathered information through

_____ personal experience?

_____ laboratory observations?

_____   library resources?

_____   computerized databases?

_____   2. Used computer technology?

_____   3. Collaborated with other people on the writing project?

Notes

1. Juanita Williams Dudley, *A Text-Workbook for English 421—Technical Writing* (West Lafayette, Ind.: Purdue Research Foundation, 1978): 15–16.
2. Craig C. Dennison, "The Effective Interview—An Important Tool," in *Proceedings*, 33d International Technical Communication Conference (Washington, D.C.: Society for Technical Communication, 1986): 381. This article provided background material for the section on interviewing.
3. Diane J. Harvego, "Measuring Productivity: A Preliminary Assessment," in *Proceedings*, 33d International Technical Communication Conference (Washington, D.C.: Society for Technical Communication, 1986: 133–134.
4. Cheryl A. Price, reference librarian, Galvin Library, Illinois Institute of Technology. Ms. Price expertly supervised and arranged material for the section on library resources and provided the example of the checklist for research.
5. Kathleen Doty, "Redefining the Writing Process: The Integration of Form and Content," in *Proceedings*, 33d International Technical Communication Conference, (Washington, D.C.: Society for Technical Communication, 1986): 425. This article provided background material for the section on computer technologies.
6. Adele T. Jones and Paul C. Jennings, "Analysis of the Process of Writing Structured Documentation in a Team Setting," in *Proceedings*, 33d International Technical Communication Conference (Washington, D.C.: Society for Technical Communication, 1986): 393–396. This article provided background material for the section on team writing.
7. Henry James, *Notebook*, F. O. Matthiessen (ed.) (Magnolia, Mass.: Peter Smith Publications, 1984).
8. Wilson Y. Gateley and Gary G. Bitter, *Basic for Beginners* (New York: McGraw-Hill, 1970): 12.
9. The Notebooks of Leonardo Da Vinci, compiled and edited from the original ms. by Jean Paul Richter, Vol. 1 (New York: Dover Publications, 1970): 145.
10. Barry N. Feinberg, *Applied Clinical Engineering* (Englewood Cliffs, N.J.: Prentice-Hall, 1986): 1.

11. Alice S. Culbert, "Getting Started on the Vax," Technical Writing 421, Illinois Institute of Technology, 1983.
12. Paul D. Leedy, *Practical Research*, 3d ed. (New York: Macmillan, 1985). The practicum in this book provided the model for the library exercise.

References

Annette N. Bradford and Merrill D. Whitburn, "Analysis of the Same Subject in Diverse Periodicals: One Method for Teaching Audience Adaptation," *The Technical Writing Teacher* 9 (1982): 58–64.

Herman A. Estrin, "The Teaching of Technical Writing: Fascinating, Fulfilling, and Rewarding," *The Technical Writing Teacher* 10 (1983): 167–173.

J. H. Potvin, R. H. Brock, and E. S. Pape, "Computer Searches Teach Research Methods in Technical Writing Courses," *Technical Communication* 13:3 (1981): 14–19.

Donna M. Hamlin and Craig Harkins, "A Model for Technical Communication," *Journal of Technical Writing and Communication* 13 (1983): 57–81.

Applying Your Knowledge

EXERCISE 2.1

Consider the passages that follow. In each passage, is the author writing for the reader or for the writer? State reasons for your opinion.

1. In pursuance of my plan of writing some very short tales—things of from 7,000 to 10,000 words, . . . I began yesterday the little story that was suggested to me some time ago by an incident related to me by George du Maurier—the lady and gentleman who called upon him with a word from Frith, an oldish, faded, ruined pair—he an officer in the army—who unable to turn a penny in any other way, were trying to find employment as models. I was struck with the pathos, the oddity and typicalness of the situation—the little tragedy of good-looking gentlefolk, who had been all their life stupid and well-dressed, living on a fixed income, at country-houses, watering places and clubs, like so many others of their class in England, and were now utterly unable to do anything, had no cleverness, no art or craft to make use of as a "gagne-pain"—could only show themselves, clumsily, for the fine, clean, well-groomed animals that they were, only hope to make a little money by—in this manner—just simply being.[7]

2. This chapter will acquaint you with a typical remote terminal used in a time-sharing computer system and with some of the mechanics and vocabulary needed to converse with the computer.

   The use of the word "typical" is regrettable but necessary. We noted in Chapter 1 the existence of many different dialects of BASIC, and we must here note the existence of several different kinds of terminals and sets of "system commands," the vocabulary used when communicating with the computer.[8]

3. The Mirror

   If the illuminated object is of the same size as the luminous body and as that in which the light is reflected, the amount of the reflected light will bear the same proportion to the intermediate light as this second light will bear to the first, if both bodies are smooth and white.[9]

4. The Hospital as a System

It is not the purpose of this section to discuss fully the organizational arrangement of a hospital or other health care facility. However, because Clinical Engineers must function within such a system it is important that they have some awareness of the complexity of the facility in which they work. While there are manifold variations of the organizational chart of any hospital, the general arrangement is given in Figure 1-1.[10]

EXERCISE 2.2

The following portions from documents are addressed to different audiences. Using the three categories of readers—expert, executive, technician—identify the audience for each portion.

A. Conclusions

Methanol concentrations up to 40 percent (v) had no significant effect on the film persistency of KG-35 in synthetic brine. Methanol concentrations of 70 percent (v) slightly reduced the integrity of the film coating. Neat methanol apparently destroys the KG-35 film integrity.

B. The American Dietetic Association (ADA) is publishing and distributing to professionals the publications *Food 2* and *Food 3* developed by the USDA. These publications offer easy-to-read food guides that emphasize low-salt, low-cholesterol, low-fat cooking. These are excellent low-cost, consumer-oriented publications that would be easily adapted to product promotion. The private sector could make these books, developed by government agencies and endorsed by a professional organization, available to the general public.

C. To Produce a Report Using EDT (by Alice S. Culbert)[11]

Equipment: Computer terminal
        Booklet "Getting Started on the VAX"
Materials: Paper
        Pencil
        Rough draft of report

Note: The report may be composed on the computer. However, composing on the computer uses up your computer budget.

To log in

1. Push BREAK key.
2. Push RETURN key two or three times. Repeat if necessary. Within two minutes the computer responds "Enter class"
3. Type VAX (or vax) <cr>, where <cr> represents the carriage RETURN. "Vax class start:"
4. Push RETURN (symbol <cr>). The computer requests "Username:"
5. Type HUM421name <cr>, using your last name instead of "name." Use no spaces. The computer responds "Password:"

EXERCISE 2.3 ═══════════════════════════════

Write an appropriate purpose statement for each of the following scenarios. You may write the statement as the writer's purpose, the reader's task, or the document's communication purpose.

1. You have studied the benefits and disadvantages of building a hospital on a forest preserve site. The hospital will bring in more revenue, but the timber stand also has a financial value. The hospital provides health services, but visiting the forest preserves also has a health value. On the whole, the community already has enough health facilities. Now you are ready to write the purpose statement for your report to the Village Board of Directors.

2. In your laboratory some components for the high-pressure liquid chromatograph recently developed mechanical difficulties. The president of your company, Mr. Desmond, asked you to investigate the economics of repair compared to replacement and to send him your evaluation. You have determined that it would be unwise to repair the chromatograph because of its age. Instead, you think that the company should buy a new chromatograph. Now write the purpose statement for your memo to Mr. Desmond.

3. The first thing you have to do in the laboratory this morning is test the Photovolt Aquatest II, Model 702 (serial no. 2453). You test the instrument and find that it is giving erratic readings. You think it will have to be repaired or replaced. Write a note in your laboratory notebook reminding yourself to tell the laboratory director that the Aquatest test device is faulty. Then write the purpose statement for a memo to your laboratory director, telling her about your findings.

4. Universal Transport is considering the purchase of an automated reservation system for passengers and freight. The company has asked you, an independent computer consultant, to evaluate its needs. You determine that the company is growing and expanding its services. However, the management staff has little or no knowledge of computers and needs assistance in selecting and operating the appropriate system. You can recommend two alternatives. The company can purchase its own computer system, or it can purchase time on a reservation service from a large trunk carrier. To the business manager of the company, write the purpose statement for your report containing your recommendations.

EXERCISE 2.4 ═══════════════════════════════

Identify the following purpose statements by indicating whether they are written as the writer's purpose, the reader's task, or the communication purpose of the document.

1. This manual instructs the user in (a) how to log on to a PST 100 terminal, (b) how to operate the terminal, and (c) how to maintain the terminal.
2. In this study I evaluate the "user friendliness" of the PST 100 terminal.
3. The purpose of the memo is to inform you of the superfund policies regarding reimbursement for travel and personal expenses.

4. To be reimbursed for travel and personal expenses, read the following directions and complete all 10 steps.
5. This report explains why the states should hold public hearings.

EXERCISE 2.5

1. Review the following table; then write a purpose statement for each of the activities. Decide whether the purpose statement should be written as the writer's purpose, the reader's task, or the document's communication purpose.
2. Add your own topic to the table and complete the table by writing four different statements for your topic, statements that explain either the reader's task, the writer's purpose, or the communication purpose of the document.

| Topic | Purpose | | | |
	To Inform	To Investigate	To Evaluate	To Persuade
EPA public hearings	To instruct the public in steps to set up a public hearing	To study EPA's budget needs for holding hearings and to present findings	To compare Ohio's and Iowa's hearing procedures and recommend improvements	To propose that states take over some of the hearing responsibilities

EXERCISE 2.6

This exercise is designed to help you become familiar with your library's resources. It is based on a practicum by Paul D. Leedy.[12]

1. Go to the reference desk or circulation desk and ask for
   - Guide to the library—Does your library use Library of Congress or the Decimal Classification System?
   - Guide to the electronic card catalog, if available.
   - Guide to an on-line search system for interlibrary loan, if available.
   - Library policy on access to computerized information retrieval systems. Some libraries have student rates or a budget to search some systems.
2. Using the lists of library resources in this module, check the electronic card catalog and the card catalog files to see if your library owns books in each of the areas listed in the Checklist for Library Research in Figure 2.16. Select titles appropriate to your field.
   - In your Checklist, write the titles next to each resource.
   - Opposite each of the titles, jot the call number of the volume. (Use Library of Congress or the Decimal Classification System.)
3. Go to the reference shelves; inspect each of the works beginning with the preface and table of contents. Then look at the section that contains your specialty.
4. Go to the reference shelves where reference books in your specialization are housed. Get acquainted with what's there.

Checklist for Library Research

Resource	Title	Call Number
Handbook		
Guide		
Dictionary		
Directory		
Encyclopedia		
Bibliography		
Professional journal (index)		
Professional journal (abstracting)		
Government publications		
Statistics		
Others		

FIGURE 2.16 Checklist for library research

Source: Cheryl A. Price, reference librarian, Galvin Library, Illinois Institute of Technology. Used with permission.

EXERCISE 2.7

Draw a map from your room to your school or job. Then write the directions for your roommate who wishes to follow the path you take to your job or school. Take into account landmarks, distance, time intervals, orientation, and any other features to help your reader follow directions. (Save these directions for the next time you have to tell someone how to get to where you live.)

In this exercise, what questions will you ask yourself about your reader? How can you design the information to help the reader understand and follow your directions?

WRITING ASSIGNMENT

Figure 2.17 is an insurance report describing an automobile accident. You work for the insurance company and have to prepare a prose account of the accident to be submitted to the home office. Your job is to describe the accident clearly, completely, and objectively for the home office.

AUTOMOBILE ACCIDENT LOSS REPORT

File Number
611-036793
(Office Use Only)

We have been informed that you were a party to an accident.
To assist us in securing all of the facts relating to the accident, complete this report and return it in envelope provided.
Your cooperation will enable us to take appropriate action

1. YOUR NAME & ADDRESS
OWNER NAME *BARNARD KLEIN*
HOME PHONE — WORK PHONE *437-8500*
FULL PERMANENT ADDRESS No. & St. or Rt. & Box No. – City or Post Office – Township – County – State – ZIP
5620 S. ASHLAND AVE. CHGO. IL. 60636
Directions if Address is Rural
Where Employed
Hours Worked *8* to *4:30* (A.M.) (P.M.)

2. YOUR VEHICLE DESCRIPTION
YEAR – MAKE – MODEL *1979 OLDS DELTA 88*
IDENTIFICATION (VIN) NUMBER *3N3749X249228*
SPECIAL EQUIPMENT

3. YOUR INSURANCE
AGENT - NAME ADDRESS *MINSKY INSURANCE AGENCY P.O. BOX 796 NORTHBROOK IL 60062*
INSURANCE COMPANY *AMER. STANDARD*
POLICY NUMBER *BAP 402530*
COVERAGES: LIABILITY ☑ MEDICAL PAYMENTS ☑ OTHER: PROPERTY DAMAGE ☑ COLLISION ☑ COMPREHENSIVE ☐

YOUR AUTO LOCATION & DAMAGE ESTIMATE *59th + CARPENTER* $*700*
COLOR
IS AUTO DRIVEABLE& YES ☐ NO ☐
WILL YOU GO TO DRIVE-IN? YES ☐ NO ☐ DATE:

DATE OF LOSS OR ACCIDENT *4-17-83*
TIME *5:05* A.M. ☐ P.M. ☑

LOCATION OF LOSS *FRONT END*
INVESTIGATING POLICE DEPARTMENT *CHICAGO*

YOUR VIOLATION
OTHER VIOLATION

I.D. NO. YOUR DRIVER NAME / ADDRESS / ZIP *SAME*
RELATION TO OWNER

INJURIES *NONE*
AGE *37*
HOME PHONE — WORK PHONE

I.D. NO. NAME / ADDRESS / ZIP OF OCCUPANTS IN YOUR AUTO *JACK KLEIN 2901 BOB-O-LINK FLOSSMOOR, IL.*
AGE / INJURIES / PHONE

I.D. NO.
AGE / INJURIES / PHONE

I.D. NO.
AGE / INJURIES / PHONE

I.D. NO. OTHER OWNER / ADDRESS / ZIP (OR PEDESTRIAN) *JOHN NELSON 9045 S. HARVARD CHGO. 60628*
HOME PHONE — WORK PHONE *569-8012*

OTHER VEHICLE DESCRIPTION* *1970 CHEV. VEGA*
DAMAGE ESTIMATE OR ESTIMATE OF DAMAGE $*LEFT FRONT #900*

I.D. NO. OTHER DRIVER / ADDRESS / ZIP *SAME*

INJURIES
AGE
HOME PHONE — WORK PHONE

OTHER AUTO LOCATION
WILL HE / SHE GO TO DRIVE-IN
DATE

OTHER INSURANCE COMPANY *UNKNOWN*
AGENT NAME
POLICY NUMBER

I.D. NO. NAME / ADDRESS / ZIP OF OCCUPANTS IN OTHER VEHICLE*
AGE / INJURIES / PHONE

I.D. NO.
AGE / INJURIES / PHONE

I.D. NO.
AGE / INJURIES / PHONE

I.D. NO. NAME / ADDRESS / ZIP FOR PROPERTY DAMAGED IN LOSS OTHER THAN VEHICLES*

*CONTINUE ON SEPARATE SHEET IF MORE VEHICLES OR PEOPLE ARE INVOLVED.
C-4   Stock No. 10835   Rev. 9/81

FIGURE 2.17 Auto accident loss report form

NAME ADDRESS ZIP OF WITNESS		PHONE
LILY WALSH 1012 CARPENTER CHGO.		568-4073
NAME ADDRESS ZIP OF WITNESS		PHONE
NAME ADDRESS ZIP OF WITNESS		PHONE

ANSWER FOLLOWING QUESTIONS BY FILLING IN THE BLANKS OR CIRCLING APPROPRIATE WORDS

What direction were you driving? EAST	On what side of the road? (Right) Left or Center	What direction was other car driving? SOUTH	On what side of the road? (Right) Left or Center
Speed of your car before the accident? 35 mph	Speed of your car at time of collision?	Did you apply your brakes before collision? YES	Were your brakes in good condition? YES
Where was other car when you first saw it? How far away?		Speed of other car before collision?	Speed of other car at time of collision?
Did other car slow down or stop before collision? STOP SIGN	What signals did you give?	What signals did other driver give?	
In what part of roadway did accident occur? Right Left (Center)	How far did your car move after the accident?	How far did other car move after the accident?	
Was either car entering or crossing an Arterial (Thru Traffic) highway? THRU	Which car? #1	Number of traffic lanes? 4	
What type of traffic control were you faced with? NONE	Other Driver?	Did you yield or make full stop as required?	Other Driver?
Was view obstructed from either direction?	If so, for what distance should you have seen the other car?	For what distance should other driver have seen your car?	
What were road conditions? (Concrete) Gravel Black top Dirt (Wet) Dry Icy Narrow Crooked Other		Weather conditions? Clear Foggy (Raining) Other	Were the lights lighted on your car? Yes On the other car? Yes
Had either driver been drinking? NO	Which car?		Intoxicated?
What statements or admissions were made by either party after the accident? (What was said and who said it?)			

STATE IN YOUR OWN WORDS HOW ACCIDENT HAPPENED

NUMBER EACH VEHICLE AND SHOW THE DIRECTION OF TRAVEL BY ARROWS. (IDENTIFY YOUR CAR AS NO. 1)

CAR #1 GOING EAST ON 59th
CAR #2 WAS SOUTHBOUND ON
CARPENTER. CAR #2 PROCEEDED
AFTER STOPPING AT SIGN AND
CAR #3 GOING WEST ON 59th
STRUCK CAR #2 ON LEFT
FRONT. CAR #2 BOUNCED
INTO CAR #1.

SHOW NORTH BY ARROW ↑

IN YOUR OPINION WHO WAS RESPONSIBLE FOR THE ACCIDENT? CAR #3, CAR #2 WHY DO YOU THINK SO?

DID DRIVER HAVE PERMISSION TO DRIVE FROM OWNER?
IF DRIVER DID NOT HAVE PERMISSION, EXPLAIN:
EXPLANATION OF LOSS IF LOSS DID NOT INVOLVE ANOTHER VEHICLE

ARE YOU MAKING AN INSURANCE CLAIM	YES	AMOUNT? $700 — DED.	
I (WE) DECLARE THAT THIS IS A FULL AND TRUTHFUL STATEMENT OF THE ACCIDENT OR LOSS	OWNER'S SIGNATURE X Bernard Klein	DRIVER'S SIGNATURE X	
REPORT MADE OUT BY		DATE 4/18/83	

FIGURE 2.17 (cont.)

MODULE 3

Organizational Strategies

From Module 2, you know how to gather information and define audience requirements. Now you will have to organize your content and present that content effectively in the text.[1]

Based on the model in Figure 3.1, this module will answer the main question, How do I organize the document and develop the content?

This module describes organizational strategies that aid you in designing the entire document as well as in developing the paragraphs that provide the content. These strategies will help the reader follow the logic of documents such as reports, policies, letters, and proposals, increasing the readability of the document. Readability is a concept that describes the reader's ability to read and understand the document. You are increasing readability when you

- Include information the reader needs to know.
- Organize the information so the reader understands the message.
- Write the document clearly and at the appropriate level for the reader.
- Lay out and use graphic techniques to clarify the information.

Module 2 presented the principle of writing at the appropriate level for the audience. This module will help you select and organize the information

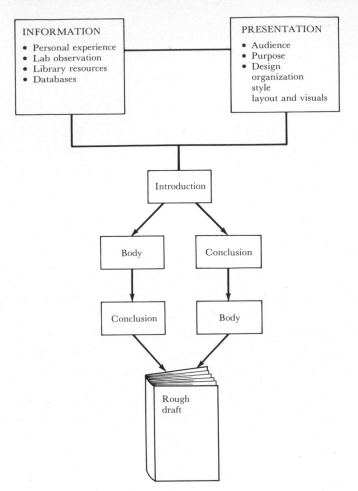

FIGURE 3.1 Using organization to shape documents

so that the reader understands the message in the document. Selection and organization depend on the audience and the purpose. The strategy you design to organize your document should help your reader grasp the information.

      To aid in the logical presentation of the information, this module introduces you to two modes of logical thinking—inductive and deductive reasoning. After considering the logical plan of your document and some conventional organizational strategies, you will be encouraged to think about the introductory section, incorporating information that will help your reader follow the order in the rest of the document. Finally, this module will help you plan and develop the paragraphs within the document. Logical thinking, organizational strategies, and paragraph development are critical components in the design of a technical document.

Scope

At the end of this module you will be able to

1. Examine your critical thinking strategies using inductive and deductive reasoning.
2. Develop organizational strategies to accommodate audience, purpose, content, and text.
3. Use strategies from conventional designs to help you organize your document.
4. Introduce the document to your reader, providing the plan to your organization.
5. Plan paragraphs to provide the information the reader needs to know.
6. Apply the organizational strategies to a conventional document—the extended definition.

Logical Thinking

Inductive and Deductive Reasoning

Inductive and deductive reasoning are two logical ways of thinking. They are also ways of organizing information. When you present your specific details and data first, followed by a conclusion based on preceding information, you are presenting information in ascending order, using the pattern for inductive reasoning. When you move from a general statement to specific sentences that present data, you are arranging information in descending order, using the pattern for deductive reasoning. You may choose to organize inductively or deductively on the basis of

1. The effect you wish the document to have on the reader.
2. The nature of the subject.

Many times, when we reason inductively, we cannot prove the conclusion; we can only infer the results by looking at the facts. Inference is a way of jumping to a logical conclusion based on preceding facts, but the conclusion has yet to be proved. People who predict what will happen to the stock market based on previous data are drawing a conclusion based on inference; still, many stock market players act on these conclusions. A coauthor and I drew the following conclusion through inference, a conclusion based on questionnaires completed by business executives asked to describe the content of a writing course.[2]

> Executives stressed the need for instructors to train people to write logically, clearly, and briefly, and to concentrate on such judgment skills as audience, tone, relevance, and timeliness. The desire to shift from traditional emphases opens a new approach to teaching business communications. It implies that there is a much greater need to base courses on real-life case studies and to use business people as guest lecturers, for both can illustrate the kind of logical thinking that is necessary to avoid communication problems.

Documents that present the data first and then draw a conclusion based on the data develop inductively or in ascending order. Figure 3.2 illustrates the inductive reasoning in a report evaluating calculators.

You are presenting information deductively when you begin with a general statement followed by specific information that supports the primary statement. This descending order of information is illustrated in Figure 3.3 in Julian Huxley's paragraph on ant warfare.

Manuals that provide instructions develop deductively because they introduce the general statement early in the document and then provide specific steps or data to accomplish the primary goal. Figure 3.4 illustrates the deductive pattern in a software documentation manual.

Organizing Inductively or Deductively

All documents must use details and/or quantifiable data and general summarizing statements to develop the content. How will you decide whether to organize the information inductively or deductively? The answer depends on the audience and on the subject.

Evaluation of Three Programmable Calculators

Discussion
Calculator X and Calculator Y are almost identical in appearance. The first preserves information in memory when the calculator is off, but it has only half as much memory as Calculator Y. The latter has a built-in card reader that stores and retrieves programs and data with small magnetic cards. This storage decreases the problem of losing memory when the machine is turned off. The card reader also permits the user to create a library of programs. Other than these features, Calculator X and Calculator Y are also almost identical in features.

Calculator Z exceeds the other two in the categories of memory size, number of instructions, alphanumeric capabilities, and speed of executing programs. Calculator Z averages about a year of use from a set of batteries; the batteries in Calculator Z lasted twice as long as those in Calculator X and one and one-half times as long as the batteries in Calculator Y. Batteries are replaceable at a cost of about $5.00. A rechargeable battery pack and charger are also available, but at a cost of $50.00. Of the machines tested, Calculator Z had the greatest number of features.

Conclusion
The evaluation indicates Calculator Z is the best performer of the three tested.

FIGURE 3.2 Evaluation developing inductively
Source: John Robin, Technical Writing 421, Illinois Institute of Technology.

In point of fact, there are only two kinds of animals that habitually make war—man and ants. Even among ants war is mainly practiced by one group, comprising only a few species among the tens of thousands that are known to science. They are the harvester ants, inhabitants of arid regions where there is little to pick up during the dry months. Accordingly, they collect the seeds of various grasses at the end of the growing season and store them in special underground granaries in their nests. It is these reserve supplies which are the object of ant warfare. The inhabitants of one nest set out deliberately to raid the supplies of another group. According to Forel and other students of ant life, they may employ quite elaborate military tactics, and the battles generally result in heavy casualities. If the attackers win, they remove the stores grain by grain to their own nest. Ant wars never last nearly so long as human wars. One campaign observed by American myrmecologist McCook in Penn Square in the centre of Philadelphia, lasted almost 3 weeks. The longest on record is 6½ weeks.[3]

FIGURE 3.3 Paragraph developing deductively

Questions to Ask Yourself About Organizing Inductively or Deductively

1. How will the reader best understand the information?
2. Does the reader have a preference for organizing one way over another?
3. How can organization help you as the writer elicit the anticipated reader response?

　　　　　To use the DISKCOPY command to make a backup copy of your diskette

1. Insert your MS-DOS Operating System diskette in drive A.
2. Type:

    diskcopy a: b:/f

3. Press the RETURN key.
4. Remove the MS-DOS diskette from drive A.
5. Insert Document Diskette in drive A and blank diskette in drive B.
6. Press the RETURN key.
    When the copy is complete, the "Copy another" prompt is displayed. Because you wish to make only one copy,
7. Press the N key.

FIGURE 3.4 Instructions developed deductively

Consider the scenarios:

Readers (executives) who make administrative decisions based on the expert opinions of others may want to know the "bottom line" of the report. They read the conclusions and recommendations first, distributing different sections of the report to experts who can evaluate methodology, product design, costs, or technical data.

Even some technical readers who are directors of research laboratories prefer the conclusions near the front of the document because they cannot pore over every detail. They may know the methodology well enough simply to glance at it in order to determine if the conclusions are appropriate. For the readers who want their conclusions and recommendations near the front of the document, you would present your general statement first.

This strategy relegates the supporting material to the back of the document rather than to the middle section of the document. The purpose of this document is to present the bottom line to that reader whose need is administrative or whose decision may lead to immediate action. This organizational strategy is deductive because it gives the conclusion first and then supports it with data or detail.

On the other hand, many scientists want to follow your experiment step-by-step, carefully reviewing your methodology, looking at your data, and finally drawing the same conclusions you drew (or drawing their own conclusions based on your data). For this reader, you would organize the content inductively. Either strategy in Figure 3.5 will help you shape your document.

Presentation Techniques

Purpose

Depending on the purpose of the document, you will want to select the most effective techniques to present your information. Your presentation techniques will contribute greatly to your reader's understanding of the information you are presenting. But, first, you must know what type of document you are writing. Will you be writing descriptive, procedural, or persuasive materials? What is your purpose or aim in this document?

You can

- *Narrate* events (tell a story).
- *Describe* the device or the situation.
- *Explain* the procedure or the steps.
- *Persuade* the reader to act on your recommendation.

In a single document, you may have all four aims. Let's say, for example, you wish to persuade your boss to permit you to develop a manual for a database management system, a project that will cost the employer some money. To persuade the boss, you describe the problems that the absence of a manual has created. You may even narrate a story or two about employee

Strategy	Design	Content
Deductive		
• Introduction	Section 1	Statement of problem and method to solve it
• Conclusion	Section 2	Summarizing statements
• Supporting material	Section 3	Body of details and data
Inductive		
• Introduction	Section 1	Statement of problem and method to solve it
• Supporting material	Section 2	Body of detail and data
• Conclusion	Section 3	Summarizing statements

FIGURE 3.5 Inductive and deductive strategies

frustration; then you compare your situation to a company with a manual for database management, and, finally, you explain the procedure for establishing the contents of the manual and give an example of the table of contents. Your proposal, essentially persuasive in its aim because you want the reader to act on your suggestion, has also used the techniques of narration, description, and explanation of procedure.

In a proposal or a feasibility report (a report that compares products or ideas and makes a recommendation), your purpose is to persuade the reader to act on the recommendation. Modules 8 and 9 illustrate the organization of the *proposal* and the *multiple evaluation/feasibility study* as persuasive documents. When your purpose is to write descriptive or procedural materials, you will narrate, describe, and explain. Modules 6, 7, and 10 present descriptive documents, instructions, and design reports. The *scientific report* in Module 11 relies on description, procedure, and especially explanation, an explanation of the rationale behind the experiments. Narration is seldom the main intention of a writer of technical documents. However, if you were writing to inform the public about the discovery of the pacemaker, as does Wilson Greatbatch in *Implantable Active Devices*, then you might want to narrate the events chronologically to tell your readers about this exciting discovery.

One way to think about these presentation techniques is to visualize them as organizational patterns. These patterns can become visual constructs, helping us present the information so that the reader recognizes the organization quickly, remembers the information vividly, and recalls it accurately.[4] Figure 3.6 presents the visual constructs for narrative, descriptive, procedural, and persuasive techniques. The visual construct for narration is a horizontal sequence of blocks; for description, the visual construct is a hier-

Purpose	Organizing Principle	Visual Construct
Narrate	Series • chronological • logical	
Describe	Levels • ladder • tree • grid • heuristic	
Explain	Lists • step-by-step • bullets • check	 1. • 2. • 3. •
Persuade	Dialogue	

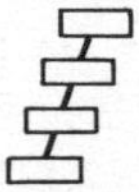

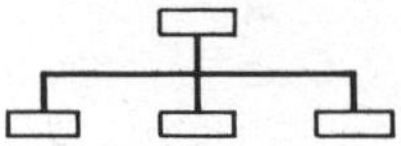

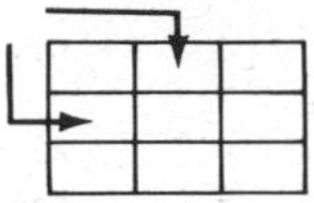

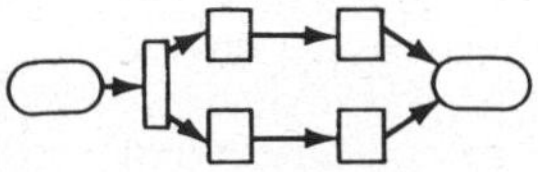

FIGURE 3.6 Visual constructs for organizing documents
Source: Adapted from William Horton, "Templates of Thought," in *Proceedings*, International Technical Communication Conference, 1986: 302–305. Used with permission of the Society for Technical Communication.

archical sequence of blocks; for explanation, the visual construct is a vertical list of blocks; and for persuasion, the visual construct is a diagonal sequence of triangles.

After you consider the audience and the purpose, you have to consider the content and the text.

Content and Physical Text

In business and industry, readers often need certain types of documents that provide information to make decisions or produce products. In the research study mentioned in Module 1, the participants in the study listed at least 13 different documents that readers needed. These documents included

style manuals	ads
procedures	reports
instructions	questionnaires
summaries	evaluations
policies	trip notes
proposals	letters/memos
descriptions	

The organization of these documents depends on content and the physical dimensions of the text as well as on audience and purpose. For example, in a manual that describes a software program, the content must include a description of some of the screens that the reader can expect to use, and the manual must lie flat so that the reader has both hands free to type at the terminal. Thus, content and text are also factors in organization.

Conventional Strategies

Before you invent or select an organizational structure, you should begin with the question, "What is the purpose of this document?" The answer will help you develop a useful organizational strategy. Some conventional strategies, however, may be guides to help you organize your content. You should consider the conventional strategies, but, remember, the final organization is your invention. All strategies are designed to help answer the question, *"What is the purpose of this document?"*

What Is the Purpose of this Document?[5]

PURPOSE: To evaluate a given object or project.
STRUCTURE: Useful for a *feasibility study* or *multiple evaluation report*
1. Introduction
   - statement of purpose
   - background
   - scope or plan of development
2. Body
   - criteria
   - procedures
   - data
   - discussion of data
3. Conclusions and Implications
4. Recommendations

PURPOSE: To provide management with a conclusion or recommendation they may act on.
STRUCTURE: Useful for *management report* or *policy statement*
1. Introduction
   - purpose
   - background

- recommendation—optional placement for this section
- plan for development

2. Factual Summary
3. Conclusions and Recommendations—may appear
   earlier in the first section
4. Annexes—any supporting material appears in this
   section, such as
   - procedures
   - data
   - evaluation
   - illustrations

For this type of structure, see the scientific report in Module 11 or the
case studies in Module 10.

PURPOSE: To tell someone how to do something.
STRUCTURE: Useful for *instructions, procedures, documentation,* or
                style manuals
                1. Introduction
                2. Theory (principle)
                3. Equipment and Materials Needed
                4. Description of Process (or mechanism)
                5. Performance Instructions
                6. Troubleshooting

PURPOSE: To answer a theoretical question or solve a problem.
STRUCTURE: Useful for *research reports* (both theoretical and
                empirical)
                1. Introduction
                2. Literature Review
                3. Materials
                4. Methods
                5. Results
                6. Discussion (review and analysis of data)
                7. Summary (significance of findings)

PURPOSE: To present a design or process.
STRUCTURE: Useful for *design documents*
                1. Introduction
                2. Standards and Specifications
                3. The Design/Process
                4. List of Materials
                5. Methods and Procedures
                6. Evaluation (state criteria)
                7. Conclusions and Recommendations

PURPOSE: To describe a situation, organization, place, and so on,
                as it presently exists, usually to recommend further
                action.
STRUCTURE: Useful for *case studies* and *status reports*
                1. Introduction

2. History
3. Present Status
4. Implications
5. Recommendations

PURPOSE: To report on the results of a trip or a meeting.
STRUCTURE: Useful for *trip reports, summaries of meetings, reports of call*
1. Purpose/Subject
2. People Attending (may be included in an appendix)
3. Scope for *trip reports* or Scope for *meetings*

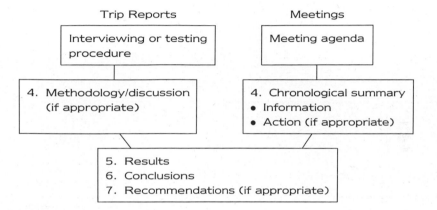

Trip Reports   Meetings

| Interviewing or testing procedure | Meeting agenda |

4. Methodology/discussion
   (if appropriate)

4. Chronological summary
   • Information
   • Action (if appropriate)

5. Results
6. Conclusions
7. Recommendations (if appropriate)

PURPOSE: To provide a laboratory analysis or evaluate a site.
STRUCTURE: Useful for *laboratory reports, research reports, field reports*, or *site visits*
1. Purpose for *laboratory report* or *field report*
   • Site
   • Participants
2. Methodology/Objectives
3. Results/Summary
4. Discussion
5. Appendixes/Attachments
6. Bibliography (if appropriate for *laboratory report*)

Note: In the *laboratory report*, often the *conclusions* or *results* appear immediately following the *purpose* statement.

PURPOSE: To offer to provide a service.
STRUCTURE: Useful for *formal* and *informal proposals, work statements, contracts*
1. Introduction
   • proposal
   • background of the problem
   • significance (if appropriate)

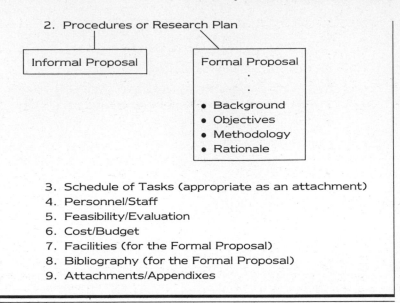

2. Procedures or Research Plan

Informal Proposal

Formal Proposal

- Background
- Objectives
- Methodology
- Rationale

3. Schedule of Tasks (appropriate as an attachment)
4. Personnel/Staff
5. Feasibility/Evaluation
6. Cost/Budget
7. Facilities (for the Formal Proposal)
8. Bibliography (for the Formal Proposal)
9. Attachments/Appendixes

The Introduction: How Will You Guide Your Reader Through the Document?

The information in the introductory section of your document prepares your reader for the rest of the document. The introduction usually includes

- the purpose
- the background
- the organizational strategy.

The **purpose** of the document is to communicate information. The opening statement for a document may be as simple as "The purpose of this report is to present . . . ." In this module and in Module 2 we considered purpose statements and reader's needs or tasks. A purpose statement makes the communication purpose of the document clear to the reader. You may omit the purpose statement when your intention is to persuade the reader to your point of view or to explain the reader's task with a self-evident purpose. For example, the purpose is self-evident in this notice: "To receive your new license plates, take this notice and $70.00 in cash or certified check to your nearest motor vehicle center."

The **background** tells the reader the problem or circumstances that led up to the document. It puts the contents of the document in context by describing the writer's assigned task or explaining the history of the study.

The **organizational strategy**, sometimes called the **plan of development**, tells the reader what information will be included in (or excluded from) the

---

Organizing

Always Provide a Context

Every document has an introduction that provides a context.

The context begins with an informative title.
The context-setting introduction should
- Introduce the topic.
- Explain the purpose of the document.
- Clarify the audience.
- Briefly state the thesis (the major point, the result or conclusion, if any).
- Lay out road map for the document or through the document.

FIGURE 3.7. Context-setting introduction (from the Document Design Center)
Source: D. Goswami et al., *Writing in the Professions*, American Institutes for Research, 1981: 77. Used with permission.

rest of the document and in what order the information will be presented. In other words, the strategy or plan provides the organizational **design** for the remainder of the document. It provides the reader with a map for following the rest of the document. In Figure 3.7 the Document Design Center provides the organizational plan for the introduction, and Figure 3.8 illustrates the content that may go into the **introduction**.

Developing the Paragraph: How Do You Give the Reader Complete Information?

After you have an organizational strategy for the main sections of your report, you will have to develop the information in paragraphs organized under the main sections. Any document is a compilation of paragraphs that you write using a variety of techniques. Some of the techniques include

- analogy
- example
- narration
- cause/effect
- definition
- classification/division

At different places in the document, you use a variety of these techniques to clarify the information for your readers. The examples that follow illustrate these techniques of paragraph development.

Designing a DX Receiver

Purpose
The purpose of this report is to present the results of a survey of radio hobbyists and to incorporate those results into a descriptive and rough design of a new DX receiver.

Background
DXing, the hobby of listening for distant stations on radio or TV bands, can be done on nearly any standard broadcast band. The most popular bands for DXing are the shortwave, medium wave (or AM), FM, and TV bands, roughly in that order. Although many DXers listen to several different bands, the method of reception on each band differs considerably from that on any other. The DXers demand high quality in any type of receiver they use. Unfortunately, not many receivers of high quality are available to the general public, so DXing remains a hobby not easily taken up by the average listener. Our objective is to create a receiver both attractive and useful to DXers and to regular listeners.

Plan of Development
The first step in the body of this report will be to analyze and interpret the results of the questionnaire. (See Appendixes I and II.) From these data we will develop a set of specifications for the receiver, and we will determine the capabilities and features of the receiver. Much of this information will be based on the multiple evaluation among four receivers. A short market analysis of the new receiver, derived from the results of the survey, will be provided. Finally, a rough sketch of the new receiver will be included, displaying the accepted features and the recommended size and design.

Introduction
- Purpose
- Background
- Plan of developmen

FIGURE 3.8 The contents for an introduction
Source: Michael Jezsiorski, Technical Writing 421, Illinois Institute of Technology.

Analogy

An analogy is a comparison between things otherwise dissimilar, but because they share some similar aspects of function or position, they may correspond in some respects. Because analogies are a good way of using the familiar to explain the unfamiliar, writers and researchers often use analogies to help the novice remember the information. In Figure 3.9, two researchers compared a computer screen to paper, a window, and a scroll.

Example

Like an analogy, an example makes a concept clearer to the reader who may be unfamiliar with the information. Usually, the writer makes a general state-

A computer display screen is something like a sheet of paper on a typewriter. As you type letters and numbers on the "typewriter" keyboard, they appear on the display screen. To start typing on a new line, you press the key labeled RETURN, just as you would on a typewriter.

A computer display screen is also something like a window. What you type into a computer doesn't get transferred to separate sheets of paper, as with a typewriter. Rather, you can think of your text as existing on a scroll of paper, more like a Dead Sea scroll than a modern book with separate sheets of paper. The display screen acts like a window through which you can look at your scroll. The window remains stationary, but you can move the scroll forward and backward to change your view.[6]

FIGURE 3.9 Paragraph developed by analogy

ment and then follows it with an example. The example supports the principle or the generalization, as it does in Figure 3.10. When Noel Mostert was describing the incredible resourcefulness of sailors to repair their ships, he used the following:

When, for example, the 5,000-ton British tramp steamer *Titania* lost her propeller during heavy gales in the South Atlantic in 1900, the ship's head was held to the wind and sea by a sea-anchor, the forward holds were flooded to raise the stern and, lurching and pounding in this dangerous position, the spare propeller was swung outboard by cargo winches and then guided onto the wildly gyrating tail shaft, threaded onto it, and then sealed into place by a locknut. The whole business took several days and was supervised by the ship's master, who was suspended outboard in a bo'sun's chair which, with the motion of the ship, alternately swung him across the skies, then plunged him into the crests. Lloyd's awarded him its medal for Meritorious Services.[7]

FIGURE 3.10 Paragraph developed by example

Narration

Narration tells a story; and, in technical writing, the events are related in chronological order. Flashback techniques are more generally reserved for fiction. The writer may relate the events using the first person *I*, a point of view that is engaging and personal; or the narrator may prefer the more detached third person point of view, one that seems more objective. In either case, the author sequences the events so that the reader understands what happened next. The narration in Figure 3.11 is written by Wilson Greatbatch, one of the inventors of the first implantable cardiac pacemaker.

> We had in Buffalo the first local chapter in the world of the Institute of Radio Engineers, Professional Group in Medical Electronics, (the IRE/PGME, now the Biomedical Engineering Society of the IEEE). Every month 25 to 75 doctors and engineers met for a technical program. We strove to attract equal numbers of doctors and engineers. We had a standing offer to send an engineering team to assist any doctor who had an instrumentation problem. I went with one team to visit Dr. Chardack on a problem dealing with a blood oximeter. Imagine my surprise to find that his assistant was my old high-school classmate, Andy Gage [now Dr. Andrew Gage]. We couldn't help Dr. Chardack much with his oximeter problem, but when I broached my pacemaker idea to him, he walked up and down the lab a couple of times, looked at me strangely and said, "If you can do that, you can save ten thousand lives a year." Three weeks later we had our first model in a dog.[8]

FIGURE 3.11 Paragraph developed by narration

Cause/Effect

When one event follows another and the second is the result of the first, then the first event starts a causal chain. This causal chain finally results in an action, and the paragraph or the document develops with sentences of cause and effect. The danger in speaking of cause and effect is that the final action may not be the result of the preceding event; it may be the result of earlier events leading up to the final action.

In logic, Copi distinguishes between remote and proximate causes that lead up to an event.[9] When an event is the result of an action described in the preceding sentence, then the preceding sentence described the proximate cause; when the event is the result of causes described much earlier in a paragraph or a document, then the event is the result of remote causes. You will have to beware of attributing the cause of a final action to a preceding sentence. In logic, this error is described as "after this, therefore, because of this." Neither the remote nor the proximate cause may produce a final action, but all the causes may produce the final action. Make sure you know the entire story before you jump to a conclusion.

In Figure 3.12, Wilson Greatbatch narrates his discovery of the transistor that permitted him to proceed with an implantable pacemaker. As is true of many other breakthroughs in science, the causes are prior experience, current knowledge of the state of the art, intuition, and accidental activities. The accidental discovery is the result of remote causes leading up to the creation of the first pacemaker.

In Figure 3.13, Garrett Hardin describes a humorous situation that shows a causal relationship between old maids and the fall of the British

My marker oscillator used a 10K base bias resistor. I reached into my resistor box for one but misread the colors and got a brown-black-green (one megohm) instead of a brown-black-orange. The circuit started to "squeg" with a 1.8 ms pulse, followed by a one second quiescent interval. During the interval, the transistor was cut off and drew practically no current. I stared at the thing in disbelief and then realized that this was exactly what was needed to drive a heart. I built a few more. For the next five years, most of the world's pacemakers were to use a blocking oscillator with a UTC DOT-1 transformer, just because I grabbed the wrong resistor.[10]

FIGURE 3.12 Paragraph based on cause and effect

Empire; the remote causes leading up to the fall of the British Empire remind you to beware of the faulty logic: "After this, therefore, because of this."

Definition

When you define a term you give its meaning. In technical writing you will use more **denotative**—factual—definitions than **connotative**—emotional—definitions. You may write two types of denotative definitions:

• formal definitions
• operational definitions.

It was pointed out, on the one hand, that cats are kept (as is well known) by old maids; and on the other, that red clover (which requires humble-bees as pollinators) is used to make the hay that nourishes the horses of the cavalry, on which the defense of the British Empire depends. Putting all this into a causal chain, we see:

Old maids keep:	→	Cats, which eat:	→	Mice, which otherwise might destroy:	→	Humble-bees; these are needed for:	→
Clover pollination; required for:		Clover hay; → required for: →		Cavalry horses; required for:		Defense of → British Empire (*Taran-tara!*)	

    Thus, "it logically follows" that the perpetuation of the British Empire is dependent on a bountiful supply of old maids![11]

FIGURE 3.13 Paragraph with faulty causal logic

Formal Definition

Denotative definitions like those found in dictionaries are also called **Aristotelian** or formal definitions. The Aristotelian definition has three elements:

Aristotelian Definition	Example
term (to be defined):	Bunsen burner
genus (class):	instrument
differentiae: (distinguishing characteristics)	used in laboratory to direct and control a gas flame

> A Bunsen burner is a **stainless steel** instrument **used in a laboratory to direct and control a gas flame**.

A single, concise sentence places the term in a class of like items such as a device, mechanism, or instrument and then distinguishes the particular item from all other items in the class by naming its unique characteristics. You can list the unique features of an item if you think of

- its construction
- its use
- its description
- its producer.

You will want to place the term in as small a class as possible to reduce the number of terms falling into that class. For example, rather than placing the term *hot pot* in the class *mechanism*, you might try the class *container*.

> A hot pot is a cylindrical, metal container used to heat liquids and cook some foods.

Operational Definition

At times, you will find it more appropriate to define a term by describing actions or events that explain the term or occur as a result of the term. This type of definition, the **operational definition**, defines the term by describing cause or effect. For example, you might prefer to give an operational definition of medical terms because the reader will have a clearer idea of the medical problem.

> Asynapsis occurs when homologous chromosomes from the male and female fail to pair during meiosis.

The operational definition usually reveals a cause/effect relationship between the term and the description or explanation, using a verb that suggests the cause/effect relationship. The linking verb **is**, used in the Aristotelian definition, is inappropriate for operational definitions because linking verbs suggest an equality rather than a cause/effect relationship. You can say

> Asynapsis **is** a genetic problem . . . . (linking the term and the class, both nouns)

But you cannot say

> Asynapsis is when . . . . (linking the term and the event, a noun and an
> adverb)

You must use a verb such as **occur** in an operational definition.

When you want to expand the definition, either the formal or the operational definition, beyond one line into a paragraph, then you have to use techniques to develop paragraphs. For example, Figure 3.14 uses contrast to expand the definition:

A hard disk is a rigid aluminum or ceramic plate with a magnetic coating used to store information in a computer. The term is generally used to contrast with diskettes, which are flexible plastic plates with slower access speed and smaller storage capacity. The hard disk is not removable whereas the diskette can be removed from the computer.

FIGURE 3.14 Paragraph developing the definition through contrast

The following techniques also help to expand a definition:

example	How to use the term in context.
etymology	Origin of the term.
negative definition	What the term does not mean or how the term is confused.
stipulative definition	How the writer plans to use the term.

A common task in business and industry is writing the **extended definition**. The extended definition uses several of these techniques to define the term and make the meaning clear to the reader. This module ends with an extended definition as a model for using several paragraphing techniques to develop a document.

Classification/Division

When you classify, you group the item or part into a larger whole, or class, according to a single principle. For example, *O* rings are fasteners, and the classifying principle is function. What is the function of *O* rings? They fasten.

> term: *O* rings
> class: fastener
> classifying principle: function

But *O* rings may also be classified as analogies to describe unfamiliar items or concepts. In this case, the classifying principle is structure. What is the shape of *O* rings? They look like the letter *O*. Other items also belong to this class of analogies: *A* frames, *S* curves, *Y* pipes.

Classifying also permits you to group items under a larger heading. For example, an eye, a solar cell, and a camera lens are all light-receiving devices. Once again, the unifying principle is function, and the class is devices. By classifying items into broad categories on the basis of a single principle, you help the reader understand the items in a logical context.

Division may accompany classification in the same document, but division and classification are opposite analytical processes and must be developed separately. An easy way to remember the concept of division is to think of various headings for grouping items or concepts. For example, you could place rings under three common headings—function, structure, composition of materials—and further partition the headings. The headings are all parallel divisions, illustrated in the chart in Figure 3.15.

Finally, when you divide a single item or concept, you are **partitioning**. Again, you can partition on the basis of a single principle, such as function, structure, or composition of material. For example, you can divide a television camera into two basic parts: the lens and the Vidicon tube. The principle for dividing the term is structure. Then you can continue to subdivide or partition the lens into its component parts. The illustration of the television camera lens in Figure 3.16 shows the structure of the components. Before you list all the component parts, you should select a starting point; if you are using an illustration, your starting point is a point in space, either from right to left, top to bottom, center radiating outward, or a circle starting at the center of the top. Select your spatial point and then proceed in a logical path. For the illustration in Figure 3.16, the listing of each component part is right to left:

the *f* scale, the iris adjustment, the focus scale, the focus adjustment

Dividing and partitioning are often illustrated in a figure called a **tree chart**. The tree chart allows you to branch into the parts of the mechanism,

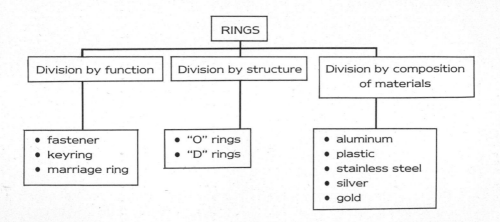

FIGURE 3.15 Division by parallel headings

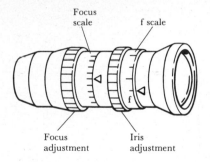

FIGURE 3.16 Television camera lens

and this branching gives the figure its name: tree chart. If you subdivide the components of the television camera lens using a tree chart analysis, you would have the division in Figure 3.17.

A tree chart is often used in computer programming. A marketing and engineering program in Figure 3.18 illustrates the concept of division. The program has two parallel applications: marketing and engineering. The marketing program has distinct uses: word processing, budget, customer service, and sales. The engineering program uses word processing, budget, and schedule.

If you compare the tree chart to the drawing of the filing cabinet, you can see the efficiency of the tree chart to convey hierarchical structures. The visuals that accompany the paragraphs, as well as the paragraphing techniques, must be applied to the entire document.

Extended Definition: Developing the Entire Document

When a reader needs to understand a term thoroughly, then definition may be the purpose of the entire document. Whether the definition is formal or

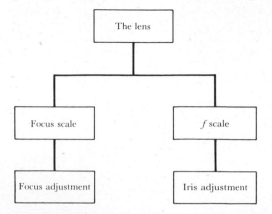

FIGURE 3.17 Tree chart for a television camera lens

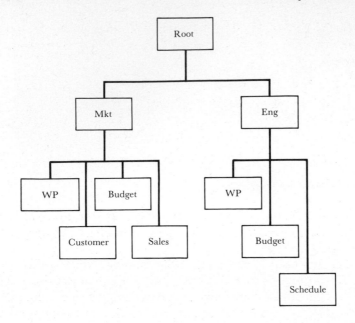

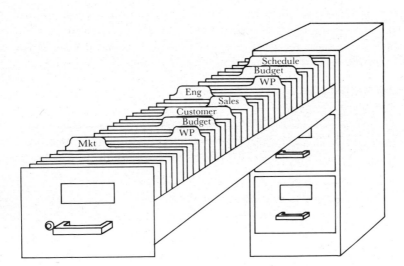

FIGURE 3.18 The tree chart for this marketing and engineering program is like a filing cabinet with information for two branches of a company's activities.
Source: Van Wolverton, *Running MS-DOS* (Bellevue, Wash.: Microsoft Press, 1984): 135. Reprinted by permission of Microsoft Press. Copyright © 1984 by Van Wolverton. All rights reserved.

operational, you will have to expand the definition by answering the reader's questions about the term:

What is it?
What does it look like?
What does it do?

To answer the reader's questions, you will have to write different types of paragraphs. In the first paragraph, you will have

• The essential (Aristotelian) definition, including term, class, differentiae.

or

• The operational definition.

Then you will need to describe it and explain what it does in detailed paragraphs:

analogy
example
comparison/contrast
division/partitioning (analysis)
etymology
stipulative
negative

The extended definition also demands attention to organization, diction, and, possibly, even to illustration.

Detailed Paragraphs

The choice of paragraphing techniques depends on the term and the reader's need. An etymological paragraph explaining the root or origin of the term may help the reader understand the appearance or function:

> phonocardiogram: cardi (Greek *kardi*: heart)
>   phono (Greek *phone*: sound)
>   gram (Greek *gramma*: a writing)

Phonocardiogram is a written recording of heart sounds. The stipulative explanation tells the reader how a term is being used for a particular situation.

> In physiology, the inferior position refers to the lower portion of an organ. For example, the inferior vena cava refers to the bottom vein feeding the heart.

The negative explanation tells the reader what the term is not, in the way of clarifying a misunderstanding.

> In physiology, the inferior vena cava does not mean that this vein is any less important than the superior vena cava.

Paragraphs of analogy, example, contrast, and analysis are described earlier in this module. All these techniques are useful for amplifying a definition, but the paragraphs must appear in a logical order.

Organization

Most extended definitions begin with the single line of definition; then you have to organize the additional information. Some of the paragraphs will have their own order, especially paragraphs organized around the division of parts. But all extended definitions will include paragraphs on the form (the appearance of the item) and the function of the term.

Diction

Careful diction and transitional words will help you move logically and coherently from paragraph to paragraph. If you have a term that you have classified as a laboratory instrument, do not change the class later in the text to a device. This attention to terminology will help to keep your document accurate and coherent by careful repetition of key words. Transitional words are words that help the reader see the connection among paragraphs. Diction, coherence, and transition are discussed in depth in Module 4. For now, the categories of transitional words will help you connect ideas from one paragraph to another.

To add:	also, and, furthermore, in addition
To contrast:	but, however, nevertheless, on the other hand
To summarize:	as a result, consequently, in summary, therefore
To exemplify:	for example, to illustrate, that is
To sequence:	first, second, in conclusion, finally
To enhance:	in fact, indeed, to highlight

Illustration

An illustration is optional, but it may supplement paragraphs describing appearance. If you use an illustration, remember to refer to it in the paragraph before you present it, and clearly label the parts to increase the reader's understanding. Module 5 provides more information about design and visual aids.

When the extended definition is part of a larger report, the definition usually appears in the introduction or introductory sections of a report rather than in the conclusion because the definition provides the reader with essential information to understand the report. On the other hand, the one-line definition appears any time the reader needs the information and especially in a glossary.

The example of an extended definition in Figure 3.19 illustrates the sole task of writing an extended definition. It fulfills the reader's need to know by describing appearance and function as well as by using accurate diction, coherent terms, transitional words, and a supplementary illustration. The purpose of the article is to explain a term used in a manufacturing company.

Change Parts

Formal definition

      Change parts are components of packaging machinery that allow the machinery to operate accurately on a particular type of container or part. Packaging machinery has many different mechanisms; each mechanism performs its specific operation on

Example

containers or parts fed into the machine. For example, in an automatic capper, one mechanism will deliver a container to the bottleholder where another mechanism screws a cap onto the container. Each mechanism in the capper can operate on many different sizes of containers. However, certain components of each mechanism must be changed to accommodate the different containers. These components, or change parts, are designed according to specifications from the dimensions of the particular container or cap they operate on. The following figure illustrates change parts.

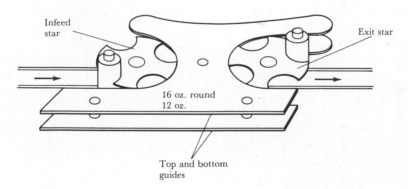

If we take the mechanism responsible for delivering a container to the bottleholder as an example, then we can easily understand the need for change

Division
Part 1

parts. Three change parts must be installed in the mechanism for this operation: two gears and a timer. The first gear adjusts the speed of the conveyor according to the size of the container. By installing sets

FIGURE 3.19 Extended definition
Source: Guy G. Gardner, Technical Writing 421, Illinois Institute of Technology.

function

of change gears with different ratios, the operator can adjust the speed of the conveyor so as to deliver each container accurately to the center of the bottleholder.

Part 2

function

The second gear moves the conveyor so that the container is removed before another one enters the bottleholder. Without this speed control, containers of different sizes would not be positioned accurately in the bottleholder, and they would eventually jam the machine.

Part 3

function

The third change part, the timer, is used to separate the containers before they reach the bottleholder. Operating the capper with the wrong timer will prevent the conveyor from positioning the container accurately in the bottleholder, and the machinery will jam immediately.

Negative

Change parts are not to be confused with spare parts. Spare parts are mass-produced and used universally on many different machines because they are not in direct contact with the container. Change parts are custom-made and designed for specific machines with mechanisms that are in direct contact with the container.

Analogy

In summary, then, the term *change parts* describes components of packaging machinery that enable one machine to adapt to different-size product parts. With change parts, a single machine becomes versatile and accurate. Human beings are considered to be one of the most versatile and adaptable species on earth. Just as people try to become more adaptable and accurate, so they attempt to make machinery more adaptable and accurate through the use of change parts.

FIGURE 3.19 (cont.)

Summary

Organizing the content of the document is important because organization helps the reader follow the logic of the document and find the information easily. When the organization, content, style, layout, and visuals aid the reader, then the ***readability*** of the document increases. Readability is an important concept in technical writing, and organization is an essential component of readability. Organization helps the reader follow the information in the document.

The overall organization depends on the audience and the purpose. Your reader's needs and your reason for writing the document shape the strategy you use to organize or design the document. All documents must use details or quantitative data and general statements. How you arrange these general statements and sentences of detail depends on logic. Logic involves *critical thinking*, and readers can follow information that is presented logically. In speaking or writing, there are two common paths for critical thinking: *inductive* and *deductive reasoning*.

Inductive and deductive reasoning provide strategies to arrange general and specific statements. When you present your details or data first, followed by a conclusion based on the data, then you are reasoning inductively. When you move from a general statement to specifics that support the statements, then you are thinking deductively. In inductive reasoning, readers follow your statements of detail and logically arrive at your conclusion (if you are persuasive in your specific statements). When you present the general statement first and support it with details, then the reader is encouraged to accept the general statement. Sometimes the general statement is called the *thesis*.

Other *presentation techniques* also help organize the document by answering the question, "What is the purpose of the document?" In technical writing, some of these techniques are used frequently because they aid in the writing of narrative, descriptive, procedural, or persuasive material. Finally, certain common documents—documents such as procedures, instructions, proposals, descriptions, reports, evaluations, and trip notes—often have content and physical text constraints. They must include certain information presented in specified sizes and structures. These organizational structures are also called *conventional* formats or designs. Conventional structures may be time-savers when you have to organize some common types of documents, but the important point to remember is that the reader's need and your reason for writing shape the document. As the writer, you are responsible for the organization and design of the document.

Because the organization must be clear to the reader from the beginning of the text, the *introduction* should include the *organizational plan* for the rest of the document. But often the reader also needs to know the *background* to understand the problem or the reason for the document. The background and the reason for the document provide your reader with a *context* for the rest of the information. And the organizational plan provides your reader with a map.

After you have an organizational strategy, you will have to provide the information in *paragraphs* organized under the main sections. Paragraphs help you develop information through a variety of techniques, including analogy, example, narration, cause/effect, formal and operative definition, and also classification, division, and partition. These techniques inform the reader, clarify the message, and enhance the readability of the document. Most technical writing combines a variety of these techniques.

An extended definition, a common technical writing task, exemplifies the organizational strategies and paragraphing techniques in a single document. The *extended definition* answers the reader's need to know what the term looks like and how it is used. Beginning with a one-line definition, the extended definition requires a variety of paragraphs, organization, attention to diction and transition, and possibly even an illustration.

Finally, you may use conventional organization or design your own strategy; you may narrate, exemplify, describe, or persuade. But you must always organize to meet your reader's needs.

Checklist for Organizational Strategies

This checklist asks you to think about how you organized your documents. Whether you organize before you write or write first to see where you are going, you should return to these questions about your organization. Check all those items that apply:

1. Basically, does the document move from

_____ general statement to specific details?

_____ specific details to a general statement?

2. Does your reader

_____ want the conclusion at the beginning of the document?

_____ expect to follow your data and arrive at your conclusion by the end of the document?

3. To make your presentation effective, do you have sections that

_____ narrate?

_____ describe?

_____ explain?

_____ persuade?

4. In your introduction have you stated the

_____ purpose?

_____ background?

_____ plan of development (also called road map or organizational strategy)?

5. To develop paragraphs with complete information, did you use

_____   analogy?

_____   example?

_____   cause/effect?

_____   definition?

_____   classification/division?

      6. Can you visualize your basic organizational pattern in

_____   chronological or logical series?

_____   list?

_____   hierarchy?

_____   tree charts?

_____   flowcharts?

_____   persuasive dialogue?

Notes

1. *Journal of Documentation Project Management,* Sandra Pakin & Associates, Inc. (Winter 1987). The excellent article, "Critical Success Factors," summarizes the skills of a successful technical writer.
2. Susan Feinberg and Irene Pritzker, "An MBA Communications Course Designed by Business Executives," *The Journal of Business Communication* 22 (Fall 1985): 75.
3. Julian Huxley, "War as a Biological Phenomenon," reprinted in McCuen and Winkler, *Readings for Writers,* 4th ed. (New York: Harcourt Brace Jovanovich, 1974): 295.
4. William Horton, "Templates of Thought," in *Proceedings,* 33d International Technical Communication Conference (Washington, D.C.: Society for Technical Communication, 1986): 302.
5. These strategies are suggested by Juanita Williams Dudley in *A Textworkbook for English 421—Technical Writing* (West Lafayette, Ind.: Purdue Research Foundation, 1978).
6. Candace Soderston and Carole German, "An Empirical Study of Analogy and Person in Computer Documentation," presented at the 32d International Technical Communication Conference, Houston, Texas, 1985.
7. Noel Mostert, *Supership* (New York: Warner Edition, 1976): 185.

8. Wilson Greatbatch, "Early People and Early Systems," *Implantable Active Devices* (Clarence, N.Y.: Greatbatch Enterprises Inc.): 1–7.
9. Irving M. Copi, *Introduction to Logic*, 3d ed. (New York: Macmillan, 1968).
10. Greatbatch, *Implantable Active Devices*, p. 7. Used with permission.
11. Garrett Hardin, "What the Hedgehog Knows," in *Exploring New Ethics for Survival* (New York: Viking, 1972).

References

Robin Battison and Dixie Goswami, "Clear Writing Today," *The Journal of Business Communication* 18: 4 (1981): 5–16.
Virginia A. Book, "Canons, Categories, and Technical Communication," *Journal of Technical Writing and Communication* 9 (1979): 303–310.
Richard T. Brucher, "Definition: The First Step in the Thinking/Writing Process," *Journal of Technical Writing and Communication* 10 (1980): 249–255.
Charles H. Sides, "Heuristics or Prescription: Synthesis Rather Than Choice," *Journal of Technical Writing and Communication* 11 (1981): 115–120.

Applying Your Knowledge

EXERCISE 3.1

In the margin, arrange these blocks in logical order for the audience and the purpose. What would you put first, second, and third?

A. *Evaluating Chairs*

_____ Six designer chairs were selected and compared in terms of price, comfort, durability, and ease of assembly. The prices ranged between $80.00 and $180.00 based on current retail prices. Specific features for the chairs are also included, when appropriate.

_____ If the budget allows, the buyer should seriously consider the Stressless chair as offering the best comfort per cost ratio. For moderate budgets, the buyer should consider the Ribbon chair. The consumer on a limited budget should consider either the Breuer or the Herman Miller chair, depending on the type of use.

_____ This report presents the results of an evaluation of selected designer chairs. Based on the findings of this report, the consumer may purchase the appropriate designer chair.

B. *Designing Forms*

_____ The basic procedure for carrying out my proposal involves three steps, which will be completed within three weeks.
Step one: Analyze the existing form and study its usage to determine the sources of the problems.

Step two: Establish standards and design forms to obtain complete information.

Step three: Submit at least two new form designs and prepare a report with recommendations on how to use the forms efficiently and effectively.

_____ The design of forms for office use and record keeping is a complex process. Not only must a form contain all essential information, but it must also be clear and concise. A properly designed form needs no additional explanation to fill it out; it is self-explanatory. As you are aware, the existing form is ambiguous, incomplete, and inaccurate, causing considerable inconvenience to both the students and the Academic Support Center. I propose to study the placement test form and its usage. Upon completion of my investigation, I will submit at least two newly designed forms for your inspection and a report detailing how to use the forms most effectively.

_____ I appreciate your consideration of my proposal. The best proof I can offer for the success of this project stems from my experience with the Office of Admissions and Records. I redesigned many of the forms used by that office, forms that originally suffered from the same problems as your placement forms. My redesigned forms are still in use.

EXERCISE 3.2

Given the following facts, move inductively to draw your conclusions.

- In 1980 the Tek Electronics company hired seven engineers.
- In 1981 the Tek Electronics company hired five engineers and one technical writer.
- In 1982 the Tek Electronics Company hired eight engineers and one technical writer.
- In 1983 the Tek Electronics Company hired six engineers and two technical writers.

EXERCISE 3.3

Beginning with the general statement, "I would be an excellent candidate for the position in your company," support the statement with data.

EXERCISE 3.4

To practice inductive reasoning, read the annual report of a company and draw some conclusions based on the facts in the report.

EXERCISE 3.5

To practice deductive reasoning, state your opinion about the safety of nuclear energy and support your opinion with facts.

EXERCISE 3.6

Use the Aristotelian method to define the following terms:

a stethoscope
a telephone
an electric car
a mousetrap
a micrometer

Use the operational method to define the following terms:

an automobile accident
an electric power failure
a computer program error

EXERCISE 3.7

Apply these questions to the following writing tasks:

- What is your purpose?
- What are your paragraphing techniques?
- What visual construct best illustrates your organization?

the campfire yarn
a quarterly report of the stock market
the sinking of the *Titanic*
a sales brochure
a playscript scenario
a handbook on protocol
assembly instructions for a toy or a nuclear power plant
technical proposal
scientific paper
philosophic or scientific dialogue
shopping or laundry list
legal brief
agenda for a meeting
decision about how to time stoplights
word processing documentation
military parts list
board game like Monopoly

EXERCISE 3.8

Using the illustration of the wheelchair, draw a tree chart to organize the parts and subparts.

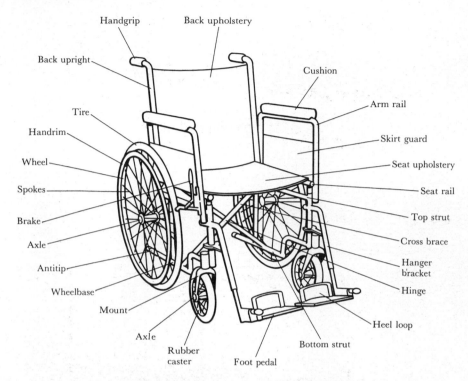

Source: Lauren S. Schwartz, Technical Writing 421, Illinois Institute of Technology.

WRITING ASSIGNMENT

Write an extended definition of a term you use frequently in your field. Use at least three paragraphing techniques to amplify your essential or operational definition. Consider your use of accurate diction, transition, and visuals, if appropriate.

M O D U L E   4

Readability and Style

This module explains some writing techniques that will help you present technical information clearly to the reader. **Clear technical writing** is difficult because often the ideas are complex and the information must be accurate. When you write clearly and consider the reader's ability to absorb information, then you enhance the **readability** of the document.

Clear writing is an important component of readability. This module explains some techniques that will help you write and edit text so that the reader comprehends the information. No matter how familiar the reader is with the subject, if the information is not presented clearly or in manageable units, then the reader will be overwhelmed or confused.

For your writing style, when you select clear words, phrases, and sentences, as well as the connections between sentences, you improve the readability of the document. Other aids to making text clearer are the computer programs that analyze the text. This module briefly describes some types of **text analysis programs** on the market, programs that provide information on grammar, spelling, syntax, and other surface features of the text. More important, though, this module emphasizes what you can do to make your writing clearer and why you should do it.

Scope

In this module you will practice

1. Writing clear sentences by
   - Finding the strong verb.
   - Completing the sentence.
   - Changing nominalizations.
   - Evaluating active versus passive voice.
   - Connecting sentences coherently.
   - Using parallel structure.
2. Editing sentences by
   - Shortening sentences.
   - Using brevity and length appropriately.
   - Unstacking nouns and adjectives.
   - Avoiding jargon and sexist language.
   - Lengthening sentences using modifiers.
3. Applying a readability formula.
4. Identifying text analyses programs.

Writing to Be Clear

Good writing depends on your skill as a writer to make the document clear and comprehensible. The reader expects the words in a sentence and the sentences in a paragraph to flow in a familiar order, just as the reader expects the document to be organized appropriately for the content. There are some basic techniques that you can practice to improve the flow of words. First, the reader expects to find the three basic parts in the majority of sentences you write. These parts are

> subject, verb, object

If you think of the parts as holding slots in a sentence, then you have a sentence with three slots:

subject	verb	object

Using these slots in a sentence and filling them in with appropriate words will help you write clear sentences. In his book, *Style: Ten Lessons in Clarity and Grace,* Joseph Williams uses these slots to help the writer develop a clear writing style.[1] Some of the advice in this module is adapted from his excellent text.

Find the Verb

The first principle for a clear and direct statement is to fill the **verb** slot in the sentence by expressing the crucial **action** as a verb. Locate the verb in the sentence by deciding on the crucial action even if you have to change a noun in the sentence to a verb. Ask yourself, What is the crucial action in the sentence?

> *Example*
> *Original sentence:* We made a decision to have a discussion on the subject.
>   **(ACTION: decide, discuss)**
> *Revised sentence:* We decided to discuss the subject.
> *Original sentence:* There was a modification of the program by the state.
>   **(ACTION: modify)**
> *Revised sentence:* The state modified the program.

Complete the Sentence

If you keep the action in the verb as often as possible, then all actions have somebody or something that acts: the **agent** or the **subject.** Once you find the verb, then ask of the verb:

Who or what does this?
or
Who or what is this?

In the preceding sentences, you would ask of the verb:

Who or what decided or discussed?
(AGENT: We)
Who or what modified?
(AGENT: The state)

The agent then moves into the subject slot in front of the verb slot that contains the crucial action. Figure 4.1 illustrates the slots.

The final slot contains the **object** of the sentence. In a sentence, most actions are followed by objects (somebody or something is acted upon) to accomplish the **goal** of the agent and action. So agent, action, and goal take up three slots in a sentence. The other words connect agents, actions, and goals or supply additional information.

Example

(Subject) Agent	(Verb) Action	(Object) Goal
We	decided to discuss	subject
The state	modified	program

FIGURE 4.1 The three slots in a sentence

To Complete the Slots in a Sentence,
Ask Yourself the Following Questions:

1. What is the crucial **action** in the sentence?
2. Who or what **agent** does this? *or* Who or what **agent** is this?
3. The action and agent accomplish what **goal?**

> *Example:* The actions of operator number 2 were observed by us.

Crucial action?	observed
What agent observed?	We
We observed what goal?	the actions of operator number 2

> *Revision:* We observed the actions of operator number 2.
>
> *Example:* Any errors on the tax returns that are created by us will be corrected or revised by us.

Action?	correct or revise	created
Agent?	we	we
Goal?	errors on tax returns [that]	

> *Revision:* We will correct or revise any errors on tax returns that we created.

Example

Agent (Subject)	Action (verb)	Goal (Object)
We	will correct or revise	errors
we	created	the actions of operator
	observed	number 2

EXERCISE 4.1

Find the crucial action and ask of the action, Who or what does this? or Who or what is this? Then place the agent in the subject slot and the action in the verb slot in the sentence, and rewrite the sentence. You may have to create an agent.

1. There was a reduction of the staff by the president.
2. The alteration of the bill was approved by the investigating committee.
3. Directions and questions directed to the user also appear on the screen.
4. Other keys are used to instruct the computer to carry out various functions.
5. The wheelchair can be pushed by an attendant from the rubber handgrips located at the top of the back uprights.
6. In this part of the report is found a presentation of the medical technicalities of the case in lay language.
7. In the way training has been done in the past, there are several deficiencies.

8. Before writing the copy for the brochure, the information to be included in it had to be acquired.
9. Such things as cost overruns, breakdowns, maintenance, and delays can be kept track of by the computer.
10. The Prints Accounts section sets up a condition, and if the condition is not met, there will be a set of operations to be performed.

Change Nominalizations

When a writer makes a noun from a verb or an adjective, the writer is nominalizing the verb. In general, **nominalizations** weaken a sentence because they detract from the verb. Sometimes nominalizations make the sentence wordy because

1. The noun is longer than the verb.
2. A prepositional phrase often follows the nominalization.

As often as possible, change the noun back to its verb form and keep the action in the verbs. You can easily distinguish the nouns that should appear as verbs because the sentence will be full of words that end in *-tion, -ence, -ing, -ment, -ness, -acy, -ity*. In the next example, the noun *evaluation* ends in *-tion* and is followed by the prepositional phrase *of the program*.

> *Not this:* An *evaluation* **of the program** has been made by the project directors that was the *motivation* **for the next round** of government funding.
> *But this:* The project directors have evaluated the program that motivated the next round of government funding.
> *Not this:* The *adoption* of **a waste management program** on the part **of the public** was due to public *awareness* of the problem.
> *But this:* The public adopted the waste management program because they were aware of the problem.

You cannot avoid all nominalizations because they summarize ideas from the preceding sentence.

> *Example:* We adjusted the interest rate on your home loan. This **adjustment** will reduce your monthly payments.

The nominalizations in the following list appear frequently. Although the list is not exhaustive, it provides you with nouns that could easily return to verbs.

failure	indications
adjustment	negotiations
occurrence	exemplification
requirement	alterability
analysis	achievement
confirmation	development
agreement	decision

When you change the nominalization to a verb, keep the subject, verb, and object fairly close together and near the beginning of the sentence.

For review, then, to reduce wordiness and make the action of the sentence clear,

1. Find the key action.
2. Change a noun to the crucial verb if necessary.
2. Add the agent.
3. Add the goal.

> *Not this:* Chuck made an **enumeration of his main points.** (8 words)
> *But this:* Chuck **enumerated** his main points. (5 words)
> *Not this:* **Analysis of the results** of the survey was done by the author. (12 words)
> *But this:* The author **analyzed** the results of the survey. (8 words)
> *Not this:* 1.5 percent **gain** over last quarter was reported by the stock market. (13 words)
> *But this:* The stock market **gained** 1.5 percent over the last quarter. (10 words)

EXERCISE 4.2

Rewrite the following sentences, eliminating as many nominalizations as possible.

1. With the emergence of wheelchair sports and the growing awareness of the needs of the disabled, new wheelchairs have been developed.
2. Careful consideration of the wheelchair options available should help match the proper wheelchair to the user's needs.
3. Success of analysis could be increased if provisions for recording all data are made.
4. Once the molten metal is in alignment with the ladle opening, molten metal is released into the pouring basin.
5. A program is a plan or procedure to code instructions of a desired operation or performance for a computer.

Evaluate Active Versus Passive Voice

When the agent is performing the action, the verb is in the **active voice.** When the agent is being acted upon, the verb is in the **passive voice.** To write clearly, we need to use both the active and the passive voices for emphasis and for exact expression.

If you want to emphasize who performed an action, place the agent in the subject slot with the goal following the verb. Then the verb is in the active voice.

Example: **Active Voice**

Agent/Subject	Action/Verb	Goal/Object
The police	threatened	the students.

If the agent is unknown or unimportant and you want to stress who was affected by the action or what happened, place the person or thing acted upon in the subject slot followed by a verb in the passive voice and the agent either in the goal slot or omitted entirely.

Example: **Passive Voice**

Subject/Agent	Verb/Passive	Goal/Object
The students	were threatened	by the police.
A brochure	is enclosed.	

Often in a sentence in the passive voice, the agent appears in a prepositional phrase, such as "by the police."

The decision as to which voice to use rests with the writer, and you must decide on the basis of your meaning and the content of the sentence. The passive voice is not forbidden. Sometimes it must be used, as it is in this and the preceding sentence, because the goal is more important than the agent. Methodology sections in research reports are often written in the passive voice because the method is more important than the performer.

But when you use the passive voice to avoid using the personal pronoun such as **I, we,** or **you,** you will overuse the passive voice and write sentences laden with repetitious verbs and prepositional phrases. If you must avoid the pronoun **I,** use the more impersonal **this office** or **the agency.** Also refer to the reader as **you** whenever you can. At least you will be writing more vigorous and more concise sentences.

In short, when either the active or the passive voice suits your purpose, use the active voice because it will increase the vigor of your writing. The active voice is simpler and more vigorous. With the active voice you will use a greater variety of verbs because the passive voice always consists of a form of the verb **be.** In many cases, you will also eliminate a prepositional phrase that contains the agent.

Example: During the audit of Mr. Green's 1988 income tax return, he **was asked by the agent** to substantiate certain deductions. He **was** also **asked** to obtain a record from his employer showing the number of trips he had made during the year. On the basis of these records, the agent arrived at an amount for each trip and a settlement **was proposed** on that basis.

Revision: During the audit of Mr. Green's 1988 income tax return, the **agent asked** him to substantiate certain deductions and to obtain a record from his employer showing the number of trips he had made during the year. On the basis of these records, the **agent arrived** at an amount for each trip and **proposed** a settlement on that basis.

We need both the active and passive voices, but when either is appropriate, select the sharpness of the active voice.

EXERCISE 4.3 ═══

Rewrite the following sentences, if necessary, to change the sentences into the active voice. Retain the passives when appropriate and defend your decisions.

1. The variable features considered in this evaluation are presented in Table 1.
2. The TV can be powered by 12V DC with the proper adapter.
3. Within the past few years, a new format has been made available to the consumer, that is, the laser compact disc (CD).
4. The most pertinent criteria for a CD player have been listed as follows.
5. The touch tone telephone can be plugged into any modular phone jack.
6. When we receive your travel request, arrangements can be made to process a cash advance.
7. The investigation will be terminated within 10 days, and we will let you know our decision 3 days after termination.
8. For the purpose of using the computers more effectively, a reorganization of the office space and personnel was initiated.

Connect Sentences Coherently

When you begin to write a series of sentences for a paragraph, you have to sequence the information in the sentences so that one sentence flows into the next one coherently. In other words, if a paragraph is **coherent,** one sentence will lead logically into the thought of the next sentence.

In his book on style, Williams suggests that to make sentences coherent, you should organize the information in a sentence into two parts: **old information** and **new information.** Put more familiar information at the beginning of the sentence to orient a reader. After the verb put the new information you intend to develop. Think of the familiar information at the beginning of the sentence as ideas already stated or readily known, in other words, as old information. Think of the information at the end of the sentence, after the verb, as the most significant and important new information.[2]

When you plan a coherent sentence, place the old information in the first half of the sentence, and place the new information in the second half of the sentence. In the second half of the sentence, you place the information you want to emphasize. Figure 4.2 organizes the sentence for coherence and emphasis.

Example		
Subject	**Verb**	**Object**
Agent	Action	Goal
Old information		New information

FIGURE 4.2 Organizing the information in a sentence

Not this: The scientists discovered the dangers of radiation at the turn of the century.

But this: At the turn of the century, the scientists discovered the dangers of radiation.

With the important information about radiation at the end of the sentence, the next sentence can use the subject of radiation as old information and supply new information about the dangers of radiation.

Plus this: Radiation damaged the bone marrow and produced leukemia.

As a general rule

- Put short old information before the verb.
- Put long new information after the verb.

As you add sentences to build a paragraph,

- Make the new information from one sentence the old information of your next sentence.

This string of linking information will help you build a **coherent** sequence of sentences in the paragraph.

Example

Sentence 1: OLD INFORMATION + NEW INFORMATION →
We know that X-radiation is produced when high-speed electrons strike a **target.**

Sentence 2: The **target** converts the energy to heat and X rays.
OLD INFORMATION + NEW INFORMATION

When a sentence contains more than one important point, you can split the sentence into a sequence of sentences, linking old information to new information.

Not this: AIDS is a paradigm of the havoc that results when the delicate balance, evolved over millions of years, between humans and their microbial environment, breaks down.

But this: Over millions of years humans and their microbial environment developed a delicate balance. When that balance breaks down, AIDS is a paradigm of the havoc that results.

Don't hesitate to repeat the same subject through a series of consecutive sentences. Repeating a subject, key words, a phrase, or a pattern will establish a coherent sequence and help your reader follow your meaning more easily. In the following example, the revision improves the original sentence by repeating a pattern.

Not this: The purpose is twofold: (1) This project should involve the public in
           sharing responsibilities for safeguarding the environment and (2) in
           developing a system that will allow the public to do so.

But this: The purpose of this project is twofold: (1) to involve the public in
           sharing responsibilities for safeguarding the environment and (2) to
           develop a system that will allow the public to participate.

Use Parallel Structure

When you write a list, an outline, or a sentence with a series of grammatical
elements, such as verbs, nouns, infinitives *(to protect)*, or gerunds *(improving)*,
you are writing in a balanced or **coordinated** pattern called **parallel structure.**
Parallel structure helps you avoid awkward sentences and lists or headings
that jar your reader. When you write a sentence with coordinate or parallel
elements, the advice is relatively simple:

> nouns = nouns; phrases = phrases; verbs = verbs; subordinate clauses =
> subordinate clauses; and so forth.

**Not this: Faulty Parallelism (present tense verb vs. noun and gerund and
noun)**
The responsibilities are that the technician **determine** the practice, **selection**
of the site, **supervising** the installation, and **certification** of the safety of
the equipment.

But this: The responsibilities are that the technician **determine** the practice,
           select the site, **supervise** the installation, and **certify** the safety of
           the equipment.

Or this: The technician's responsibilities are **determining** the practice,
           selecting the site, **supervising** the installation, and **certifying** the
           safety of the equipment.

Not this: Faulty parallelism (subordinate clause vs. noun)
The main criteria for the grant are **that the company** has laboratories and **its
experienced personnel.**

But this: The main criteria for the grant are **that the company has laboratories**
           and **that the personnel have experience.**

Or this: The main criteria for the grant are the company's **laboratories** and
           experienced personnel.

Other coordinating or parallel elements in a sentence are called **correlative conjunctions,** and these conjunctions work in pairs to show words or
ideas that are parallel in structure. Among the correlative conjunctions are

either . . . or   neither . . . nor
not only . . . but also   if . . . then
both . . . and   because . . . therefore

If *not only* is followed by an adjective, then *but also* must be followed by an
adjective:

Not this: The reply was not only **prompt** but also **it was complete.**
But this: The reply was not only prompt but also complete.

With headings in outlines or in text, the organization should also be parallel. You would have a faulty outline if your headings were

  I. Lung Malignancy
 II. Heart Disease
III. Gathering Data
IV. Liver Disorder

Gathering Data is important, but it does not fit in grammatically or logically with the other items (organs in the body, all nouns) in the list. You would have to revise your organizing principle to include gathering data or remove the topic and insert it under one or all of the other relevant topics.

Lists are used so frequently in technical writing that it is important to remember the principle of parallel structure. Make sure your lists have the same grammatical constructions:

All gerunds: Finding strong verbs.
                 Completing sentences.
                 Changing nominalizations.
                 Evaluating active vs. passive voice.
                 Using parallel structure.
All imperative verbs: Hold the can securely.
                 Lift the lever at the top of the can opener.
                 Place the rim of the can between the gear with the teeth
                    and the sharpened, circular blade.
                 Press down on the lever . . .
All abbreviated sentences: Facilities Inadequate
                 Personnel Inexperienced
All questions: How Can You Improve Facilities?
                 How Can You Train Personnel?

EXERCISE 4.4

Correct the problems in faulty parallelism.

1. As a consumer, you should follow these procedures:
   a. Shop more before you buy.
   b. Your complaint should be brought first to the seller.
   c. Reporting false advertising to the media should be done.
   d. Deception should be reported to the local organization concerned with better business standards.
   e. The Fair Trade Commission should be written and told the facts as a last resort.
2. The chapters in the manual discuss
   a. Determining the need for the service.
   b. Selecting the site.
   c. Supervising the installation.
   d. Performance of the personnel.

3. Many business letters are unwieldy because of content, some are too long, or then, too, there are some of a legal nature.
4. The finance committee will not only study the problem, but also recommendations will be made as to the solutions.
5. Please advise us if our assumption is incorrect, and a further investigation of your claim will be made.
6. The report is not only a presentation of a list of problems facing us but also designates personnel who can assist with the problems.
7. One of the supervisors complimented the staff not only on their systematic approach to data processing but also he was impressed with their promptness.

Editing Sentences

You can now apply your knowledge of clear sentence patterns to editing your own documents and the documents of others. Factors other than sentence patterns also affect the readability of information and are important when editing documents. For example, the length of sentences and the complexity of the terminology affect the amount of information a reader can absorb. Of course, familiarity with the subject matter makes a difference in the reader's understanding, but even readers who are familiar with the subject may be overwhelmed with sentences laden with too many words.

Shorten Sentences

Sentences grow longer when you add clauses to the basic sentence pattern of agent, action, and goal. Words such as **which** and **that** introduce clauses that confuse reader and writer alike. Few writers remember the difference between *which* and *that*. A simple rule of thumb is to use the word *that* to introduce a restrictive clause. A restrictive clause is vital to the sentence because the clause provides the reader with more complete information. If you are adding essential information to a sentence, introduce the information in a *that* clause and use no additional punctuation.

> **Example:** Before you go on to the next page, answer the questions **that** review Section 1.

On the other hand, if you are adding information that is nonessential to the sentence, then you are adding a nonrestrictive clause. The nonrestrictive clause is introduced by the word *which* and a comma before *which*.

> **Example:** The user can delete the unit of text by using the define function, **which** is also useful for deleting large blocks of text.

The comma before the *which* clause tells the reader the information is unessential and could be dropped out of the sentence. In technical writing, unessential information can be omitted. So the clause after the comma can be omitted. In other words, use the *which* clause sparingly in technical writing. Instead, use *that* and make all your information essential.

Not only do *which* and *that* clauses cause trouble for the writer, but they also affect the reader because they may decrease readability. Clauses increase the length of sentences. In their research on training manuals, Bell Laboratories discovered that the average sentence length is between 13 and 20 words. If sentence after sentence exceeds 20 words, look at the sentences closely. Often you can split a sentence if the sentence has *and, but,* or *because* in it or if the sentence has a *who, which,* or *that* clause. If a long sentence becomes confusing, place slashes before these words, as the example in Figure 4.3 indicates.

Then look at each segment of the divided sentence, and determine the crucial action of the segment. Remember to change a noun to a verb if possible. After locating the action, add an agent that acts and complete the sentence with the goal. Figure 4.4 revises the long sentences, and Figure 4.5 adds connectors to reduce the monotonous sentence patterns and improve coherence.

Example

However, it was soon realized that the peculiar nonexperimental nature of the economic process rendered classical methods inappropriate,//because the variables appearing on the right-hand side of the econometrician's equations are not subject to his or her control//but are jointly determined by the simultaneous interaction of the equations in the system,// so that these variables will not be independent of the error terms in the equations//and hence classical least square methods will produce biased and inconsistent estimates of structural parameters.

FIGURE 4.3 Slashes before coordinating conjunctions and connectives
Source: John Kirkman, consultant in communication.

Example

However, the advisers soon realized that the peculiar nonexperimental nature of the economic process made classical methods inappropriate. Classical methods are inappropriate because the variables appearing on the right-hand side of the econometrician's equations are not subject to his or her control. The variables are jointly determined by the simultaneous interaction of the equations in the system. Thus, these variables will depend on the error terms in the equations. As a result, classical least squares methods will produce biased and inconsistent estimates of structural parameters.

FIGURE 4.4 Revised version

The two preceding examples and the final version in Figure 4.5 illustrate four aspects of editing long sentences:

1. Break the sentence into segments, usually at words such as **and, but, because, who, which, that.**
2. Locate the crucial action in each segment even if you change a noun to a verb.
3. Add an agent and a goal to each segment.
4. If the sentences in the resulting sequence are too short and monotonous, add connectors between some of the segments.

Example

However, the advisers soon realized that the peculiar nonexperimental nature of the economic process made the classical methods inappropriate. The methods are inappropriate because the variables appearing on the right-hand side of the econometrician's equations are not under his or her control. The variables are jointly determined by the simultaneous interaction of the equations in the system. Accordingly, these variables will depend on the error terms in the equations, and classical least squares methods will produce biased and inconsistent estimates of structural parameters.

FIGURE 4.5 Final version

A final word on shortening sentences cautions you about the use of **expletives.** Avoid using *there are, these are, this is,* and *it is* because these expletives add no information to the text and lengthen the sentence.

Not: There are no known solutions to this problem.
But: Scientists know no solutions to this problem.
Not: It is this state of ambiguity that increases the user's confusion.
But: This ambiguity confuses the user.

EXERCISE 4.5 ═══

All these sentences are too long. Split them into smaller units; then edit them using the four steps just given.

1. Use the information here to learn what qualities to look for in a tree that is hardy, and then locate a good nursery worker to help you expand your choices within the range of those trees that will grow in your climate.
2. There are over 60 million metric tons of nonradioactive hazardous waste generated each year by the manufacturing industry alone, and when one considers the fact that over 80 percent of all hazardous waste ever produced has been disposed of in environmentally unsound methods, this translates into an awesome problem that has only begun to surface (in more than one sense).
3. The bureau will decentralize functions to two regional offices that will establish their own operating procedures to reorganize to be completed by October 1 and retaining only the original mission of federal control of toxic waste.
4. All the adaptations in living beings, like all the artifacts they produce, are the fulfillment of particular projects that may be seen as so many aspects of a unique primary project, which is the preservation and multiplication of the species.
5. The Quadra Fold overall rated the best, but the Rolls 500 did nearly as well and offered some features that may make it more attractive to many users such as the availability of the open-locked position.
6. A mechanism is provided for conveniently removing the inner electrode so that a sample can be introduced and then returning the inner electrode so that the sample floods the gap between the two electrodes.

Unstack Nouns

Sometimes even short sentences can be too densely packed. When the writer stacks too many modifiers in a string of words or links too many noun phrases together in a sentence, then the short sentence may still be difficult for the reader to digest. Readers are often confused by a string of more than three nouns and modifiers, especially if the short sentence has two such strings of words. You can edit these densely packed short sentences by (1) unstacking the phrases and then (2) placing the agents and actions into the subject and verb positions in the sentence. Unstack the nouns by

• Changing nouns into verbs whenever possible.
• Rewriting the string with the last noun first.
• Adding a prepositional phrase.

Example

The system is an interactive computer network with extensive information storage capabilities.
    4   3   2   1
capabilities storage information extensive
capable (of) storing large amounts (of) information
The system is an interactive computer network
capable of storing large amounts of information.

In scientific and technical writing, we often find a sentence that strings nouns together and uses nominalizations instead of verbs. Although these sentences may seem to be economical in total number of words, they are ambiguous and confuse the reader. Many times the content-laden nouns need the little words—the conjunction **and,** the preposition **of,** the article **an**—to hold the content together. A pamphlet published by the United States Environmental Protection Agency discusses several of the writing problems in this module, including the ambiguity that arises when writers string nouns together.[3]

Example: Inferior product labeling requirements
Does the example mean
Inferior requirements for product labeling
or
Requirements for labeling inferior products?

Unstacking noun strings will solve the problem of ambiguity for the reader. Furthermore, unstacking noun strings will avoid some hyphens. *Hyphenation* is dying because it adds clutter to the text. Many words that were once hyphenated are being written *without* hyphenation, just as lines are being eliminated in the drawing of tables.

Example: solutionlike; multidisc; uppercase; shutdown; juxtanuclear

---

Because most word processing programs tend to move words automatically to the next line and use proportional spacing to eliminate hyphenating words, when you are tempted to hyphenate, check the spelling of the word in a current dictionary.

To Edit a Sentence with Noun Strings, Try the Following Remedies

1. Place the last noun in the phrase first as an aid to unstacking.
2. Change nominalizations into verbs if appropriate.
3. Add prepositional phrases to connect nouns.

> *Not this:* Last week's meeting was devoted to surface water quality protection procedures development.
>
> *But this:* At the meeting last week we developed the procedures to protect the quality of surface water.

EXERCISE 4.6 ===========

Edit the following packed sentences. Turn the stacked nouns into verbs and prepositional phrases; then place agents and actions into a sentence, inventing agents when necessary.

1. This aspect of the system is separated into two parts: a signal initiating heat detection device and the signal carrying wires.
2. I submit the accompanying report, entitled "Computer Needs Analysis for Central Photo Shop."
3. Advertising rate sheet information is available on request.
4. The results of the solutionlike conformation surface area calculation is closer to the observed nitroxyl rate than the crystal structure.

Use Brevity and Length Appropriately

It is important to distinguish between sentences that are needlessly wordy or inflated and sentences that should repeat words or phrases for the reader's ease of understanding. Short sentences are not necessarily clear, and long sentences are not necessarily obscure. When a writer achieves brevity by packing a short sentence with confusing noun strings, then obviously the writer is practicing a false economy. Similarly, when the sentence repeats a word or when a passage from a text repeats a pronoun or a phrase, the repetition may promote clarity for the reader. Remember that information may be repeated in a sentence to establish coherent thought in the passage. Take, for example, a coherent passage from Strunk and White's famous book, *The Elements of Style.*[4]

> *Sentence 1*
> Vigorous writing is concise.
> **OLD INFORMATION + NEW INFORMATION**

> *Sentence 2 (OLD INFORMATION)* +
> A sentence should contain no unnecessary words; a paragraph, no unnecessary sentences, (+)

(NEW INFORMATION)
for the same reason that a drawing should have no unnecessary lines; and a
machine, no unnecessary parts.

On the other hand, think of editing for brevity when the sentence contains **inflated language.** Inflated language is an attempt to impress the reader
and is the opposite of slang, but, like slang, it usually interferes with the
message the reader receives and decreases readability.

Not this: translocate   *But this:* move
Not this: juxta-arterial position   *But this:* next to the artery
Not this: The batches experienced a color change during storage.
But this: The batches changed color during storage.

Edit for brevity when the sentence uses nominalizations rather than verbs

Not this: Terminals can employ transmission verification.
But this: Terminals can verify transmission.

or when the agent in a sentence can be moved to the beginning of the sentence or can be added to the sentence to aid the reader's understanding of
the information.

Not this: Removal of the coating can be affected by the application of Z.
But this: Z will remove the coating.
Not this: Calculations of the yield were performed that revealed the original
           weight.
But this: We calculated the yield and found the original weight.
Not this: No experiments have been conducted on the rats.
But this: We have not experimented on the rats.

Avoid Jargon and Sexist Language

Like inflated language, jargon makes a sentence more complex and confusing. When you use the less familiar word, even though it may be short, it
interrupts the reader's progress with the information. Jargon jars the reader;
the reader may be unfamiliar with the special terminology used in the professional field. Remember that jargon is appropriate for communication between
experts. If the reader is unfamiliar with the jargon or uncomfortable with
the vocabulary, then the writer must edit the sentence.

It would be impossible to list all the words that might be jargon. The
reason is the language itself. Words are appropriate for a certain audience
within a special environment. One person's technical language is another
person's jargon or **shoptalk.** The government is notorious for using bureau-
cratese, legalese, or acronyms (words formed from the initial letters of a
name). The U.S. Environmental Protection Agency (EPA) reminds writers
that people who work together become inbred. They develop their own language to communicate with each other accurately. For example, mathema-
ticians use **parameter** and **optimize** to refer to special concepts; lawyers use

litigate and **proximate cause;** computer specialists need **input, interface,** and **database.**

But when these languages creep into public announcements, the announcements become unintelligible to the audience. If you keep your audience in mind, you will be conscious of words special to your field and try to define them when writing to an audience outside your field or your environment.

At EPA people made a list of jargon used frequently and disliked heartily.[5]

to impact on — to affect or influence
    prioritize — assign priorities or rank by priority
   implement — do, carry out, perform
      finalize — make final, complete, finish
  necessitate — compel, must
    facilitate — make . . . easier

John Kirkman, an internationally known linguist, consultant, and writer in the field of scientific and technical communication, compiled a list of inflated vocabulary and inefficient jargon. These words and phrases should be edited for the reader's convenience:[6]

Vocabulary

utilize	= use
manifests	= shows
initiate manual shutdown	= begin the shutdown of the (equipment) manually
occupies a juxtanuclear position	= is next to the nucleus
unidirectional heat flow	= one-way heat flow
endeavor to ameliorate	= try to improve
in the event of fire, evacuation of the building	= leave the
it is visualized that no servicing	= we do not see (think) that . . .
homologous	= alike
pervasively	= throughout

Jargon

solar energy	= sun
enhances	= improves, increases
parameters	= variables
increased by a factor of 2	= doubled
aggregate	= total
with regard to	= regarding
boot a system	= start a system
ceiling	= limit
optimum	= best
economically disadvantaged	= poor

Specialists need to use their own technical vocabularies when they communicate with other specialists in the same environment, but you must remember that a large part of your communication will travel not only beyond your field, but far beyond your workplace. Perhaps Mark Twain had the final word on terminology: "Avoid obfuscation."

A problem related to terminology is the **gender-specific** confusion. People who write for the government are particularly sensitive to the problem and offer some good advice. This advice, adapted from the EPA pamphlet, explains the problem of gender-specific pronouns and **sexist language.**[7]

Example 1: As chairman, (chairperson? chairwoman? chair? head?) of the task force, I believe. . . .

Example 2: Every regional administrator should send his (her? his/her? their?) forms in by June 30.

On the one hand, some people believe that forms like *chairman* in Example 1 and *his* in Example 2 subtly bias our thinking against women—that masculine gender encourages us to think first about placing men in these positions. On the other hand, contortions to avoid the problem often lead to incorrect grammar, as in the next example, with its singular subject and plural pronoun *their:*

Example 3: Each respondent should send in *their* comments within 30 days.

One solution is to avoid sex-linked nouns and titles: chairperson has become acceptable, but

Instead of	**Use**
man years or person years	work years
fireman	fire fighter
spokesman or spokesperson	representative, speaker, or head representative

Not: The manpower for whale sitings came from Earth Watch.
But: The personnel for whale sitings came from Earth Watch.

Another solution is to avoid the problem. For Example 4, regional administrators may be both men and women. Thus

---

Example 4A: Each regional administrator should send his or her forms in by June 30.

---

is acceptable, but not as good as

Example 4B: Regional administrators should send their forms in by June 30.

(Be careful, though, about substituting plurals for singulars. Example 5A does not mean the same thing as 5B).

Example 5A: Each regional administrator will deliver his or her conclusions at the meeting.

Example 5B: Regional administrators will deliver their conclusions at the meeting.

(Will the administrators deliver conclusions individually or collectively?)

EXERCISE 4.7

Edit the following sentences for vocabulary appropriate to the general reader.

1. When touched, the typewriter tabs will sink to become level to the surface.
2. Stephen Brown made an assessment of the revenue requirements for the bank's financial integrity.
3. Life-style innovation may also be a basis for design innovation.
4. The oil-lubricated, multidisc clutch packs for the 12-bolt rear end are enhancements for road performance.
5. After the driver did not properly execute the maneuver, it was thought that the movement of the pylons was a good idea.

EXERCISE 4.8

Select an article from a journal either in your field or in an area of your outside interest. Ask a classmate to read the article, highlight sentences and words that are inappropriate for the classmate-reader, and return the article to you. All of us have difficulty determining what readers may or may not understand about our professional fields or our particular interests. This exercise will indicate terminology and jargon, sentence length, and complexity that may confuse the general or executive reader outside your field. Make notes here of those highlighted sentences and words; then edit them for the general/executive reader.

Edit the following sentences for brevity and the reader's convenience.

1. Automating the testing of the CX2 hybrids will give the technician time to work on the other hybrids and help her stay on schedule.
2. High strength and resistance to wear are needed to support the weight of a train that is transmitted through the wheel over a constant area of about 0.5 in.
3. The precision of measurement now allows more accurate identification of earthquake faults.
4. Withdrawal prior to maturity will be permitted only with the consent of the bank, which may be given only at the time withdrawal is sought.
5. With this ski binding you get upper-boot radius contact points at the toe and lateral boot holders at the heel for increased retention.

Lengthen Sentences

At times you will have to write longer sentences to present complex ideas. When writing or editing a sentence with a complex thought, help the reader understand the idea by repeating a key word or a phrase within the sentence. The repetition may lengthen the sentence, but it will also clarify the information in the sentence. Williams identifies a few devices you can use to repeat and clarify a complex thought, devices that also add variety to your sentences. Two of these techniques are especially useful.[8]

1. The **resumptive modifier** lets you repeat a key word and then resume the line of thought, elaborating on what went on before.

Example: Williams identifies a few **devices** you can use to repeat and clarify a complex thought, **devices** that also add variety to your sentences. (The resumptive modifier is **device**.)

---

2. The **summative modifier** is used after you end a segment of a sentence with a comma, sum up in a phrase what you have just said, and continue to the end of the sentence with a clause.

Example: The project could be considered an extension of the report I wrote, **an initial inquiry** that may be used as background information for the research on corrosion. (The summative modifier, **an initial inquiry**, sums up in a phrase the first segment of the sentence.)

You may remember that the advice on shortening sentences tells you to end a sentence in front of a **which** clause and to begin a new sentence. The summative modifier or resumptive modifier is a way of retaining the length of a sentence for variety's sake while avoiding the ambiguity of a vague **which** or **this.**

> *Not this:* The project could be considered an extension of the report that I wrote //which was used as background information for the research on corrosion.
>
> *But this:* The project could be considered an extension of the report that I wrote, a report that I used as background information for the research on corrosion. (This sentence uses a resumptive modifier.)

These two techniques, resumptive and summative modifiers, help you lengthen sentences, allowing you to add variety while still controlling readability.

EXERCISE 4.10

Add resumptive and summative modifiers to each of the sentences below.

> *Example:* The bureau will decentralize functions to two regional offices, (resumptive modifier)
> ... offices that will establish their own operating procedures, (summative modifier)
> ... a reorganization that will be completed by October 1.

1. The sensor is connected as part of an oscillator circuit that provides an output frequency that is in proportion to the dielectric content of the ink mixture, which in turn is determined by the mixture's water content.
2. A small cuff concentrates the pressure in a small area that can cause pain and possibly nerve damage.
3. It has one flow port on the bottom that is used for loading and unloading the system with protein test solution.
4. The monitored parts of the rotating disc surface will experience fluid flow and mass transport conditions which are completely understood and well controlled.

Applying a Readability Formula

A **readability formula** is a numerical standard against which your document may be read. The formula is not the same as the concept of readability that takes into account audience, purpose, typography, layout, clear sentences, and coherence. The formula is based on the length of the sentences and the number of polysyllabic words in the prose. Robert Gunning, an internationally known writing consultant, developed one such formula for measuring the readability of a document.[9] The *Gunning Fog Index,* as the formula is called, measures the readability of the prose and compares it to the average academic grade level of the reader. The purpose of evaluating your document against such a standard is to predict the difficulty a reader might have with the document.

The Fog Index corresponds with the reader's years of education. For example, a Fog Index of 8 corresponds with an eighth-grade reading level. Of course, the Fog Index tells us nothing about the coherence of the prose or the complexity of the ideas in the passage. The words may be simple and the sentences short, and still the passage may not make any sense. On the other hand, a readability formula may be a useful tool for writers initially insensitive to the needs of the reader. According to Gunning, if the prose has a Fog Index of more than 12, the writer may be "putting his communication under a handicap," especially for lay readers. The Gunning Fog Index permits you to measure the grade level of the sentences and words in the passage.

The Gunning Fog Index has this formula:

1. Jot down the number of words in successive sentences. If the piece is long, you may wish to take several samples of 100 words, spaced evenly throughout the long piece. If you do, stop the word count with the sentence that ends nearest the 100-word total. Treat independent clauses as separate sentences. (For example, count as three sentences: In school we studied: we learned; we improved.) Divide the total number of words in the passage by the number of sentences. This product gives the average length of the sentences in the passage.
2. Count the number of words of three syllables or more per 100 words. Don't count the words (1) that are proper names, (2) that are combinations of short, easy words (like *bookkeeper* and *shutdown*), (3) that are verb forms made three syllables by adding *-ed* or *-es* (like *created* or *trespasses*). This gives you the percentage of hard words in the passage.
3. To get the Fog Index, total the two factors just counted and multiply by 0.4. The resulting number corresponds roughly to the years of schooling needed to understand the piece of writing.
4. Check the result against this scale from Gunning's standard.

Fog Index = Number of years of schooling	Rating
5	.... fairly easy
7 or 8	.... standard
9 to 11	.... fairly difficult
12 to 15	.... difficult
17 or above	.... very difficult

We can apply the formula to a passage written by author Tracy Kidder from his book *The Soul of a New Machine*.[10]

Example

[Computer engineers call a single high or low voltage a bit, and it symbolizes one piece of information. One bit can't symbolize much; it has only two possible states, so it can, for instance, be used to stand for only two integers. Put many bits in a row, however, and the number of things that can be represented increases exponentially. By the way of analogy, think of telephone numbers. Using only four digits, the phone company could make up enough unique numbers to give one to everybody in a small town. But what if the company wants to give everyone in a large region a unique phone number?] By using seven instead of four digits, Ma Bell can generate a vast array of unique numbers, enough so that everyone in the New York metropolitan area or in the state of Montana can have one of his own.

Total words = 108 (count 100 words or to the end of the
sentence nearest 100 words)

Total sentences = 7
Average sentence length = 15.4
Total polysyllabic words = 13

$$15.4 + 13 = 28.4$$
$$28.4 \times 0.4 = 11.3$$

FOG INDEX = 11.3 (fairly difficult)

Gunning developed his formula and the standards for the Fog Index almost 20 years ago, but we know that the reading level has declined nationally. So, as writers, we must still consider the reading level of the audience. But we now have other ways of improving readability and increasing comprehension.

If the idea is complex or the information includes difficult terminology, as it often must, especially in technical writing, then the writer must use other techniques along with shorter sentences. The organizational patterns in Module 3 and the techniques for clear writing discussed in this module will help present information clearly and coherently. Dividing the content into smaller passages under headings increases comprehension and clarifies the message for the reader. Subdividing still further by making a list with circles, also called bullets, in front of each item will enhance readability, too. So far we have used the following techniques for improving comprehension and readability:

- Consider the audience.
- State the purpose.
- Organize the content.
- Use parallel headings and lists.
- Write clear sentences.

I. INTRODUCTION

Throughout 1980 and 1981, Environmental Services, Eastern District Office (EDO), has investigated the Region V area in support of the Clean Water Act (CWA), Resource Conservation and Recovery Act (RCRA), Toxic Substances Control Act (TSCA), and the Clean Air Act (CAA). EDO visited a total of 18 industrial and disposal sites and conducted the following types of inspections:

- RCRA Reconnaissance Inspections
- Compliance Sampling Inspections—Toxics
- Compliance Evaluation Inspections
- PCB Inspections
- NESHAP Inspections

II. PURPOSE

The purpose of this report is to summarize the results of the investigative efforts of the Eastern District Office during 1980–1981.

FIGURE 4.6 A readable introduction

Figure 4.6 illustrates the use of organization, division, headings, and lists, as well as sentence length and word choice, to increase understanding and readability. The Fog Index is an inappropriate measure for this text because the passage is too short (the prose must have at least 100 words) and lists cannot be counted as sentences.

EXERCISE 4.11 ═══════════════════════════════════════

1. Using an article from a journal in your field, select a passage of approximately 100 words. Apply the Gunning formula to the passage to determine the Fog Index. Remember that the passage must have consecutive exposition unbroken by lists or headings. As you consider the audience and the subject matter, is the Fog Index appropriate, or should the passage be geared to a lower grade level?

   If you have a readability program on a computer to which you have access, type in the passage from a journal and have the computer run a readability test on the passage.

2. Select a passage from one of your own reports and apply the Gunning Fog Index to this passage. Compare your style to the style of the preceding passage. Consider the average length of sentences, the number of difficult words, and the appropriateness of the Fog Index to the subject matter and to the intended audience.

3. How would you improve the following letter? Rewrite the entire letter, reorganizing and revising it to improve the comprehension and readability for people who have to supply the information.

Authorized and empowered by the Public Works Act of 1967 and pursuant to its provisions, consideration is being given by the Urban Development

Administration to the design and development of a prospectus at the present time for a construction project at Cicero, Illinois, for the purpose of full and complete review by the Bureau of the Budget and for the purpose of submitting said prospectus to the Committees on Public Works of the Congress.

Under and subject to said provisions, our planning contemplates the future construction of a multiagency federal building on an ecological site, located in the central business district; said site of such a nature as to be deemed accommodating to the sole and exclusive requirements of the U.S. Office of Business Administration and/or other federal activities in the aforementioned community. Eventual disposal of the extant post office and courthouse building is contemplated when the construction of the before-mentioned proposed new federal building is finalized and completed.

In order more easily to facilitate the early and expeditious transmittal of the said prospectus, it is hereby requested that your current total space requirements be submitted on the format, UBA Form 342, which is attached herewith. Each and every change that you deem significant and that you can anticipate for and during the period of the next five years should also be furnished.

For the purpose of lending us assistance in connection with the discharge of our responsibilities in reference to the development of this project, it will be appreciated if this information can be submitted as expeditiously as possible and with a minimum of delay.

Identifying Text Analysis Programs

Other researchers have studied the readability of documents and developed formulas to count additional features such as the passive voice and verbs that are used as nouns. For example, Bell Laboratories uses the Kincaid formula, named after J. Peter Kincaid, to rate training documents. The results are compared to the Bell Lab standards for good training documents. Figure 4.7 describes these standards.[11]

Average sentence length: .... 12.3 to 20.2 words
Average length of content words: .... 5.5 to 6.8 letters
Percentage of short sentences: .... 23.1% to 31.4%
Percentage of long sentences: .... 7.3% to 12.8%
Passives should be fewer than: 28.7%
Nominalizations should be fewer than: 3.4%

FIGURE 4.7 Bell Lab standards for training documents. Used with permission.

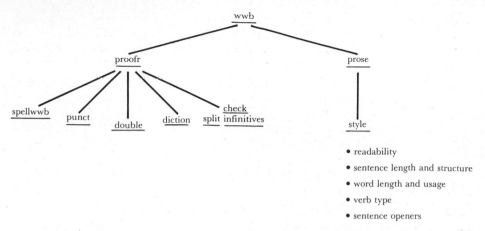

FIGURE 4.8 Features of the WRITER'S WORKBENCH (wwb)™ program. Used with permission.

The numerical readability formulas are too time-consuming for the writer to apply. But a computer programmer can incorporate them into a program to do what a computer does well—count. Computer programmers now write programs that (1) count the length and type of sentences and words, (2) identify other surface features of writing such as spelling and grammar, and (3) compare these results to standards. These programs, called **text analysis programs or prose analyzers,** provide us with an analysis of the surface characteristics of our prose.

When you type your prose passage on the computer and run a text analysis program on your text, the program analyzes your prose. One of many such programs on the market, Writer's Workbench (AT & T Technologies), is used here to illustrate the general features of text analysis programs. This program analyzes spelling, punctuation, double typing of words, diction, split infinitives, and style; and it also provides you with the results of the analysis. Figure 4.8 provides the tree chart for the Writer's Workbench program.

Text analysis programs are tools to aid us as writers, tools that analyze the surface features of our prose. Programmers are incorporating these text analysis programs into word processing programs. Text analysis programs are available for personal computers as well as for large computers.

Summary

How you write is an element of *style;* in technical writing the style has to be clear and readable. One way to be clear is to arrange your words to flow in an order familiar to the reader. In a sentence, the familiar order is to begin with a subject (an *agent*) followed by a verb (an *action*) and completed by an object (the **goal**). To write vigorous sentences, select the verb first by locating the crucial action. Often you will find the crucial action embedded in a noun form of the verb. This noun form is called a **nominalization.** Nominalizations weaken a sentence by detracting from the verb and making the sentence wordy. You cannot avoid all nominalizations because they often summarize an idea from a preceding sentence. But, whenever possible, change the nominalization back to the verb.

To write effectively, writers need to use both the **active** and the **passive** voices. When the agent is performing the action, the verb is in the active voice; when the agent is acted upon, the verb is in the passive voice. Use the passive voice when the goal is more important than the agent or when the agent is unknown, but when either the active or the passive voice suits your purpose, use the active voice.

When you write a series of sentences for a paragraph, you have to sequence the information in the sentences so that they form a **coherent** paragraph. To make sentences coherent, put more familiar or **old information** at the beginning of the sentence to orient the reader. After the verb put the **new information** you intend to develop. Then, as you add a sentence to build a paragraph, make the new information from your preceding sentence the old information of your next sentence. This string of linking information will help you build a coherent sequence of sentences in the paragraph. Repeating a key word or a grammatical pattern will also help establish a coherent sequence. When you repeat a grammatical pattern (using verbs, nouns, infinitives, gerunds, phrases, subordinate clauses, and so forth) throughout a list, an outline, or a sentence, you are writing in a **coordinated** or balanced structure called **parallel structure.**

Factors other than sentence patterns affect the readability of documents. The length of your sentences is a factor, but not all long sentences are confusing, and not all short sentences are clear. To edit a long, confusing sentence, split it before *and, but, because* or a *who, which, that* clause. Then edit each segment to create a sequence of sentences. Expletives *(there are, these are, this is, it is)* also add length and are unnecessary. Sometimes even short sentences can be too densely packed with a string of modifiers or nouns. **Unstack** the phrase by changing a nominalization into a verb whenever possible, rewriting the string with the last noun first, and adding a prepositional phrase. Unstacking noun strings solves the problem of ambiguity for the reader and the tendency to use **hyphens,** a writer's tendency that adds clutter to the text.

Edit sentences for readability when the sentences contain **inflated language** (language that attempts to impress the reader) or **jargon** (vocabulary appropriate for a certain audience within a special environment). **Sexist language** is another problem that may bias readers' thinking by encouraging them to think about placing only a man or only a woman into a position. Try to avoid sex-linked nouns and titles such as *spokesman* and *his.* Use instead *representative* and *their* (use *their* only after a plural subject).

When you want to write longer sentences to add variety or to present complex ideas, then help the reader follow the idea by using a **resumptive** *modifier* (a key word or phrase that you repeat before you resume the next segment of the sentence) or a *summative modifier* (a phrase that you create to summarize the idea in the first segment before you continue the next segment of the sentence).

Readability formulas and *text analysis programs* are mechanical tools that may aid you in diagnosing surface problems of prose. One readability formula is the *Gunning Fog Index,* a formula that counts the length of sentences and type of words in a passage and compares the numerical results to the academic grade level of the reader. Computer programs that (1) count the length and type of sentences and words; (2) identify other surface features of writing such as spelling, punctuation, split infinitives, and so forth; and (3) compare these results to standards are called text analysis programs. But you must remember that, so far, these mechanical tools do not deal effectively with the logic or the coherence of the prose.

As the writer, you have to write coherently. When you follow the pattern of old information plus new information from sentence to sentence, you can ensure coherence in a paragraph. How long should your sentences be? How brief? We do have standards for documents, standards that a good text analysis program can compare to your document. But you have to develop a sentence sense—that's style. If you know how to shorten and lengthen sentences and make them more vigorous, clearer, and less jarring to the reader, in short, if you understand the techniques in this module and apply them, you are in control of style.

Checklist for Style

TO WRITE CLEARLY

yes   no

———   ———   1. Does the sentence use a strong verb instead of a nominalizaton to express the crucial action?

———   ———   2. Does the agent precede the action in the sentence?

———   ———   3. In the sentence do the agent and action accomplish the goal?

———   ———   4. Are the majority of sentences in the active voice with the agent performing the action?

                    5. Are the sentences in the passive voice appropriate because

———   ———   the goal is more important than the agent?

____ ____ the agent is unknown?

____ ____ 6. Do the sentences move from old information to new information, repeating the topic so that the passage is coherent?

7. Is there parallel structure

____ ____ in the grammatical elements of a sentence?

____ ____ in a list?

____ ____ in an outline?

____ ____ in headings?

TO EDIT

____ ____ 1. Are the vital clauses introduced with *that?*

____ ____ 2. Should you shorten some sentences by splitting them before *and, but, because, who, which, that?* (Remember to include an agent, action, and goal for each segment.)

____ ____ 3. Can you omit expletives *(there are, these are, this is, it is)?*

____ ____ 4. Can you add little words *(and, of, an)* to unstack noun strings?

____ ____ 5. Does the sentence contain inflated language, jargon, or sexist language?

6. To add variety or handle complexity in a sentence, can you

____ ____ repeat a key word in a resumptive modifier?

____ ____ sum up the first segment in a summative modifier?

TO APPLY MECHANICAL STANDARDS

____ ____ 1. Would a readability formula provide pertinent information?

____ ____ 2. Would a text analysis program identify additional errors?

Notes

1. Joseph M. Williams, *Style: Ten Lessons in Clarity and Grace,* 2d ed. (Glenview, Ill.: Scott, Foresman, 1985):14.
2. Williams, *Style,* pp. 33–34.
3. United States Environmental Protection Agency, *Be a Better Writer* (Washington, D.C.: Printing Management Office, March 1980):17.
4. William Strunk, Jr., and E. B. White, *The Elements of Style,* 3d ed. (New York: Macmillan, 1978).
5. *Be a Better Writer,* p. 28.
6. John Kirkman, The John Kirkman Communication Consultancy, Wiltshire, England. In 1981, I received this list from John Kirkman during my trip to Cardiff, U.K.
7. *Be a Better Writer,* pp. 20–22.
8. Williams, *Style,* pp. 135–136.
9. Robert Gunning, *The Techniques of Clear Writing* (New York: McGraw-Hill, 1968):38–40. Used with permission.
10. Tracy Kidder, *The Soul of a New Machine* (New York: Little, Brown, 1981):33.
11. *Unix® Writers Workbench™ Software User's Manual* (Piscataway, N.J.: Systems Training Department, Bell Laboratories, 1982):2–8.

References

James DeGeorge, Gary A. Olson, and Richard Ray, *Style and Readability in Technical Writing* (New York: Random House, 1984).

James B. Maggiore, "Quality Measurement Forms: Write in the Active Voice," in *Proceedings,* 33d International Technical Communication Conference (Washington, D.C.: Society for Technical Communication, 1986):443–446.

M O D U L E 5

Design and Visual Aids

The spatial design of a page also contributes to the way humans obtain information. A page printed from top to bottom and right to left margins will probably weary the reader and obscure the message. Most readers benefit from white space, space in which no printing appears. If a page has too little white space, typeface that is too small, or graphs that are too complicated, the reader may become confused or miss the message altogether. On the other hand, excessive design with a number of typefaces, sentences all in capital letters, or visual elements that simply repeat the text may prevent the reader from focusing on the most important information. Too much page design can be distracting to the reader, and too little can obscure the information. Whereas designers are the experts in presenting visual information, writers can be knowledgeable about the effects of visual presentation. In fact, writers should consider the physical presentation of the document at the same time they are considering the content.

This module will provide you with basic information abut page design and visual aids so that you can confidently discuss the production of your work with a designer and make informed decisions about the visual aids you use to present your information to your reader. Typography, page layout, and visual aids all contribute to the message of the document. With the layout and graphics capability of many of the computers, you can design and enhance the visual effects of your own documents.

Scope

In this module you will learn to

1. Consider visual presentation from the point of view of the reader and the purpose of the document.
2. Define the typography of the document.
3. Lay out the content and visual aids.
4. Select appropriate visual aids, including tables, graphs, and figures.

Theory of Visuals

The visual presentation of information aids the reader and contributes to the message of the document. If you evaluate the documents that you find interesting and lively, you will discover that the visual presentation, as well as the style, makes the difference. In fact, the same words may seem even clearer in a well-designed document. The illustrations in Figure 5.1 demonstrate an example of an original document redesigned to improve the visual presentation and to accommodate the older reader who uses the equipment. In the first illustration of the microwave oven, the numbers on the touch control panel are too small to see clearly. In the illustration of the time pad, the numbers are much larger and the touch control panel is enlarged.

Readers are becoming more visually oriented. One writer and designer says, "As communicators, we know that humans would rather look at pictures than words. Their understanding of pictures is instantaneous and holistic. Their understanding of words is linear and time-consuming."[1]

But some visuals are not entirely self-explanatory and cannot carry the entire weight of technical information. In most cases, unless you are describing a simple procedure that can be done by illustrations alone, words will still communicate the important information. Visual aids enhance the purpose and the readability of the document.

Audience and Purpose

In situations where the audience is diverse or international and you want to convey the message immediately, a picture may indeed be worth a thousand words. Consider the international pictoral symbols in Figure 5.2.

But most of the time the purpose of the document determines the design and the type of visual aids.

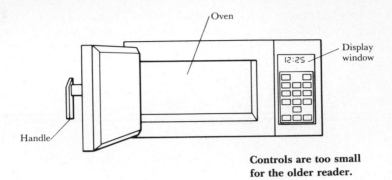

**Controls are too small
for the older reader.**

To set time
1. Press the "Time" pad on the touch control panel.
2. Set desired cooking time by pressing appropriate number pads.
   (For example, 1-0-0 = one minute; 1-3-0 = one minute thirty seconds.
   Time set will appear in the display window.

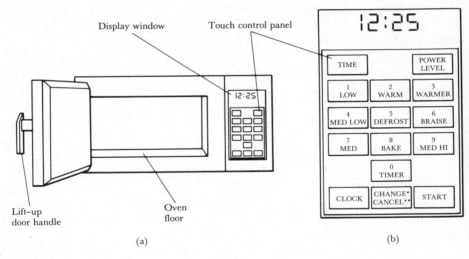

(a)   (b)

**Large time pad helps the
older reader see the
number.**

To set time—see (b).
1. Press the "Time" pad on the touch control panel
2. Set desired cooking time by pressing appropriate number pads.
   For example, one minute = 1-0-0; one minute thirty seconds = 1-3-0.
   Time set will appear in the display window.

FIGURE 5.1 Original and revised document
Source: Adapted from Jo Ellen Nielsen, Technical Writing 421,
Illinois Institute of Technology.

No Smoking

FIGURE 5.2 International symbols
Source: Adapted from Robert C. Bring, Jr., and
S. Gayle Wyman, "Developing Nonverbal
Operating Instructions," in *Proceedings,* 32d
International Technical Communication
Conference, 1985: VC-19. Used with the
permission of the Society for Technical
Communications.

Readability

When the reader has to follow instructions, it is better to group information into manageable units or **chunks** of information that the reader can remember. Many times you can chunk or divide this information under headings and subheadings; division is explained more thoroughly in Modules 3, 4, and 7. A chunk of information may be thought of as a portion of information that the human can process comfortably while following directions. Research indicates that humans can remember numbers or items in a sequence up to seven numbers plus or minus two numbers. Figure 5.3 illustrates a partial list of steps that continue for four pages. Even thought the text is in a list form with numbers or bullets (darkened circles appearing before separate items in a list), the steps are still too numerous for the reader to absorb. You would have to chunk the list under main headings.

When a single illustration is used at the end of a set of instructions, the reader may not even see the illustration until after struggling with the instructions. On the other hand, if you place the line drawing on page 1 of the manual, and the instruction on page 4 tells the reader to refer to the illustration on page 1, the reader may lose his place and become frustrated. You will have to accommodate the reader and use several illustrations, perhaps selecting a two-column layout so that the appropriate illustrations appear in

Fuselage assembly (cont.)

22. Bevel the bottom edges of canopy formers C-2 and C-5 to match the required angles at the rear C-2 canopy fairing and the rear C-5 angled former F-10.

    Glue these two formers in place on the canopy base. Also lightly tack-glue them to their matting surfaces.

23. Glue the two remaining canopy formers, C-3 and C-2 in place on the base.

    • Use the pencil marks you made earlier on the fuselage sides for location. These two formers should be inset 1/8" from the edge of the base on each side.

24. Use a flat surface to glue and pin the 1/4" triangular balsa stock provided to the inside top edge of canopy sides C-1. Be sure to make a right and left side.

    • When dry, carefully fit the canopy sides in place. Trim if needed to get a good fit.

    • Glue and pin the sides in place.

    • When dry, sheet the top of the canopy with cross-grain 1/8".

    • Raise from the back face of C-2 to the forward face of C-5.

    • Pin and allow to dry completely.

    • Use your sanding block to sand the canopy/fuselage sides flush and smooth.

25. You must now decide whether to go with the fixed towhook

25. (cont.). provided or with the option. The installation shown on the plans works very nicely and is quite simple. In fact, when we used this system, we slotted the ply floor, installed the mounting rails and secured the towhook in place on them and then installed the ply floor to the fuselage.

    • To install the towhook
        —Position and hold the 1/16" ply forward floor in place and mark fuselage outline in pencil.
        —Trim off the excess with a hobby saw.
        —Glue the ply floor in place from the center of the cross brace beneath F-7 forward and on to the nose block. Tape and allow to dry.
        —Epoxy a length of 1/16" by 1/2" ply (provided for you in an 8" length) to the inside center of the ply floor, between the cross brace and the back of F-6. This is the towhook plate doubler.
        —Determine the location of F-6 and mark its rear edge location across the bottom of the fuselage in light pencil.
        —Draw a light centerline of the fuselage on the bottom from the F-6 line back.
        —Measure back 1/2" and drill a 3/32" die hole through the ply floor and the ply doubler.
        —Epoxy the 2–56 blind mounting nut provided onto this hole from the inside of the fuselage.

FIGURE 5.3 Instructions with too many steps for the reader to follow

Electronic Camera

This camera is composed of seven basic parts: the casing, a lens, an electroarray (electrophotosensitive array), a viewing screen, function buttons, a record-chip (microchip), and a battery case.

Camera Components

Casing. The hard, plastic casing provides a watertight rigid framework that houses the camera's electronic components. The lens, function buttons, record-chip, and battery lid all fit onto the case and are connected to the inner components of the camera. The casing is also designed to fit comfortably in the hand, utilizing a smooth, rounded bottom and a lens-to-hand angle of 60 degrees. The angle relieves the wrist of the stress caused by the weight of the camera. The angle also serves to steady the wrist and camera when recording an image.

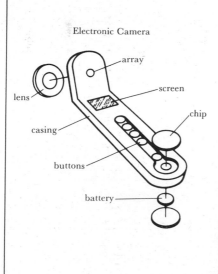

Electronic Camera — array, screen, chip, lens, casing, buttons, battery

FIGURE 5.4 Two-column layout with illustration
Source: Shin Takeda, Technical Writing 421, Illinois Institute of Technology.

the left-hand column next to the instructions. Figure 5.4 shows the two-column layout with illustrations.

If the purpose of the document is to provide the reader with instructions for filling out a form, you should include an example of the completed form; the example should be as close to the instructions as possible. If the illustration cannot be on the same page as the instructions, it should be on the facing page (the page opposite the instructions). Certainly the illustration should be no farther from the instructions than the very next page.

You might even consider detailing the illustration further by more specific graphics for a section of the device; this specific detailing of a section of an illustration is called **breaking out** or enlarging a section. Figure 5.5 illustrates an example of breaking out a section of an illustration to explain further a part of the device.

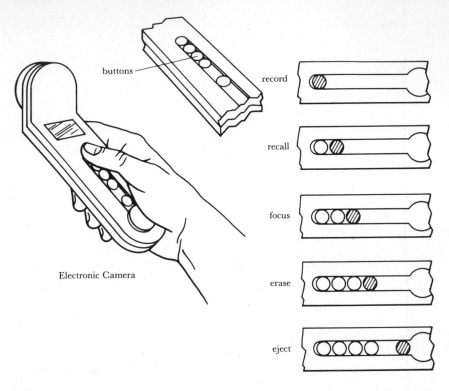

FIGURE 5.5 Breaking out a section of an illustration to explain the part
Source: Shin Takeda, Technical Writing 421, Illinois Institute of Technology.

Appropriate design and illustration serve two important functions in a document:

- To support the purpose for writing the document.
- To provide white space and visual aids to help the reader grasp and use the information.

Typography

Designing a printed document involves knowledge and skills that take designers, illustrators, and printers years to acquire. As writers, we want to have some of these tools and skills for assisting the reader, skills we can acquire by learning some essential definitions and concepts associated with typography and design. Typography is the art and technique of composing type. This information will not make you a design specialist, but it will give you some basic facts that will help you take advantage of the benefits of good design.

presenting FIGURE 5.6 Bodoni typeface

FIGURE 5.7 Serif typeface

Typeface

Each letter, number, or punctuation mark on this page is a character of type. A typeface is a complete alphabet of characters in one style of type. Typeface comes in hundreds of styles, Bodoni, Futura, and Helvetica, to name a few. Bodoni is illustrated in Figure 5.6

But all typefaces fall into two basic categories:

• serif
• sans serif

Serif typeface has fine lines projecting from the major strokes of the letter, as it does in Figure 5.7.

Coming from the French word *sans,* meaning "without," sans serif lacks the projections. Sans serif is illustrated in Figure 5.8.

Some research indicates that readers recognize serif letters faster than sans serif letters because the projections help the reader distinguish the letters in the word. The serif typeface is usually used in textbooks and magazines. Sans serif typefaces, designed in this century, tend to be more modern looking without their extra lines. They follow the modern design in architecture with the adage that "less is more." With cleaner lines the letters appear larger.

The fact is that both typefaces have their advantages and should be chosen for their appropriateness to the document as well as for their readability. Sans serif typeface in a demanding text may become too bold and inflexible whereas serif typeface in a straightforward text with a simple purpose may interfere with the message. If you have a typewriter or a printer with interchangeable type style, you should select the appropriate typeface for the purpose and readability of your document. Some personal computers and printers permit you to experiment with typeface and type size, as well as with other print features.

FIGURE 5.8 Sans serif typeface

Type Size

The size of the type also affects the document, and, taken together, the typeface and type size make up a block of type. The block of type goes back to medieval times when Johannes Gutenberg, the German inventor of movable type, hand-set the first block of type for the famous Gutenberg Bible. The block of type had a face and a body, illustrated in Figure 5.9. The face is, of course, the typeface, such as Univers.

Printers measure the body to determine the type size and then refer to the measurement as the **point size.** An easy way to remember type size is to think of a line of type with the letters all one inch tall; that line of type is 72 points high. Of course, only large displays would have letters that tall. Most text types are 14 points or smaller. You will want to remember the concept of type size because some states set the minimum type size for documents, especially legal documents and insurance documents. Clear text should be printed in at least 8-point type or larger, but not larger than 12-point type.[2]

Most typewriters and printers come in pica and elite type size. The pica type looks larger because it has only 10 characters to the horizontal inch whereas the elite type has 12 characters to the inch. The important point to remember about type size is that the visual effect of the typeface is most important, and not the point size. Two typefaces could have the same point size, as they do in Figure 5.10, and yet 12-point Helvetica looks larger than 12-point Bodoni.

Layout

With the typewriter or the computer and printer, you can design and enhance the visual effects of your own document. For example, you can arrange the lines of your text so that the left margin is always **justified.** That means the

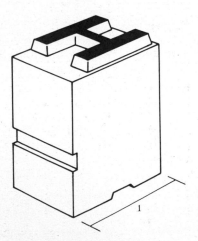

FIGURE 5.9 Block of type

C S A   C S A

FIGURE 5.10 12-point Helvetica versus 12-point Bodoni

first character on the left side of the page is always aligned with the left margin. A manuscript usually has **ragged** right margin; the space at the end of the line is dependent on the length of the last word on the line. On a computer you can justify both the left and right margins because the computer will proportion the words on the line, inserting spaces between words so that the right side is always aligned with the right margin. Sometimes aligning the right margin creates a river of white space in the text, a situation that distracts the reader. Figure 5.11 illustrates the right and left justified margins with the river of white spaces.

Line Length

The length of the line affects readability and is something you can control on the typewriter or computer. Long lines of type are difficult to read because the margins are small and make the page look crowded. So if the line lengths are long, the reader does not receive the cues to process the information, and the reader's eye may wander in the course of the sentence. On the other hand, short sentences require more eye movement and create distracting breaks in the text. The Document Design Center recommends a line length containing 50 to 70 letters and spaces.[3]

```
On  a  standard  typewriter,  each  letter takes up a uniform amount of
space, and so no  disproportionate number  of white  spaces are created
within the  text.    But, in  typesetting and on computers, you have the
option of proportional spacing.   When  you  select  justified margins,
spaces are  added between  words to  proportion the line of text.  This
paragraph has justified type, type aligned at both  the left  and right
margins, but in proportioning these lines of text, you will also notice
the river of white space in this passage.
```

FIGURE 5.11 Left and right justified margins, with rivers of white space

Leading

You can also control the space between your lines. In typesetting, the space between lines is referred to as leading (pronounced "ledding"). Of course, on a typewriter or computer you indicate **spacing** rather than leading between lines, and you can set single, double, or space and a half spacing. Spacing depends on (1) typeface, (2) length and kind of publication, and (3) visual effect desired; and it can also help you produce a document that is easy to read.

White Space

White space, the space without any type, contributes to the visual effect of the page. When a page has long lines of text with small margins and very little leading, as illustrated in Figure 5.12, the text is difficult to read.

Text with spacing between sections helps the reader remember the content by providing the information in manageable segments of information or chunks. Spacing between lines makes the information more visually appealing. When you use wide margins or columns on the sides or at the top or bottom of your page, you can add an illustration to accompany your text, as in Figure 5.4. Or, as I have done in Figure 5.13, you can insert headings in the wide left-hand column, headings that help the reader find information quickly.

Grids

Now that you know you need white space as an important part of page design, you have to consider the total page layout. Designers use a grid to place their type and visual aids on a page. A grid is a floor plan for a page and divides a page into horizontal and vertical rows. Using the grid, designers proportion the text and visuals within the margins and borders of the page. Most commonly, grids have from two to six columns and are designed for flexibility. Figure 5.14 shows a four-column grid.

A flexible grid allows the designer to have uniform pages so that the finished product has continuity, but at the same time each page has a flexibility, illustrated in Figure 5.14. Your sense of spacing the elements on your page will increase the legibility of your document and remind you of the value of white space. If your text and illustrations are clumped together or spread sparsely around the page, then your document will be more difficult

The space between words

Thespacebetweenwords

FIGURE 5.12 Type with very little leading between words

1. Three Principles
   of Technical Writing
      Audience
      Purpose
      Design

1.1 The concept of AUDIENCE is important in technical writing. We use the term to refer to the types of readers who may be reading our documents. Later in this module, in Section 3, we analyze the different categories of readers. Now let us say briefly that, to present technical information, you have to consider the background of the audience, their educational level, their experience, their need to know certain kinds of information. In most cases, you will have to develop a design plan and a style to suit the background of your audience.

FIGURE 5.13 Headings in the left-hand columns

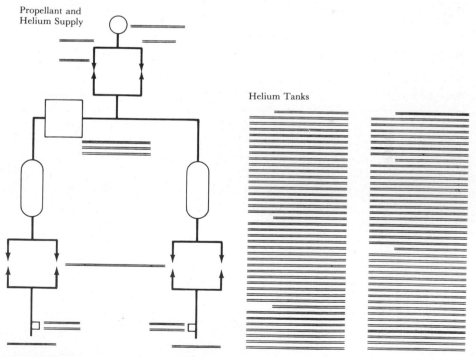

Propellant and
Helium Supply

Helium Tanks

FIGURE 5.14 A four-column grid

Source: M. F. McKay, A. J. Petro, R. L. Magin, and J. A. Resnik, "High-Flying Training Manuals," in *Proceedings*, 32d International Technical Communication Conference, 1985: VC-42

Format for Scanning

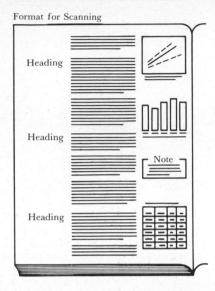

FIGURE 5.15 Grid used for scanning information
Source: William Horton, "Quick-Relief Documentation," in *Proceedings*, 32d International Technical Communication Conference, 1985: WE-6. Used with permission of the Society for Technical Communication.

to read. Whether you select the two-column grid with even or uneven horizontal rows or the grid with three equal columns, which encourages shorter, more readable lines of type, your choice depends on the purpose of your document. Figure 5.15 illustrates a grid that is useful for scanning. The first column helps headings stand out; the second column provides detailed information; the third column places tables and illustrations near to the text. Each column presents a different type of information.

Visual Aids

Text is often linear and time-consuming to understand. On the other hand, with the exception of tables, visual aids quickly provide the reader with an overall picture, illustrated in the efficient message of Figure 5.16. But different visual aids require different levels of effort from the reader. Consider the difference between a table and other visual aids in Figure 5.17.

Summarize Essential Facts

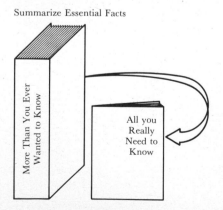

FIGURE 5.16 Efficient visual message
Source: William Horton, "Quick-Relief Documentation," in *Proceedings*, 32d International Technical Communication Conference, 1985: WE-5. Used with permission of the Society for Technical Communication.

Table 1 City of Rochester, Indiana—Average Daily Water
Consumption (1982) (gallons in millions)

Month	Business and industry	Private homes	Schools and colleges
January	4.256	3.608	1.910
February	4.310	3.673	2.296
March	4.318	4.127	2.501
April	4.325	4.980	2.507
May	4.331	5.641	2.610
June	4.417	6.775	2.192
July	4.484	8.926	.807
August	4.491	9.681	.762
September	4.369	8.810	1.418
October	4.323	5.604	2.298
November	4.298	4.254	2.304
December	4.243	3.672	1.641

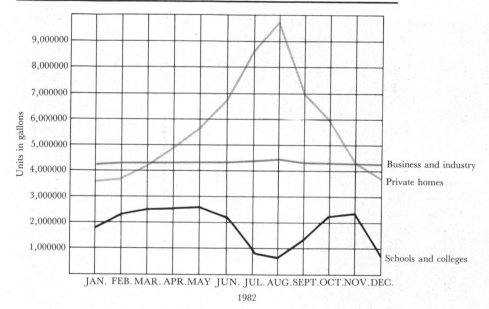

City of Rochester, Indiana—Average daily water consumption (graph)

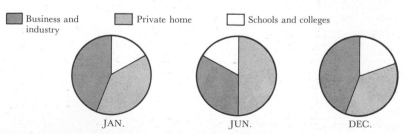

City of Rochester, Indiana—Average daily water consumption (pie charts) 1982

FIGURE 5.17 Table versus other visual aids

Year	1980	1984
City	Population in Millions	
New York	3.4	7.6
Chicago	1.7	3.6
Philadelphia	1.3	2.0
Detroit	0.3	1.8
Los Angeles	0.1	2.0

FIGURE 5.18 Quantitative data in a clear visual
Source: Nancy C. Corbin, "The Well-Dressed Posterboard," in *Proceedings*, 32d International Technical Communication Conference, 1985: VC-28. Used with permission of the Society for Technical Communication.

Illustrations supplement the text and help the reader perceive the information in a different mode. Charts, photos, drawings, maps are all alternatives to text; but you should have a reason to use these, and other, visual aids. When you want to describe or clarify a point you are writing about or when you wish to highlight or make a point more memorable or when you wish to present ideas that are quantitative, then you should use the appropriate visual aid, preferably an aid as clear and readable as the one in Figure 5.18.

In general, visual aids enhance the text in a document and are useful if they support the written content and help the reader remember, understand, or apply the information. All visual aids should be relevant to the written text and should be appropriate to the specific point, as Figure 5.19 illustrates.

Each type of visual aid has advantages and disadvantages. Once again you have to consider the purpose for the illustration and the needs of the reader. Every visual aid that is not a table is considered a figure, and figure numbers and captions go beneath the illustration. Table numbers and captions go above the table. When you decide to use a visual aid, you must also

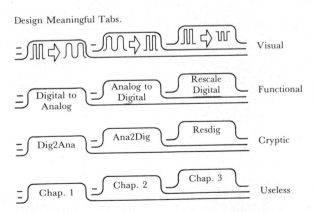

Design Meaningful Tabs.

FIGURE 5.19 Visual relevant to the text's major point
Source: William Horton, "Quick-Relief Documentation," in *Proceedings*, 32d International Technical Communication Conference, 1985: WE-7. Used with permission of the Society for Technical Communication.

- Refer to it in the text.
- Place it close to the initial reference.
- Label it with a figure or table number and caption.

Tables

Tables are useful in reports that must give exact data for the purpose of comparison or computation. If you want to compare data in your own report, or know that the reader wants to compare exact values, then a table is a convenient way to present a large amount of data in a small amount of space. You should consider a table when you want to

- Present a large amount of numerical data.
- Emphasize discrete values for the purpose of comparison.
- Organize and list conditions that would take a great many words to explain.

Figure 5.20 compares a paragraph of data with its corresponding table, illustrating the advantage of a table over prose.

After you decide that a table will suit your purpose, you will have to consider

- Where to place the table.
- How to design the table.

Where to Place a Table

When you need to give quantities of exact data, you may want to put the table in an Appendix because a reader must study the exact values. If the reader needs the table while reading the report, then the table should be

---

When the HP EGS software was tested to determine the user's need for outside help to install the software, with the HP EGS 2.0 (original version), out of six users, 100% needed help. With the interim version, out of seven users, 57% needed outside help to install the software. With the HP EGS 2.1 (final version), out of six users, none needed outside help installing the software.

Table 1. Outside Help Needed to Install HP EGS

Software Tested	Subjects Needing Help
HP EGS 2.0 (original version)	100% (n6)
Interim Version	57% (n7)
HP EGS 2.1 (final version)	0% (n6)

FIGURE 5.20 Comparing a paragraph of data with a table
Source: J. Eyre, M. A. Dohn Moore, and T. Rideout, "Testing Software Installation Procedures: An Integrated Approach," in *Proceedings*, 33d International Technical Communication Conference, 1986: 377. Used with permission of the Society for Technical Communication.

Table 5.1 Table Included Within Body of Document

Method of Evaluation
The data were organized to compare the features of each backpack in terms of five standards. This information is shown in Table I. Loading time was evaluated on a pass/fail basis.

Table I Backpacks: Comparison of Features

| Feature | Manufacturers | | |
	Coleman	Academy	Rangeley
A. Material	Plastic frame; nylon pack w/urethane coating; padded shoulder strap	Aluminum frame nylon pack; padded shoulder straps	Aluminum frame; nylon pack with coating; padded shoulder straps
B. Weight	33 oz.	20 oz.	60 oz.
C. Adjustability range	4'5"–6'0"	4'5"–5'2"	5'1"–6'1"
D. Cost	$75.00	$30.00	$58.00
E. Loading time/15 min.	pass	fail	pass

Source: Terryl Washburn-Shouba, Technical Writing 421, Illinois Institute of Technology.

inserted into the document as near to the first reference to the table as possible. In this case, because Table 5.1 is emphasizing discrete information to help the reader decide which backpack to purchase, the table is included in the body of the document rather than in the Appendix. Remember that the table number and caption appear at the top of the table.

If you insert the table in the discussion, make it as short as possible. You should consider using a summary table in the text of the document and placing a full table in the appendix. When a table goes to a second page, you should repeat the column heads for the reader's easy reference.

How to Design the Table

Because a table is more linear and time-consuming than other visual aids, the reader will appreciate a properly designed table. If you think of a table as presenting information in rows and columns, you will design a rectangle or a box with a field for the actual data and then row and column headings for the main parts of the table. A description of the parts of a table looks like Table 5.2. Table 5.3 violates the following principles of constructing a good table whereas Table 5.4 demonstrates them. The vertical numbers in Table 5.4 are also appropriately aligned on the decimal point.

Table 5.2 Parts of a Table

How we read a table			
head	*head*	*head*	*head*
stub	item	item	item	item
stub	item	item	item	item
stub	item	item	item	item
stub	item	item	item	item
stub	item	item	item	item

Source: William Horton, "Templates of Thought," in *Proceedings*, 33d International Technical Communication Conference, 1986:304. Used with permission of the Society for Technical Communication.

Not this: Table 5.3.

Table 5.3 A Table That Violates the Principles of Design

Model	Test 1	Test 2	Test 3
A	5.666 min.	4.034 min.	3.224 min.
B	3.800 min.	2.231 min.	4.357 min.
C	2.677 min.	1.968 min.	1.971 min.

But this: Table 5.4.

Table 5.4 Test Results for Warm-up Time of Automobile Models (in minutes)

Test Number	Model Warm-up Time (in minutes)		
	A	B	C
1	5.66	3.80	2.67
2	4.03	2.23	1.96
3	3.22	4.35	1.97

Principles of Constructing a Good Table
- Put units of measurement in boxhead, not in field.
- Round numbers to second decimal; include no more than two decimal places.
- Align vertical numbers on the decimal point.
- Use white space, not lines, to make numbers distinct.
- Avoid unnecessary repetition in stub and column headings.
- Use columns to compare the important data.

Table 5.5 Words in a table format (decision table)

Temperature	Precipitation	Wear . . . Raincoat	Overcoat	Boots
Warm	none			
	rain	X		
	none		X	
Cold	rain	X		
	snow		X	X

Source: William Horton, "Templates of Thought," in *Proceedings*, 33d International Technical Communication Conference, 1986: 305. Used with permission of the Society for Technical Communication.

You can also present words or sentences in table formats. When you are writing conditions or procedures similar to those in Table 5.5, you can organize words into rows and columns, saving lengthy discussions and summarizing complex ideas in a few words.

Task Completion Times

Another measure of ease of installation was the time required to completely install the system. Reducing installation time benefits both the customer and the system engineer in terms of time and money lost or spent. Installation time was cut in half for the interim release of the software, and cut an additional 10% for the final release of the software. Table 2 shows the average time to completion for all the subjects who finished the specified subtasks. If you consider the amount of time devoted to machine processing of the discs, the task-related time savings from the first test to the third test appear even greater than total time savings.

Table 2 Installing HP EGS—Task Completion Times

Task	Completion Time (Minutes) HP EGS 2.0	Interim	HP EGS 2.1
Install hardware	41	41*	41*
Install Pascal	86	30	17
Install software	201	98	78
Install codeword	58	20	15
Total	386	189	151
(Machine processing time)		(64)	

*Estimate only

FIGURE 5.21 Table within text
Source: J. Eyre, M. A. Dohn Moore, and T. Rideout, "Testing Software Installation Procedures: An Integrated Approach," in *Proceedings*, 33d International Technical Communication Conference, 1986: 377. Used with permission of the Society for Technical Communication.

Finally, after you introduce the table in the text, take a little more time to explain the table briefly. Then provide a precise title, or caption, for the table. Figure 5.21 illustrates the introduction of the table in the text as well as the explanation and a precise title.

Because tables make more of a mental impact than a visual one, you must keep the reader in mind.

Design the Table with the Following Points in Mind

For your reader:

- For the general audience use brief, simple tables; audiences such as scientists and engineers who use tables frequently can benefit from more complex tables.
- At the head of each column use a clear caption and include the units of measurement (See Table 5.4). If the table continues to a second page, repeat the column headings.
- Cite every table in the text, and place the table as close to the citation as possible (unless the table is long and should go into the appendix).

For your design:

- Keep the table as "open" as possible by eliminating unnecessary vertical and horizontal lines.
- Use as few columns as possible.
- Place the table number and a descriptive table title at the top of every table even if there is only one.
- Align vertical numbers on the decimal point.
- Insert footnotes to the table or explanatory comments beneath the table, not at the bottom of the page.

Graphs

Graphs are similar to tables in some ways and different in others. Whereas tables give exact data for comparisons of numerical values, graphs give a picture of relationships or trends. Both tables and graphs have a horizontal and a vertical scale. On a graph the horizontal scale is called the x-axis. Usually an independent variable such as time—a variable that changes predictably— is plotted on the horizontal axis. The vertical scale, called the y-axis, depicts the dependent variable, which is affected by changes on the x-axis. See Figure 5.22 for the graphic scale.

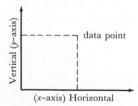

FIGURE 5.22 Graph with x- and y-axis

The type of graph you use depends on your reader and the point you want to stress. Line graphs depict trends or movement over a period of time, as well as magnitude or rate of change. You can introduce the major trend in words and then use the line graph to clarify the relationship of the two functions and emphasize the direction of the trend. Line graphs stress

- Continuity as opposed to individual points.
- Change in one function in relation to a change in another function.

The functions most frequently appearing on the horizontal and vertical scales are

- time
- temperature
- erosion
- cost
- strength
- distance
- speed

Functions, whether dependent or independent variables, and units of measurement must be given on both the x- and y-axis, as they are in Figure 5.23. Remember that graphs—and all visual aids—must be cited in the text and placed as near to the citation as possible.

Designing a Graph

Line graphs may have a single curve or multiple curves. Figure 5.23 shows a **single curve** with one relationship between two functions. **Multiple curves** show more than one relationship between two functions. When the graph contains more than three curves, it is probably too crowded. You should keep in mind that graphs with multiple curves are difficult to interpret because of their data points. Multiple curves are more appropriate for readers who want quantitative data rather than for the general reader. You must distinguish

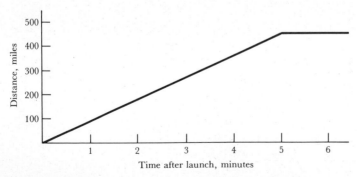

Distance of Missile over Period of Time (minutes)

FIGURE 5.23 Graph with single curve

each line on a multiple curve graph by making each line different, as Figure 5.24 illustrates.

Color is expensive, but it directs attention, creates emphasis, and distinguishes between difficult factors. For example, on a multiple curve graph, color helps differentiate among the lines. Most of the time, however, black and white visual aids are easy to prepare and are as effective as color. **Coded bands** in Figure 5.25 represent a range of data and enhance the comparison among the ranges, making comparison easier and saving space and words.

Remember that only tables have table numbers and titles at the top of the visual aid. All other visual aids including graphs are considered figures, with figure numbers and captions beneath the graphs. When composing the **title** for the graph, describe the dependent variable first in comparison to the independent variable. For example, the title for Figure 5.23 is "Distance of Missile over Period of Time (minutes)."

If you are using a graph with grids, you must be precise at the **data points.** On a graph without grids, you may wish to emphasize the data points by using an enclosed triangle or an x.

A final word stresses *simplicity* for graphs and, indeed, for all visual aids. The purpose of visual aids is to provide an alternative to prose when the

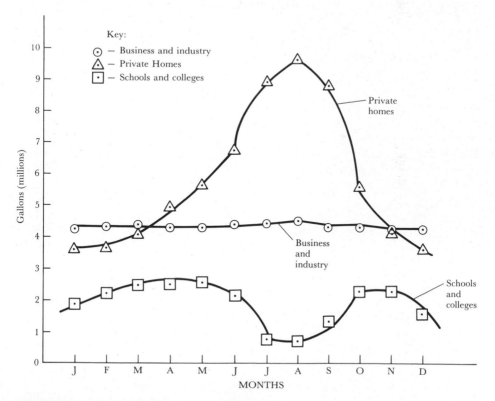

FIGURE 5.24 Graph with multiple curves

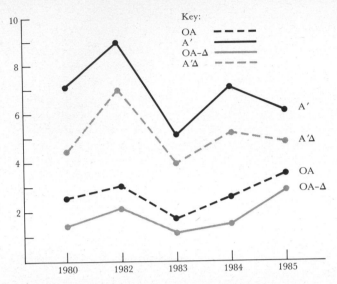

FIGURE 5.25 Graph with coded bands
Source: R. B. Stoner and R. H. Amend, "Documentation Practices in ITCC Proceedings," in *Proceedings,* 33d International Technical Communication Conference, 1986. Used with permission of the Society for Technical Communication.

information would be difficult to describe by words alone. As a visual aid, graphs can effectively support and clarify what you have written, but each graph should present one idea in an easy-to-read figure.

Remember the Following Points About Graphs

When constructing the scale,

- Start the scale at zero. If you fail to write in the zero, you will create a visual distortion of the truth. When a large part of the grid is unnecessary, break the grid, but retain the zero baseline and make the break obvious (see Figure 5.26).
- Select the size of the grid intervals carefully because an exaggerated length in either the horizontal or vertical scale will distort the shape of the curve. The most common grid interval is in units of 10.
- Label the function and the unit of measurement on the x- and y-axis.

When labeling the curves,

- Give each curve a different type of line.
- Be sure each curve represents a different type of data.
- Identify each curve.

When identifying the graph,

- Give the graph a figure number and a caption. Figure numbers and captions go beneath the graph.

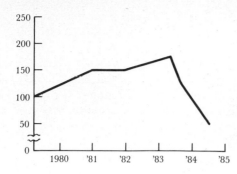

FIGURE 5.26 Comparison of graphs: broken grid

Charts

Charts are simple, adaptable, and suitable for a general audience. They are used for simple comparisons, to compare magnitude or size, or to emphasize differences in an item at various periods of time.

Bar Charts

Bar charts effectively illustrate separate points as opposed to the continuous line of the graph. Bar charts are most useful to contrast similarities and differences between similar numerical facts. Figure 5.27 shows the percentage of people involved in producing graphics for documents. But bar charts are less accurate than numbers on a table, so for absolute values, use a table; for complicated relationships or trends between variables, use a graph.

Charts can be constructed horizontally or vertically. As a rule of thumb, vertical charts clearly depict the difference in one item at various periods in time whereas horizontal charts emphasize the difference between many items at one specific time. Figure 5.28 illustrates horizontal and vertical charts. You

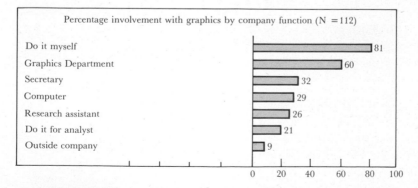

FIGURE 5.27 Bar charts

Source: Renee K. Barnow, "A Methodology for Addressing Needs for Computer Graphics," in *Proceedings,* 32d International Technical Communication Conference, 1985: VC-12. Used with permission of the Society for Technical Communication.

can add bars to provide more information, but you should limit the number of bars in one group to three unless you provide a clear key, as both bar charts demonstrate in Figure 5.28.

Additionally, the bars can be subdivided and then shaded to indicate comparisons within each factor being considered, as they are in Figure 5.28. On a subdivided bar chart, also called a component or segmented bar chart, the segment on the bottom should be chosen on the basis of its importance

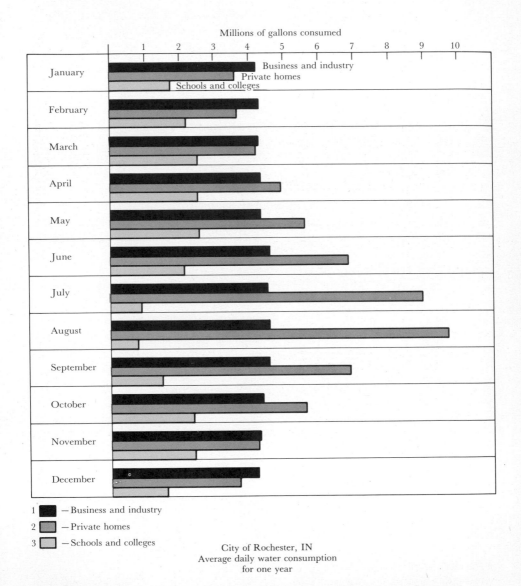

FIGURE 5.28(a) Bar chart: Horizontal, City of Rochester, Indiana, Average daily water consumption for one year

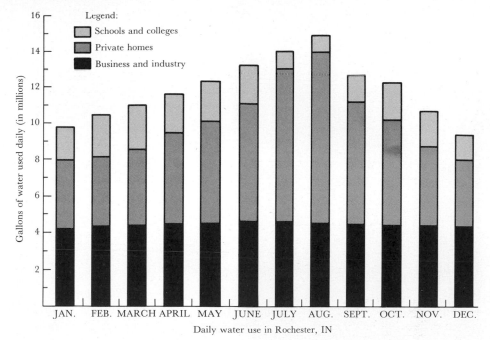

Daily water use in Rochester, IN

Note: This chart shows the average daily use for each month of 1982.

FIGURE 5.28(b) Bar chart: Vertical, Daily water use in Rochester, Indiana,
Note: This chart shows the average daily use for each month of 1982.

(most important first), its size (largest first), or its constancy. The shaded portions should be labeled to help the reader identify what each shade represents.

When constructing a bar chart, keep the bars separated by a constant width. As in all visual aids, do not pack too much information into one chart, and use prose to explain the major relationship, citing the figure number in the text and placing the chart as near to the citation as possible. Label all bars and scales, and give the figure a caption or title.

Design the Bar Chart with the Following Points in Mind

- Avoid using squares, cubes, circles, or spheres in a bar chart. They are too difficult to compare visually.
- Shade all the bars. Do not let one bar or portion be white.
- Make the most important bar the darkest or the lightest, *but* make all bars of equal width (see Figure 5.28).
- Place the most important segment first at the bottom or first at the left end of the axis (see Figure 5.29).
- Line up the right end of bar legends with the axis (see Figure 5.29).

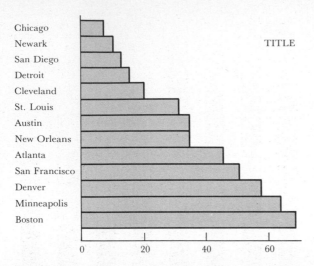

FIGURE 5.29 Bar chart: Long segments and legends

- When there are many bars, eliminate the spaces **only if** the bars can be clearly labeled (see Figure 5.29). Otherwise, limit the number of bars in a group to three (see Figure 5.28).
- If one bar or column is unusually longer than the others, break the bar *and* the axis (see Figure 5.30).
- When the scale is omitted, indicate the amounts within the bar or outside the axis lines (see Figure 5.30).

Pie Charts

A pie chart shows the relation of component parts that total 100 percent. The pie chart is especially useful to show differences and similarities between large and small percentages, but the pie chart will not show absolute values of small differences between factors. For this reason, the pie chart is appropriate for a general audience.

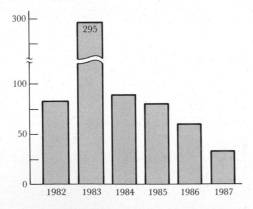

FIGURE 5.30 Break the bar and the axis

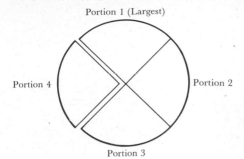

FIGURE 5.31 Pie chart with a separated segment

To construct a pie chart, arrange sectors according to size with the largest at the central point of the top half of the circle. If possible, limit the number of sectors to five, and place labels outside the circle. You may separate one segment to give it emphasis, but, as a general rule, do not separate more than one segment, as Figure 5.31 illustrates. When you have to divide the pie into more than five segments, use a legend to label the sections, illustrated in Figure 5.32.

Pictorial Charts

Pictorial symbols can communicate abstract ideas or concepts and have great audience appeal. Because the symbols must have a strong association with the idea they represent, they are nearly a universal language. Pictorial symbols have two purposes:

- As numerical counting units with each symbol representing a specific number.
- As support for another figure to add emphasis or differentiate.

Figure 5.33 illustrates the pictorial symbol as a numerical unit.

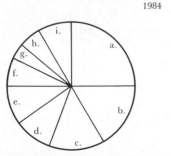

Conference Attendance
1984

Who Attended:

a.	Scientists	25.5%
b.	Engineers	11.8%
c.	Programmers	18.3%
d.	Info developers	10.3%
e.	Teachers	9.4%
f.	Doctors	7.0%
g.	Lawyers	4.1%
h.	Accountants	2.9%
i.	Miscellaneous	10.7%

FIGURE 5.32 Pie chart with legend

Source: Nancy C. Corbin, "The Well-Dressed Posterboard," in *Proceedings*, 32d International Technical Communication Conference, 1985: VC-27. Used with permission of the Society of Technical Communication.

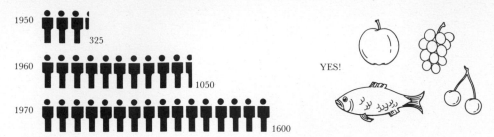

FIGURE 5.33 Pictures used as counting units
Source: A. J. MacGregor, *Graphics Simplified* (Toronto: University of Toronto Press, 1979):19. Reproduced by permission of University of Toronto Press. © University of Toronto Press, 1979.

A general audience readily understands symbols, but these symbols must be well designed and simple and support the prose. Symbols should not be used to depict volume or size because the pictures are one-dimensional whereas volume requires two dimensions. Two important cautions about drawing symbols are these:

- Avoid comparison of size of symbol because readers cannot compare symbols whose size varies. Change the number of symbols instead of the size.
- Use contrasting shapes to compare or contrast. Do not rely on minor differences to differentiate between symbols, as they do in Figure 5.34.

Diagrams

Diagrams are charts that display detailed procedures or complex relationships. Diagrams such as flowcharts, time lines (Gant charts), logic trees, matrices, or organization charts simplify complicated relationships or functions and save you writing time. These diagrams probably save the reader long, tedious explanations of the interrelationships between units. More complex diagrams such as schematics and circuitry should probably be placed in an appendix for the reader who wishes to build or repair the product. Information specialists encourage using diagrams when you want to show the following:[4]

- data flow (path of data)
- major phases and parts of a process
- sequence of operation
- logic flow
- relationship between parts of a process or program

A template, a simple design tool with various sizes of circles, squares, rectangles, and triangles, will permit you to design flowcharts and other il-

NOT THIS

NO!

BUT THIS

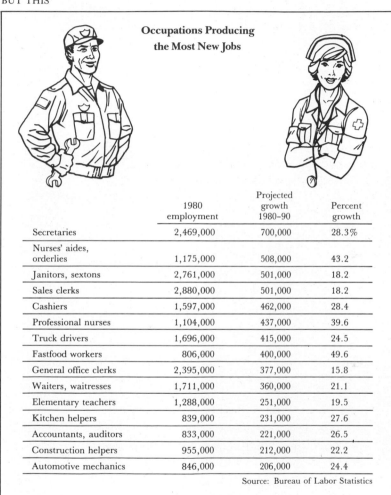

**Occupations Producing
the Most New Jobs**

	1980 employment	Projected growth 1980–90	Percent growth
Secretaries	2,469,000	700,000	28.3%
Nurses' aides, orderlies	1,175,000	508,000	43.2
Janitors, sextons	2,761,000	501,000	18.2
Sales clerks	2,880,000	501,000	18.2
Cashiers	1,597,000	462,000	28.4
Professional nurses	1,104,000	437,000	39.6
Truck drivers	1,696,000	415,000	24.5
Fastfood workers	806,000	400,000	49.6
General office clerks	2,395,000	377,000	15.8
Waiters, waitresses	1,711,000	360,000	21.1
Elementary teachers	1,288,000	251,000	19.5
Kitchen helpers	839,000	231,000	27.6
Accountants, auditors	833,000	221,000	26.5
Construction helpers	955,000	212,000	22.2
Automotive mechanics	846,000	206,000	24.4

Source: Bureau of Labor Statistics

FIGURE 5.34 Symbols must have contrasting shapes
Source: A. J. MacGregor, *Graphics Simplified* (Toronto: University of Toronto Press, 1979):19.
Reproduced by permission of University of Toronto Press. © University of Toronto Press, 1979.

lustrations easily and quickly. When you draw the arrows to indicate flow, make sure you connect the heads to the shafts and point all the heads in one direction. Figure 5.35 illustrates a variety of diagrams.

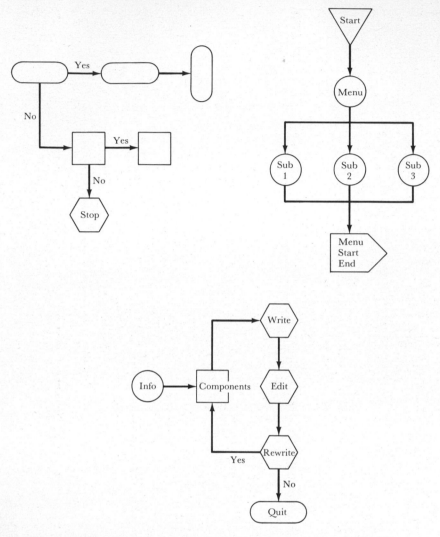

FIGURE 5.35 Arrows used to indicate flow of diagram

Other Figures: Photographs, Line Drawings

Photographs

Photographs provide an authentic illustration or scientific proof of an item. They are useful when you want to give your reader the visual appearance of an item without focusing on a particular aspect of the item. Figure 5.36 is a photograph of a pacemaker. Because photos are difficult to copy and print, you should select a photo that is clear and contains no extraneous information to distract the reader. For reproduction, use a black and white glossy print, usually 8 × 10 in size so that the printer can reduce the photo to fit the allotted space.

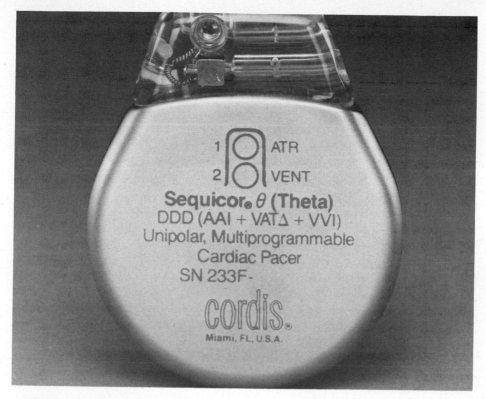

FIGURE 5.36 Photograph of a heart pacemaker
(Courtesy of Cordis Corp., Miami, Florida). Used with permission.

Line Drawings

Line drawings like the Bunsen burner in Figure 5.37 have one major advantage over photos; they show essential details of an object or emphasize important points and are useful when you want to clarify certain points of a

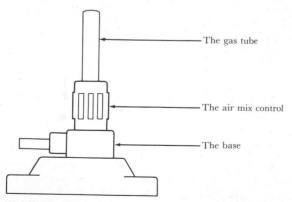

FIGURE 5.37 Line drawing of a Bunsen burner

complex topic. Although a photograph captures all detail to produce a holistic effect, the line drawing omits excessive detail to simplify a point or highlights a detail to clarify a function. You can draw your own illustration using simple,

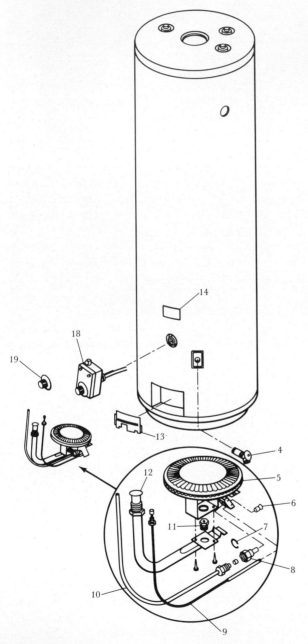

FIGURE 5.38 A line drawing: Exploded view.
Used with the permission of Sears, Roebuck and Co.

straight, and angular lines; and you will save many words by illustrating your text.

The line drawing is particularly useful when you wish to present a hidden part of an object or focus on a detail in an **exploded drawing,** a view enlarging a part of a more complicated object, as illustrated in Figure 5.38.

Summary

The visual presentation of information can help the reader understand your message. In a well-designed document, the words may seem even clearer. The words communicate the important information, but the visuals and the layout aid the reader's grasp of the words.

The audience and the purpose of the document determine the layout and the type of visual aids, but design and visuals are also based on concepts of readability. For example, readers grasp information more efficiently when it is grouped or *chunked* in a section on the page. Surrounding this chunk of information is *white space,* space in which no print appears so that the space frames the important information. Visual aids also support the purpose for writing the document by illustrating information; if the illustration is complex, you may wish to *break out* or focus on a detailed or hidden segment of the illustration in an *enlarged view,* a view enlarging a part of a more complicated object.

Knowing some facts about design will enable you to take advantage of the benefits of good design. *Typography* is the technique of composing type. Each character of type belongs to a *typeface,* a complete alphabet of characters in one style of type. All typeface is either *serif,* a typeface with fine lines projecting from the major strokes of the letter, or *sans serif,* a typeface that lacks the projections. The serif projections help the reader distinguish letters in the word, but without extra lines the sans serif typefaces appear larger. The height or size of the type, measured in *point size,* also affects the readability of the document, and some states set the minimum type size for legal and insurance documents. Clear text should be printed in from 8-point to 12-point type size. The horizontal measurement of the type is measured in *pica* or *elite.* The pica type has 10 characters to the horizontal inch, whereas elite has 12. The important point to remember about type size is that the visual effect of the typeface is more important than the point size.

Layout is the arrangement of lines of text. Right margins can be *justified* (the last character is aligned with the margins) or *ragged* (space at the end of the line depends on the length of the last word on the line). The left margin is usually justified. The line length also affects readability. Long lines of type are difficult to read because the margins are small and the page looks crowded. Short sentences require more eye movement and create distracting breaks in the text. The recommended line length is 50 to 70 letters and spaces. *Spacing* between the lines, called *leading* in typesetting, also helps produce a document that is easy to read. *White space* can help readers find information quickly, and a *grid* helps you plan the white space for the page. A grid is the floor plan for a page and divides the page into horizontal and vertical rows.

Visual aids supplement the text and present the information in a different mode. Every visual aid that is not a *table* is considered a *figure.* Table numbers and captions belong above the table whereas figure numbers and captions go below the visual. You must refer to visual aids in the text, place them close to the initial reference, and label them. Tables present a large amount of data in a small space and are useful to present comparative data. To design a table, think of a box with rows and columns. The rows and columns need headings, including the units of measurement.

Graphs are figures that depict a continuous relationship between two or more functions, such as time, cost, distance. Like tables, graphs have a horizontal scale called the *x-axis* and a vertical scale, the *y-axis.* Line graphs have *single* or *multiple curves* that can be confusing to the reader. When designing a graph, start the scale at zero, use a common grid interval such as units of 10, and label the function and the measurement unit on the x- and y-axis. On a graph with multiple curves (no more than three, though), identify each curve with a different type of line or shaded band.

Charts illustrate separate points for simple comparisons. *Bar charts* can be constructed horizontally or vertically, but the bars should all be a constant width and shaded to indicate comparisons. Label all bars and scales or provide a bar legend. *Pie charts* show the relationship of parts that total 100 percent. When designing a pie chart, arrange the largest sector at the center of the top of the circle. *Pictorial charts* communicate abstract ideas through symbols. Do not use symbols to depict size or volume; simply increase the number of symbols to indicate gain. When using comparative symbols, make sure the differences are easy to distinguish. *Diagrams* show the relationships between units by using circles, squares, rectangles, triangles, straight lines, and arrows. With the help of a *template,* a simple design tool, you can draw flowcharts, logic trees, matrices, organization charts, and other yet-to-be invented charts.

Other visual aids are *photographs,* useful for authenticity; *line drawings* are popular because they can show essential details of an object or highlight a detail in an *exploded view.* In short, visual aids are versatile aids to the content, and along with layout and typography, contribute to the readability of the text.

Checklist for Visual Aids

The checklist serves as a summary of visual aids. Before constructing a visual aid of any kind, ask yourself the following questions:

yes   **no**

_____ _____ 1. Does the illustration help the reader better understand the point you are trying to make in the document?

————— —————   2. Is the visual aid cited in the text before it is presented to the reader, explained, and located near the citation?

————— —————   3. Is the type of illustration the appropriate one to add, reinforce, or clarify the prose?

————— —————   4. Would another visual aid be better for the purpose or for the reader—a line drawing rather than a photo, a chart rather than a table?

————— —————   5. Does the visual aid have a table or figure number and an informative heading?

————— —————   6. Is the visual aid limited to one subject, with enough labels and white space?

————— —————   7. If the figure has a scale, does the scale begin at zero so as not to distort the data? If you must break the
————— —————   scale, is the broken segment clearly marked?

Notes

1. Patricia Caernarvon-Smith, *Page Design for Writers and Editors,* Workshop presentation at the 30th International Technical Communication Conference (St. Louis, Mo., May 1983).
2. Dixie Goswami, Janice C. Redish, Daniel B. Felker, Alan Siegal, *Writing in the Professions* (Washington, D.C.: American Institutes for Research, 1981): 142.
3. Goswami et al., *Writing in the Professions,* p. 144.
4. Herbert E. Vogt, "Graphic Ways to Eliminate Problems Associated with Translating Technical Documentation," in *Proceedings,* 33d International Technical Communication Conference (Washington, D.C.: Society for Technical Communication, 1986):331.

References

Denise Arai, "Design Handout," Technical Writing Seminar 423, Illinois Institute of Technology, 1983. This report provided the background material on typography.
Mary Fran Buehler, *Report Construction* (Sierra Madre, Calif.: Foothill Publications, 1970). This handbook provided invaluable material for the sections on graphs and figures.

Daniel B. Felker et al., *Guidelines for Document Designers* (Washington, D.C.: American Institutes for Research, 1981).

William Horton, "Templates of Thought," in *Proceedings,* 33d International Technical Communication Conference (Washington, D.C.: Society for Technical Communication, 1986):302–305.

A. J. MacGregor, *Graphics Simplified* (Toronto, Canada: University of Toronto Press, 1979). This text provided exemplary models for clear visual aids.

James A. Mann and John B. Ketchum, "The Multi-Use Concept: A Cost-Effective Way to Present Technical Material in a Number of Forms," in *Proceedings,* 31st International Technical Communication Conference (Washington, D.C.: Society for Technical Communication, 1984): WE 164–167.

Leslie A. Olsen, "Visual Aids," Paper presented at the 1985 NCTE/CCCC Winter Workshop, Clearwater, Fla. This paper provided the organization for the section on visual aids.

Herbert E. Vogt, "Wordless Instructions—Say It with Pictures," in *Proceedings,* 31st International Technical Communication Conference (Washington, D.C.: Society for Technical Communication, 1984): VC 23–26.

Applying Your Knowledge

EXERCISE 5.1

How would you improve the readability of the following text? Redesign the page to accommodate the purpose and the reader.

MEDICAL INSTRUMENTATION SERVICES, INC.
7143 Lincoln Avenue
St. Louis, Missouri 80076

Date: May 15, 1989

Subject: Medical Instrument Service Program

Director of Medical Instrumentation Laboratory:

Medical Instrumentation Services, Inc., specializes in providing quality engineering support services to medical instrumentation laboratories throughout the Southeastern United States. In response to requests from several major hospitals in your area, we are opening an office in the Houston area. Servicing primarily ventilators and blood gas analyzers, we also repair respirometers, ultrasonic nebulizers, oxygen blenders and analyzers, and related equipment. In addition to providing emergency repairs on a 24-hour basis, we have developed a comprehensive preventive maintenance program for most critical care instruments. This includes periodic testing and calibration assuring continued quality control and compliance with all current Joint Commission for Accreditation of Hospitals (JCAH) standards. All work is scheduled in advance and performed in a professional manner by factory-trained, certified biomedical engineers, who provide complete documentation for all services rendered.

To assist you further in meeting your patient's needs, we rent all popular ventilators on a 24-hour basis and generally provide delivery within one hour of your call. And we can arrange for 10,000-hour remanufacturing for your Bennett MA-I. Our service is prompt and professional, and our prices are very competitive. For more information on our program and a detailed price quotation for your hospital, please complete and return the enclosed questionnaire.

Yours very truly,

Service Manager

EXERCISE 5.2

Select one article from a popular magazine and one section from a textbook and analyze them for the following features:

- typeface
  serif
  sans serif
- type size
  vertical points
  horizontal points (pica or elite)
- layout (ragged *or* justified)
- leading
- grid (column)

EXERCISE 5.3

Create a page of copy for a hot pot. Make a rough sketch of the layout, including location and size of illustration, heading or headings, as well as any other elements you think should appear on the page. Write the heading or headings and body copy from the list of features. Limit the size to one 8½ × 11-inch page.

Item: Hot Pot
Price: $16.95
FEATURES:
- aluminum body—orange
- bakelite plastic base, handle, and lid—black
- holds 36 oz.
- 5 heat settings
- weighs 2 lbs.
- measures 7 inches high
- UL listed for 110-120-v. 60-Hz. ac.
- 2-foot rubber cord
- lid consists of grip, spout, and lock
- lid designed to keep heat in and prevent liquid from bubbling out
- heating time less than 15 minutes
- warning light when pot is hot
- heats chili, soup, water for dorm room

EXERCISE 5.4

Create a page of copy for one of the products listed. The purpose of the copy is to sell the product. Make a rough sketch of the product and layout. Write the heading or headings and body copy.

PRODUCT:
hand-held can/bottle opener
telephone
children's toy
food blender
coffee maker
any kitchen appliance
gumball machine
clock radio
popcorn popper
any item of your own choice

EXERCISE 5.5

You have been asked to prepare the graphics for two documents: a technical report and a magazine. The business managers want accurate data, the executives want readable indexes, and the marketing department wants the information to be attractive and accessible to the general reader. What visuals will you use for the two documents? Create the visuals based on the information provided.

From 1976 to 1982 small businesses grew and created a large number of jobs. Businesses with a maximum of 19 employees in 1976 had increased the number of employees by 29.3 percent in 1982. Those with a maximum of 99 employees in 1976 had increased employment by 13.1 percent in 1982. In 1976 companies with up to 500 employees had increased employment only by 10.7 percent in 1982 and companies with over 500 employees in 1976 had grown in employment by 12.2 percent in 1982.

EXERCISE 5.6

What visuals would you use to present the following information?

Audience: Journal of Rehabilitation Physiology readers
In 1988, of the people who attended the Rehabilitation Conference, 14.3 percent came from New York, 10 percent came from Florida, 6.7 percent came from Nevada, 50 percent came from Maine, and 20 percent came from California.

Audience: newspaper readers
In 1984 the average department size was 10.5 people; in 1983 the average department size was 10 people; in 1982 the average department size was 8.5 people; in 1981 the average department size was 6.75 people.

Audience: general readers
In 1980 through 1984 the social security taxes rose from 4.0 percent to 10 percent of the total income of low-income families; in the same time period the social security taxes rose from 9 percent to 23 percent among medium-income families; in the same time period, among the high income families, the taxes rose from 15 percent to 25 percent.

Audience: professionals in the field

One way to pare down a large manual is to write a series of smaller documents, giving the users what they need to perform their tasks: Buyers need to know the advantages of the product; operators need to know the operations and start-up of the product; programmers need to know the programming and operations of the product; repair personnel need to know the installation, operations, start-up, and repair of the product.

U N I T 2

The Components of Technical Reports

M O D U L E 6

Descriptions: Mechanism, Place, and Process

If your customer wants to know what a crescent wrench looks like before ordering 10 gross to sell in the hardware shop, then you have to write a physical description. When your client wants to know how to solve computer hardware problems, then you have to write a process description. This module helps you write these two descriptions by explaining the purpose behind each and the procedures for writing descriptions.

A physical description of a mechanism helps your customer visualize the crescent wrench, evaluate it, and compare it to other devices. A physical description of a place helps your reader visualize the setting, evaluate it, and compare it to other settings. Descriptions of mechanisms or laboratory instruments appear frequently in experimental research reports or other scientific reports. A description of a place or environment often is necessary in a case report or a design report.

Unlike the physical description, which is static, a process description describes an action involving a sequence of events, such as reading flowcharts to solve computer problems so that your client can understand the procedure and replicate the process if appropriate. Process descriptions are an important part of the methodology section in a scientific report or of a feasibility section in a management report.

Both the physical description and the process description require analysis—usually by division and partition, explained in Module 3. They often appear in the same document, also. But, they are separate writing tasks and must be treated individually.

Scope

In this module you will learn to

1. Organize a physical description.
2. Describe the parts of a mechanism.
3. Arrange the details for a place description.
4. Describe a sequence of events for the process description.
5. List the steps for performing a process.
6. Choose a style for accuracy and coherence.
7. Integrate visuals into the text.

Description of a Mechanism (Physical Description)

A description of a mechanism answers two questions for the reader: What does it look like, and what does it do?

What does it look like?
The answer to this question follows an organizational strategy that includes

- definition of the mechanism
- overview of the whole
- division into parts
- description of each part

What does it do?
This answer must include

- description of mechanism in use
- its advantages, disadvantages, uniqueness, and applications

Organizing for a Description of a Mechanism

The Introduction
The description begins with an introduction that describes what the mechanism looks like by placing the mechanism in a context with other mechanisms. In other words, the introduction begins with a definition that includes the class and the function of the mechanism. The advice on definitions in Module 3 is to make the class as narrow as possible.

Not: mechanism   *But:* draftsman's tool
Not: device   *But:* laboratory instrument
Not: equipment   *But:* vehicle

The introduction also includes an overview, that is, a description of the size, shape, and composition of the mechanism. The overview is usually accompanied by a visual so that the reader sees the mechanism. Following the overview is a clear division of the mechanism into its major parts. Again, Module 3 offers advice on dividing an item into parts: Divide the item into parts according to a principle of organization, such as assembly, location, or importance.

Finally, the introduction also lists the parts and subparts before describing each one in the next section. The example in Figure 6.1 illustrates the introduction to a description of a mechanism.[1]

Double Bar Ankle Foot Orthosis

A double bar ankle foot orthosis [see (a)] is a bracing system for the foot and ankle. This device is applied to the exterior of the leg (below the knee) to restrict or enhance motion of the foot and ankle. This type of orthosis is custom-fit to the user's leg and shoe so it varies in both size and shape. The length of the device is measured from the top of the calf to the bottom of the sole of the shoe. Its width and depth are determined by the shape of the user's calf. This orthosis is made of leather, plastic, velcro, foam rubber, steel, aluminum, and stainless steel. It consists of four major components: a calf cuff, two uprights, and a stirrup [see (a)].

Double Bar Ankle Foot Orthosis

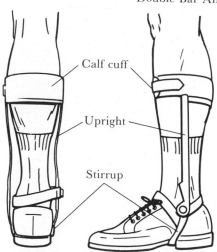

(a) Orthosis

FIGURE 6.1 Introduction to a description of a mechanism
Source: Dorothy Greenberg, Technical Writing 421, Illinois Institute of Technology.

Description of Parts

The next section of the description describes and explains each of the parts in order, repeating the organizational pattern in the introduction:

Part 1 and subparts:
  Definition—class and function
  Overview—description with quantitative data of size, shape, composition
  Subparts—with definition, overview, description
Part 2 and subparts

Figure 6.2 illustrates the second section of the description of a mechanism, the section that describes each of the parts. The parts description must include accurate data, detail, and, depending on the complexity or uniqueness of the item, visuals. Remember that the reader may want to evaluate this item and compare it to similar items.

	Description of Parts
Part 1	The calf cuff [see (b)], the first part of the orthosis, is a device that secures the upper portion of the orthosis to the calf. It keeps the orthosis rigid and the uprights correctly aligned. The large surface area of the calf cuff allows the forces that build up in the orthosis to be distributed over a greater area of tissue than would be possible if the cuff were small. A small cuff concentrates the pressure in a small area, which can cause pain and possibly nerve damage.
	The calf cuff is 2″ wide and has an interior diameter that is slightly larger than the diameter of the calf. It is ⅜″ thick. The cylindrically shaped calf cuff is contoured by the orthotist (the person who builds orthoses) to conform to the shape of the calf. The calf cuff is made of leather, plastic, velcro, foam rubber, and steel.
Subpart	Inside the calf cuff is a calf band (c). It is 1½″ wide and 1/16″ thick. The calf band is bent to fit the back of the calf and is shaped like half of a cylinder. It is made of steel. The calf band is lined with a ⅛″ thick piece of foam rubber cut to fit it. The calf band and foam rubber pad are covered with soft leather that is glued and stitched to keep it in place. A ⅝″ square buckle is riveted with a ⅛″ steel rivet to the calf cuff (b). A ½″ wide by 6″ long piece of velcro is used to make the tab that fits through the buckle. The end of the velcro is tapered so that it fits through the buckle easily. The velcro is also attached with two steel rivets to the calf cuff.
	Attached below the calf cuff, on each end of the calf band is an upright [see (c)]. The two uprights that are similar to each other are the second and third parts

Parts 2 and 3

of the orthosis. The tops of the uprights keep the calf cuff at a distance from the ankle. This is necessary for the type of force an orthosis uses to brace a foot and ankle. The bottom end of the upright contains a joint (d). This part of the upright acts as a substitute for the user's deficient ankle joint and leg muscles.

Subpart

The two uprights are ¾" wide and ⅛" thick. The uprights are ½" wider and ¼" thicker at the bottom. The very bottom end of the upright is rounded. Its length is measured from the top of the calf band to the malleolus (the protruding bone of the ankle). The upright is bent and twisted so that it will lie flat on the calf. The center of the joint is aligned by bending and twisting the upright. The center of the upright's joint must align with the anatomical ankle joint of its user. The upright is made of polished aluminum.

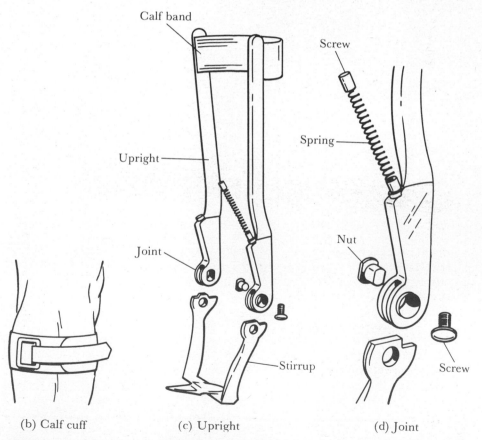

(b) Calf cuff   (c) Upright   (d) Joint

FIGURE 6.2 Section of the description that describes each part
Source: Dorothy Greenberg, Technical Writing 421, Illinois Institute of Technology.

Description of the Mechanism in Use

The third section of the description explains the mechanism in use. This section uses the third person and the indicative mood to explain the operation of the mechanism.

Description of the mechanism in use
(indicative mood)

To use the double bar ankle foot orthosis, the wearer puts on the shoe with the stirrup permanently attached. Then the wearer adjusts the calf band, if necessary, and the uprights so that the mechanical joint aligns with the wearer's anatomical joint.

Conclusion

The fourth section concludes the description by explaining

uniqueness
advantages *versus* disadvantages
similarities *or* applications

Figure 6.3 illustrates the conclusion of the description of the double bar ankle orthosis.

Conclusion

This orthosis is distinguished from other ankle foot orthoses by the presence of two uprights instead of only one. If there are two uprights, then an ankle-controlling strap can be attached to either one. The strap applies corrective pressure to either the inside or outside of the ankle, depending on the direction of the force. One upright allows pressure to be applied only to one side of the ankle.

Two uprights also result in an orthosis stronger than one with only a single bar. However, two uprights are more visible than one, so the double bar orthosis is more noticeable than other kinds. Usually the wearer prefers it not to be noticed. Also, the permanent attachment of the stirrup to the shoe permits the wearer to use only one pair of shoes. A different type of stirrup permits shoe interchanging but is not as durable.

The joint in the double bar orthosis is very versatile. It permits a very large range of motion and by its particular design can compensate for deficiencies of the muscles of the lower leg and foot. It can help lift the foot and prevent the foot from dragging on the ground. The double bar ankle foot orthosis is a very useful device to those for whom it is prescribed. It helps them walk as normally as possible.

FIGURE 6.3 Conclusion of the description of a mechanism
Source: Dorothy Greenberg, Technical Writing 421, Illinois Institute of Technology.

Summing Up the Description of a Mechanism

Instead of summarizing in prose the conventional format for a report about mechanisms, Figure 6.4 uses a visual, a hierarchy, to illustrate the parts of a report about mechanisms.

Then Figure 6.5 provides a model of a complete description of a mechanism.[2]

Description of a Place

Just as in mechanism description, the introduction of a place description includes a definition, description of the physical appearance, and function. As always, definition includes class and differentiae. The class may be a building, a forest preserve, or any area or environment. The differentiae provide details on an exact location, such as an address or points on a map. Finally, the overview is important because it orients the reader to the place's size, shape, and function.

Even more than with the mechanism description, the logical ordering of detail in a place description requires the careful selection of an organizing principle because the place may include people as well as parts; it is still possible to use assembly, location, or importance as the organizing principle. A visual, such as a map or layout, is crucial to the reader.

A place description carefully describes each part with its subparts, perhaps followed by a description of the place or environment in use. An example can show how people use the environment. Usually, the description

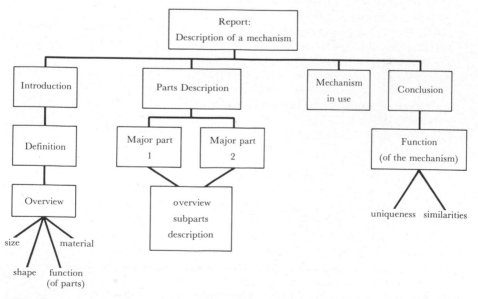

FIGURE 6.4 Hierarchy for a report about a mechanism

The Crescent Wrench

Definition

A crescent wrench is a hand tool made of heavy metal. It has a long handle and a flat, clawlike head with an adjustable lower jaw for gripping and turning nuts and bolts.

Overview

The crescent wrench ranges in weight from $\frac{1}{4}$ pound to 2 pounds and varies in length from 5 inches to 24 inches. The shape resembles a lollipop because of its two main parts: the handle and the head. An average, all-purpose, adjustable wrench for home use, it is 10 inches long and $2\frac{1}{2}$ inches at the widest part of the head. Even the small, all-purpose wrench is heavy, weighing $8\frac{1}{2}$ ounces, because the tool is commonly made of forged steel.

Description of Parts

The drawing (a) illustrates the parts of the crescent wrench. The handle of a 10-inch wrench is smooth, flat with a uniform thickness of $\frac{3}{8}$ inch, and $7\frac{1}{2}$ inches long, tapering from 1 inch at the base end to $\frac{3}{4}$ inches near the head.

A large hole at the base end of the handle allows the user to store the wrench on a hook near the workbench area.

The head of a 10-inch wrench is $2\frac{1}{2}$ inches at its widest point, $2\frac{1}{2}$ inches long, and $\frac{1}{2}$ inch thick. The wrench head has a stationary upper jaw and two moving parts that comprise the adjustment mechanism: the adjustable jaw and the threaded turning gear and teeth.

(a) **Crescent wrench**

The stationary upper jaw has a flat jaw surface and simply acts in opposition to the adjustable jaw.

The adjustable jaw also has a flat surface, but it can be raised or lowered by the threaded turning gear and the teeth. [See (b).]

(b) **Adjustment mechanism**

The gear, housed at the base of the wrench head, fits into the teeth and rotates through the teeth to move the adjustable jaw toward or away from the stationary jaw.

The Mechanism in Use

To use the open-ended wrench, the operator fits the open jaws around the bolt to be loosened or tightened. With the thumb pressing down and backward on the threaded turning gear, the operator moves the adjustable jaw toward the stationary jaw. [See (c).]

When the jaws tightly grip the bolt, the operator turns the handle to loosen or tighten the bolt. The handle turns clockwise to tighten and counterclockwise to loosen.

To release the jaws, the operator reverses the direction of the threaded turning gear, pushing up on it, to separate the jaws from the bolt head. The jaws of the wrench will need to be repositioned continuously around the bolt head with each turn of the bolt.

(c) Mechanism in use

Conclusion

The all-purpose crescent wrench can be used for numerous simple home repairs on bicycles, appliances, plumbing, and hardware on doors and windows. The size of the bolt, nut, screw, or pipe fitting determines the size of the wrench to use.

Other wrenches include the sprocket, ratchet, monkey, pipe, and stillson—all wrenches with specialized uses and various means of adjustment; but the primary purpose of wrenches remains the tightening and loosening of nuts and bolts.

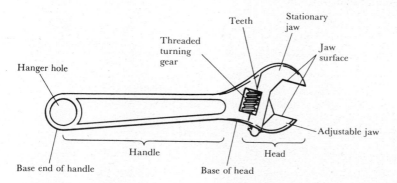

(a) Parts of the adjustable crescent wrench

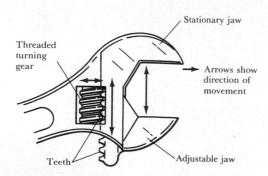

(b) Adjustment mechanism of the threaded turning gear

FIGURE 6.5 Description of a crescent wrench
Source: Terry Washburn-Shouba, Technical Writing 421, Illinois Institute of Technology.

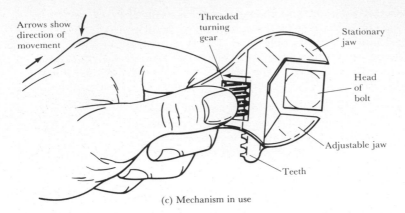

(c) Mechanism in use

FIGURE 6.5 (cont.)

of a place is part of a larger report for assessing, designing or redesigning, or managing the environment; thus, the conclusion is relevant to the purpose or reason for the report. Remember, for orientation, that the reader depends on the logical ordering of detail and the accompanying visual, as exemplified in Figure 6.6[3]

My neighborhood is located in Vernon Park, Chicago, Illinois, and consists of six blocks. What makes this area uniquely my neighborhood is its three boundaries: (1) physical, (2) housing, and (3) family.

This area is bounded by railroad tracks to the north, 95th Street to the south, King Drive to the west, and St. Lawrence to the east [see (a)].

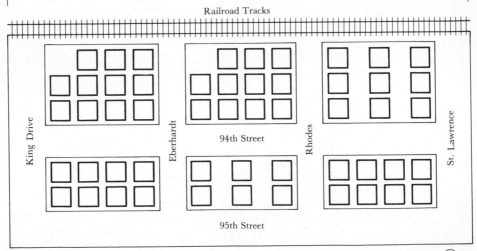

(a)

The railroad tracks, King Drive, St. Lawrence, and 95th Street—all main thoroughfares—are the physical boundaries that totally encompass my neighborhood.

The housing within this neighborhood is predominantly single-fam-lly. These single family homes have been there at least 20 to 30 years. The main material for the structure is brick. To the east and outside my neighborhood, the predominant housing consists of three-story walk-ups. This housing has been built of a wood construction within the past 8 to 14 years. To the west of my neighborhood, the housing consists of predominantly one- and two-story single-family contemporary homes (ranch homes) constructed of brick and wood.

The family structure within my neighborhood consists mainly of older parents whose children are grown and live with them or are mar-ried and have moved away from home. A few families have moved in recently, but their children are teenagers. To the east of the neighbor-hood, the family structure is a single-parent one with children or teen-agers who have children of their own. This area has a large child popu-lation. To the west of my neighborhood, the family structure is similar to the one in my neighborhood, but the parents are older, and the grown children do not live at home.

These boundaries provide a brief description of my neighborhood and can be used to predict the achievement, the politics, and the econ-omy of the people living within and outside my neighborhood.

FIGURE 6.6 Description of a place
Source: Adapted from Renee Hearn, Technical Writing 421, Illinois Institute of Technology.

> Description of a Process

Like the mechanism description, the process description answers the reader's questions, What is the process, and how does it work? You frequently find a process description preceding a set of instructions.

What is the process?

The answer to this question follows an organizational strategy that is similar to the strategy for a mechanism description:

- definition (formal or operational) of process
- overview of the whole process
- explanation or theory behind process
- description of equipment, mechanisms, and preparation, if necessary
- explanation of sequence of actions (events)

How does it work?

To answer this question, you have to use a different technique than the one you used for the mechanism description. The process description uses

- performance steps/set of instructions
- conclusion, only if necessary

Organizing for a Process Description

The Introduction

The introduction provides the context for the process description. An operational definition may be more appropriate than a formal definition because it describes what happens when the process is initiated. The overview explains the principle or concepts and usually includes a visual such as a flowchart or an example. The introduction also identifies the steps in the process. The example in Figure 6.7 illustrates the introduction for a process description.

Explanation of Equipment

The second section of the process description explains any equipment, mechanisms, or preparation needed to perform the process. If the equipment is self-evident, you do not have to describe it. But if the mechanisms are unfamiliar, you will have to describe them; and if the preparation is complex, you will have to analyze it and break it into steps. All equipment and preparation must be related to the overall process, as it is in the example of the flowchart:

Example:
Materials Required:
To understand some of the terminology in the text on the flowchart, you will need the FTX 3000 Troubleshooting Guide for Operators. Besides having a table of contents and an index, this guide has an extensive glossary to help you interpret the text.

Performance Instructions

The third section of the process description has instructions for performing the process. This section is quite different from the third section of the mechanism description because the mechanism description is fixed or static whereas the performance steps are a fluid or moving action using narration techniques. You will remember from the mechanism description that the section on the mechanism in use must always be in the indicative mood, using the third person.

The performance instructions in the process description use the imperative rather than the indicative mood. The imperative mood is sometimes called the command mode because the second person is understood and omitted from the sentence.

Instructions for performing the process
(imperative mood—command)

To read flowcharts:
1. Start at the top and work your way to the bottom.
2. As you progress through the chart, interpret the meanings of the symbols and the text within the symbols.

Problem Determination Flowcharts

A flowchart is a visual that graphically presents the steps in a procedure. A problem determination flowchart helps users diagnose a problem and find the appropriate action. A problem determination flowchart
for a computer helps users diagnose a computer hardware problem and
find the appropriate action. Computer operators who suspect a computer system failure or an operating system failure can get assistance
from a problem determination flowchart. Flowcharts are becoming so
popular that every reader should be acquainted with the process of reading a computer flowchart [see (a)].

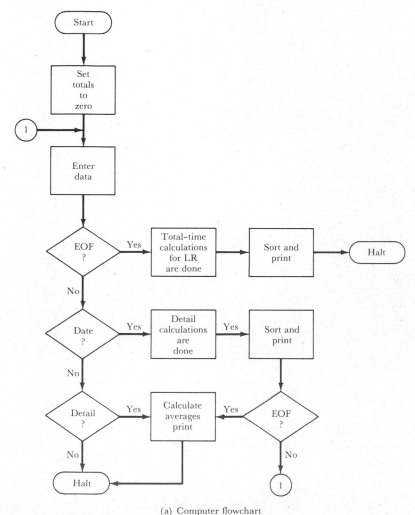

(a) Computer flowchart

FIGURE 6.7 Introduction for a process description

General Principles

Reading a computer flowchart proceeds along logical lines and uses some major elements that are standard in the computer industry. It is important to know these major elements in order to understand the process of reading the flowchart. The major elements of a flowchart are symbols, flow lines, and text.

—Symbols
- The rectangle, sometimes called a process block, represents a process or a single activity.
- The diamond, sometimes called a decision block, represents a point in the procedure where a decision must be made. The diamond contains a question and provides alternative paths to follow depending on the answer to the question.
- *Start* represents the starting point of the procedure.
- The circle, called a connector, is used for reentry at a block in the flowchart.

—Flow lines
- Set up paths for you to follow when reading the procedure.
- Connect the bottom of a block to the top of the next block.
- Several flow lines may extend from decision blocks, one for each alternative path.

—Text
- Provides explanatory information (in process blocks).
- Asks a question (in decision blocks).

FIGURE 6.7 (cont.)

The set of instructions for reading a flowchart is very brief, but writing instructions is so important in technical writing that the next module, Module 7, is devoted to writing instructions.

Conclusion or Summary

In a process description, a conclusion or summary is usually unnecessary because the reader can look back at the steps. You might use a summary only if the steps are complex or if the process has unique applications unfamiliar to the reader. Otherwise, most process descriptions end with the final step under performance instructions.

Exemplifying the Process Description

Figure 6.8 provides a report about a process, a report that exemplifies the organization of the process description.[4]

How a Xerographic Process Works

Definition

    Xerography is an electrostatic process used to duplicate original documents. The word *xerography* comes from the Greek words *xeros* and *graphe* meaning "dry writing." The process of xerography consists of the following six steps:

List of steps

Step 1: Charging
Step 2: Exposing
Step 3: Developing
Step 4: Transferring
Step 5: Fusing
Step 6: Cleaning

Description and function of step 1

    The first step is to charge the whole surface of the drum electrostatically by rotating it under a corotron. The corotron is a bare wire to which a 7,000 positive voltage is applied. This voltage ionizes the air, producing the blue cloud often seen around the wire.

    The second step is to project the image of the original to be copied onto the drum by a series of lenses and mirrors. The white areas of the original reflect a large amount of light, which destroys the charge on the drum, whereas the black areas do not reflect and leave the charge intact.

Description of step 3

    The third step is to develop with a special dry developer. The developer consists of a mass of tiny glass beads, sand, or metal shot, coated with thermoplastic (melts with heat) resin car-

material

bon. The black powder mixture is called the toner. When the glass beads and the toner rub together, they create static electricity, making a layer of toner that covers the glass beads. The

function

developer is poured over the drum; then the beads covered with toner roll over the drum surface. The toner adheres to the charged areas of the drum because the positive charge of the image on the drum is greater than that of the bead.

Description and function of step 4

    The fourth step is to transfer the toner from the drum to the paper. If the toner is to be removed from the drum and onto the paper, the paper must possess a positive charge greater than the charge on the toner. The corotron charges the paper as it is pressed against the drum, causing the toner to adhere to the paper.

FIGURE 6.8 A complete process description
Source: Michael D. Jones, Technical Writing 421, Illinois Institute of Technology.

Description of step 5

    The fifth step is to fuse the toner into fibers of the paper. This fusion is done by passing the copy through heated pressure rollers.

Description and function of step 6

    The sixth step is to clean the drum. The transfer of toner is never complete, and the drum must be cleaned before another copy can be made. The drum is charged with a negative corotron to destroy the positive residual charge, making it easier for the toner to be brushed off the drum. This brushing effect may induce a static charge on the drum so that the drum is exposed to light to neutralize any charge left.

List of Materials

Following is the list of materials needed to perform the unique xerographic process.

paper cutter
matt knife
flat straight edge
drafting tape
Scotch tape

Performance Instructions

To reproduce black-line or blue-line prints:
    Step 1: Cut the sheet to be reproduced into three 12″ sections.
    Step 2: Cut the 14″ wide roll of 1020 or 1000H paper 3″ longer than the section to be reproduced (the extra length is to allow for the elongation by the machine).
    Step 3: Flatten the edge of the 14″ wide paper with the straight edge to prevent the paper from curling and getting caught in machine. [See (a)].

(a) Preparing paper for machine

Step 4: Unlatch the paper cassette by raising the paper cassette latch to the REMOVE position; then, using both hands, grasp the cassette and pull it straight out. [See (b)].

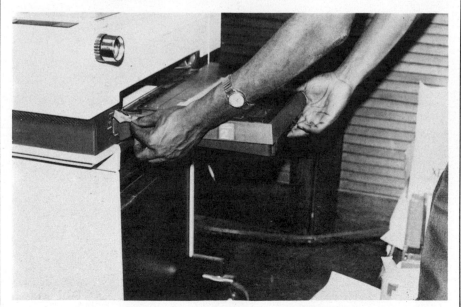

(b) Removing paper cassette

Step 5: Place the paper from step 3 into the large paper cassette. [See (c).]

FIGURE 6.8 (cont.)

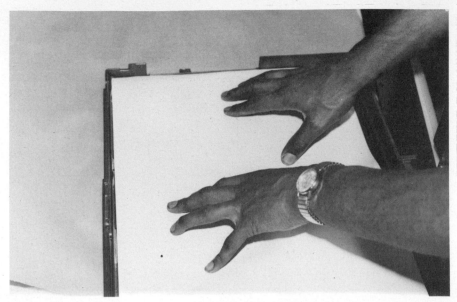

(c) Placing paper in cassette

Step 6: Replace the paper cassette and lower the paper cassette latch to the OPERATE position.

Note: If the latch does not move, the cassette is not fully inserted.

Step 7: Raise document cover and pull lever forward to put machine into the stream feeding mode. [See (d).]

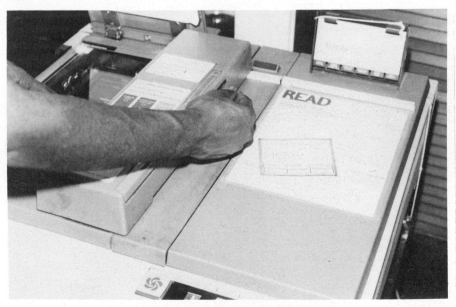

(d) Activating stream feed mode

Step 8: Place the original face down, aligning the long edge of the original against the DOCUMENT GUIDE; then slide the original into the DOCUMENT FEEDER. [See (e).]

174

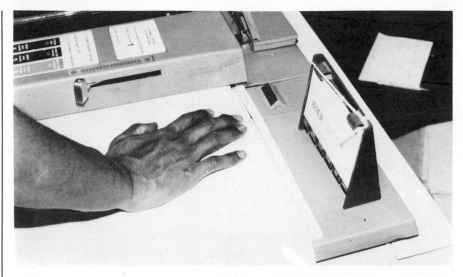

(e) Sliding original into document feeder

Note: When a misfeed occurs, the copier will stop, and the words CLEAR PAPER PATH will be visible on the control console. Turn the release knob to unlatch the copier [see (f)], lift open the copier, and, without touching the drum, gently remove the jammed paper. Close the copier and begin again from step 3.

FIGURE 6.8 (cont.)   (f) Clearing paper path

Step 9: Repeat steps 3, 4, 5, 6, and 8 for the remaining two sections.
Step 10: Match the lines of the newly reproduced sheets together, and tape with brown tape on front.
Step 11: Cut along matching lines with a matt knife, and discard waste paper.
Step 12: Tape remaining paper on the back with transparent tape.
Step 13: Tape together the original sheet on the back with either brown or transparent tape.

FIGURE 6.8 (cont.)

Using Good Style

Accuracy in diction is important in descriptions. You have to help the reader visualize the mechanism by narrowing the class to which the mechanism belongs, measuring the parts to provide quantitative data, and describing the parts using analogy (*O* ring, *U*-shaped head are just two of the analogies discussed in Module 3) if your reader will benefit from comparing the unfamiliar to the familiar.

In a mechanism description, the section on the description of a mechanism in use uses the indicative mood and the third person. In a process description, the section on performance instructions uses the imperative, the command, mood and the second person. The second person is implied.

Finally, as each part or subpart is described and each step or substep is explained, you will have to relate them to previous parts and steps. The relationship of subparts to parts and parts to the whole maintains coherence throughout the descriptions. As you remember from Module 4, coherence is achieved by repeating information from the first sentence to the second sentence and by using transitional words such as *finally, the fourth step,* and *however, unlike the previous part.*

Integrating Visuals into the Text

In mechanism descriptions and place descriptions, visuals are essential. In the process description, too, readers must have flowcharts or diagrams as well as photographs and other visuals. You can use a simple line drawing to illustrate the mechanism with the major parts clearly labeled. Remember to mention the figure in the text even if you are using only one figure and to place the visual at the side or in the text as near to the reference as possible. Do not place the visual on the bottom of page 2 because your reader may not see it until after struggling through the description.

If you illustrate parts and subparts, illustrate them in relation to the

whole mechanism or in relation to a human user. Human hands or feet place
the mechanism in perspective and help the reader see the orientation of the
mechanism in use.

Summary

A description of a mechanism or place helps the reader visualize the mechanism or place, evaluate it, and compare it to other similar mechanisms or
places. A process description explains how a process works so that the reader
can understand and replicate the procedure. These descriptions require analysis, usually by *division and partition,* and frequently appear in the same
report. For example, in a scientific report the materials section may require
a mechanism description whereas in the methodology section a process description is necessary. But the descriptions are separate writing tasks and must
be treated individually.

A *mechanism description* tells the reader what the device looks like and
what it does by beginning with a definition in the introduction. The introduction also includes an *overview* that describes the size, shape, and composition of the device. The overview is usually accompanied by a *visual.* Following the overview is a division of parts, arranged according to a principle of
assembly, location, or importance, and a list of the major parts.

The second section of the mechanism description describes and explains
each of the parts in order, repeating the organizational pattern in the introduction. The description of each part should include such details as *exact
size, shape,* and *composition.*

The third section describes the *mechanism in use* by using the third
person in the indicative mood. The user of the mechanism may be called the
operator, the wearer, the technician, and so on. The fourth section concludes
the mechanism description by explaining the device's uniqueness, *advantages
and disadvantages,* similarities, or applications.

The *place description* follows most of the advice for the mechanism
description because both are physical descriptions. But the reader relies heav-
ily on a detailed overview that orients the reader to the environment. Listing
the components of a place is often difficult because the parts may be more
fluid in a place description than in a mechanism description. For example, a
place description often includes people who provide a perspective on the
place description. But an *ordering principle* of assembly, location, or importance is useful. An accompanying visual, a map or a layout, will also assist the
reader. Usually, a place description is part of a larger report for assessing,
designing, or managing the environment; thus, the conclusion of the place
description should be relevant to the purpose for the report.

A *process description* tells the reader what the process is and how it
works. Like the mechanism description, a process description begins with an
introductory definition. An *operational definition* may be more appropriate
than a formal definition because it describes what happens when the process

is initiated. Following the definition is an overview that explains the principle, accompanied by a flowchart or other visual, and a list or description of the steps in the process.

The second section of the process description explains any equipment, mechanism, or preparations needed to perform the process; and the third section provides the instructions for performing the process. Unlike the third section in the mechanism description, this section uses a *narrative technique* that requires using the second person in the imperative mood. In fact, the set of instructions omits the *you* from the command; for example: Start at the top and work your way to the bottom.

In a process description, a conclusion or summary is usually unnecessary, and the process description ends with the final step under performance instructions.

Checklist for Descriptions of Mechanism, Place, and Process

Review your description section by section. Check only those items to which you can give a positive response.

MECHANISM DESCRIPTION
Does the introduction include
_____ definition?

_____ overview with accompanying visual?

_____ division of parts?

_____ list of parts?

Does the description of parts section define and describe
_____ Part 1?

_____ Subparts?

_____ Part 2?

_____ Subparts?

Is the mechanism in use section
_____ in the indicative mood?

_____ in the third person?

Does the conclusion explain
_____ uniqueness?

_____ advantages versus disadvantages?

_____ similarities?

_____ applications?

PLACE DESCRIPTION
Does the place description have
_____ a detailed overview?

_____ a logical ordering of parts?

_____ an accompanying map or layout?

PROCESS DESCRIPTION
Does the introduction include
_____ definition?

_____ overview of the theory or principle?

_____ identification of the steps?

_____ an accompanying visual, such as a flowchart?

_____ Is a section on equipment, mechanism, or preparation necessary?

Is the section on performance steps
_____ in the second person (implied)?

_____ in a logical sequence from step 1 (including substeps) to step 2, and so on?

For all descriptions, have you edited for **stylistic and visual techniques,** using
_____ quantitative data?

_____ strategies for coherence, such as transition?

_____ headings?

_____ numbered or bulleted (●) lists?

_____ visuals?

Notes

1. Dorothy Greenberg, "Double Bar Ankle Foot Orthosis," Technical Writing 421, Illinois Institute of Technology, 1985.
2. Terry Washburn-Shouba, "The Crescent Wrench," Technical Writing 421, Illinois Institute of Technology, 1983.
3. Adapted from a report by Renee Hearn, "My Neighborhood," Technical Writing 421, Illinois Institute of Technology, 1985.
4. Michael D. Jones, "How a Xerographic Process Works," Technical Writing 421, Illinois Institute of Technology, 1980.

References

Sandra Pakin and Associates, Inc., *Documentation Development Methodology* (Englewood Cliffs, N.J.: Prentice-Hall, 1984).

Applying Your Knowledge

EXERCISE 6.1

Using classification and division, divide and subdivide parts of the modular office phone under broader headings. Try to indicate where you might use illustrations.

A modular office telephone is a telecommunications instrument that enables two or more people to communicate from different locations. Every telephone is composed of three basic parts: receiver, base, and cord. The receiver of a telephone is composed of durable, molded plastic. It has three parts: handle, earpiece, and mouthpiece. The handle is used to hold the telephone. Its component parts—the earpiece and mouthpiece—serve as methods of transmitting voice and sound by wire. The earpiece is found on the upper portion of the handle. Its shape is circular, with holes in it. It is the part of this instrument to which the ear is applied to hear the voice of the other party. The mouthpiece is found on the lower portion of the handle. Its shape is also circular, with holes in it. It is the part of this instrument to which the mouth is applied to speak through. The base serves as the rigid framework on which other parts of the telephone are mounted. It is composed of two distinct parts: the face and the cradle. The face is composed of touch-tone buttons, a hold button, and a com-line button. All buttons are composed of clear plastic and are square in shape. Touch-tone buttons are used to dial telephone numbers in both long distance and local areas. Extension buttons are used to gain access to five unique extensions. They are arranged horizontally along the bottom of the face. There is one hold button. It is used to put a caller on hold when there is another incoming call to answer. The com-line button is used to reach other telephones in the same office area. The cradle, about three inches in width, holds the telephone receiver. On the cradle, a receiver button may be used to transfer calls to other extensions on the same telephone line. The cord is composed of a flexible plastic substance. It is coiled and is approximately 10 inches in length. A modular phone must use an adapter and a jack. An adapter is a device for connecting two parts of an apparatus. The adapter is plugged into a jack in the wall, and the cord is plugged into the adapter. There are many advantages to using an office phone. Its five extension buttons, hold button, and com-line button provide efficiency in answering calls within the office area. The hold button is very useful when there is an incoming call. It allows you to put the first caller on hold while answering the second caller. Com-lines are also useful when you want to talk to a co-worker on the same line but at a different extension. This telephone is unique because of its ability to receive several calls simultaneously. [Source: Cynthia Moore, Technical Writing 421, Illinois Institute of Technology.]

EXERCISE 6.2

The figure, Figure 6.9, accompanying this exercise is called a ladder of abstraction. The ladder moves from the most abstract category to the most specific item. After studying the ladder, describe in a paragraph the process that the ladder is illustrating of determining resources.

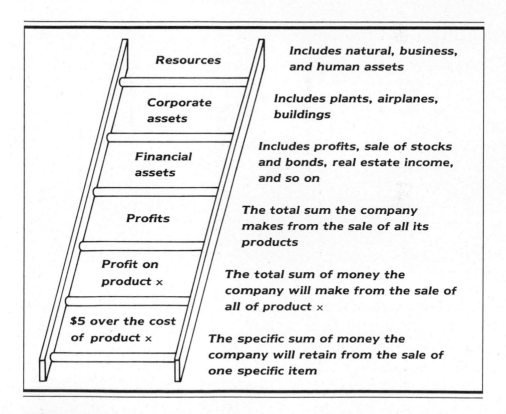

FIGURE 6.9 Ladder of abstraction
Source: Unknown.

EXERCISE 6.3 ═══

Rewrite the following paragraph on the description of a flashlight in use. Avoid mixing mood and person; indicate where you would integrate visuals.

First, the user should make sure the flashlight has batteries. Unscrew the end cap in a counterclockwise direction, and look into the body cavity. If batteries are present, the flashlight is ready for operation. If not, the user should insert two batteries into the body cavity, positive end up (toward the lamp housing). The positive end is marked with a "+". When batteries are inserted, screw the end cap back on until snug. The flashlight is now ready to be used.

To operate the flashlight, if you hold the entire mechanism, with the on/off switch facing up, in the palm of one hand, you can turn the flashlight on by sliding the on/off switch forward (toward the lamp housing) to the "on" position.

With the flashlight on, the user can now point the lens or top portion in the desired direction and illuminate the area.

EXERCISE 6.4 ═══

What is missing from the following mechanism description?

The device has six main parts (see Figure 1). Two handles, one flat and one round, are joined at one end by a rivet to comprise a hinged arrangement. The actual cutting mechanism is a steel cutter connected to the round handle and rivet in such a manner as to allow the cutter to be pivoted into place by moving the two handles together. When the two handles are squeezed together, the cutter is positioned against a toothed gear, which is fastened to the riveted end of the flat handle. A turnkey is attached to the gear and causes the gear to turn.

What is missing from the following place description?

The locker/office cores are 44 ft. long by 6 ft. wide except at the center, where the offices are located. The office spaces are 9½ ft. by 7 ft. There are two offices to each core, and each core provides room for two instructors. The lockers are connected to the offices and stacked 10 over 10. At one end of the core, there is space for a computer and storage of architectural references. At the other end there is space for either a computer, a public telephone, or more storage. All 4 new cores will replace the 4 old cores in the exact location, giving a total of 8 new offices with room for 16 instructors.

EXERCISE 6.5 ═══

In this exercise, convert the explanation of the procedure to a set of instructions.

A request for a change in scope of work is required when

1. Grantee deletes one energy conservation measure (ECM) and substitutes another ECM.
2. Grantee deletes one or more ECMs to pick up cost overruns on remaining ECMs.

3. Grantee completes all original ECMs funded and has cost underruns and wants to do additional work.
4. Grantee completes all work and wants to transfer funds to another ECM project to pick up cost overruns.

All of the above requests are made on a case-by-case basis.

WRITING ASSIGNMENT

Write a description of a mechanism, place, or process. Pay particular attention to these factors:

organizational structure
description by analogy or example
quantitative data
coherence
mood and person
headings and visuals

M O D U L E | 7

Instructions and Evaluations

This module will acquaint you with the basic principles of writing and evaluating clear, accurate, readable instructions. One important type of instructions is computer documentation, discussed in a subdivision of this module. When writing the text for instruction manuals, documentation, and procedures, you have to consider sections on (1) the theory or principle behind the process or the product, (2) an overview, (3) performance instructions, and (4) troubleshooting. This module describes these sections as well as some issues pertinent to writing instructions, issues such as analyzing audience, determining tasks, organizing steps in the process, assessing readability, planning layout and visual aids, and evaluating the document.

This model also discusses testing measures that ask users to evaluate a document intended for their use. Testing offers valuable data about documents, but testing is a complex field. The test designer has to clarify the purpose of the measure, determine that every question or task supports the objectives, plan a method to evaluate the data, and, finally, design the measure and select the users. The success of some documents depends on data from consumers who are asked to evaluate documents, and this module offers some guidelines on evaluating documents.

You may have to instruct readers on how to use a piece of equipment, how to run a computer program, how to compute some figures for their income tax forms, or how to initiate a plan or project. The most difficult part of writing instructions or documentation is putting yourself in the reader's place. Usually, if you write the instructions, you know quite a bit about operating the device or the program, and you have forgotten what it is like to be totally unfamiliar with how an object works. You may even have difficulty stating the steps involved in a thought process. It is important that you exercise your sympathetic imagination, remembering what it is like to be introduced to an object or a process for the first time.

When you write instructions, you will often be writing for the novice user. Of course, if your reader is experienced with the subject of your instructions, then you can take some information for granted. But you must carefully consider the experience of your reader and then provide the appropriate level of instruction. Because written instructions are so crucial to the success of a product or project, you should practice writing instructions for a variety of products and projects.

Scope

In this module you will learn to

1. Identify the level of the audience's knowledge.
2. Organize the document to include necessary sections.
3. Determine the tasks and the steps in the process.
4. Consider readability.
5. Lay out the text and the visual aids.
6. Apply these techniques to job aids and computer documentation.
7. Evaluate the document for the reader's use:
   - State the objectives of the measurement.
   - Convert the objectives to tasks for instructional and informational documents.
   - Establish criteria for evaluating the effectiveness of a document.
   - Choose the measurement for usability (field) testing.
   - Select users to test a document.
   - Collect data using testing methods.
   - Use the results to improve the document.

Identify the Novice Versus Advanced User

Usually, with a set of instructions the reader just wants to know how to use the equipment or how to follow the process. In this case, when the reader simply wants to know how to put Tab A in Slot A, the reader is essentially performing on the technician level. The reader wants to get the job done; the task, rather than the method, is important here, and why the process works may be of little or no importance. In a longer document, such as a

Drawings of Parts of the Computer

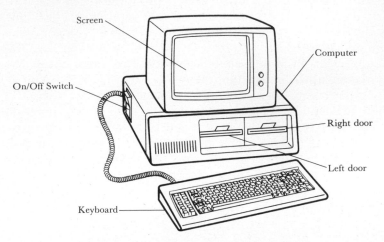

Drawing 1   The computer with keyboard and screen

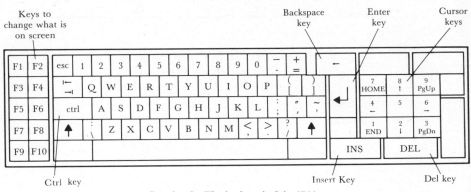

Drawing 2   The keyboard of the IBMpc

The Diskettes

DOS diskette   Writing Assistant diskette   File diskette

Drawing 3   The diskettes

FIGURE 7.1 Manual for children

Adapted from Linda Parsons, Technical Writing 421, Illinois Institute of Technology.

manual of operating instructions or a reference manual, the reader may want to know the theory behind the instructions. But, for a brief set of instructions, perhaps one to three pages, the reader wants to follow the steps quickly and accurately. The cookbook set of instructions illustrates the involvement of the

Performance Instructions

Section A

How to Turn on Computer

1. Make sure computer is turned off. Look at the drawing of the computer.

2. Put DOS diskette* in left door.*

3. Close the door.

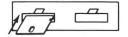

4. Turn on computer.

5. Wait. The computer will ask for the date and time.

Current date is_____
Enter new date:

Section B

How to Get to Writing Screen*

You do not have to type in the date or time. If you want
to skip the date and time, do instructions 6 and 7. If
you do want to type in the date and time, do instructions
8 through 19.

How to skip the date and time

6. Press* the enter key* two times.

7. Go to instruction 20.

FIGURE 7.1 (cont.)

audience in this type of document. Generally, the audience level of knowledge
has little to do with education and much more to do with experience about
the subject.

The instructions in Figure 7.1 are directed to children, but the children
still want to follow these directions accurately and efficiently.

If you are writing a manual on illustration techniques, you will have to identify your readers as beginners or technically advanced or both. You may have to reserve different sections in a manual for the technically advanced, as exemplified in Figure 7.2.

If the document is entitled _Basic Illustration,_ write for the new user, and write as though you were talking to a real person about how to use your product or how to follow your steps. When you are writing for an experienced user, indicate the audience in the preface or in the title of the document. In that way, an unsuspecting novice will be forewarned. Of course, when writing for the general consumer, assume little prior knowledge or experience and write for the new user.

Oblique Projection

This section of _Basic Illustration_ is for the person who has mastered orthographic and isometric projections. You will need to review sections 3 and 4 on circles, angles, and ellipses. Oblique projection is a combination of orthographic and isometric projections. It takes an orthographic projection and adds an artificial depth to it.

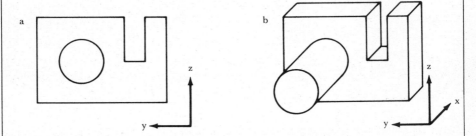

Figure 0.1 Transformation of orthographic into oblique

Figure 0.1a shows a shape drawn in orthographic projection. No information is given about the depth. Figure 0.1b shows the same object transformed into an oblique projection. Not only the feeling of depth, but also information is conveyed in oblique projection. Notice, the circle in Figure 0.1a could very well have been a hole instead of a protruding cylinder. Figure 0.1b gives no doubt as to what the nature of the circle is.

Figure 0.1a shows the y and the z axes, and Figure 0.1b shows the y, z, and x axes. In these figures, the depth direction is the x direction. All lines going in the x direction were drawn at an angle of 45 degrees. Any angle may be chosen but angles between 30 and 60 degrees produce the most pleasant results.

FIGURE 7.2 Section in a manual for the technically advanced
Source: Adapted from Tony Yu, Technical Writing 421, Illinois Institute of Technology.

Organize the Document

If the reader is going to need or want information besides the steps in the process, you have to plan the contents of the entire document.

Should the Document Have the Following Sections?

Introduction   To define the audience, explain the background, and describe the contents of the document.

Theory (principle)   To explain the concepts behind the process so that the reader has a better understanding of the way the process or product works.

Overview   To describe the overall process or product, divide it into its major parts, and divide it further into its subparts so that the reader has a general idea of the process or a picture of the product and its component parts. Module 6 on description provides a detailed discussion and illustrative model on dividing major sections into headings and listing the parts under those headings. Figure 7.3 illustrates the first three sections of the manual entitled *Basic Illustration.*

Troubleshooting   To explain to the users how to recover from an error.

A section on troubleshooting is probably one of the most important sections in a manual of instructions. How does the user recover from the error of pressing the wrong button or omitting a step? In an instructions or procedures manual, you should plan for the following:

Basic Illustration

This manual is designed to introduce you to various drafting techniques, techniques that will allow you to illustrate your documents. Because you are not expected to be experienced with drafting, this manual outlines the basics of drafting and presents examples to help you understand how to draw the finished illustrations.

With mechanical pencils and a few types of pencil lead, a drawing board, a T Square and compass, several templates and triangles, you can produce geometrically simple line drawings that will look like professional illustrations. These illustrations begin with defining shapes and contours and move to designing pictures to enhance your text. Geometric line drawings are the basis for the formal design of pictures.

An Overview of This Manual
This manual contains several topics illustrating the methods and procedures draftsmen and illustrators use to draw shapes that are geometrically simple. Although ink and color are very important aspects of illus-

tration, they are beyond the scope of this manual. The following is a list
of topics that will be covered in this manual.

- cost of equipment
- proper use of equipment
- types of lines
- projection from infinity (orthographic, isometric)
- projection from finite distances (perspective projection)
- lettering methods

FIGURE 7.3 The introduction to a manual, including theory
and overview
Source: Adapted from Tony Yu, Technical Writing 421, Illinois Institute of Technology.

⊖ The document must have appropriate task procedures, as well as

- set of instructions
- warnings, cautions, notes
- materials, equipment
- troubleshooting or error recovery.

Determine the Tasks for the Set of Instructions

Once you have identified the audience, you have to assess the reader's tasks
and determine how to organize and present them. When the reader's steps
are numerous and the instructions or procedures are complex, you should
organize the steps into tasks or headings with a brief list of instructions under
each heading. Think of tasks as chapters in a table of contents. You can't
teach a reader everything at once, so you organize the material into chapters
and present related material in that chapter.

When the list of instructions exceeds nine steps, you should consider
classifying the steps into two or more major tasks and listing these steps under
the appropriate task. When you list information in units that readers can
easily manage, you are using a learning principle called *chunking;* this principle suggests that you group information into manageable packages that
readers can remember.[1] Researchers have discovered that readers can remember a certain number of items, approximately seven items or numbers
plus or minus two. When the information exceeds this number, readers may
forget the material or become confused. Figure 7.4 classifies the tasks necessary to operate a crescent wrench and organizes the steps under each task.

The tasks or headings preceding the list of instructions serve as captions
or purpose statements and help the reader focus on the objective of a particular portion of the instructions. Figure 7.5 illustrates the several purpose
statements throughout a complete set of instructions.

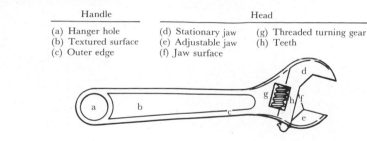

Handle

(a) Hanger hole
(b) Textured surface
(c) Outer edge

Head

(d) Stationary jaw   (g) Threaded turning gear
(e) Adjustable jaw   (h) Teeth
(f) Jaw surface

Base end of handle   Base end of head

How to Use the Crescent Wrench

To adjust the jaws around the bolt:
1. Fit the open jaws around the bolt.
2. Press your thumb down on the threaded turning gear.
3. Stroke the turning gear backward away from the head.
4. Continue this motion until the adjustable jaw and stationary jaw touch the bolt.

To loosen the bolt:
1. Turn the handle counterclockwise.
2. When it is inconvenient to continue turning, reposition the wrench around the bolt.
3. Repeat steps 1 and 2 until the bolt is loose.

To tighten the bolt:
1. Turn the handle clockwise.
2. When it is inconvenient to continue turning, reposition the wrench around the bolt.
3. Repeat steps 1 and 2 until the bolt is tight.

To release the jaws from the bolt:
1. Press your thumb down on the threaded turning gear.
2. Stroke the turning gear forward toward the head.
3. Continue this motion until the adjustable jaw and stationary jaw are loosened from the bolt.
4. Remove the open jaws from the bolt.

FIGURE 7.4 Steps organized under major tasks to use a crescent wrench
Source: Adapted from Annette O. Vujovich, Technical Writing 421, Illinois Institute of Technology.

Issue Warnings, Cautions, Notes

Do not assume that your readers know the dangers in using a piece of equipment or the pitfalls in a thought process. Forewarn them with *warning* and/ or *caution* statements. Giving this information before you begin the set of

Instructions on how to operate a gas mantle lantern

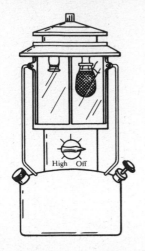

Warning:

Materials needed:

To replace the mantle:
Caution:

To refuel the lantern
Warning:
Caution:

To light the lantern:
Warning:
Caution:

To turn off the lantern:

To maintain the lantern:

Illustration of gas mantle lantern

FIGURE 7.5 Outline of purpose statements throughout a set of instructions
Source: Sierk J. Oudemans, Technical Writing 421, Illinois Institute of Technology.

instructions may save you or your company from a lawsuit. *Warning* statements are used to alert people to situations that may injure them:

> *WARNING:* Use glue in a well-ventilated room.
> *WARNING:* Use heat-resistant gloves to handle the melting pot.

Caution statements alert people to situations that may damage the product.

> *CAUTION:* Do not immerse the electric frying pan in water.
> *CAUTION:* Use specified AC adapter only. Wrong adapter may cause serious damage to this set.

Note statements alert readers to possible problems or conditions, as well as informing them of any prior knowledge they are expected to have.

> *NOTE:* Detach and retain the pink copy for your files before submitting the voucher to our office.
> *NOTE:* Before completing this application, you will need to familiarize yourself with the Report on Short-Term Investments for the Novice Investor.

Gather Materials

If the reader is going to need any additional equipment, materials, or prior knowledge, you will have to identify this material and encourage the reader to have the material on hand, if appropriate. For example, if the user is following instructions to change the oil in a car and will need a bucket to catch the dirty oil, you should tell the user to assemble the materials, including the bucket, before beginning the instructions. Users will become very angry if they discover they need a bucket after they have removed the cap to the oil filter and the dirty oil is flowing onto the garage floor. The best place to tell the readers what additional materials they will need is under a caption entitled *Materials Needed* or **You will need**

> *MATERIALS NEEDED:*   Coleman lantern fuel (4 oz.)
> Mantles (part # 1234)
> Wooden matches

Anticipate Problems

If you try to give the readers the steps they need when these are needed, then you may have to repeat certain steps that you have mentioned before. But it is better to repeat steps than have the readers lose their place in the instructions by having to refer to another part of the manual, as the readers are forced to do with the instructions in Figure 7.6.

Setting the Program Timer

For unattended recording the Timer needs to know what day to make the recording, the time to start, the time to stop, and the channel to be recorded.

Recording While You Are Away

The programmable electronic Clock/Timer permits the unattended recording of up to 6 preselected programs. It can be preset 14 days in advance to record your favorite programs. Once you have set the built-in timer for unattended recording you can forget about it. The timer will turn your VCR on and off at the time you set. However, if the tape runs out, the VCR will stop automatically.

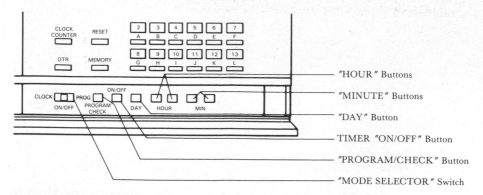

FIGURE 7.6. Instructions referring to another part of the VCR manual
Source: Adapted from *VHS Video Cassette Recorder* Operation, Sears, Roebuck and Co. Chicago, Illinois. Used with permission.

1. Be sure that the clock is set to the present time. (Refer to "SETTING THE CLOCK." See page 17.)
2. "POWER" Button may be "ON" or "OFF."
3. Set "TAPE SPEED" switch to "EP," "LP," or "SP." MOVE THE "AUX/TU-NER" Switch to the "TUNER" position.
4. Set the program timer for "Record-starting time," "Record-stopping time," and "Channel." Refer to "SETTING THE PROGRAM TIMER." (See below on this page and pages 17 and 18.)

FIGURE 7.6. (cont.)

It is not easy to predict how or where the reader will be using your product. If you consider the usefulness of the product, you may be able to imagine the various conditions under which the user may be using the product, and then you can write these considerations into the instructions. For example, in telling the reader how to set a mousetrap, you should consider where the reader is likely to place the mousetrap. Often mice are found in basements, and it is safer for the user to carry the unset trap to the basement rather than precariously balance a set trap down a flight of stairs into the basement. Also, if the reader sets the trap and then places the bait on the trap, the weight of the bait will probably spring the trap, so you have to tell the reader to bait the trap first and then begin to set the trap.

Organize the Steps in the Process Logically

In a set of instructions, the reader expects to be addressed in the second person:

Example: You stroke the turning gear away from the head.

or in the command mode, with *you* understood:

Example: Press your thumb down on the threaded turning gear.

When you are unable to use the second person because the reader-writer relationship is more formal or objective than the informal use of the pronoun *you,* then use an alternative third person.

Example: The account executive examines all check voucher ledgers.

Usually, you will write your instructions in the command mode with *you* understood, and always organize the steps sequentially. Use only one instruction per step, and number the steps to help the readers find their place if they look away from the instructions in order to perform a step. Although numbering the steps is standard, you have other options. You may use bullets (●), asterisks (*), or some other symbol to indicate the sequence of the steps.

Whatever method you use to sequence the steps, you may have to reorganize after thinking through the steps. Writing good instructions involves preplanning and design. You have to collect all the information that the reader needs to know and be prepared later on to revise your first draft after inexperienced users have tested your document. Consider the questions for writing good instructions.

Questions to Help You Write Useful Instructions

1. Have you considered your **audience** by asking
   - What is the level of the reader's experience with the subject?
   - How will the reader use the product?

2. Have you organized the **tasks** by asking
   - What information will you need to write the text?
   - What tasks will the reader accomplish by following the set of instructions?
   - Are the tasks presented clearly as captions or headings to help the reader organize and sequence information?

3. Do your **instructions** consider the following:
   - Are there *warning* or *caution* statements?
   - Does the reader know about your assumptions of prior knowledge as stated in a *note*?
   - What materials or equipment must the reader supply before following the instructions?
   - Are the instructions (a) in the command mode with *you* understood, (b) in the proper sequence, and (c) in separate steps with one instruction per step?

Now let's look at Figure 7.7 and a document that follows the advice for writing instructions.

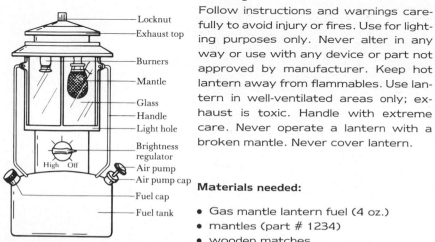

(Instructions on how to operate a gas mantle lantern. [See (a)]

Locknut
Exhaust top
Burners
Mantle
Glass
Handle
Light hole
Brightness regulator
High Off
Air pump
Air pump cap
Fuel cap
Fuel tank

Warning:
Follow instructions and warnings carefully to avoid injury or fires. Use for lighting purposes only. Never alter in any way or use with any device or part not approved by manufacturer. Keep hot lantern away from flammables. Use lantern in well-ventilated areas only; exhaust is toxic. Handle with extreme care. Never operate a lantern with a broken mantle. Never cover lantern.

Materials needed:

- Gas mantle lantern fuel (4 oz.)
- mantles (part # 1234)
- wooden matches

(a) Gas mantle lantern

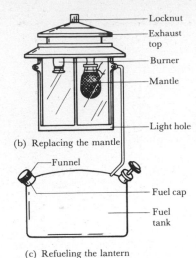

(b) Replacing the mantle

(c) Refueling the lantern

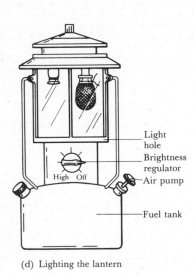

(d) Lighting the lantern

To Replace the Mantle:

- Unscrew locknut above exhaust top.
- Remove exhaust top and glass by pulling both up.

Caution: Glass is breakable.

- Clean both burners thoroughly.
- Tie new mantles to burners [see (b).].
- Replace glass, exhaust top, and locknut.
- Light both mantles through light hole until they appear ash white.

Caution: Do not use fuel while burning the mantles.

- Lantern is now ready for use.

Caution: The mantles are fragile; handle lantern with care.

To Refuel the Lantern: [See (c).]

Warning:
Lantern fuel is extremely flammable. Always fill lantern in an upright level position and in a well-ventilated area. Never fill lantern or open fuel cap near open flame source or while lantern is hot. Use lantern fuel only.

- Open fuel cap.
- Using a funnel, pour in fuel.

Caution: Use recommended dosage of fuel. Do not overfill.

- Close fuel cap.

To Light the Lantern: [See (d).]

Warning: Place lantern in an upright position. Light and use lantern in a well-ventilated area only.

- Turn brightness regulator to "off" position.
- Open air pump by unscrewing air pump counterclockwise. One full turn is sufficient.
- Cover hole in air pump with thumb and pump 30 full strokes.
- Close air pump by turning air pump clockwise.
- Hold burning match through the lighting hole near the mantle.
- Turn the brightness regulator to high.

Caution: Flames other than at mantle indicate a lantern or user malfunction.

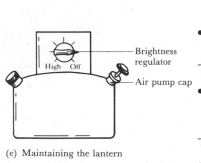

Turn brightness regulator to "off" position and review the instructions carefully.

- Pump additional air in the tank. (instructions 3, 4, 5.) Pump until pressure makes pumping difficult.
- Adjust brightness regulator to desired brightness.

To Turn Off the Lantern:

- Turn brightness regulator to "off" position. Lamp will go out in 1 or 2 minutes.

To Maintain the Lantern: [See (e).]

- Oil air pump regularly by putting a few drops through hole in air pump cap about once a month.
- To clean tip inside brightness regulator, turn brightness regulator from "off" to "high" and back several times.

(e) Maintaining the lantern

FIGURE 7.7 Instructions for a gas mantle lantern
Source: Adapted from Sierk J. Oudemans, Technical Writing 421,
Illinois Institute of Technology.

Consider Readability

Once again, readability is an important factor in writing instructions and documentation. This section summarizes guidelines for readability, a topic discussed more completely in Modules 4 and 5.

1. Alert your readers to the tasks by using consistent headings and captions, illustrated in Figure 7.8.

2. Use parallel construction for your headings and instructions, and write in complete sentences or in fragments, but be consistent.

   Not this Mantle Replacement Instructions
   Lighting Lantern Instructions
   To Turn Lantern Off
   But this To Replace Mantle
   To Light Lantern
   To Turn Lantern Off

3. Use the second person, either implied or stated, to give instructions to

---

Example

OPERATING INSTRUCTIONS FOR A VACUUM CLEANER
Table of Contents

FIGURE 7.8 Consistent headings for readability

your readers. In most cases—and especially in instructions—readers prefer to be addressed as *you.*

> *Not this* One should depress the return key on the typewriter.
> *But this* Press the return key on the typewriter.

4. Avoid multiple phrases and clauses. Because readers are performing tasks while reading instructions, sentences should be short. Each sentence or segment should contain a single instruction. If sentences are lengthened with phrases and clauses, the reader who looks away from the instructions may become lost and move to the next numbered instruction, perhaps missing an important step in a clause. Long sentences defeat readability, especially if the long sentence is long because it has too many phrases and clauses.

The two preceding sentences are too long, as is the next one.

> *Not this:* Sometimes you will find that adhesive tape has been used on the handlebars of the bicycle, in which case get a sharp knife and, following the contour of the handlebars make a cut from one end of the tape to the other, at right angles to the wrapping, so that, with a bit of luck, you can peel the whole lot off in one easy motion.

Rewrite the sentence so that the reader can follow the instructions easily:

> *But this:* If adhesive tape has been used on the handle bars,

- Get a sharp knife.
- Cut the tape at right angles to the wrapping.
- Extend the cut from end to end of the tape, following the contours of the bars.
- Try to peel off all the tape in one motion.

5. Select appropriate terminology. Obviously, the words you select to explain

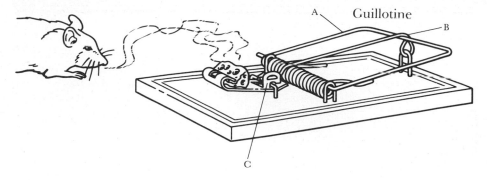

FIGURE 7.9 Mousetrap with humorous terminology

the steps of instruction must be precise and realistic. *Terminology* can have a humorous effect, as it does with the term *guillotine* in the example in Figure 7.9. Once you select the terminology, use it consistently. Synonyms encourage the readers to consider shades of difference in meaning when none exists. Consistent terminology and conventions eliminate confusion and increase clarity.

6. When labeling the parts of a figure, select the labels carefully so that the readers easily associate the part with the label. Whenever possible, name the part by describing it, such as the *S*-shaped hook. These descriptive labels, metaphors for technical names, are easy for the reader to remember and are often used in technical descriptions. The following list describes some of the useful labels.[2]

A frame	*S* curve
C clamp	*T* bolt
D ring	*U* bolt
H beam	*V* block
I beam	*X* brace
O ring	*Y* pipe

Plan Layout and Visual Aids

Visual aids and **examples** are crucial to good instructions and documentation. The reader benefits from a clear example of how a process works as well as from a drawing of the product and the labeling of parts. When giving a reader instructions for calculating a quantity or completing a form, you should give the reader enough **space** to work out the solution or fill in the answers. Space becomes a layout problem, and so you have to divide your page into text and space, allowing enough space for the reader to respond

BIO-RHYTHM

Frequently you can find bio-rhythm machines in movie theaters and arcades. Using the birth date of the person, these machines calculate the bio-rhythm, a quantity that indicates whether a person is having a good day physically, emotionally, and intellectually. Although the bio-rhythms are not very reliable, they can be fun to play around with if you know how to calculate them.

Determining Bio-rhythm:

Birth date: April 25, 1965
Date: September 14, 1984

1. Multiply the person's age by 365.

   $19 \times 365 = 6935$

2. Add the number of leap years lived through to the quantity in step 1.

   $6935 + 5 = 6940$

3. To the new total, add the number of days since the person's last birthday. This quantity is the total number of days the person has been alive.

   $6940 + 5 + 31 + 30 + 31 + 31 + 14 = 7082$

Determining Physical Bio-rhythm:

4. Divide the total number of days lived by 23. Round the decimal to five digits.

   $7082/23 = 307.91304$

5. Subtract the integer portion of step 4 from the quantity calculated in step 4.

   $307.91304 - 307 = 0.91304$

6. Multiply this decimal by 23.

   $.91304 \times 23 = 20.99992$
   The day is bad physically.

7. If the number is:
   a. between 0 and 11.5, the day is good for the person physically.
   b. between 11.51 and 23, the day is bad for the person physically.

Determining Emotional Bio-rhythm:

8. Divide the total number of days alive by 28.

   $7082/28 = 25.28572$

9. Subtract the integer portion of step 8 from the quantity calculated in step 8.

   $25.28572 - 25 = .28572$

10. Multiply the number from step 9 by 28.

    $0.28572 \times 28 = 8.00016$
    The day is good emotionally.

11. If the number is:
    a. between 0 and 14, the day is good for the person emotionally.

> b. between 14.01 and 28, the
>   day is bad for the person
>   emotionally.
>
> *Determining Intellectual Bio-*
> *rhythm:*
> 12. Divide the total number of $7082/33 = 21.46061$
>   days alive by 33.
> 13. Subtract the integer portion of $21.46061 - 21 = 0.46061$
>   step 12 from the quantity cal-
>   culated in step 12.
> 14. Multiply the number in step 13 $0.46061 \times 33 = 15.0013$
>   by 33.
> 15. If the product is: The day is good intellectually.
>   a. between 0 and 16.5, the
>   day is good for the person
>   intellectually.
>   b. between 16.51 and 33, the
>   day is bad for the person in-
>   tellectually.

FIGURE 7.10 Instructions with example
Source: Adapted from Theresa Pastore, Technical Writing 421,
Illinois Institute of Technology.

to the instructions. The instructions in Figure 7.10 involve sequential calculations and the readers may want to compare their products with an example. The bio-rhythm document begins with a brief introduction and definition but then moves immediately into instructions.

If you are designing a **form** and writing the instructions for completing the form, you will want to plan for three basic principles:

- Leave enough space for the user to fill in the slots.
- Arrange the questions logically so that the user follows the questions sequentially.
- Keep the illustrations near the instructions.

Of course **breaking out** parts of a form to describe or illustrate a difficult step requires space, but if you have the space for illustrations, you might want to consider the format in Figure 7.11 for writing instructions. Figure 7.11 illustrates an original and revised version of a form. Remember that in instructions an illustration is worth many paragraphs of explanation.

Illustrations to accompany instructions should be planned during the designing of the document. When an illustration appears at the end of a two-page document, the reader may not even know the illustration exists until after struggling with all the instructions.

Instructions for Completing the Purchase Order Requisition Form (original)

The following are step-by-step instructions on how to fill out the Purchase Order (P.O.) Requisition Form. Any squares not addressed in this instruction sheet will be completed by the Purchasing Department. The (a) figure illustrates the completed P.O. requisition.

ILLINOIS INSTITUTE OF TECHNOLOGY
PURCHASE REQUISITION

INSTRUCTIONS

Execute form in duplicate and forward original to Department Head or Dean. Properly authorized requisition should be addressed to the Purchasing Department. Direct all inquiries regarding requisition or purchase order to the Purchasing Department.

RESERVED TIME STAMP

FOR PURCHASING DEPARTMENT USE ONLY

REQ. NO. **51955**

P. O. NUMBER

PHONED IN	MAIL CONFIRM.	DO NOT MAIL CONFIRM.	MAIL ORIG.
☐	☐	☐	☐

BY   DATE

PLEASE TYPE OR PRINT ALL INFORMATION

SUGGESTED SOURCE:
John Doe Corporation
123 Randolph Street
Chicago, Illinois 60601

DELIVER TO:
3300 S. Michigan
Farr Hall   567-3638
Placement & Coop   Room 407
Lisa Mechnic

DATE ORDERED	DATE NEEDED	ACCOUNT NUMBER	ESTIMATED COST	BUDGET APPROVAL	TERMS	SHIP VIA
4/18/88	A.S.A.P.	0-00000-000	$50.00			

REQUISITIONED BY
Dr. Robert Bonthron
PHONE 567-3637

APPROVALS

DEPARTMENT HEAD	DEAN	V P BUSINESS AFFAIRS	PURCHASING
R.J. Bonthron			

QUANTITY	PART OR CAT. NO	COMPLETE DESCRIPTION	AMOUNT
3	S21167134	IBM Courier 10/72 Typing Element	

Form PF 100 Revised 2/79 Quality Business Forms, 821-1600   78165-8

(a) P.O. requisition

1. **Suggested Source** —the requisitioner (the person ordering the items) can suggest a source to the purchasing department. This information is helpful to the buyer or purchasing agent when extremely complicated or scientific items are being requested. Enter the

	name, street address, city and state, and zip code number of the suggested source.	 none of the figures are near the instruc- tions
2. Deliver to	—Completely fill in *ALL* delivery information.	
3. Date Ordered	Enter the date the requisition is prepared.	
4. Date Needed	Enter the date goods or services are needed.	
5. Account Number	Enter the requisitioning department's 9-digit university account number. This number is assigned by the Comptroller's Office.	
6. Estimated Cost	Enter the estimated cost for the entire order including shipping and handling charges. The estimated cost will be used to encumber funds from the account number given.	
Department Head or Supervisor	The head of the department, his or her assignee, or the supervisor should approve the requisition. NOTE: All assignees must have a signature card on file in the Purchasing Office.	
Dean	On large academic departmental purchases over $1,000, the dean of the college should approve the requisition.	
Vice President	On purchases of $500 or over, the business manager and/or the vice president for finance will review and approve or return the requisition.	
Quantity	Enter the desired quantity. Remember to put the type of units (pieces, gallons, dozens or boxes, and so on). NOTE: Prepackaging may lower prices.	
Part or Catalog Number	Enter the part number or the known catalog number of the items requested.	
Description	Enter the complete description of the goods or services being ordered. INCLUDE COLOR, MATERIAL, AND SIZE.	

| Amount | Enter the single-unit price of each individual item stated on the requisition. | **reader must turn pages to complete forms** |

Send the completed and approved purchase requisition to the Purchasing Department. Because the buyer or purchasing agent may need to contact the requisitioner, if you have flexible office hours, include that information with your phone number.

PURCHASE REQUISITIONS SHOULD NOT BE CONFIRMED BY THE DEPARTMENT WITHOUT APPROVAL OF THE PURCHASING DEPARTMENT.

Purchase requisitions drawn on project accounts will be sent to Project Accounting for approval.

Purchase requisitions drawn on restricted accounts will be sent to the comptroller for approval.

Form and Instructions (revised)

The following are step-by-step instructions on how to fill out the Purchase Order Requisition Form. Any squares not addressed in this instruction sheet will be filled out by the Purchasing Department. A completed P.O. requisition can be seen in (Q).

iiT PURCHASE REQUISITION

RESERVED — TIME STAMP

FOR PURCHASING DEPARTMENT USE ONLY

REQ. NO. **50152**

INSTRUCTIONS
Complete this form in duplicate and have the Department Head/Dean sign the original. Forward the authorized requisition to the Purchasing Department. Direct all requisition inquiries to the Purchasing Department.

CONFIRMATION / MAIL ORIGINAL
BY / DATE
PURCHASE ORDER NO.

PLEASE PRINT ALL INFORMATION PLAINLY

SUGGESTED SOURCE:
John Doe Corporation
123 Randolph Street
Chicago, Illinois 60601

DELIVER TO:
BUILDING: Farr Hall
STREET ADDRESS: 3300 S. Michigan
DEPT. AND ROOM: Placement & Coop Room 407

DATE ORDERED	DATE NEEDED	ACCOUNT NUMBER	ESTIMATED COST	FREIGHT ALLOWED	TERMS	SPECIAL INSTRUCTIONS
4/18/88	A.S.A.P.	0-00000-000	$50.00	PREPAID ADD CHARGES		

REQUISITIONED BY
Dr. Robert Bonthron
PHONE 567-3637

APPROVALS
DEPARTMENT HEAD: R.S. Bonthron | DEAN | VP BUSINESS AFFAIRS | PURCHASING

QUANTITY	PART OR CAT NO.	COMPLETE DESCRIPTION	AMOUNT
3	S21167134	IBM Courier 10/72 Typing Element	

The Purchasing Department Secures Price Quotations, Competitive Bids; Determines The Best Source Of Supply, And Negotiates Purchases Consistent With The Specifications And Quality Desired.

(q) Revised P.O. requisition form

Suggested Source   —The requisitioner (the person ordering the item or items) can suggest a source to the Purchasing Department. This information is helpful to the buyer or purchasing agent when extremely complicated or scientific items are being requested. Enter the name, street address, city and state, and zip code number of the suggested source. [See (b).]

Deliver to   —Completely fill in *all* delivery information. [See (b).]

S U G G E S T E D S O U R C E	John Doe Corporation 123 Randolph Street Chicago, Illinois 60601	D E L I V E R T O	BUILDING: Farr Hall STREET ADDRESS: 3300 S. Michigan DEPT. AND ROOM: Placement & Coop Room 407	

(b) Suggested source and delivery information

Date Ordered   —Enter the date the requisition is prepared. [See (c).]   **figure is near instruction**

Date Needed   —Enter the date goods or services are needed. [See (c).]

Account Number   —Enter the requisitioning department's 9-digit university account number. This number is assigned by the Comptroller's Office. [See (c).]

DATE ORDERED	DATE NEEDED	ACCOUNT NUMBER	ESTIMATED COST	FREIGHT ALLOWED / PREPAID ADD CHARGES	TERMS	SPECIAL INSTRUCTIONS
4/18/88	A.S.A.P.	0-00000-000	$50.00			

(c) Dates and accounting information

Estimated Cost	—Enter the estimated cost for the entire order including shipping and handling charges. The estimated cost will be used to encumber funds from the account number given. [See (c).]

Department Head or Supervisor	—The head of the department, his or her assignee, or the supervisor should approve the requisition. [See (d).] NOTE: All assignees must have a signature card on file in the Purchasing Office.
Dean	—On large academic departmental purchases over $1,000, the dean of the college should approve the requisition. [See (d).]
Vice President	—On purchases of $500 or over, the business manager and/or the vice president for finance will review and approve or return the requisition. [See (d).]

REQUISITIONED BY	APPROVALS			
	DEPARTMENT HEAD	DEAN	VP BUSINESS AFFAIRS	PURCHASING
Dr. Robert Bonthron PHONE 567-3637	R. J. Bonthron			

(d) Approval procedures

Quantity	—Enter the desired quantity. Remember to put the type of units (pieces, gallons, dozens or boxes, and so on). NOTE: Prepackaging may lower prices. [See (e).]	**each line of the form is integrated into the text**
Part or Catalog Number	—Enter the part number or the known catalog number of the item or items requested. [See (e).]	
Description	—Enter the complete description of the goods or services being ordered. Include COLOR, MATERIAL, AND SIZE. [See (e).]	

Amount   —Enter the single-unit price of each individual item stated on the requisition. [See (e).]

QUANTITY	PART OR CAT NO	COMPLETE DESCRIPTION	AMOUNT
3	S21167134	IBM Courier 10/72 Typing Element	

(e) Descriptions and price information

Send the completed and approved purchase requisition to the Purchasing Department. Because the buyer or purchasing agent may need to contact the requisitioner, if you have flexible office hours, include that information with your phone number.

PURCHASE REQUISITIONS SHOULD NOT BE CONFIRMED BY THE DEPARTMENT WITHOUT APPROVAL OF THE PURCHASING DEPARTMENT.

FIGURE 7.11 Original and revised form
Source: Adapted from Lisa Mechnic, Writing Workshop 425, Illinois Institute of Technology.

When planning illustrations, for the reader's sake consider

- the placement of the illustration
    top
    right section
    left section
    bottom
- the type of illustration
    overview
    exploded parts
    sequence
    flowchart
    table

Remember to consult Module 5 on design and visual aids for additional advice on illustrations.

The *overview illustration* of taping papers in Figure 7.12. demonstrates the way a writer uses the figure at the top, properly labeled, to provide the reader with an overview of the product.

The *sequence of illustrations* for using the asthma inhaler in Figure 7.13 shows the user how to hold the product while following instructions. Picturing hands on the product provides the reader with a perspective on the size and the operation of the product. Hands provide the reader additional information.

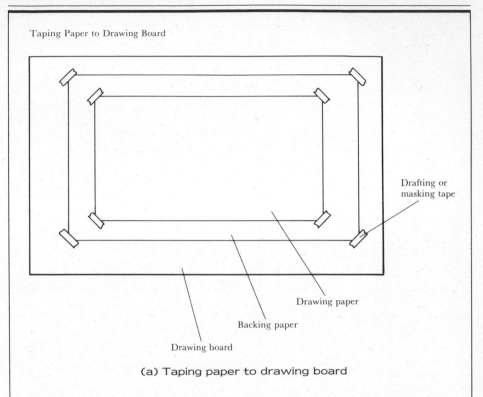

Taping Paper to Drawing Board

Drafting or masking tape

Drawing paper

Backing paper

Drawing board

(a) Taping paper to drawing board

To start drawing, use backing paper to produce good line quality. First, tape backing paper to the board, and then tape the drawing paper to the backing.

1. Place a thick piece of paper on the drawing board as backing. [See (a).] Any heavy paper will do.
2. Tape the backing paper to the board as shown in (a).
3. Place a piece of drawing paper on top of the backing paper.
4. Line up the top edge of the paper with the top edge of the T square.
5. Tape the four corners of the drawing paper to the backing paper as shown in (a).

FIGURE 7.12 Overview illustration for a set of instructions
Source: Adapted from Tony Yu, Technical Writing 421, Illinois Institute of Technology.

The illustration in Figure 7.14 shows the *exploded parts* of a Rapidograph pen. The reader can easily see the assembly of the pen, which is important because the reader will be taking the pen apart. The illustrator can show more detail in an illustration with exploded parts.

For relief of bronchial asthma spasms, carefully follow directions for proper use of apparatus.

Warning:
- Do not repeat this process more than twice daily.
- Wait at least two minutes to apply medication If you are not relieved after the first attempt.
- Do not use if physician has not diagnosed you as an asthmatic.

Caution:
- Do not puncture or incinerate container.
- Do not expose to heat or store at temperature above 120°F.
- Keep out of reach of children.

(a)

To prepare asthma inhalator:

1. Remove dust cap. [See (a).]
2. Remove the metal container (A) from the plastic mouthpiece (B).
3. Insert metal container into the short end of the mouthpiece so that the nozzle (C) is engaged in the small hole (D). [See (b).]
4. Shake the container with combined mouthpiece.

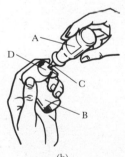

(b)

To apply medication:

5. Hold the apparatus so that the metal container is upside down.
6. Place the mouthpiece into the mouth; close lips tightly over it.
7. Clear lungs of foreign particles by breathing out through the nose.
8. Breathe in deeply through the mouth while firmly pressing the container down into the mouthpiece to release the medication. [See (c).]
9. Hold your breath for a few seconds after medication is released.
10. Remove the mouthpiece and breathe out slowly.

(c)

FIGURE 7.13 Illustration using hands to provide perspective
Source: Cynthia L. Moore, Technical Writing 421, Illinois Institute of Technology.

How to Use and Care for the
Rapidograph Pen

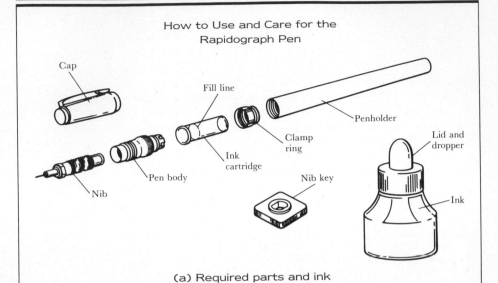

(a) Required parts and ink

CAUTION: Do not let ink remain in pen body or nib during long periods of
disuse. Clean before storing for more than one week.

To Fill
1. Unscrew both the penholder and clamp ring from the unit
   and set aside.
2. Pull the ink cartridge from the pen body and nib.
3. Shake the ink slightly, unscrew the top dropper, and
   squeeze gently to fill with ink.
4. Hold the ink cartridge upright, and fill from the dropper
   only to the fill line.
5. Slip the pen body and nib down into the filled ink
   cartridge. [See (b)].

(b) Ink cartridge on pen body and nib

6. Screw on the clamp ring and penholder.
7. The pen is now assembled. Keep the cap on when not
   in use to keep the ink from drying out.

To Use

1. Hold the pen horizontally and shake lightly a few times, away from clothing or other fabric, to start the ink flowing.
2. Try to write with the point on scrap paper.
3. If the pen fails to write, shake it lightly again.
4. Clean the pen before each refilling.

To Clean

1. Prepare a small workspace covered with a paper towel.
2. Carefully disassemble the pen:
   a. Unscrew the cap.
   b. Unscrew the penholder from the clamp ring.
   c. Unscrew the clamp ring from the pen body.
   d. Pull the ink cartridge from the nib being careful of any ink residue that might stain fabric.
   e. Gently tap the open end of the pen body against the paper towel to remove excess ink.
   f. Unscrew the nib from the pen body using the nib key. [See (c)].

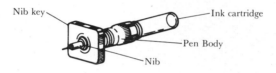

(c) Use of the nib key

3. Hold the nib and pen body under running lukewarm water. Dry the parts well with paper towel.
4. The pen is ready to store or be filled again.

FIGURE 7.14 Illustration with exploded parts
Source: Adapted from Terry Washburn-Shouba, Technical Writing 421, Illinois Institute of Technology.

In documentation, *flowcharts* frequently accompany the text. The flowcharts should be meaningful and uncluttered. Figure 7.15 shows the difference between a meaningful and meaningless flowchart, and Figure 7.16 demonstrates the cluttered versus uncluttered flowchart.

Some final points about illustration are worth repeating here:

- An illustration should appear as close to the explanatory note as possible.
- Illustrations should remain uncluttered.
- Illustrations should augment the information, not just add variety.

NOT THIS

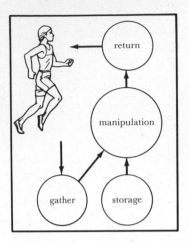

Flowchart for computerized health system

BUT THIS

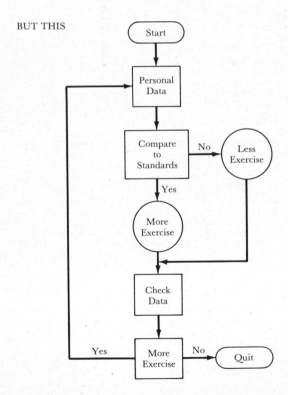

FIGURE 7.15 Meaningless versus meaningful flowchart

NOT THIS

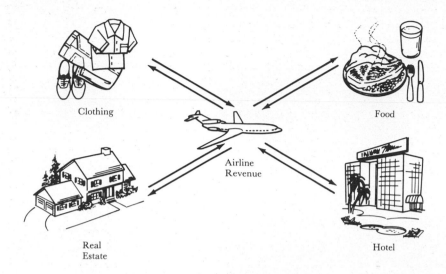

BUT THIS

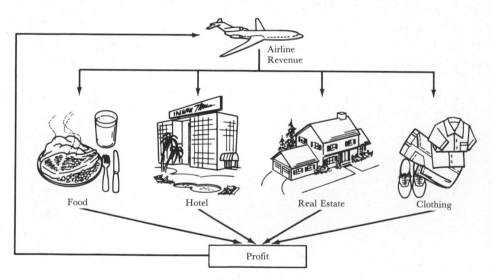

FIGURE 7.16 Reducing clutter in flowcharts

In some user's manuals for documentation, it is difficult to know how much illustration is too much. Space is always a constraint in a manual, but remember that a good illustration can replace several paragraphs of explanation. Figure 7.17 illustrates a page from a manual for adult readers.

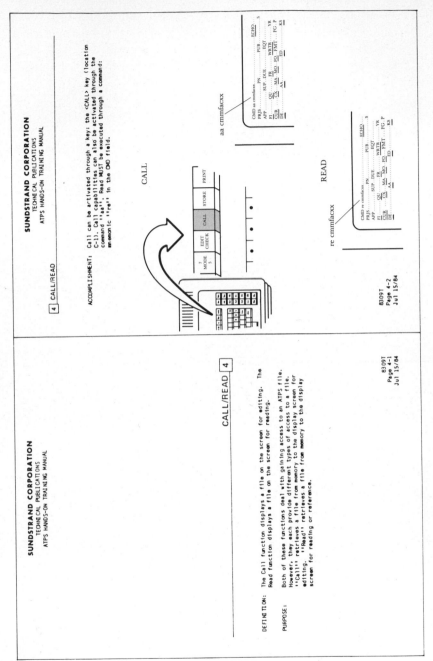

FIGURE 7.17 Manual for adult readers
Source: Sundstrand Corporation, Rockford, IL. Used with permission.

Apply Techniques to Job Aids

A job aid is an instructional tool that tells the user what to do, how to do it, the order in which to do it, or the standards to meet.[3] It is a reminder, a checklist, a cheat sheet. But, unlike the usual instructions, it often has to be durable, so the job aid is frequently laminated in plastic. For example, a job aid is used at the gas pump when you fill your gas tank, at the garage when greasy fingers handle it while repairing your fuel pump, at the computer when you tape it to your keyboard to jog your memory about word processing commands. Job aids are step-by-step instructions that are

- succinct
- visual
- skill based

as illustrated in Figure 7.18.

If hands are used to do complex tasks, show them

Powerful job aids show motion and direction with arrows

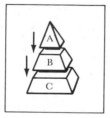

Powerful job aids have lots of white space

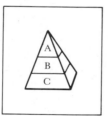

FIGURE 7.18 Job aids (Courtesy of Caterpillar-Joliet Plant Training Division)

Approach Computer Documentation Cautiously

Computer documentation consists of explanations and instructions that help the reader understand and use computer equipment and accompanying computer programs. Whereas everything that has been said so far is relevant to writing instructions for the computer, computer documentation involves some special writing problems that require additional discussion. In her book *Guide to Effective Software Technical Writing*, Christine Browning offers some excellent advice on computer documentation for software, and some of this advice is adapted for this section.[4]

Who Is Your Reader?

If you are writing a user's manual for a word processing program, you will have to identify your readers carefully. Most users' manuals are written for novice users. Sometimes the manual has a very special audience, as exemplified in Figure 7.19.

INTRODUCTION

Purpose

    This instruction manual tells you how to operate the ABC personal computer (ABCpc). It is written for you, kids between the ages of 8 and 13.

Background

    Many of you could work with an ABCpc, but you do not have the chance. A main reason is that instruction manuals are usually written for adults, and few adults have the time to teach you computer skills.

    This manual is written especially for you, so that you can have the chance to work with the ABCpc, too. You will learn how to work with the ABCpc and operate it by yourself.

FIGURE 7.19 A children's manual for using word processing on the personal computer
Source: Adapted from Linda Parsons, Technical Writing 421, Illinois Institute of Technology.

    Frequently, manuals began as procedures for those who were closely associated with the program's design and installation. The procedures were nothing more than a notepad. Then, as the computer consultants departed and more novices used the program, the new users needed a manual written for readers with no technical expertise. Because users change over a period of time, it is prudent to write for the novice user.

Organize the Reader's Text

Every text requires an outline that establishes and meets the goals for the text. Of course, the goals are determined by the user's tasks. How will your readers use the text? What do they need to know? Assess the information you have gathered from programmers, analysts, specifications, and listings. Then organize the information under the major tasks. Sharing the organi-

INTRODUCTION

Some students in the technical writing class had problems using the personal computer to do word processing. This manual presents a thorough set of descriptions, explanations, and instructions to help solve many of their problems. It includes the following information:

1. A description of computer and printer hardware and various processes and terminology associated with them.
2. An explanation of word processing and software with a detailed set of instructions for preparing the computer to use WRITING ASSISTANT.
3. A brief set of instructions for preparing the computer to use WRITING ASSISTANT.

This manual assumes that the user has had no previous experience with personal computers or word processing.

FIGURE 7.20 A manual for novice users
Source: Adapted from Helen Peck, Technical Writing 421, Illinois Institute of Technology.

zation with the reader by **highlighting the tasks** gives the reader the large picture of what the manual contains. The portion of the manual in Figure 7.20 demonstrates audience awareness, organization of the manual, and the major tasks of the text.

Begin at the Beginning

Before writing the set of instructions, begin by using the product yourself. That way you can teach and not just describe. First, caution your reader about damaging the program or the diskettes.

> *EXAMPLE:* Do not write on this diskette with a ballpoint pen. The impression will damage the surface of the diskette.

Also inform readers of any prior knowledge they are expected to have:

> *NOTE:* The computer is assumed to be OFF. If the unit is ON, disregard steps 1, 2, and 3.
> *NOTE:* You will need to familiarize yourself with the FPSE 430 LAB MANUAL before operating this program.

If appropriate, forewarn your readers to have materials on hand before they begin to run the program.

> *EXAMPLE:* For this section you will need
> - housekeeping diskette
> - self-study guide

Organize the steps under the major tasks:

- TO BEGIN THE PROGRAM
- TO ENTER DATA
- TO SAVE DATA
- TO RECALL DATA
- TO PRINT DATA

When you write the steps, remember that it is better to repeat steps than to have the readers lose their place by referring to other sections in the manual. As a general rule, user manuals are written in the second person with *you* implied.

Consider Readability Again

The problems with readability in computer documentation often revolve around ill-conceived concepts, terminology, or jargon that started in the computer field but entered the public domain.

1. Evaluate *user friendly*. Often the term *user friendly* becomes synonymous with overdone humor or a folksy writing style; on the contrary, **user friendly** instructions refer to intelligent, clear statements that assist the uninitiated user and do not offend the experienced user. Remember that instructions and documentation accompany products sold worldwide. For example, foreign readers do not like contractions, and your user friendly contraction might alienate a foreign reader. Clear, precise instructions make a document **user friendly.**

Of course, **user friendly** instructions also take into account what you already know about readability, illustrations, and organization. Figure 7.21 illustrates the integration of organization, style, illustration, and layout.

2. Select terminology carefully and use it consistently. When you talk about entering information into the computer, use PRESS or TYPE or STRIKE, but choose one term and use it throughout the document. Slang and jargon confuse inexperienced users and hinder communication. Furthermore, some of the common Americanisms do not translate overseas. Even in a computer manual, avoid computer jargon.

Not this	But this
initiate manual shutdown	shut down [the system] manually
monostation configuration is upgradable	one-station arrangement can be upgraded (increased)

3. In documentation, the words *may, can, might* lead to frustration and confusion. Browning suggests that the word *may* is used extensively in wills, insurance policies, and government publications, leaving the precise meaning open to interpretation by lawyers or arbitration. In documentation as well as in technical writing in general, ambiguities defeat clear communication. Readers do not want to guess at a possible interpretation of an instruction.

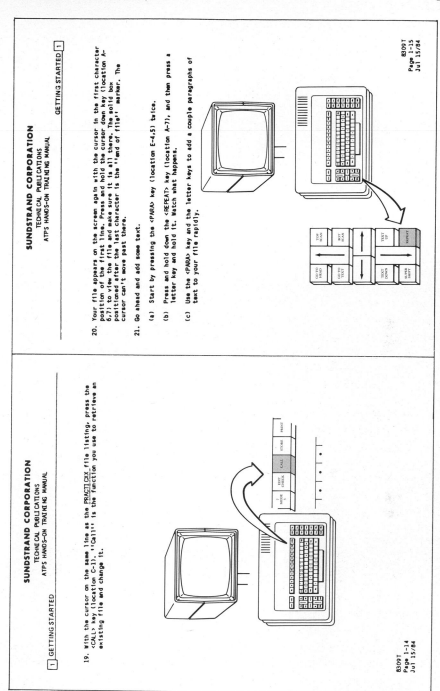

FIGURE 7.21 The integration of instruction, layout, and illustration in a training manual

Source: From Sundstrand Corporation, Rockford, IL. Used with permission.

> *EXAMPLE* (of ambiguous *may* statement):
> The account specialist may enter invoice numbers and amount with any corrections on the "Check Voucher Sheet."

If you really want to imply the possibility of options, then use *might* or *could*. Otherwise, use *must* or *can* to tell your readers what they have to do or what they have the capability of doing with the procedure, equipment, or software. In the example about the account specialist, the person must enter the invoice numbers and amount on the Check Voucher Sheet.

> *EXAMPLE* (of optional statement using *can*)
> Once the computer is on, you can start the operating system from the beginning again by turning the computer OFF and ON or by pressing three keys—CTRL, ALT, DEL—simultaneously.

To follow Browning's advice: Never say *may; may* guarantees ambiguity.

4. *Eliminate quotation marks.* Quotation marks create a problem in documentation because readers will wonder if the marks are key strokes. When you want your reader to type in

> "PRINT"

then you say to your reader

> TYPE "PRINT"

The quotation marks are keyboard entries in a computer program. Otherwise, eliminate quotation marks from your instructions. Do not use the marks to indicate slang because, in technical writing, writers should be avoiding slang. To emphasize a point, use italics, underline, or rewrite the sentence to achieve emphasis.

> *EXAMPLE: Getting Started on the Vax:*
> At $ Enter HUM NAME (not "HUM NAME")

Evaluate the Document

After you have written the document, you will want to know whether the intended audience can understand and use it. Instructions, training manuals, and documents such as handbooks that provide information (informational documents) all benefit from having inexperienced users pilot-test the material. Although this module covers instructional documents, you should also evaluate informational documents that explain safety to life and health (for example, *Rules of the Road*). This section on evaluation offers advice on both types of documents.

You are asking the people for whom the document was written to review it and provide information so that you can rewrite and improve the document. This end user review is called usability testing, field testing, or audience-centered evaluation. Users test the document and tell you whether or not the document is easy to use. If they evaluate the document early in the developmental stage, their responses can influence the rest of the writing. Companies that produce manuals for products try to create documents for users that are[5]

usable
motivating
complete
inviting
friendly
accurate.

How Do You Evaluate? A Model and a Method

The Document Design Center has created a process model of document design. It appears in Module 1. A process model of document evaluation seems to be an equally good idea because evaluation is also an iterative and dynamic process. Figure 7.22 illustrates the dynamics of document evaluation.

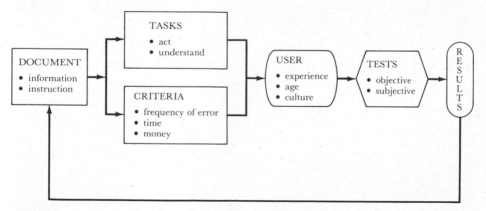

FIGURE 7.22 Model for evaluating documents

Based on researcher's findings, we learn that a testing method called *reader protocols* provides valuable information about revisions a writer should make to the documents.[6] A reader protocol is a recording of the comments a reader makes while performing the tasks. If the reader "talks aloud" into a tape recorder while following the instructions, then later a transcription can be made of the tape. According to researchers, by analyzing the tape, the tester learns where

- To break the material because the user becomes fatigued.
- To use visuals to clarify content.
- To describe less ambiguously and more clearly.
- To assume less and explain more.

- To summarize or forecast.
- To improve the punctuation.

Of course, reader protocols take time, and the document should have an extensive circulation to warrant this protocol testing.

If the testing is run early in the development of the training materials, the writer can benefit from reader protocols and apply the information to the rest of the document, avoiding some of the problems. Reader protocols help the writer in revising the materials.

A less rigorous way to test the instructions is to have a user apply the instructions and simply tell the writer where problems exist with

- the organization of the instructions
- the visuals
- the terminology or descriptions
- the punctuation
- the management of the product or hardware.

Regardless of the testing procedure, evaluation should be a part of writing instructions. *No training materials should be distributed until they have been tested and revised.* The rest of this module will provide more details about evaluating documents.

What Documents Should You Evaluate?

Any document the user has to read and follow as instructions or read and remember is a prime document for audience-centered evaluation. Instructional documents tell us how to operate equipment, fill out forms, test for leaded gasoline, arrive at decisions, and manage everything from our money to our time. The computer industry provides us with computer manuals that are ideal for usability testing. An example of an informational document users read and remember is *Rules of the Road,* a booklet of facts for people who want to obtain a driver's license. We read and remember informational documents when the documents are handbooks, policies, textbooks, announcements, and so on. Figure 7.23 presents a page of information from *Rules of the Road,* information a driver must read and remember.

How Do You Define the Tasks?

The tasks are the objectives of the document, what the intended user is supposed to remember or perform after reading the document or while reading the document. In a set of instructions, the reader must be able to perform each step, and each step is a task the user can perform. Figure 7.24 demonstrates part of a set of instructions and questions to evaluate the tasks.

When evaluating an entire project, you may have to break the objectives down into tasks and subtasks. For example, tasks and subtasks for evaluating turn signals may be flashed at the same time, however, to indicate a possible hazard on the highway.

Illegal Signals. It is against the law to flash turn signals as a courtesy or "do-pass" signal to other drivers in the rear.

Stopping. When stopping, or slowing down suddenly, the proper hand and arm signal (left hand and arm extended downward), or electric brake light must be displayed if there is another vehicle close to the rear of the vehicle you are driving.

SPEED

Speed is a major factor in many motor vehicle accidents. Although excessive speed itself may not be the primary cause, when it is combined with other violations, mechanical failure, or errors in judgment, it becomes the added ingredient which often brings about disaster.

Illinois law provides for absolute maximum speed limits, and in some cases, minimum speed limits as well. When minimum limits are not posted, drivers still may not drive so slowly that they interfere with the normal movement of traffic.

You may drive at maximum allowable speed only under safe conditions. Regardless of the limits which may be posted, the law also provides that no person shall drive at a speed which is greater than is reasonable and proper with regard to traffic conditions

and the use of the highway, or which endangers the safety of any person or property.

Speed must also be decreased, if necessary for safety, when:
1. Approaching and crossing an intersection.
2. Approaching and going around a curve.
3. Approaching the top of a hill.
4. Traveling on a narrow or winding roadway.
5. Hazards exist due to pedestrians, traffic, weather, or road conditions.
6. It is necessary for the purpose of avoiding a collision with pedestrians or other vehicles.

LEGAL SPEED LIMITS	
Rural Areas	55 m.p.h. (unless otherwise posted) 50 m.p.h. (trucks over 4 tons) (Speed limit will be 55 m.p.h. beginning July 1, 1986)
Urban Areas	30 m.p.h. (unless otherwise posted)
School Zones	20 m.p.h. (on school days between the hours of 7 a.m. and 4 p.m. when children are present and signs are posted)
In Alleys	15 m.p.h.

FIGURE 7.23 Information from a driver's license manual
Source: Illinois *Rules of the Road*, State of Illinois, March 1986.

Instructions for Disjointing Poultry

WARNING: 1. When using a knife always cut away from yourself making sure to keep fingers away from blade.
2. Wooden cutting boards should be cleaned thoroughly
with soap and water after using.

Getting Started

You'll need a sharp knife, a cutting board, and
the chicken. Refer to the diagrams to the right
to locate parts of the chicken and further explanation of instructions. When you are done, you
will have 10 pieces of chicken.

To separate thigh from leg

- Squeeze thigh-leg together, running finger
over top until two adjoining ridges are found.
- Place knife between ridges and cut halfway
through. Finish cutting through with thigh-leg
lying on cutting board.

Problems?	Solutions
• Knife wants to slide off the skin instead of cutting through.	Try a sharper knife.
	Make sure chicken has not warmed to room temperature before starting.
• Bones, not joints, are being cut.	Readjust the angle of the knife to lie across the center of the joint.

Rating Scale for Instructions for Disjointing Poultry

1. Were terms easily understood?   Yes   No
2. Where, if any place were you   Wing separation
   confused about what to do?   Thigh-leg separation
                                      Preparation of thigh from leg
                                      Back-breast separation
                                      Breast separation
                                      Back separation
3. Where, if any place, were you   Wing separation
   not able to do as instructed?   Thigh-leg separation
                                      Separation of thigh from leg
                                      Back-breast separation
                                      Breast separation
                                      Back separation
4. At any point were you afraid   Yes   No
   you might hurt yourself if you   Wing separation
   followed instructions? If so,   Thigh-leg separation
   where?   Separation of thigh from leg
                                      Back-breast separation

FIGURE 7.24 Evaluating instructions
Source: Helen Peck, Technical Writing 421, Illinois Institute of Technology.

	Breast separation		
	Back separation		
5. Was it easy to move from step to step?		Yes	No
6. How were the illustrations?	Good	O.K.	Poor
7. How would you rate these instructions overall?	Good	O.K.	Poor

Suggestions: _____

Signature

FIGURE 7.24 (cont.)

training manuals include the following features of a computer software product.[7]

>   *EXAMPLE*
>
> ### Basic Tasks
> - Typing information in a file.
> - Using return and control keys.
>   move the cursor
>   scroll   } Subtasks
>   insert and delete characters, words, lines }
> - Correcting typos.

Informational documents have facts, concepts, or items of information the user must understand or remember, either for future reference or for performance. For example, a brochure on cholesterol may tell the reader what cholesterol is, why it may be dangerous, who is susceptible, when and where to measure it, and, finally, how to control it. These items of information all become tasks for the users to demonstrate they have learned. Figure 7.25 demonstrates the concepts, the facts, the items of information a reader should understand or know after reading the document.

What Are the Criteria for Determining a Document's Success?

When you are evaluating the usability of a document, if all the users have difficulty performing step 3, then step 3 has to be rewritten. But seldom will every user fail to perform step 3 or miss question 5. Thus, you have to establish criteria for rewriting a document before you begin testing. If the document contains information or instructions that are life-threatening—for example, instructions for implanting a pacemaker—then the criteria are clear. All users must understand all the tasks. On the other hand, if a company

STUDY QUESTIONS

Here are questions to help you study the chapter on Traffic Laws. Turn to the page indicated for information which will give you the answer. Some of these questions will appear on the written test when you take your driver's examination.

1. What is the speed limit (unless otherwise posted)
   —On city streets? (30)
   —For passenger cars on rural highways? (30)
2. When and where must you slow down below the legal limit, if necessary for safety? (30)
3. If the speed limit is 55 and you are driving 40 could you be breaking the law? Why? (30)
4. Could you be breaking the speed law if you are driving too slowly? Why? (30)

FIGURE 7.25 Questions for an informational document
Source: Illinois *Rules of the Road*, State of Illinois, March 1986.

wants to reduce customer calls for help on operating equipment to less than 10 percent of total sales, then only 10 percent or less of the evaluators/users can ask for help on any part of the document.[8]

In industry, time and money are usually criteria for making decisions. Starting with the most crucial tasks first, writers can rewrite documents until time and money run out. IBM also suggests the following items as criteria for rewriting documentation:[9]

Quantitative Criteria
- time to complete tasks
- calls for help
- number and type of errors
- frequency of errors
- time to recover from errors

Qualitative Criteria
- perception of user after completing task

Who Are the User/Evaluators, and When Do You Need Them?

Users are the intended readers of the document. They should be people who share the same characteristics as those likely to use the documents. If a document is written for people who know little or nothing about the product, then the user/evaluator should have the same level of experience. If engineers, business managers, and technical writers have to use the manuals, then the test subjects should come from all three fields. If senior citizens have to follow the social security instructions, then the instructions should be tested by that age group, with additional regard for sex, race, ethnicity, and education.

Researchers agree that users should read the document early in the developmental stage of the document. Furthermore, testing a document should be done early and often during the drafting so that responses can shape the document. This interaction between drafting, evaluating, and rewriting is an iterative part of document development. If users test the document too late in the cycle, you may have time to rewrite only one or two of the sections. Although tests can be run with 1 or 2 users, 10 or more will provide more information about the product while reducing the effect of an idiosyncratic response.

What Types of Tests Produce Usable Data?

Testing is a field rich in its own concepts and techniques. For the purposes of technical communication, some testing methods offer data that improve technical documents, testing methods that may incorporate reader protocols mentioned earlier.

Tests for Instructional Documents

For instructional documents, usability testing supplies information from users who read the document while performing a typical task. Two researchers from the American Institutes for Research cite three types of usability tests.[10]

1. **LOGS:** An evaluator records the user's actions while the user reads and performs the tasks. Often the user is videotaped so that the evaluator can observe the videotape of the test. If you are the evaluator and you observe the user stopping at a particular task in the document and unable to proceed further without searching back in the document, then you know where the user has encountered a problem.

A variation of this type of usability test is called the "think-aloud" method. Users are asked to talk aloud while they are reading and performing the tasks; this type of log provides information about what an individual is thinking, information unavailable from performance measures alone. If you are using a tape recorder to capture the thinking aloud of the user, then you can study the thought process as well as the user's comments on very specific problems such as an unfamiliar word or a confusing phrase. With the thinking-aloud method, the user's comments tell you why the reader is having trouble. These performance and verbal logs are also called reader protocols because they record reader behavior and reactions.

2. **OBJECTIVE MEASURES:** These measures are quantitative because the evaluator counts the number of errors a user makes while reading and performing the task, as well as the time and the amount of help required. (During the test, the user can ask the evaluator for help.)

Instruction Evaluation for How to Cook a Microwave Meal

1. Did you successfully accomplish the tasks described by the instructions?   (Y)(es)   N(o)
2. Were the instructions easy to read?   (Y)   N
3. If you answered no above, circle section or sections where the instructions are confusing.

- To prepare
- To set time
- To set power level
- To cook food
- To change time set before or while cooking

- To change power level set before or while cooking
- To cancel operation
- To maintain

4. Were the illustrations accurate?   (Y)   N
5. Did you find the illustrations helpful?   (Y)   N
6. Overall, you would rate these instructions (circle)

Poor	Satisfactory	(Good)
(Hard to follow)	(need refinement)	(easy to follow)

7. Do you consider yourself a novice user (having used the item never or seldom) or an expert user (having used the item frequently)? (circle)

(Novice)   Expert

Comments (if any):

If food is not hot enough before repeating steps 5-9, turn food 180°.

Thank you for taking the time to complete this evaluation. Your input will be used to help refine the set of instructions.

FIGURE 7.26 Questionnaire on attitude
Source: Adapted from JoEllen Nielsen, Technical Writing 421, Illinois Institute of Technology.

3. **SUBJECTIVE MEASURES:** The user supplies feelings and opinions about a document by responding to an oral interview or questionnaire like the one in Figure 7.26 or by participating in a focus group, a group devoted to evaluating a single document. In Module 10, which discusses case studies and design reports, a focus group evaluates a manual for an electric blanket.

You can use any or all of the measures discussed earlier to evaluate a document presenting technical instructions. A testing technique called the thinking-aloud method can be used with a very small number of users and still give valuable results.[11] These users pinpoint specific problems and their data are useful. The instructions to the participants are very simple: "Tell me what you are thinking about as you work." The instructions to the evaluator are also simple:

- Remain an observer, not an interviewer, as you record the user.
- Prompt the user to keep talking.
- Don't worry about equipment; you can collect useful data with a notepad.

The performance measures require a larger number of users to see if a problem area is recursive, but if a group of users identify a problem area, then the usability testing has determined that the document (or a portion of the document) is *not* easy to use.

Tests for Informational Documents

The Document Design Center of the American Institutes for Research suggests two different audience-centered methods to evaluate documents.

1. **VALIDATION METHOD:** This test is designed to find out if the document does what it is supposed to do, that is, test to see if the user has understood the information. Of course, the validation method is a testing method that follows other steps in the evaluation process, illustrated in part here in Figure 7.27.

The tests are usually objective tests with items that measure the important points presented in the document. A guidebook on evaluating documents describes four common formats for test items:[12]

- true-false items
- multiple choice items
- short answer items
- fill-in items

For all four formats, the test questions should be paraphrased from the document, avoiding the exact wording.

The criteria for scoring the test should be established before the test is administered. You will have to

- Assign a numerical value to each item.

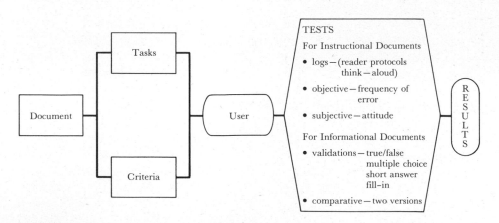

FIGURE 7.27 Evaluation process

Multiple choice	Number of Respondents Selecting Test Item No. (based on 100 respondents)					
answer	1.1	1.2	2.1	2.2	3	4
a	(82)	6	12	10	(82)	20
b	11	(71)	(87)	7	19	(80)
c	7	23	1	83	0	0
Total % correct	82	71	87	(83)	82	80

FIGURE 7.28 Frequency distribution of responses to questions on Illinois *Rules of the Road*

- Determine the number of times a single item is missed (the frequency of a missed item can be tabulated in a frequency distribution table, as illustrated in Figure 7.28.
- Determine mean and median scores.
- Establish performance standards for the percentage of readers who take the test. (How many people must pass the test with what score to determine whether the document is effective?)

Before you distribute the test to a large number of people, you should pilot the test to discover misleading questions that encourage incorrect answers.

2. **COMPARATIVE METHOD:** Readers compare two versions of a document, using any of the methods described under validation, as long as the same test is used to test both documents. Then you can apply the criteria to measure the effectiveness of a document and determine which is superior to the other. If you want to measure the success of the document with different audiences, you can create two groups on the basis of characteristics, such as age or education, and test the same document with both groups. The comparative method can also be used to test instructional documents to see if users perform tasks faster using Document X rather than Document Y (or vice versa).

What Do the Results of the Evaluation Tell You?

Evaluation tells you what is wrong with the document and how to improve it. Usability testing tells you whether or not the document is easy to use; it identifies problem areas that you can rewrite and retest, time and money permitting. Practically speaking, not every document should be tested—only those with a large circulation or a message with life-threatening ramifications. The benefits of testing also accrue after the document is released. A successful document will save time and money because the user has fewer questions and complaints and less need for service calls.

Summary

You must consider the reader whether you are writing a user's manual or a brief set of instructions. In both cases, the reader needs the information and wants to get the job done. So the reader performs essentially as a *technician*. But, depending on the experience of the reader and the reader's use for the document, you may have to include a section on the *theory* of the process and an *overview* of the process or product. The overview is a description of the process or product and its *component parts*.

The next step is to assess the reader's *tasks* and determine how to organize and present them. The tasks become the *headings* for the *set of instructions* and help to organize the *steps*. The set of instructions also requires preplanning to

- Issue warnings, cautions, and notes.
- List materials or equipment needed.
- Plan a troubleshooting/error recovery section.
- Organize the steps logically.
- Chunk the steps.
- Use the second person *you*, either stated or implied.
- State one instruction per step.

Readability is an important factor in writing instructions and documentation. Besides following the advice listed under the set of instructions, you can improve readability if you alert your readers to the tasks by using *headings* and *captions* that are *consistent* in typography and in *parallel construction*. Because readers are performing tasks while reading instructions, it is important that you keep your *sentences short* and *avoid multiple phrases and clauses*. Finally, you must select appropriate *terminology* and use it consistently (for example, PRESS the key). Synonyms encourage readers to seek differences in words when none exist. The most appropriate terminology is to name the part by describing it (for example, *Y* pipe).

Layout and *visual aids* are crucial to good instructions and documentation. *Space* is a layout problem when the reader has to respond in writing to the instructions as well as when visual aids and examples accompany the instructions. But, an *uncluttered* visual aid can replace several paragraphs of instructions. Visual aids are meaningful when they are near to and augment instructions. For instructions and documentation, some successful visual aids are overview drawings, exploded parts, sequence drawings, flowcharts, and tables.

Job aids and *computer documentation* are a special type of instructions. The advice for writing instructions also applies to computer documentation, but some additional advice will alert you to special problems. How your readers will use the text will help you plan the content. Often you will have to *gather the information* from programmers and analysts as well as specification and listing sheets. After *assessing the information,* you can give the reader the *large picture* of what the manual contains, and *organize* the text under major *tasks.* Then you can begin the instructions with the proper *cautions* and *notes,* again using techniques that enhance *readability. User friendly* documentation is instruction that is clear and precise, instruction that avoids even computer *jargon* (for example, monostation configuration); *Americanisms* (for example, awesome programming capabilities); and *contractions;* instruction that uses the words *can* and *must* (instead of *may* and *might*) to avoid ambiguity.

Finally, evaluating documents that give instruction or information, especially if the material is life-threatening, is important to both the company and the consumer. Asking people to use and review a document written for them is called *usability testing,* field testing, or audience-centered evaluations. A type of testing called *reader protocols* is a recording of the comments a reader makes while performing the tasks. This type of testing helps the writer revise the text by identifying problems. A less rigorous test is to have the user apply the instructions and answer a questionnaire.

To design a *measurement,* the writer establishes *criteria* for rewriting the document and then breaks the document down into *objectives,* asking users to complete *tasks* that demonstrate that the user understands the objectives. Usually, time and money are the criteria for rewriting documents that fail the consumer usability testing. Users should test the document early and often during the drafting stage, with 10 or more users providing information about the document.

Some testing methods that offer data for instructional documents are *logs, objective measures* of error, and *subjective responses* to questionnaires or *group interviews.* With logs, an evaluator or a videotape recorder records the user's actions while the user reads and performs tasks. To measure error, the evaluator counts the number of errors a user makes as well as the time and the amount of help required. With subjective measures, the users supply feelings and opinions about a document.

Evaluators often use the *validation method* or the *comparative method* with users who test informational documents. The validation is a test designed to find out if the document does what it is supposed to do. An objective test, such as true-false and multiple choice as well as short answer or fill-in tests, questions users about the important points in the document. As is true of the needs assessment, the criteria for scoring the test should be established when the test is administered. With the comparative method, two sets of readers compare two versions of a document, using any of the objective tests as long as the same test is used to test both documents.

Data from testing methods help writers create and improve documents. *Usability testing* identifies problem areas that writers can revise and improve.

Complete the Checklist

The following checklist has two parts, a section for you to complete and a section for your reader to complete. If you hand Part II to your reader with your written set of instructions, you will have data to analyze. From this information, you can then revise the first version of your document.

PART I—CHECKLIST FOR THE WRITER

Yes (good) On Content, Organization, and Layout

_____ 1. Did you provide the overview (the big picture)?

_____ 2. Are the major tasks clearly highlighted?

_____ 3. Are long sets of instructions subdivided under the tasks?

_____ 4. Did you include warning, caution, notes, and equipment if necessary?

_____ 5. Did you plan a troubleshooting/error recovery section?

_____ 6. Have you considered the illustration and where to place it?

_____ 7. Did you refer to the illustration in the steps?

_____ 8. Are the steps well organized?

_____ 9. Is each step a single instruction without multiple phrases or clauses?

_____ 10. Have you repeated instructions when steps recur on following pages?

Yes (good) On Readability and Right Words

_____ 1. Did you write the instructions and headings in parallel construction?

_____ 2. Have you used the second person *you,* either implied or stated?

3. Did you edit for

_____ multiple phrases and clauses?

_____ terminology?

_____ consistent words?

_____ slang/jargon?

_____ may/ought/should?

_____ quotation marks?

On Evaluating Documents
4. The document I want the user to evaluate is

_____   instructional.

_____   informational.

_____   life-threatening.

5. Before designing a measurement, I have

_____   clarified the objectives of the document.

_____   broken down the objectives into measurable tasks.

_____   established the criteria for judging the success of the document.

_____   identified the users who will evaluate the document.

6. For instructional documents, the testing measure I used is

_____   logs (including video and tape recorders).

_____   objective measures (user errors, time and amount of help required).

_____   subjective measures (interview, questionnaire, survey, focus group).

7. For informational documents, the testing measure I used is

_____   validation method (true-false, multiple choice, short answer, fill-in).

_____   comparative method.

PART II—MEASUREMENT FOR USERS
1. Do you have a clear picture of the overall process?   yes   no
2. Do you understand the terms?   yes   no
3. Where, if any place, were you confused about what to do?

                                                Step 1
                                                Step 2
                                                Step 3
                                                Step 4
                                                and so on

4. Where, if any place, were you unable to do as
   instructed?   Step 1
                                                          Step 2
                                                          Step 3
                                                          Step 4

5. At any place were you afraid you might hurt
   yourself or damage the equipment if you fol-
   lowed the instructions?   yes   no
   If so, where?   (Step X)

6. Was it natural to move from step to step?   yes   no

7. How were the illustrations?   clear   cluttered
                                  Figure 1
                                  Figure 2
                                  Figure 3

8. How would you rate these instructions overall?   good   O.K.   poor

Suggestions: _____
                                                               x

                              Signature

Notes

1. Suzanne Watzman, "New Electronic Publishing Technology Solutions for Documentation," in *Proceedings,* 33d International Technical Communication Conference (Washington, D.C.: Society for Technical Communication, 1986):14–16.

2. John Sterling Harris, "Metaphor in Technical Writing," *The Teaching of Technical Writing* (NCTE: Urbana, Ill., 1975):193.

3. Patricia Lawson, "Job Aids: Give the Readers What They Want," in *Proceedings,* 33d International Technical Communication Conference (Washington, D.C.: Society for Technical Communication, 1986):339–342.

4. Christine Browning, *Guide to Effective Software Technical Writing* (Englewood Cliffs, N.J.: Prentice-Hall, 1984), © 1984, pp. 28–30. Reprinted by permission of Prentice-Hall, Inc., Englewood Cliffs, N.J.

5. Tania Wilke, a speaker from Atlanta Staff, IBM Corporation, provided these notes on usable documents.

6. Victoria M. Winkler, Richard Ferguson, Diane Youngquist, "Procedures for Designing and Evaluating Training Materials," in *Proceedings,* 32d International Technical Communication Conference (Washington, D.C.: Society for Technical Communication, 1985): RET 6–9.

7. Winkler et al., "Procedures for Designing and Evaluating Training Materials," RET 6–9.

8. Dixie Goswami, Janice C. Redish, Daniel B. Felker, Alan Siegel, *Writing in the Professions* (Washington, D.C.: American Institutes for Research, 1981). Chapter 9 of this guide was used as background material for the discussion of evaluating documents.

9. John M. Morgan, advisory information developer, Atlanta Technical Staff, IBM Corporation, "The Usability Lab—A New Tool for Making Easy-to-Use Manuals."
10. Carol Bergfield Mills and Kenneth L. Dye, "Usability Testing: User Review," *Technical Communication* 32 (Fourth Quarter 1985):40–44.
11. Clayton Lewis, "Using the 'Thinking-aloud' Method in Cognitive Interface Design," IBM Thomas J. Watson Research Center, Yorktown Heights, N.Y.
12. Goswami et al., *Writing in the Professions*, Chapter 9 on evaluating the document.

References

George T. Bowman, "Applying Theory to Develop Task-Oriented Documents," in *Proceedings*, 33d International Technical Communication Conference (Washington, D.C.: Society for Technical Communication, 1986):174–76.

Renee K. Barnow, "A Methodology for Assessing Needs for Computer Graphics," in *Proceedings*, 32d International Technical Communication Conference (Washington, D.C.: Society for Technical Communication, 1985): VC 11–13.

P. Benson, "Writing Visually: Design Considerations for Technical Publications," *Technical Communication* 32:4 (Fourth Quarter 1985).

Donald Cunningham and Gerald Cohen, *Creating Technical Manuals* (New York: McGraw-Hill, 1984).

David Dobrin, "What's Technical About Technical Writing?"; L. Flower, J. R. Hayes, and H. Swarts, "Revising Functional Documents: The Scenario Principle"; and J. Seltzer, "What Constitutes a 'Readable' Technical Style?" in *New Essays in Technical and Scientific Communication: Research, Theory, Practice,* Paul V. Anderson, R. John Brockmann, and Carolyn R. Miller (eds.) (Farmingdale, N.Y.: Baywood Publishing Company, 1983).

L. Flower and J. R. Hayes, "Identifying the Organization of Writing Processes," in *Cognitive Processes in Writing: An Interdisciplinary Approach,* Lee Gregg and Erwin R. Steinberg (eds.) (Hillsdale, N.J.: Lawrence Erlbaum, 1983).

Roger A. Grice, "User Testing as an Information Development Activity: Writing with Pen and Screwdriver," in *Proceedings*, 31st International Technical Communication Conference (Washington, D.C.: Society for Technical Communication, 1985): MPD 18–21.

T. N. Huckin, "A Cognitive Approach to Readability," *New Essays in Scientific and Technical Communication* (Farmingdale, N.Y.: Baywood Publishing Company, 1983).

Patricia Lawson, "Job Aids: Give the Readers What They Want," in *Proceedings*, 33d International Technical Communication Conference (Washington, D.C.: Society for Technical Communication, 1986):339–342.

Mary M. Lay, "Procedures, Instructions, and Specifications: A Challenge in Audience Analysis," *Journal of Technical Writing and Communication* 12 (1982):235–242.

Yarusso Lowell, "Job Aids—Panacea or Placebo," *Performance and Instruction Journal,* National Society for Performance and Instruction (October 1984):1.

Maril McDonald, "Using Examples in Software Documentation," in *Proceedings*, 33d International Technical Communication Conference (Washington, D.C.: Society for Technical Communication, 1986):430–433.

B. D. Meyer, "The ABCs of New-look Publications," *Technical Communication* 33 (First
    Quarter 1986):16–20.
Carolyn R. Miller, "Rules, Context, and Technical Communication," *Journal of Tech-
    nical Writing and Communication* 10 (1980):149–158.
J. C. Redish and J. Selzer, "The Place of Readability Formulas in Technical Com-
    munication," *Technical Communication* 32:4 (Fourth Quarter 1985).
Amy Simpson, "Task Oriented Writing: Using Action Sentences to Get the Job Done,"
    in *Proceedings*, 33d International Technical Communication Conference (Wash-
    ington, D.C.: Society for Technical Communication, 1986):447–449.
William V. Van Pelt, "Teaching Technical Writing for the Computer Sciences," *The
    Technical Writing Teacher* 10 (1981):189–194.

Applying Your Knowledge

EXERCISE 7.1

*Reorganize the steps to demonstrate a logical order. Consider the possibility of
using headings to group or chunk the steps under tasks. Prepare a flowchart
to present the same information in the order you arranged.*

- Guide user through steps.
- Avoid jargon and slang.
- Collect all necessary information first to write complete instructions.
- Be precise.
- Anticipate new user questions.
- Avoid interpretation.
- Reinforce instruction with example or visual aid.
- Use short sentences and one instruction/sentence.
- Use second person; for example, "You divide the number by 2," or implied
  second person, "Divide the number by 2," instead of, "One should divide the
  number by 2."
- Repeat information if necessary instead of sending reader to another part
  of the document.
- *Highlight crucial information.*
- Present steps logically, chronologically, or sequentially.
- Revise instructions after inexperienced users test document.
- Use headings (purpose statements) to separate sections of instructions.

EXERCISE 7.2

For the following exercises, work in groups of three.

1. Bring an item that can be handheld.

    For example: mousetrap, box of building blocks, can opener, heating pad,
        micrometer

2. Select one item to write "how to use" instructions.
3. Appoint a recorder for the group.
4. Follow steps to write instructions.
5. Produce document.
6. Field-test the document following the suggestions under the section on
   field testing.

EXERCISE 7.3

You are in the accounting department of your power company. For several months you have prepared checks and vouchers for Accounts Payable. Now your department is reorganizing and you have been asked to prepare a job aid. Using the description provided, write the job aid.

> Procedure to Prepare Checks and Vouchers for the Current
> Accounts Payable System

You have to prepare the checks, the Check Register (three copies), the Voucher Distribution Sheets (three copies), and the Special Handling Report (two copies). The Control Clerk provides you with the initial Cash Voucher numbers so that you can determine the number of checks that you have to run. After you print the checks, you have to compare each check to the Check Register data, noting especially agreement between data on checks and data on vouchers. If any checks are blank, spoiled, or inaccurate, you have to hand-punch the signature area on each check, note the number and date of the spoiled check on C & R Section's copy of the Check Register, and store the discarded check in the file in the filing drawer.

EXERCISE 7.4 REDESIGN THE DOCUMENT

Redesign the cover letter and set of instructions provided. Because the cover letter is long, you will have to read the entire document before you revise it. Be sure you consider audience, readability, instructions for writing procedures, layout, and illustration.

UNITED STATES
ENVIRONMENTAL PROTECTION AGENCY
REGION V
230 SOUTH DEARBORN ST.
CHICAGO, ILLINOIS 60604

Dear Vehicle Owner:

Thank you for your recent inquiry to the U.S. Environmental Protection Agency (U.S. EPA) concerning vehicles designed to use unleaded fuel which may have been misfueled with leaded gasoline. Because of the number of retail gasoline stations in the Chicago area which have allegedly sold leaded represented as unleaded, U.S. EPA is concerned that misfueling may have detrimental effects on many vehicle emission control systems.

We have enclosed the following information to assist you in determining if leaded gasoline may have been used in your vehicle:

1) A U.S. EPA press release of March 21, 1983, with a list of gasoline stations and distributors that allegedly sold mislabeled gasoline;

2) instructions on how to administer the test using test paper to determine if there is lead in the tailpipe; and

3) the lead detection test paper you requested.

If, after performing the test, the test paper changes to a pink color, leaded gasoline has probably been used in your car. If the test indicates that leaded gasoline has been used in your car and you have purchased gasoline from one of the retail outlets listed during the time period in which the violations are alleged to have occurred, we would appreciate you doing the following:

1) Place each individual piece of lead detection test paper back into the plastic bag it came in and either staple or clip the plastic bag onto a sheet of paper. On the paper, write your name, address, telephone number (during the day), make, model, year and vehicle identification number of the car. Also, note the date the lead test was performed, and the name(s) and address(es) of the station(s) listed in the press release at which you purchased gasoline labeled as unleaded.

2) Make clear copies of any receipts for gasoline purchases from those stations listed in the press release around the dates specified in the release. (This will show that you purchased gasoline from one or more of those stations during the period those stations allegedly were selling mislabeled gasoline.)

3) If you do not have a record of gasoline purchases, write on a separate sheet of paper those stations listed in the press release where you believe you purchased gasoline during the time period involved, and the approximate date and amount of each purchase.

4) Make copies of any receipts for repair work performed on any portion of your emission control system (especially the catalytic converter) in 1982 or 1983.

5) Send all the above information and any other information you feel may be useful to the following person:

U.S. EPA (EN-397)
401 M Street, S.W.
Washington, D.C. 20460

The case resolution procedures which will be used to process these cases are often time-consuming and could take from three months to a year or more. All alleged violators will be given an opportunity to settle their cases with U.S. EPA. A key focus of all settlement negotiations will be an attempt to get damaged catalytic converters and/or other portions of emission control systems replaced on vehicles where there is substantial information showing that leaded gasoline from specific stations listed in the press release is responsible.

We caution, however, that we cannot predict whether our efforts to achieve such settlements will succeed, and, in fact, they may not be successful in all cases. You will be notified how you can get your vehicle repaired or otherwise be compensated if we are successful in achieving such a settlement and if there is sufficient information showing that gasoline purchases from one of the identified retail outlets damaged the emission control system.

If the test paper does not turn pink or violet, it indicates your vehicle has not received leaded gasoline and your vehicle's emission control system has not been damaged. <u>Please do not return the lead test paper if a color change does not occur.</u>

Once again, thank you for your inquiry. We are pleased to provide you with the lead detection test paper and urge you to read the instructions thoroughly and perform the test carefully. Should the test indicate that leaded gasoline has been used, please send the information requested as soon as possible. Because of the large number of inquiries, we will be contacting you only if and when we achieve a settlement which involves you.

Sincerely,

Air Management Division

Instructions for Use of Lead Detection Paper

CAUTION: FOR SAFETY REASONS USE TEST PAPER ONLY WHEN ENGINE IS OFF AND THE TAILPIPE IS COOL TO THE TOUCH.

The purpose of this test is to determine if there are any lead deposits in a vehicle tailpipe. These deposits may be present if your vehicle has had leaded gasoline introduced into it. The test results will provide a good indication whether leaded fuel has been used in the vehicle.

Step-by-step Instructions: Read all seven steps before undertaking the test.

1. Wash and dry hands before using the lead test paper. Dirt or other debris on your hands may have an adverse effect on the lead test paper and invalidate the test.
2. Cut the lead test paper in half. This will allow you to conduct two tests with one sheet of lead test paper.
3. You are now ready to conduct the test. With a paper towel or clean rag, wipe away a portion of the soot accumulated on the inside of your vehicle's tailpipe. (This is to ensure that soot from the inside of the tailpipe will not mask any color change of the lead test paper.)
4. Moisten the lead test paper with a few drops of distilled water. Do not soak the lead test paper as it may ruin it.
5. Immediately (within 10 seconds) apply the lead test paper to the cleaned portion inside the tailpipe. The tailpipe should be cool. Hold the lead test paper in contact with the tailpipe for approximately 60 seconds. Remove the paper from the tailpipe.

A test indicating the presence of lead deposits on the tailpipe will cause a color change of the test paper from light yellow to pink or red-violet. The intensity of the color depends upon the concentration of lead in the tailpipe.

6. When conducting more than one test, care must be taken not to contaminate any subsequent tests. Always wash hands between tests. Be careful not to drop test paper on the ground as lead concentrations and other contaminants on the ground could invalidate the test.
7. If the test indicates the presence of lead, place each individual test paper back into the small plastic bag it came in and either staple or clip the plastic

bag onto a sheet of paper. On the paper, write your name, address, telephone number (during the day), make, model, year, and vehicle identification number of the car. Also, note the date of the test, and the name(s) and address(es) of the station(s) listed in the press release at which you purchased gasoline labeled as unleaded.

See other side to receive additional amounts of lead test paper.

To receive additional quantities of lead test paper, contact the following sources:

1. Gailard-Schlesinger Chemical Mfg. Corp.
   584 Mineola Avenue
   Carle Place, NY 11514
   (516) 333-5600 Contact: Henry Madollo

Paper is available in 40 sheets per box as well as individually wrapped pieces; call for current price.

2. Galileo Enterprises
   P.O. Box 2772
   Livonia, MI 48150
   (313) 322-7270 Contact: John Holman

Paper is available 40 sheets per box; call for current price. Individually wrapped sheets of paper with instructions cost $1.00.

3. Lead Test Paper
   c/o Chicago Lung Association
   1440 West Washington Blvd.
   Chicago, IL 60607

Paper is available free of charge for individually wrapped sheets only.

EXERCISE 7.5

In Exercise 7.4, you revised an instructional document on testing for leaded gasoline. Now state the users' tasks for the instructions, and write some test items. Using the comparative method to evaluate the two documents, determine which document is more effective.

EXERCISE 7.6

Manuals on obtaining a driver's license do contain lifesaving information. Obtain a copy of the manual for your state; select a few pages of information and five users. Then evaluate the effectiveness of those pages in the manual by determining the percentage of users who understood all the tasks associated with the information.

WRITING ASSIGNMENT 1

Write a set of instructions, a job aid, computer documentation, or a procedure. Select your own subject, but remember to consider your audience's knowledge, the purpose of the text and the reader's tasks, the set of instructions, reada-

bility, layout, and illustration. Then ask a new user to field-test your instructions by following the procedure. Observe the field test, and take notes on the user's performance of each step in the instructions. Ask the user to comment on these:

- organization of the document
- visuals
- terminology or descriptions
- punctuation
- management of task

WRITING ASSIGNMENT 2

Collaborate with two other people on this assignment. Select an instructional or informational document distributed by the state or federal government and prepare to revise it by doing the following:

- Establishing tasks and criteria to evaluate it.
- Writing a set of objective questions or planning a field test.
- User-testing the document (use three people on another team).
- Analyzing the results.
- Revising the document.

MODULE 8

Proposals and Progress Reports

A proposal is an offer to perform a service. You are trying to convince your reader that you can do a job, do it well, and that you are the best person to do the job. All kinds of organizations and people need services performed: Industries ask employees to study and recommend new ways to solve old problems or to advance the organization; government agencies need outside consultants to evaluate their software needs; individuals want their houses painted.

Because the proposal is a persuasive piece of writing, you must organize your information in such a way that you encourage your employer or client to act on your proposal and accept your offer. Your client will want to know what it is that you are proposing to do, how you are going to do it, and how much it will cost. The visual techniques or headings and steps in a list, as well as the stylistic techniques of precise purpose statements and procedures in parallel structure, will enhance the proposal.

The proposal sells the employer or client on a project that will solve a problem, a project constrained by both time and money. In actuality, a proposal is a low-pressure sales document. As the writer, you try to establish your credibility, maintain a factual, problem-solving tone, and assure your client that you can succeed. The purpose of this module is to help you write the informal proposal and acquaint you with the formal proposal. It is possible that the informal proposal you write for this module will become the project you work on for the course in technical writing, leading to the final technical report for the course.

After the proposal is accepted, clients or the sponsoring agency may want progress reports that keep them informed about the project. Progress reports keep track of the project tasks and help the proposer appraise and forecast the completion of the project.

Scope

In this module you will learn to

1. Identify the informal and formal proposal as well as the solicited and unsolicited proposal.
2. Cite the main elements of a proposal.
3. Write an informal proposal with attention to
   • introduction.
   • details about procedure, time, and materials.
   • credentials.
4. Enhance readability with
   • a precise purpose statement.
   • headings.
   • procedures in parallel structure.
5. Outline the primary and secondary elements of a formal proposal by
   • examining the guidelines and checklist.
   • reviewing the criteria for evaluation.
   • organizing the sections.
6. Track project tasks in a progress report.

Identifying the Proposal

A proposal is an offer to perform a service. You can make the offer informally in a letter or memo or formally in a report.

Informal Versus Formal Proposals

Both informal and formal proposals require the same technical information: what you propose to do, how you propose to do it, including costs, and why you can do the job. In an informal proposal, you can provide this information in two to four pages without needing a table of contents or a list of appended materials. In other words, unless you are working on a large project with a group of colleagues or co-workers, you will frequently submit at least your initial proposal as a memo or letter.

The formal proposal, discussed in detail later in this module, is much longer than the informal proposal. Because of its length, detail, and supporting materials, the formal proposal is usually submitted as a formal report. The sections in the report run to pages rather than paragraphs, requiring the report to have a cover letter, a table of contents, a list of appended material, a bibliography, vitae, and so forth. The formal and informal proposals originate in two ways: They are solicited or unsolicited.

Solicited Versus Unsolicited Proposals

If a client (or your employer) defines a problem and requests a solution, then the client initiates the request for a solicited proposal. For example, if you own a company that tests soil for acidity and if a potential customer calls you, describes a problem she is having with brown spots in her grass, and requests your services to analyze and solve the problem, then you are responding to a request for services. You will probably respond with an informal proposal, that is, a follow-up letter offering to analyze the problem and solve it, all for a certain fee. If the customer accepts and signs the proposal to have the work done, the proposal becomes a contract. A proposal done on a standard form is illustrated in Figure 8.1.

Unsolicited Proposal

If you are working for a company, the company probably initiates the offer for services to clients. Many times the company produces a letter or a brochure that sells the services or products of the company. These letters or marketing brochures are unsolicited proposals in that they describe the service that is for sale. They describe a problem and offer the company's services to solve the problem. Figure 8.2 is an unsolicited proposal, a letter, that offers consulting services.

You may have to write an unsolicited proposal in your company, especially if you perceive a problem and think that you can solve it or if you have an idea for a new product and think that the company should produce it. You may decide to write the proposal as a memo to your supervisor; if you are head of your own company, you may have to write a letter to a potential client, proposing to solve the client's problem and offering your company's services. If you want to solve a problem that requires extensive research and a lot of money to cover research costs, then you may have to write an unsolicited proposal such as a report to a government agency that funds research projects in your field of expertise.

Determining the Contents of the Proposal

Whether you or the buyer initiates the proposal, your proposal must be accurate and convincing. The proposal is going to cost someone money if it is accepted, so you will want to include all the elements to persuade the buyers that they are going to get something for their money.

Proposal	Proposal No.
	Sheet No.
	Date

Proposal Submitted To	Work To Be Performed At
Name_____	Street_____
Street_____	City_____ State_____
City_____	Date of Plans_____
State_____	Architect_____
Telephone Number_____	

We hereby propose to furnish all the materials and perform all the labor necessary for the completion of

_____ Library cabinetry - plans marked B or C (choice of): _____

_____ This proposal includes Cherry Cabinetry installed only. _____

_____ (Retrimming of windows, doors, and architectural paneling
_____ not included.)

Cabinetry Delivered and Installed	$6,753.00
Terms: 50% deposit to put job into production schedule	$3,376.50
50 % due upon completion	$3,376.50

All material is guaranteed to be as specified, and the above work to be performed in accordance with the drawings and specifications submitted for above work and completed in a substantial workmanlike manner for the sum of

Dollars ($ 6,753.00   ).

with payments to be made as follows:

_____ See terms above _____

Any alteration or deviation from above specifications involving extra costs, will be executed only upon written orders, and will become an extra charge over and above the estimate. All agreements contingent upon strikes, accidents or delays beyond our control. Owner to carry fire, tornado and other necessary insurance upon above work. Workmen's Compensation and Public Liability Insurance on above work to be taken out by_____

Respectfully submitted_____

Per_____

Note — This proposal may be withdrawn by us if not accepted within 15   days

ACCEPTANCE OF PROPOSAL

The above prices, specifications and conditions are satisfactory and are hereby accepted. You are authorized to do the work as specified. Payment will be made as outlined above.

Accepted_____   Signature_____

Date_____   Signature_____

FIGURE 8.1 Solicited proposal on standard form

Questions That You Must Answer in Your Proposal

1. What's the problem?
2. What are you proposing to do about the problem?
3. How are you going to do it?

4. How long will it take?
5. How much will it cost?
6. What are your credentials or facts that demonstrate your ability to solve the problem?

Your answers to these questions must convince the potential buyer that you or your company is the best one to perform the service. These answers provide the content for the sections in the proposal:

- introduction
- procedures
- credentials

The answers to the first two questions appear in the introduction to your proposal.

CENTER FOR ENGINEERING ANALYSIS

Who are we and how can we help you?
The staff of **Center for Engineering Analysis** has 15 years of experience providing professional engineering expertise to the legal, industrial, and health care professions. The center provides both expert engineering and consultations as well as testing and analysis of **medical, electrical,** and **electronic devices** involved in the following areas of litigation:

1. medical malpractice
2. hospital accidents
3. wrongful death
4. personal injury
5. product liability

The **Center for Engineering Analysis** specializes in medical, electrical, and electronic device testing and analysis. It also offers a comprehensive range of professional engineering services such as the following:

- Prelaw suit technical analysis of client claims to determine if there is sufficient merit for further investment of time in the case.
- Analysis of patent infringement cases.
- Analysis of tape recordings.
- Analysis and interpretation of cases involved with violation of one or more technical codes or standards.
- Complete forensic photography to document problems and defects for record keeping and use in courtroom procedures.

Additional services include the review of a device's **design, documentation,** and **safety.**

All cases are handled by a **Registered Professional Engineer** and reviewed by a Ph.D. in engineering. Our engineers are experienced in giving depositions and providing testimony in court.

When your case requires technical assistance, The **Center for Engineering Analysis** can help you settle your cases quickly. Before you have invested your time in the case, call the center for the technical advice you need.

FIGURE 8.2 Unsolicited proposal

Preparing the Proposal

The Background

Let's consider a situation in which you are a self-employed mechanical engineer with an expertise in pump problems. One day you are reading an article in *The Wrap-Up* and discover that Chemicals International is having a problem with a viscose pumping system. Some internal pump parts are being corroded, and the flow rate of the pumps is inaccurate. With your knowledge of pump design and pump equipment, you determine that you could solve Chemicals International's problem if you studied their needs and their present pumping system. So you decide to submit a proposal to study their viscose pumping system, redesign the system, and initiate the redesigned system.

The Introduction

Essentially, the introduction allows you to introduce yourself and your company to your potential client, state the problem, and propose a project. In other words, the introduction provides the context for the rest of the proposal, a context that focuses on the client's needs. In a letter format, this introduction is a pleasant and factual way to begin an informal proposal. The introduction is the place to include the following information:

- your reason for writing, including
    the background of the problem
    the significance of the project to the company
- your interest in the project
- your precise proposal

Because your client is always the most important factor in a proposal, you want to state your interest in the project in terms of your client's needs or problem and gain the early confidence of your potential buyer by assuring him or her that you have studied his or her particular problem. Next you want to indicate your reason for writing and propose to perform a service. You may itemize very specifically what you propose to do.

For example, to return to the situation of the pump specialist, the expert pump specialist proposes to

1. Study the client's pumps and their use.
2. Redesign the pumps on the basis of their use.
3. Submit a plan for implementing the redesigned pumps.

The background of the problem, the significance of the project to the company, your interest in the project, and the precise proposal constitute the introduction or opening section of the proposal. In a proposal submitted as a letter, you should not use the heading *Introduction*. But after identifying yourself and your reason for writing, you can direct your reader's attention to *Background, Proposal,* and *Significance* by using these headings in your introduction.

Detailing the Procedure

After the introduction, the next section of your proposal tells your reader how you are going to solve the problem, how long it will take, and how much it will cost. This section gives your reader your procedure for solving the problem.

The Plan for Solving the Problem

The part of your document setting forth a plan to solve the problem provides the technical details that describe what you propose to do for your reader and how you propose to do it. As you itemize the steps you will take to solve the client's problem, you focus on the client's needs. Being the expert in the field, you know how to proceed technically to solve the problem, but the client will want the solution tailored especially to the client's situation. To return to the example of the pumps, before the engineer can design the pump, he or she must study the company's present system and determine the specific requirements for a new pumping system.

The Time Schedule

For all proposals, you will have to analyze the steps involved in completing the project and prepare a schedule you intend to follow. How long will it take you to complete the project? You can measure a project in weeks and hours as well as months or years, depending on the extent of the project.

Using time and the technical steps, you may want to illustrate the schedule for the project in a chart. Then both you and the client will have a clear understanding of the work to be accomplished in a given period of time. To establish a schedule, you have to consider

- The amount of time you have to complete the project.
- The number of tasks.
- The start date and the completion date.
- The personnel working on the project.

Figure 8.3 illustrates a schedule, or timetable, for a research project. A timetable or timeline presented in a chart is called a Gant chart.

The Cost

You will also have to determine the cost of the project. The cost depends on the price of the goods and services, and the buyer will want to know the price of these goods and services. So you will have to prepare a budget. Your

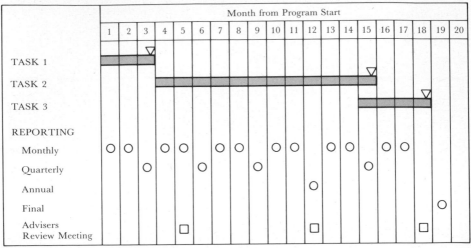

FIGURE 8.3 Schedule for a research project

budget lists as *services* your time on the project and the time of others; the materials you will have to use to complete the project are *goods*. Remember that the buyer will want the project completed on time and at the price you indicated in your proposal.

Questions to Consider Before You Submit Your Budget

1. What steps will you take to complete the project?
2. How long will each step take?
3. What are your fees for your time?
4. How much will the total project cost the buyer?
    a. your time and the time of others
    b. materials

In the example with pumps, the pump specialist calculates that the project will take about 40 hours of his time, approximately a full working week. But he has other commitments and would like to devote only 5 hours a week to this project, so he proposes to complete the project in 8 weeks and bill the company for a total of 40 hours of his time plus other costs such as goods and the services of others involved in the completion of the project.

Establishing Credentials

The final section of the proposal summarizes the credentials of the persons involved in performing and managing the project and assures the client that your company can do what you have proposed. This section answers the client's final question: What are your credentials that demonstrate your ability to solve the problem?

Personnel Qualifications

Describing the credentials may range from a paragraph on the personnel involved to an attached page describing the qualifications. It is a good idea to have copies of your résumé so that you can enclose one with your proposal. Companies often keep updated employee résumés on file just for situations when they have to submit credentials with their proposals. Advice on writing résumés appears in Module 12.

Feasibility of Completing the Project

A statement on the likelihood of your successfully solving the problem and completing the project provides the content for the feasibility statement, a statement supported with a list of references or in a paragraph describing the success you have had with similar projects. Previous successes indicate the probability of your being successful with the current proposal.

The *Qualifications* paragraph and the *Feasibility* paragraph are the last items in the proposal before you close the proposal letter by indicating a readiness to discuss or clarify any points in the proposal. Figure 8.4 presents the proposal for designing a pumping system and includes headings to help the reader follow the organization of the proposal. Of course, the headings coincide with the questions the client has about the proposal and convince the client that you have answered all the important questions.

Precision Products and Services, Inc.
7700 S. Mobile
Burbank, Illinois 60459

February 17, 19XX

Mr. Alan Fremer
Production Superintendent
Chemicals International
6733 West 65 Street
Redford Park, Illinois 60638

Dear Mr. Fremer:

I recently read an article in The Wrap-Up in which you reported the problem that Chemicals International is having with their viscose pumping system. You described the corrosion of internal pump parts as well as the inaccurate flow rates of the pumps. With my background in pumping high viscosity, corrosive chemicals, I believe that I may be of some service to you in solving your pump problems.

Background
Pumping systems have become more and more sophisticated. The various types of pumping systems perform a wide variety of services. Some processes demand that the fluid be pumped at a high flow rate. Others require pressure from a large outlet or need an accurate flow rate under variable conditions. Some even require the pumping of solids and liquids together (slurry). Our role is to meet a particular need with a particular design.

Significance
The need for efficient production and a high-quality product is essential today. In most chemical plants, a substantial amount of time and money goes toward processing corrosive chemicals. The containers, piping system, and pumping systems have to be specially made for corrosive chemicals. Still, pumps usually fail because their bearings, shafts, and impeller blades corrode. These problems are increasing with the rising demand for high acidic and high caustic chemicals.

Most of these pumping problems can be solved, however, by a careful study of what exactly is demanded from your pumping system. By making some changes in the design and equipment, we can improve your pumping system so that it operates efficiently, has less down time, and improves the quality of your product. My firm has solved many problems similar to yours. With a vast knowledge of today's pumping systems and many recent successes, I make the following proposal.

Proposal
I propose that Precision Products and Services, Inc., examine your viscose pumping system. Upon completion of this study, I will submit a report containing a plan for redesigning your system and recommendations for initiating that plan.

Procedure
The basic procedure for this study involves five steps, to be completed in eight weeks.

Step 1: Determine the requirements for flow, pressure, and accuracy that your production department needs from its pumping system.

Step 2: Analyze the degree of corrosiveness of your viscose chemical.

Step 3: Select at least three prototype pumps that meet our pumping requirements and evaluate their performance in the field. (All the pumps will be made of the proper noncorrosive material.)

Step 4: Evaluate the data and select one pump that performs the best.

Step 5: Prepare a design for a new pumping system using this pump and provide instructions for its installation.

The design and the instructions will be submitted with the final report.

Cost
The cost for this study is small compared to the amount of money saved by having a system that requires less maintenance and replacement of parts. The costs include expenses, labor, and parts.

Labor—40 hours at $50.00/hr.	$2000.00
Travel	100.00
Secretarial fees	100.00
Prototype pumps	1500.00
Total cost	$3700.00

Personnel and Qualifications

I have a B.S.M.E. degree from the Texas State University. After spending five years with the Tuthill Pump Co., I started my own firm, which has been in operation for four years. I have specialized in pumping corrosive chemicals for the last three years. My previous assignments have included major development projects at Nalco Chemical Co., Monsanto, and Martin Seymour Paints.

I hope you will seriously consider this proposal and accept it. If you have any questions about this proposal, please call me at (687) 287-9193.

Sincerely yours,

Robert W. Phillips
President

FIGURE 8.4 An informal proposal
Source: Adapted from a document by Robert W. Phillips, Technical Writing 421, Illinois Institute of Technology.

Examining Variations of the Informal Proposal

Whereas all proposals use headings to help the readers find answers to their questions about

- the precise proposal (including background and significance)
- the procedure (including time schedule and cost)
- the credentials (including qualifications and feasibility)

the organizational strategies they use to answer the questions as well as the length and detail devoted to each section set the tone of formality or informality. Compared to reports and letters, memos are the most informal. Regardless of the strategy or the informality, the headings help the clients find answers to their questions.

On-the-Job Proposals (Intradepartmental)

On-the-job proposals will obviously have variations in organizational strategies and headings because they are written for a specific reader who is acquainted with the proposer, the environment, and, probably, the problem. For these reasons, some of the information, such as qualifications or feasibility, may be inappropriate. Figure 8.5 is an example of an internal proposal

To: Dr. Philip Bartok

From: Lisa G. Mechnic
         Summer/Alumni Coordinator

Subject: Proposal to Improve the Purchase Order Requisition Form and Instruction Section in the Purchasing Policy and Procedures Manual.

PROJECT SUMMARY
A form used frequently is the purchase order requisition. I propose to review and redesign this form and revise the instructions in the *Manual* to assist the user in completing this form.

PROJECT DESCRIPTION
The *Purchasing Policy and Procedures Manual* is a reference document including purchasing forms used by every department on campus. However, the present structure of the manual complicates its use and effectiveness. One of the forms in the manual is the purchase order requisition (P.O. requisition). I propose to evaluate and redesign this form and revise the format and instructions for the P.O. requisition.

RATIONALE AND SIGNIFICANCE
In the daily functions of a department it is necessary to purchase items off campus. Generally, a P.O. requisition is used to process off-campus purchases. The P.O. requisition is sent to the Purchasing Department, which then orders the items described on the P.O. requisition.

Last year the Purchasing Department produced an instruction manual to aid campus personnel in the proper use of these forms. However, the manual does not present the material in a simple, clear format. A person writing the P.O. requisition may become confused and spend an excessive amount of time on the form, making sure the information is correct. I will redesign the P.O. form and improve the structure of the instruction section in the *Manual*, all revisions calculated to make the Purchasing Policy and Procedures Manual easy to read and simple to use.

The administrative staff on campus changes periodically. There are always some individuals who are using the P.O. requisition for the first time. Therefore, the *Manual* must present the form and the instructions clearly and concisely.

PLAN OF WORK
1. Establish standards for designing and writing clear documents.
2. Analyze the present P.O. form and improve its language and structure.
3. Evaluate the instruction section for the P.O. form and revise it.
4. Submit the revised P.O. form and instructions for inclusion in the manual.

I will present the original version of the P.O. form and discuss its weak points based on document design standards. Then I will present and discuss the revised form. The same procedure will be applied to the instructions. I will ask people to test the new form and instructions, incorporating any suggestions that are appropriate. The final product is a new P.O. requisition form and a revised and restructured set of instructions.

PERSONAL QUALIFICATIONS

In my position, I monitor the budget and review all purchase orders for our department; thus, I use the P.O. requisition frequently. At first, I had difficulty with the form and the instructions. Then, as new staff was added to our department, I had to instruct them in the use of this material, and I observed the difficulties they had with the documents. As an aspiring technical writer, I have studied document design and completed other projects on revising documents.

BUDGET

No budget other than the costs for paper and duplicating is required for this project. If the Purchasing Department wishes to incorporate the revised material, it can be reproduced at the department's own expense.

FIGURE 8.5 An on-the-job proposal
Source: Adapted from Lisa G. Mechnic, Writing Workshop 425, Illinois Institute of Technology.

submitted in memo format; that is, it was written by an employee to improve a situation within an organization. But though the sections have equivalent information, the strategy and headings are different.

Interdepartmental Proposals

Some proposals have variations in strategy and headings when the reader is associated with the company (or institution) but unfamiliar with the proposer or the problem. Figure 8.6 is an example of such a proposal submitted in letter format. It is an unsolicited proposal with variations in organizational strategy and headings.

TO: Dr. Susan Thomas
         Director of Finances
         Lewis College of Arts and Sciences
         Wishnick Hall, Illinois Institute of Technology

FROM: Douglas White
         Department of Chemistry

SUBJECT: Proposal regarding care of infrared spectroscopes.

PROJECT SUMMARY

    I propose to study the Perkin-Elmer Infrared Spectroscope Model 727-B and its accessories and develop an effective care program for both.

PROJECT BACKGROUND

The importance of identifying unknown compounds in today's society cannot be overstressed. The problem of identification is one that affects chemists, physicians, police officials, and many fields related to chemistry. A valuable tool used in this process is infrared spectroscopy, in which a portion of the unknown compound is subjected to various frequencies of infrared light, and a graph is made of its transparency. Every organic compound has a distinct infrared spectrograph. Running a simple test with an infrared spectroscope can provide a chemist with invaluable clues needed to identify the unknown.

However, an infrared spectroscope is a delicate machine. It requires a large amount of accessory equipment and chemicals to keep it running smoothly. A major problem with spectroscopy is that the machine or its accessories are not kept in good condition, a situation that leads to a poorly resolved or inaccurate spectrograph, effectively making the machine useless.

I am proposing to study a common model infrared spectroscope, the Perkin-Elmer 727-B, and write a simple, effective care program that will keep it functioning smoothly. I chose this model of the Perkin Elmer to study because it is a very popular machine, used extensively in schools and laboratories. It is relatively inexpensive and easy to use, and it provides very accurate results. Although my research will be based solely on this machine, my care program could be applied, with little modification, to virtually any machine of its type. Problems with accessory equipment would also be common to any infrared spectroscope.

The Chemistry Department at Illinois Institute of Technology owns several Perkin-Elmer Spectroscopes and would certainly benefit from an easily understood care program that students could follow. With such a program, money spent on repairs and maintenance time could be cut drastically. I could design this program with a modicum of work, and I feel that in the long run it would be well worth the cost.

PLAN OF WORK

My proposed study consists of five parts:

I. Research the Perkin-Elmer 727-B Infrared Spectroscope operating manuals and history of past repairs and determine how best to keep the spectroscope running.
II. Research the accessories needed to operate the machine and maintain it and then determine the best method of storage and use for the accessories.
III. Establish procedures for maintaining the scope and accessories in good condition.
IV. Write the instructions.
V. Submit these instructions.

The finished product of my report will be a set of guidelines and instructions on how to care for the Perkin-Elmer Spectroscope that can easily be followed by an undergraduate who is marginally familiar with the machine. It will not include instructions on the care of the electronics of the machine, nor will it include a troubleshooting manual for a malfunctioning machine.

FACILITIES AND EQUIPMENT

I will mainly be using the Perkin-Elmer Model 727-B located in Room 317 of Wishnick Hall at Illinois Institute of Technology. As a chemistry student, I have access to the machine and its accessory equipment. Operating manuals and records of past repairs can be borrowed from the Chemistry Department at no cost.

BUDGET

In this budget, the number of hours needed for research and operating time are estimates. Should the project require more time to complete, the fees will not be raised. The final cost of the project will not exceed the figure shown.

Research (8 hours @ $15.00/hour)	$120.00
Operating time (8 hours @ $15.00/hour)	120.00
Secretarial fees	50.00
TOTAL COST:	$290.00

Payment is due within 30 days of the delivery of the report.

PERSONAL QUALIFICATIONS

I am currently an undergraduate student and a candidate for a B.S. in chemistry at Illinois Institute of Technology. I am familiar with the machine to be studied, and I have used it to do numerous spectrographs. I have taken courses that require knowledge in the theory and use of the machine (Chemistry 240, Chemistry 334, Chemistry 335).

I believe these guidelines and instructions will help future students using the spectroscope and preserve the life of the equipment. If you have any questions, please call me at 334-5674.

FIGURE 8.6 Interdepartmental proposal
Source: Adapted from Douglas H. White, Technical Writing 421, Illinois Institute of Technology.

Evaluating the Informal Proposal

Writers who fail to make convincing arguments for their proposal may see their good ideas doomed. Often proposals fail because of the writer's presentation and not because of the idea itself. When you draft the proposal, carefully edit the sections under *Proposal, Procedure,* and *Qualifications.*

Not this: (The proposal indicates a predetermined solution.)
I will test the feasibility of buying a new copier versus repairing the present machine and recommend replacements for the copier.

But this: I will study the feasibility of buying a new copier versus repairing the present machine, evaluate the options on the basis of efficiency and cost, and make a recommendation.

Not this: (The proposal gives away the solution.)
I propose to improve the versatility of the copier by dividing our

architectural plans into four sections, copying each section, and taping the sections together.

But this: I propose to study ways to copy large architectural plans using our existing equipment.

Not this: (The procedures are not in parallel structure.)

Step 1: Analysis of hazard.

Step 2: Sizing of the gas reserves.

Step 3: Layout and size piping to deliver the exact concentration of gas determined by analysis.

Step 4: Mechanical/electrical specs to control doors and ventilation systems in the room.

Step 5: Put together package that will constitute a specification to be used in bid proposals.

But this: Step 1: Analyze hazards.

Step 2: Size gas reserves.

Step 3: Design layout and size piping to deliver the exact concentrations of gas determined by Step 1.

Step 4: Specify mechanical/electrical equipment to control doors and ventilation systems in the room.

Step 5: Compile the complete specifications to submit to outside bidder.

Not this: (The qualifications indicate a lack of technical information.)

I have not studied the recent developments in this area, but your problem is one easily solved with conventional methods, methods I have used in five other companies.

But this: A review of the current literature indicates that the conventional methods of solving this problem are still the most successful.

The example in Figure 8.7 combines the introduction, the proposal, part of the procedure, and possible solutions in the first three paragraphs. The writing reveals a lack of focus, and the client has no cues as to which questions are being answered in the proposal. In fact, the client may have difficulty determining exactly what the writer is proposing to do for the client.

Information Systems Design, Inc.
1311 South Parkview Drive
Los Angeles, California 55008

September 17, 19XX

Ted Armstrong
President
Advanced Airlines, Inc.
Palo Alto, California 55037

Dear Mr. Armstrong:

It is my understanding that Advanced Airlines is considering the purchase of an automated reservation system for passengers and freight. The need for a

computer system arises from the continual growth
and expansion your company has experienced over
the years. However, because your management company consists of pilots with little exposure to computers, assistance is needed in selecting an appropriate system. I have two proposals to make. The first is
to obtain a package system from a computer manufacturer. The second alternative is to purchase a reservation from a large trunk carrier.

**These ideas are possible
solutions, not a proposal.
First offer to perform
the study.**

The acquisition of a package system involves leasing
or buying a computer. The package itself can be obtained from a computer software vendor. Considerable
effort is needed to install and initialize a package system. The major advantage of this alternative is the
flexibility it offers in terms of future program expansion and availability of computer storage space. The
second alternative involves purchasing excess computer capacity from a large trunk carrier that owns
and operates a reservation service. No installation or
initialization is required if this alternative is chosen.
More important, this system is available for immediate use. Should you desire to expand your computer
capacity to include other functions, space may not
be available.

**This information goes
into the report if the
client accepts the pro-
posal.**

The steps involved in developing a computer system
are as follows:

Is this the proposal?

     1. Careful examination of your company's activi-
ties to determine the type of information needed.

     2. Determining the frequency of this informa-
tion, its source, and desired input/output methods.

     3. Designing a system which will not exceed
your projected budget.

**These procedures are in-
consistent in style and
suggest a confusion in
thinking. Are your steps
accurate and prove you
know how to solve the
problem?**

Information regarding different computers and packages will be furnished, along with the names of several computer manufacturers, software vendors, and
companies operating extensive reservations services.

**Will the company still
have work to do after
you finish?**

FIGURE 8.7 A faulty proposal

To Evaluate Your Own Proposal, Ask Yourself

1. Did I separate my proposal from my introduction,
   - Stating my proposal precisely?
   - Using headings in the introduction and throughout the proposal?
   - Without providing the solution?

2. Did I include the significance of the project to the company?
3. Did I organize my procedure in a separate, detailed section,
   - Using parallel structure for the steps in the procedure?
   - Scheduling a time line for the project?
4. Did I justify costs in the budget
   - For time?
   - For materials?
5. Have I established my credentials and ability to complete the project?

Preparing the Formal Proposal

The formal proposal is not only more detailed and longer than the informal proposal, but, frequently, the formal proposal is a team effort. More than one person in the company may contribute to the writing, and one section of a proposal may have to be written by specialists who will have little to do with writing the other sections of the proposal. Because proposals have sections that run to pages and even to chapters rather than just to paragraphs, the formal proposal is usually presented in a report format. Accompanying the report are secondary elements, such as a cover letter explaining the subject of the proposal, providing a road map to the document, and identifying the proposer. Often a long proposal will have a table of contents so that the reader can find the sections easily.

If you work for a company that submits formal proposals, you may be writing a report or collaborating on a section of a proposal going to another company in the private sector or to a federal agency in the public sector. Frequently, these companies or agencies solicit proposals to perform services and issue guidelines to follow when submitting proposals. When the company or agency publishes guidelines, you must follow their outline.

Examine the Guidelines

The federal government is a large employer that needs external goods and services. Because the U.S. government may not legally favor one external supplier over another, government agencies needing external services or goods furnished issue a *request for a proposal,* abbreviated as an RFP. The RFP is usually a set of instructions and guidelines for writing the proposal. The federal government announces RFP's in a publication entitled the *Commerce Business Daily.* An individual reads this publication and decides that she or her company can provide the service. A section from the *Commerce Business Daily* is reproduced in Figure 8.8.

Then the potential proposer contacts the government agency and requests the RFP packet of instructions and guidelines. Usually, the guidelines are very specific about what services the agency needs and what information should go into a proposal. An RFP from the government is presented in part in Figure 8.9.

Commerce Business Daily

WEDNESDAY, December 17, 1986

Issue No. PSA-9238

A daily list of U.S. Government procurement invitations, contract awards, subcontracting leads, sales of surplus property and foreign business opportunities

U.S. GOVERNMENT PROCUREMENTS

Services

A Experimental, Developmental, Test and Research Work (research includes both basic and applied research)

Aeronautical Systems Div, Wright-Patterson AFB, OH 45433-6503

A -- ENGINEERING, ANALYSIS AND SYSTEMS ENGINEERING TECHNICAL ASSISTANCE IN SUPPORT OF CLASS II ACFT MODIFICATIONS The successful contractor shall be tasked from time to time to provide intermittent quick reaction in regards to structural, functional, system, electronic and electrical studies and engineering design, structural loads analysis, stress analysis, electrical loads analysis, drafting and provide computer assistance required to accomplish the document Class II acft modifications. The contractor shall provide the computer software and programming support required to maintain, develop, debug and document computer programs. This support shall also be applied to Computer Aided Design and Computer Aided Manufacturing Systems. The Government shall retain ownership of and unlimited rights to use software developed under this contr. All designs must use standard practices and follow applicable Government directives. To qualify to receive an RFP, if and when issued, the response must include the following as a minimum: (1) Describe previous related experience with C-135, C-141, C-130, T-39, HH-53, C-18A, and EC-18B type acft to include contr no., dollar value, DOD or commercial procuring activity and a POC (customer for verification); (2) Describe the facilities avail to perform the required effort; (3) Do you have an approved quality program IAW MIL-Q-9858A? If so, how is it implemented?; (4) Discuss the availability of skilled personnel; i.e., engineers with experience in C-135, C-141, C-130, T-39, HH-53, C-18A, and EC-18B acft, drafting personnel, etc.; (5) Discuss the extent of your experience with military reliability, system safety and configuration control; (6) Systems and engineering capability is required and should be discussed in detail so as to cover qualifications and experience in Systems Engineering. The info contained herein is for planning purposes and does not constitute an invitation for bid or a request for proposal. It is not to be construed as a commitment by the Government. After screening the submittal statements of capability, requests for proposals will be issued to those prospective bidders who in the sole judgment of the Government contr activity have the greatest potential of successfully fulfilling the requirements of the planned procuremet. Receipt of responses will not be acknowledged. It is contemplated a multiple award may be made using a call-type procurement arrangement. Interested sources are requested to submit their response within 30 days after publication of this notice. Contact Attn ASD/PMWB, Richard D. Claussen, 513/255-6134. (347)

Frank M Fountain, Cont Specialist, Cont Mgmt Branch, NIAID, NIH, Westwood Bldg, Rm 707, 5333 Westbard Ave, Bethesda, MD 20892

A -- TARGETING DRUGS FOR AIDS THERAPY TO CENTRAL NERVOUS SYSTEM RFP NIH-NIAID-AIDSP-87-16. Avail approx 1-5-87 with response due approx 3-3-87. The Treatment Branch, AIDS Program, Natl Institute of Allergy and Infectious Diseases, NIH, has a requirement for targeting drugs for AIDS therapy to the central nervous system. The mod to antiviral drugs identified as effective against HTLV-III/LAV/HIV in vitro by the screening efforts of NIAID or drug discovery groups may be required to allow the delivery of drugs to the central nervous system (CNS). The objective of this proposed project is to ensure that efforts will be made now to develop the expertise necessary to deliver drugs to the CNS. The NIAID, in collaboration with the US Army Research Development Command, has established a rapid, large scale, in vitro screening program to evaluate the effectiveness of potential HTLV-III/LAV/HIV drugs. NIAID will undertake the lead role this yr, in collaboration with the NCI, in organizing scientists into groups focused on the discovery of novel drugs for the treatment of AIDS. Thru these efforts and other independent efforts, drugs which will prevent the replication of retroviruses will be identified and developed by the AIDS Program. Drugs which prevent HTLV-III/LAV/HIV replication may cross the blood-brain barrier rapidly (Azidothymidine), slowly (Dideoxycytidine, Ribavirin), or not at all. Recent reports have shown the abiliy to make dihydropyridine derivatives of nucleosides by the attachment of a chemical carrier thru an ester linkage. These modified drugs (termed prodrugs) are greatly enhanced in their ability to cross the blood-brain barrier. The successful development of improved methods for delivery and targeting of effective agents to the CNS will be especially beneficial to halt the progression of the diseases, the spread of the infection, and control a reservoir of the virus. The purpose of this sol is two-fold: First, to modify known antiretroviral drugs to increase their ability to cross the blood-brain barrier; second, to encourage the development of innovative approaches for targeting drugs to the central nervous system. To receive a copy of the RFP supply this office with two self-addressed mailing labels. All inquiries must be in writing: Tel inquiries will not be honored. All responsible sources may submit a proposal which shall be considered by the NIAID. This advertisement does not commit the Govt to award a cont. (349)

Dept of Commerce, Mountain Administrative Suppot Center, Procurement Div, RAS/MC3, 325 Broadway, Boulder, CO 80303-3328

A -- DETERMINATION OF ACCURACY OF TWO-WAY TIME TRANSFER THROUGH KU-BAND SATELLITES. Sol 524-7-00399M. Margaret Shelly 303/497-5101. The National Bureau of Standards (NBS) plans to support the operation of a satellite link to a high stability time scale in order to demonstrate the accuracy of time transfer using the two-way method at KU band. Specific tasks include: configuraton of a KU-band earth station for spread spectrum communication of timing signals using a Hartl-Mitrex modem; operation of the terminal for time comparisons with the NBS system in Boulder, CO and the US Naval Observatory (USNO) system in Washington, DC, and del of time data comparing the resident time scale with both USNO and NBS. Both short-term and long-term stability of the time comparison sys is to be studied. Qualfications include experience with absolute time interval measurements and with operation of satellite earth stations. Work under this contract requires access to a time scale (with stability comparable to that of the time scales at NBS and USNO) as well as a KU band satellite terminal. Place of perform: Ottawa, CN; Period: One yr. It is the Govt's belief that the National Research Council in Canada provides the only other site on this continent (aside from NBS and USNO) with the reqd time scale stability and KU-band satellite station needed to demonstrate the accuracy of this sys thru determination of timing closure between three separate stations. This is not a formal Sol. Interested firms and/or individuals may request to receive a copy of the Req for Quotes when/if it becomes avail. Reqs should ref Synop 524-7-00399M and include a written qualification statement clearly establishing capability to meet the above requirement. Responses will be evaluated and must be recd by the above procurement office within 30 days from the date of this synopsis. In the absence of other qualified sources, it is the intent of the Govt to awd a sole source contract under small purchase procedures to the National Research Council of Canada. This notice may represent the only official notice of such a Sol. See Notes 88 and 22, except that 45 days is changed to read 30 days. (346)

ESD/PKRD (AFSC), Attn: 2Lt Lori Angelillo, Hanscom AFB, MA 01731-5320

A -- CLOUD MEASUREMENTS BY 94GHZ RADAR Contact 2Lt Lori Angelillo 617/377-4894. Contracting Officer: William Manchester 617/377-2257. ESD intends to issue a competitive request for proposal in support of Air Foce Geophysics Laboratory (AFGL) to acquire ground-based meteorological Doppler Radar data at 94GHz frequency (3.2 mm wavelenght) in eastern Massachusetts in conjunction with other radar measurements by the Laboratory. Contractor must provide a transportable radar which can be installed for the winter and spring of 1987. The date which will be generated by these measurements are reflectivity and mean Doppler velocity recorded at muultiple ranges, derived from scans in azimuth and in elevation angle. Data are to be analyzed and delivered in reduced form. Respondents must demonstrate availability of suitable radar equipment and familiarity with meteorological Doppler radar. The forecasted RFP release date is scheduled on or about 6 Dec 86. This subject was previously synopsized 31 Jul 86. Organizations that responded to the 31 Jul 86 sysnopsis need not respond to this contract action. A twenty month effort is contemplated. Organizations with required experience who are interested in receiving an RFP should respond in writing within fifteen days of this publication. Reference RFP F19628-87-R-0028. Tel 617/377-4894. Firms responding should indicate if they are qualified as socially or economically disadvantaged. Respondents should also identify a POC regarding this action. See Note 68. (347)

Rome Air Development Center (PKRL), Griffiss AFB, NY 13441-5700

A -- TERRAIN INTELLIGENCE PROCESSING SYSTEM (TIPS) Sol F30602-87-R-0060. Contact Nancy McCann, 315/330-3844, Contr Specialist, Stanley Damon, 315/330-4827, Program Manager. This acquisition is set aside 100% for small business participation with a size standard of 1,000 employees. Completion 12 months. Perform the implementation of terrain intelligence process to support on and off road movement capability predictions for a variety of vehicles. Included in the implementation is the refinement of the mobility models to provide true-to-life results for specific vehicle types. Contr performance will require storage and facility clearances at the Secret level. Offerors are urged to review the read file by making an appointment 48 hrs in advance by contacting Stanley Damon, 315/330-4827. Read file consists of Terrain Analysis Production System (TAPS) Interim Technical Report; Test Plan; Test Plan APP E Host Background Function Menus; TAPS Host Programmer and Operation Training Matls; TAPS Computer Ops Manuals Vol I Host Subsystem, Vol II Graphics Subsystem and APP C Micro-descriptor Data Dictionary; TAPS Program Maint Manuals Vol I Host Subsystem, Vol II Host Batch Applications, and Vol III Graphic Subsystem; RADC TR 82-167 Dynamic Ground Target Assessment Techniques Project. All responsible sources may submit a proposal which shall be considered. Responses must reference Code I-7-4742-L. (347)

US Dept of Energy, Environmental Measurements Lab, 376 Hudson St, New York, NY 10014

A -- CORRECTION: ULTRA LOW-LEVEL ANALYSIS OF FRESHWATER SEDIMENT SAMPLES due 02-09-87. POC Richard C Tyson, Contr Officer, 212/620-3604. Analysis of approx 300 sediment samples of 21 elements: Al, As, Be, Ca, Cd, Cr, Cu, Fe, Hg, Mn, Ni, Pb, Sb, Sc, Se, Sn, Sr, Ti, Tl, V, Zn and total organic carbon. Total solution by normal or high pressure digetion of fusion with a flux, as well as acid leaching should be used to analyze Al, Fe, Mn, Sc, Ti, and V. Hydride generation, cold vapor atomic absorption spectrometry, combustion technique, or other appropriate methods should be used for As, Hg and Se. Other elements are to be analyzed according to acceptable methods suggested by the contractor. Ea sample will consist of 5 to 25 grams of dry sediment or the equivalent set sediment. The RFP will be issued approx 15 days from publication of this notice, deadline for receipt of proposals will be approx 45 days from issuance of the RFP. Written requests only will be honored for the RFP on a first-come first-served basis until the supply of 50 copies is exhausted. The Environmental Measurements Lab anticipates that no more than $100,000 will be avail for this contr; a fixed price contr is contemplated. Selection of contractor will be based on evaluation of proposals by an evaluation panel. (349)

Rome Air Development Center, (PKRL), Griffis AFB, NY 13441-5700

A -- FUSION PROCESSING SUPPORT STUDY Sol F30602-87-R-0051. Contact Nancy McCann, 315/330-3844, Contract Specialists; Joseph Antonik, 315/330-2344, Program Manager. Completion twelve months. Perform an analysis to determine the display requirements for advanced sensor correlation and fusion algorithms and analyze state-of-the-art display methodologies such as animation, 3-D, perspective displays and other unique graphical representations of information to determine their applicability to

Content

FIGURE 8.8 *Commerce Business Daily*

Locate the Criteria for Evaluation

Because the proposal is evaluated against other proposals, if you are the proposer, then you will want to follow the instructions and supply all the requested information. Your proposal will be evaluated on the basis of your responses to the guidelines. For the evaluation, some guidelines even provide

```
2/5/4
0996511
 TRAINING AND TECHNICAL ASSISTANCE FOR IMPROVING THE EFFICIENCY AND
EFFECTIVENESS OF THE JUVENILE JUSTICE SYSTEM IN COMBATING SERIOUS,
HABITUAL JUVENILE CRIME.   The contractor will be  required to perform
tasks consisting of Project Design and Orientation, Design and Delivery
of Technical Assistance, Design  and  Delivery of  Training Activity,
Curriculum  Development,  etc.    The  period of performance will be 12
months, with options for extensions not to exceed a total of 36 months.
The proposals  will be  evaluated by the following criteria:  Key Staff
Qualifications  (25%),   Organization  and   Management   Plan  (30%),
Organizational  Experience   and  Capability  (25%),  Understanding  of
Juvenile Justice/Criminal Justice Issues and Objectives of Training and
Technical  Assistance  (10%),  and  Cost  and Budget (10%).  Interested
offerors should submit request in writing  for RFP  No. OJP-85-R-009 to
the above address.  See note 64 and 65. (149)
 Sponsor:  Office  of  Justice  Programs,  Office  of  the Comptroller,
Contracts Division, 633 Indiana  Avenue,  N.W.  Room  1207, Washington,
D.C. 20531.  Attn: George Moody
 Subfile: PSE (U.S. GOVERNMENT PROCUREMENTS, SERVICES)
 Section Heading: H Expert and Consultant Services
CBD Date: June 5, 1987
```

FIGURE 8.9 A government RFP

the number of points you can receive for each section of your proposal. The Department of Education provides an example of evaluation guidelines in Figure 8.10.

§745.29 Evaluation criteria.

   The evaluation criteria in §§ 745.30–745.34 apply to an application for a general grant. The evaluation criteria in §§ 745.30–745.35 apply to an application for a small grant. The number of points awarded for each criterion depends on how well the application addresses all the factors under the criterion. The total possible score for a general grant application is 100 points. The total possible score for a small grant application is 105 points.

Sec.
745.30 Evaluation criterion: Need and impact. (24 points)
745.31 Evaluation criterion: Objectives. (16 points)
745.32 Evaluation criterion: Plan of operation. (40 points)
745.33 Evaluation criterion: Applicant's commitment to educational
          equity for women. (10 points)
745.34 Evaluation criterion: Staff qualifications. (10 points)
745.35 Evaluation criterion: Innovative approaches. (5 points)

FIGURE 8.10 Evaluation criteria for a government grant

Organize the Sections of the Proposal

When the government issues an RFP for the design and construction of a space shuttle to take people to the moon, for example, large companies like Rockwell International respond with a proposal to do the project. The proposal may be well over a hundred pages long. Many people contribute to the information that goes into the proposal, and the sections are written by different people. Eventually, the sections and supporting materials are compiled into a single document that is submitted in response to the government's request for a proposal to design and construct the space shuttle.

Because of the complexity and size of a formal proposal, an outline is an essential step. The outline provides an overview of the proposal and a schedule for the contributors. Most formal proposals include the customary sections found in any proposal plus subsections that vary with the nature of the proposal. The outline for a formal proposal has to be adaptable, but standard parts of the proposal, as well as secondary elements, are presented in Figure 8.11.[1] Module 9 discusses in detail the secondary elements that accompany formal proposals and reports.

Typically, the parts of a proposal are these:

    Executive Summary
    Introduction
    Objective(s) ⎫
    Scope   ⎬ May be combined
    Benefits to the Client
    Statement of the Problem
    Technical Approach
    Program Organization ⎫
    Program Management ⎬ May be combined
    Biographical Sketches of Assigned Personnel
    Time and Price
    Description of Proposing Organization
      (Related Experience, Related Facilities)
    Appendixes (if needed).

usually preceded by

    Letter of Transmittal
    Cover Page
    Table of Contents

FIGURE 8.11 Parts of a formal proposal
Source: Adalene S. Flechtner, "The Marketable Proposal," in *Proceedings*, 33d International Technical Communication Conference, 1986: 417. Used with permission of the Society for Technical Communication.

Whether you combine some of these parts to compile a separate section or change the order, all this information must be presented.

Professional proposal writers suggest using an "annotated outline" with headings for the proposal on the left-hand side and discussion and selling points on the right-hand side, illustrated in Figure 8.12.

Outline	Content
EXECUTIVE SUMMARY	Nontechnical summary of proposal.
INTRODUCTION	Why this document at this time. What is offered. Understanding of the problem.
TECHNICAL APPROACH	
Task 1. Evaluation of . . . Objective Proposed Approach Anticipated Result	Be specific about what you are going to do. Cite recent experience to support proposed approach, for example, "This method was successfully used/developed in work on. . . ." "On the basis of our experience with. . . ." Be specific about expected result or deliverable item. Show relationship to other tasks.
Task 2. Investigation of. . . . Objective Proposed Approach Anticipated Result	
PROGRAM ORGANIZATION AND MANAGEMENT	Program organization chart. Qualify supervisory staff in one or two sentences. Describe management procedures to be used to control schedule and costs. Include schedule chart.
KEY PERSONNEL	Include biographical sketch for each proposed team member, tailored to his or her particular role in the project.
RELATED EXPERIENCE	Demonstrate by specific examples.

FACILITIES	Describe those that will be used, for example, computer, chemistry laboratories.
	Photographs.
PROPOSING ORGANIZATION	Brief description of company and its capabilities.

FIGURE 8.12 Annotated outline for a proposal

Source: Adalene S. Flechtner, "The Marketable Proposal," in *Proceedings*, 33d International Technical Communication Conference, 1986: 418. Used with permission of the Society for Technical Communication.

When the proposal is a team effort, the technical authors and managers write the technical approach and the program management sections; the technical writer can also write the nontechnical portions of the proposal, such as the executive summary, the introduction, the facilities, and the description of the company. The executive summary precedes the introduction and emphasizes the results, conclusions, and recommendations. It is written for decision makers who want to read a thorough but brief review of the major points and have enough information to make a decision. Module 10 further explains the executive summary.

The introduction includes the background, the problem, the objectives of the proposal and the significance to the company—all those elements already discussed in the informal proposal. The facilities include descriptions of the laboratory or other places in which the work will be accomplished as well as descriptions of the mechanisms that will be used for the project. These descriptions of mechanisms and facilities are discussed in detail in Module 6. A description of the company is usually a combination of the history of the company (see Module 10) and a description of what the company does. Most companies keep updated descriptions of their company (and employees' résumés) on file so that they may incorporate these descriptions into proposals and reports.

The writer can also start collecting résumés and drafting the table of contents (if needed), the cover page, and the letter of transmittal. Each section in the proposal should contribute to the total marketing impact, with all writers alert "for any opportunity to reinforce the marketing message," suggested in Figure 8.13.[2]

Make a Checklist of Material to Accompany the Proposal

The National Science Foundation (NSF) issues a booklet on submitting proposals to the government. This booklet provides clear instructions on the content of the proposal and a checklist for ensuring that you are enclosing

Proposal Section	Marketing Strategy
Executive Summary	This is the opportunity to sell top management. Be sure to point out features that will possibly influence a decision to buy—such as features that competing firms cannot offer. Summarize the benefits.
Introduction	If your technical staff has made a particularly insightful analysis of the work to be done, use it to demonstrate that you really understand the problem.
Objective and Scope	Be sure your objective is the customer's objective; that it is realistic and achievable. Scope should be manageable within time and money proposed.
Benefits to Customer	Benefits may be enumerated in a separate section, or woven into the text. If appropriate, do both.
Technical Approach	The technical authors who write this part are very good at describing what they will do and how they will do it. What often is overlooked is "why"—and this could be a determining factor in acceptance or rejection. It is sometimes effective to describe several possible approaches, and the advantages and disadvantages of each. Then, "We have proposed this approach because. . . ."
Program Organization	The strategy here should be to show that you have a feasible plan for getting the work done and have identified qualified people to do it.
Program Management	Tell the customer that his work will be reviewed by a top manager and will not be treated routinely. Assure him that adequate controls for costs and schedule are in place. If you plan to use a sophisticated, computerized management system, describe it. Describe reporting plans for keeping the customer informed of progress. Point out milestones where customer can change direction if he wishes.
Key Personnel	The bios present an excellent opportunity to improve the marketability of the proposal. Each one should be tailored to the specific

	requirements of the assignment, to convince the customer that the staff can do the work. Don't be modest; if your man has an international reputation in his field, say so. Use the same format for all bios.
Time and Cost	Estimates must be reasonable in light of work proposed.
Related Experience	Point out that your company has successfully performed work directly related to what is being proposed—and say how it is related.
Related Facilities	Emphasize particularly any facilities you have that others may not have, or equipment you have that will not have to be acquired.
Proposing Organization	Describe capabilities that relate to the proposed work, call attention to the combination of skills you can provide, your overseas staff if the scope of work is international, or whatever will give you a competitive edge.

FIGURE 8.13 Marketing strategies within the proposal
Source: Adalene S. Flechtner, "The Marketable Proposal," in *Proceedings*, 33d International Technical Communication Conference, 1986:419. Used with permission of the Society for Technical Communication.

all necessary information with the proposal. Figure 8.14 reproduces some of the information from the **NSF Guidelines for Preparation of Proposals.** These guidelines begin to give you some idea of the length and complexity of a formal proposal.

Remaining on Schedule—The Progress Report

Proposals require an expenditure of time, effort, and money. Often the sponsoring agency, the client, or the employer wants to know how the project is progressing. A progress report provides this information. Some proposals have progress reports listed among the tasks for the project. In Figure 8.3, the schedule for the proposal included monthly reports on the progress of the project. Besides keeping the agency or client informed, progress reports are also another checklist for the proposer, who can evaluate the tasks against a timetable and assess the current and future activities.

Checklist for Proposal Submission

Complete proposals help to expedite review and assist the applicant to meet a planned program. To assure that research proposals submitted to the Foundation are complete, an administrative check should be made before mailing.

☐ Cover page (use required format in Appendix II), addressed to specific NSF program, if known.

☐ Appropriate boxes under REMARKS on cover page checked.

☐ All required signatures (principal investigator, co-principal investigators, and organizational) on Cover Page.

☐ NSF Form 1153, Appendix III.

☐ Human Subjects Certification, if required.

☐ Recombinant DNA Certification, if required.

☐ Table of contents.

☐ Project summary (less than 200 words) is required but use of format in Appendix IV is optional.

☐ Summary of progress to date and its relation to proposed work (renewals only).

☐ Detailed description of proposed research.

☐ Bibliography of pertinent literature.

☐ Vitae of all senior personnel.

☐ Current list of main publications (in last 5 years) of senior personnel (major publications currently in press may be listed).

☐ Budget in requested format.

☐ Brief description and justification of major items of requested equipment.

☐ Current and pending support (see Appendix VI).

☐ List or description of available facilities and major items of equipment to be used in the proposed research.

☐ Required number of copies of the proposal, including the original signed copy (see Appendix VIII and IX).

☐ Residual Funds Statement, if required.

☐ Proposal packages addressed to Data Support Services Section, NSF (See Where to Submit, p. 2.)

FIGURE 8.14 Checklist from the NSF guidelines for preparing proposals

Progress reports include

- introduction
- work statement
- summary of tasks completed and tasks remaining
- timetable
- appraisal and forecast

Introduction
The introduction briefly reviews the contract between the agency or client and the proposer. It restates the date and purpose of the agreement and the procedure for accomplishing the goal.

Work Statement
The work statement essentially repeats the precise proposal and the procedures section of the proposal.

Summary of Tasks Completed and Tasks Remaining
The section of the progress report summarizing tasks discusses each of the tasks. For the tasks completed, you should describe what was accomplished, how long it took, and whether there were any difficulties. Under tasks remaining, you will have to describe what has yet to be done and how the remaining activities will affect the completion of the project. Because this section of the report is the most important, you should consider a visual, a timetable, or a schedule to supplement your discussion of tasks completed and tasks remaining.

Appraisal and Forecast
The appraisal summarizes the report and evaluates the progress to date; the forecast describes the future activities and predicts the success of the project.
The report in Figure 8.15 illustrates an informal progress report.

Glowiak & Associates   Consulting Engineers   LaGrange, Illinois 60678

September 19, 19XX

Mr. Lloyd Alton
Chief Engineer
Alton Engineering
LaGrange, Illinois 60678

Dear Mr. Alton:

After receiving your acceptance of our proposal on July 19, 19XX, Glowiak & Associates began work immediately on designing the automobile turntable for your showroom. This letter reports on the progress to date.

PROPOSAL
We proposed to study existing designs and to design an automobile turntable that is lightweight and easily portable and can be operated continuously over long periods of time at a minimum cost.

PROCEDURE
The basic procedure for formulating this design involves five tasks, to be completed within three months from the date of the agreement.
    Task one: Conduct a patent and literature search to determine previous work accomplished.

Task two: Perform finite element stress analysis to determine structural support requirements to sustain a 4-ton vehicle.

Task three: Compare and evaluate types of roller element packages and motor drive systems.

Task four: Select motor drive system and roller element package.

Task five: Build scale model of turntable and provide design specs.

TASKS COMPLETED

Task one: Essentially, we have completed our literature search and analysis of prior art turntables.

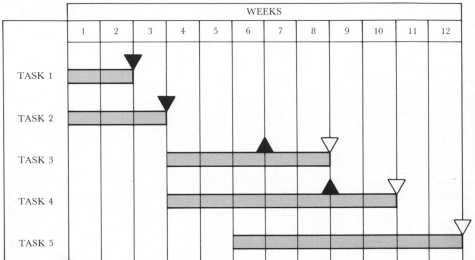

▼ Completed

▲ Progress to date

▽ Expected completion date

Schedule for automobile turntable

Task two: We have completed our stress analysis on structures to support 4-ton vehicles. The display turntable will have a capacity of 4 tons, diameter of 18 feet, and height of 14 inches. The turntable will be completely enclosed and will provide a device so that electricity will be available on the surface of the turntable. Safety will be a primary consideration in this design.

TASKS REMAINING

Tasks three and four: We have evaluated roller element packages and motor drive systems and narrowed our selection to two packages and two systems. But we will not make a final decision until we test the packages and systems on structures. We are presently doing this testing and will probably modify both the roller element package and motor drive system. Depending on availability of parts, we do not see any problems with our schedule.

Task five: We are building the turntable to scale. When we have finished, we will compile the design specs.

FORECAST
We are on schedule with all tasks (see attached schedule). Because we will have to modify the roller element package and the motor drive system, we will have to spend more time testing these components than we originally predicted. However, we are beginning our testing sooner than we originally planned, and we are adding another designer to the project of building the turntable to scale. We expect to complete the project on time.

If you have any questions about this project, please do not hesitate to call me at (412) 569-3478.

Sincerely yours,

Pat Moore
Project Engineer

FIGURE 8.15 Progress report
Source: Adapted from Suzanne Glowiak, Technical Writing 421, Illinois Institute of Technology.

Summary

A proposal is an offer to perform a service. Either the proposer or the client can initiate a proposal. If the client requests a service, the proposal is *solicited.* If the proposer offers a service, the proposal is *unsolicited.* The proposal may be submitted as a letter, a memo, or a report, but whatever the format, the proposal answers three basic questions: What do you propose to do? How do you propose to do it? How much will it cost the buyer?

The letter and memo are considered *informal* proposals, the memo more informal than the letter, because of their brief length. In the letter, the *introduction* is the place to introduce yourself and your company to your potential client, state the *problem* and propose a *project.* Because the client is the most important factor in the proposal, you have to stress the *significance* of the project to the client and state your *interest* in the client's problem. *Headings* in the introduction and throughout the proposal help the readers find answers to their questions about you and your proposal.

After the introduction the next section provides technical details about the *procedures* to solve the problem. The procedures include the *steps* you will follow, the *schedule* to complete the project, and the *cost* to the buyer for goods and services. The final section of the proposal summarizes the proposer's *credentials* and explains the *feasibility* of accomplishing the project.

On-the-job proposals are often submitted as memos; although they usually do not have to include credentials, they do include the other sections presented under the appropriate headings. *Evaluate* proposals for a purpose statement that is precise but does not provide the solution before the project begins, procedures listed in parallel structure, and assurance of expertise in the problem.

The *formal* proposal is presented in a *report* format; frequently, it is long, detailed, and requires a team effort. When the government or a private company issues a request for services, the request is called a *request for a proposal (RFP)*. The RFP usually includes *guidelines* for writing and submitting the proposal. The *Commerce Business Daily* announces services that the federal government needs. The guidelines establish the sections and the *evaluation criteria* for the proposal. Because formal proposals may be long and detailed collaborative efforts, it is important to organize the contents of the proposal, annotating the outline with points to be discussed and marketing strategies within the proposal. Finally, before submitting the proposal, review the *checklist* to ensure that all the necessary primary and secondary elements accompany the proposal.

After the sponsoring agency or the client accepts the proposal, the agreement may call for *progress reports*. Progress reports keep the agency or client informed and provide a checklist for the proposer who can evaluate the past, current, and future activities against a timetable. Progress reports include an introduction, a work statement, a summary of tasks completed and tasks remaining, a timetable, and an appraisal and forecast of the completion of the project.

Checklist for a Proposal

You should review your proposal section by section. Some of the items that follow are more appropriate for the formal proposal than for the informal letter or memo proposal. Those items are marked with an asterisk (*). Check only those items to which you can give a positive response.

THE PRIMARY SECTIONS
Does the **introduction** include
_____ background?

_____ problem?

_____ precise proposal?

_____ significance?

Has the **procedures** section
_____ *theory?

_____ detailed steps and objectives?

_____ *rationale?

_____   time schedule?

_____   Does the **budget** section cover
           goods?

_____   services?

_____   *Is the **bibliography** section current?

_____   Is the **credentials** section credible?

_____   *Is the **facilities** section adequate?

***THE SECONDARY ELEMENTS
(FOR A FORMAL PROPOSAL ONLY)**
Does the formal proposal require

_____   transmittal letter?

_____   title page?

_____   abstract?

_____   table of contents?

_____   list of illustrations?

_____   glossary (optional)?

_____   attachments?

THE PROGRESS REPORT
Does the progress report

_____   restate the agreement and the date?

_____   describe the purpose and procedure for the project?

_____   review the tasks completed and the tasks remaining?

_____   provide a schedule or timetable for the remaining tasks?

_____   summarize the work to date?

_____   predict the completion of the project?

_____   Have you edited for *visual* and *stylistic techniques,* using
           headings and subheadings?

_____   numbered or bulleted lists?

_____   visual figure of the project schedule?

_____   parallel structure?

Notes

1. Adalene S. Flechtner, "The Marketable Proposal," in *Proceedings*, 33d International Technical Communication Conference (Washington, D.C.: Society for Technical Communication, 1986): 417–420. This article provided the background material for the section on organizing the formal proposal.
2. Flechtner, "The Marketable Proposal."

References

R. Dennis Green, "The Graphics Oriented (GO) Proposal Primer: Harnessing the Power of Data in Graphics," in *Proceedings*, 32d International Technical Communication Conference (Washington, D.C.: Society for Technical Communication, 1985): VC 30–33. This article suggests using a graphic presentation for a proposal.

Michael P. Jordan, "The Thread of Continuity in Functional Writing," *The Journal of Business Communication* 19:4 (1982):5–22.

George E. Kennedy, "Teaching Formal Proposals: A Versatile Minicourse in Technical Writing," *Journal of Technical Writing and Communication* 13 (1983): 123–137.

Norton J. Kiritz, "The Proposal Summary," The Grantsmanship Center News 8 (October–November 1974).

Judith H. Marcus, "Proposal Management in a Small Organization—Everyone's Responsibility," in *Proceedings*, 31st International Technical Communication Conference (Washington, D.C.: Society for Technical Communication, 1984): MPD 69–72.

Applying Your Knowledge

EXERCISE 8.1

After reading the faulty proposal in Figure 8.7, edit the content and redesign the propoal. Use headings and formatting techniques. If necessary, see Module 5—Design and Visual Aids—for techniques.

For the next two exercises, collaborate with another writer.

EXERCISE 8.2

What tone do you think the headings achieve for Figure 8.4 and Figure 8.6? What headings do you prefer and why? Describe the audience and purpose that determine your headings.

After you consider the headings, design two charts, one to illustrate the schedule for Figure 8.4 and another to illustrate the schedule for Figure 8.6. Compare the two illustrations; are they substantially different despite the headings?

EXERCISE 8.3

Using the following information, write a proposal to perform the service needed by the Medical Records Transcription Department. Be sure to include who is doing the service and why (background), what is being done (purpose), and how to do it (procedure).

The Medical Records Transcription Department has expressed a desire to study its system for recording transcriptions, with an eye toward motivating typists to maximize production while minimizing cost to the hospital. Presently, the system includes sending excess transcription work to outside typing agencies. As the management director of MacNeal Memorial Hospital, you are aware that an equitable incentive pay system can raise output by rewarding employees (typists and word processors) for their extra effort. A higher level of production results in a savings to the hospital. An incentive system shares the portion of the savings generated by an employee with the employee, thus increasing motivation to produce even more. A further benefit of the wage incentive system is a more satisfied employee who will stay on the job longer and do a better job while there. Most industrial concerns use some sort of wage incentive plan, and in the past few years many nonprofit institutions have been examining this area as a way to contain costs.

After establishing standards for a wage incentive system, you have to apply the standards to the transcription area of MacNeal Memorial Hospital. At some time in the project you must calculate the costs to the hospital for the new system and compare them to the present system of sending excess transcription work to outside typing service agencies. Finally, if the system is accepted, you will provide instructions to implement the wage incentive system.

EXERCISE 8.4

After reading the following document, use a typewriter or computer and
1. Write a proposal to your boss offering to do the project.
2. Invent a procedure to follow to complete the project.
3. Place the appropriate details under the main procedures.

In preparing texts for various technical papers, many writers are frustrated because they do not understand the design process that turns their text into a final, printed form for brochures, style sheets, or simply a printed page.

They need a basic understanding of the process and terms used by the designer and typographer to prepare a mechanical. A mechanical is the final design form that contains all the text and art copy, ready to be reproduced. At this point in the reproduction process, the designer may consult with the writer about questions concerning the text, and it is helpful if the writer understands the design terms. (State your purpose and organizational strategy here.)

Procedures
Information retrieval (2 weeks)
Report design (2 weeks)
Final draft (2 weeks)

Details
- Search the literature.
- Read and gather information.
- Edit the material.
- Organize the information.
- Write rough draft.
- Evaluate the document.
- Prepare final draft.

WRITING ASSIGNMENT

Write an informal proposal to perform a service, manage a project, conduct research, examine a problem, or recommend a solution. This proposal should be realistic because its content may become the subject of your final report for the course in technical writing. Your instructor may accept the proposal and ask you to complete the project. If so, then the proposal becomes the contract to complete the work and to evaluate your final project.

MODULE 9

Evaluation/ Feasibility Reports: Primary and Secondary Elements

When you have to consider options or products and choose one, then you have an evaluation to write. This module explains how to evaluate products or plans. A multiple evaluation compares the features of two or more products; a feasibility study compares two or more plans or ideas. In business and industry, this type of report is common because companies have to purchase products to continue their operations and consider alternate plans or ideas to improve their services. Both reports require the same elements: a needs analysis, the selection of criteria, a method of evaluation, a discussion, a recommendation, visual aids, and headings to focus the reader's attention. This module describes each of these elements.

The reader uses the evaluation to choose the most appropriate product or desirable plan based on qualitative and quantitative factors. Depending on the reader, the organization follows one of two persuasive strategies: inductive or deductive organizing. Both strategies require the careful and thorough selection of standards and specifications. This module will aid you in the selection of those criteria and in the presentation and discussion of your data and results.

Although these studies of products or plans may be written in memo or letter format, they are usually submitted as formal reports. For a formal report, the primary sections remain the same, but some secondary elements accompany the multiple evaluation/feasibility study. These secondary elements are discussed in this module, but they may accompany any formal report. When submitting a formal report, you should make a checklist of secondary elements that will accompany your report.

Scope

In this module you will learn to

1. Conduct a needs analysis.
2. Organize the report to meet the reader's needs.
3. Explain the difference between standards and specifications.
4. Write a list of criteria in parallel structure.
5. Develop a method to evaluate the product/plan.
6. Construct tables to present data and evaluations.
7. Use the discussion to explain constraints and judgments.
8. Make a recommendation based on the criteria and evaluations.
9. Draft a checklist of secondary elements to accompany the report.

Preparing Information for the Evaluation

Let's say that you are the clinical engineer at St. Anthony Hospital, and Nurse Pearlman has asked you to recommend an electrocardiograph (ECG) monitor/defibrillator that will cost no more than $6,500.00. How will you begin to review the available units on the market, evaluate them, and recommend one for purchase? This problem is the main concern of multiple evaluation and feasibility studies. Given two or more plans or products, how will you select the one most appropriate for the project? First, you must assess needs and establish relevant criteria to meet these needs. Then you have to list the possible plans or products, and finally you have to evaluate each of the plans or products against the criteria and recommend the one likely to be the most successful for the project.

To break the project into its tasks, ask a number of questions:

1. Am I evaluating products or plans (ideas)?
2. What do the users need the product/plan to do?
3. Does the product/plan fit into a larger project, or is it an end in itself?
4. Are several products/plans available on the market?
5. Will I present options only or make a recommendation?
6. In my report, what information does the decision maker need first?
7. How will the clients evaluate my recommendation for product/plan?

Usually, when you are evaluating products, you will write an evaluation report; when you study plans or ideas, you will write a feasibility report.

Assessing Needs

Before you can evaluate the products on the market, you must analyze the needs of the users. A needs analysis or assessment

- Surveys people who are going to buy and use the product/plan.
- Reviews the options available on the market.
- Attempts to assign priorities to the list of needs.

In the example of the ECG monitor, you will have to interview the nurses, doctors, engineers, and business managers who are going to buy, use, or repair the instrument.

The engineers want an ECG monitor that

- Operates on an AC line instead of on batteries that can fail.
- Isolates the patient leads from the ground to achieve low leakage current.
- Charges the defibrillator in less than 15 seconds.
- Has a low repair record and excellent service manuals.

The nurses and physicians want an ECG monitor that has

- A nonfade digital display with **freeze** capability.
- A digital heart rate meter with high and low alarm settings.
- Defibrillator energy delivering an output greater than 300 joules.
- A hard copy recording of the ECG signal.

The business manager wants a report that recommends the two best instruments within the budget and allows the nurses and doctors to choose one.

Interviewing the people who buy, use, and repair the instrument tells you about their priorities and their preferences as well as their needs. You can also review the options available on the market. At least 10 companies make ECG monitors/defibrillators, and they all produce brochures describing their instrument and praising their reliability. These brochures may describe other features you can add to the users' list of needs. After you compile this list of needs, distribute it to your users and ask them to assign priorities to the items on the list. With this information, you are now ready to establish criteria to measure the product/plan and organize your report-writing tasks.

Organizing the Report

Once you assess the needs of the consumers and gather data on the products/ plans available, you can begin to analyze the information you have collected and organize it for your study. Your overall plan is to include information on

- the client's problem
- the purpose for the evaluation
- available products or plans on the market
- standards and specifications

- your method of evaluation
- your rationale for your selection
- your recommendation.

In organizing this study, your report, like most reports, begins with an introduction. The introduction establishes the context for the report by providing information on the background of the problem, the purpose of the evaluation, and an overview of your organizational strategy.

The next section in your report depends on the consumer. To be fair and objective, you have to present the reader with a number of feasible options. When you present several options and draw a conclusion, you are developing a persuasive piece of writing. Because an evaluation or feasibility study is a persuasive piece of writing, you have to decide how to present your information so that the reader accepts your decision.

Persuasive writing is introduced in Module 3 on organization and appears again in Modules 8 and 12. Whereas the information you present must be accurate and complete, the order in which you present the information can influence the reader. The consumer may want to know the results of the evaluation immediately without having to read the entire document. In that case, your recommendation should follow the introduction section. When the conclusion precedes the data, you are using the **deductive** strategy of organizing information, a strategy that presents a general statement first and then supports it with specific information. Or your technical consumer may prefer the more conventional strategy of stating the problem, gathering data, and then drawing a conclusion. The strategy of presenting the detailed information first and then drawing a conclusion is **inductive.**

Figure 9.1 drafts the flowchart for both organizational strategies, depending on the needs of the reader. Whatever organization you use, notice that both strategies include sections on standards and specifications, method of evaluation, and a discussion (your rationale) of your selection.

Establishing Standards and Specifications

Criteria are the yardsticks for evaluating all the items under consideration. When evaluating products or plans for a project, you must evaluate each item against the same criteria. The criteria are determined by the needs of the consumer or the goals of the project. You establish the criteria for evaluating the product or plan by analyzing the needs and listing them. In technical writing, the criteria for measuring and describing items, particularly scientific and technical items, are called **standards** and **specifications.**

Standards are the general categories for scientific and technical measure, such as portability and durability; specifications are the actual measurements and accurate data, such as maximum weight of 4.5 kg. If you wanted to help a consumer select the most suitable calculator for a science laboratory, for example, you might determine that the calculator must be

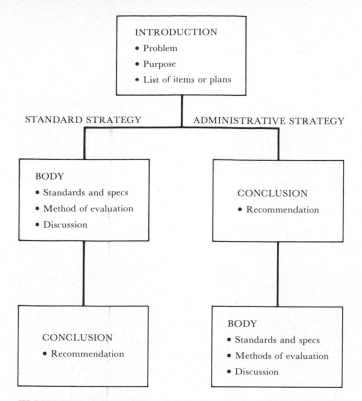

FIGURE 9.1 Flowchart for an evaluation report

pocket-size and economical, perform basic scientific functions, and have a battery with a long life—all standards for the calculator.

When listing the standards and specifications, you should decide on a stylistic structure for presenting them. You may list them either in sentences or in partial statements, but they must be listed in consistent and *parallel structure*. Module 4 on style discusses parallel structure in detail. For standards listed in sentences, you may use the following style for parallel structure:

- The calculator must have basic scientific functions.
- The calculator must be programmable.
- It must have a number of memories.
- It must have a long-life battery.
- It must be pocket-size.
- It must be cost-efficient.

To list the standards in phrases, you should use the following construction:

The calculator must have

- basic scientific functions
- programmable steps
- several memories

- lifetime or energy-saving batteries
- appropriate size to fit into a pocket
- reasonable cost

SPECIFICATIONS

Print Speed

- 180 characters per second (cps) @ 10 characters per inch (cpi) (high speed)
- 108 cps @ 12 cpi (Elite)
- 154 cps @ 17 cpi (condensed)
- 90 cps @ 10 cpi (correspondence)
- 30 cps @ 10 cpi (NLQ)

Print Method

- Impact, 18 pin dot-matrix, 2x9 staggered arrangement

Print Head Life

- 200 million impressions per pin

Print Matrix

- Pica dual pass — 21x18
- Elite dual pass — 19x14
- Pica high density — 13x9
- Elite high speed — 11x7
- Pica high speed — 7x9
- Expanded characters — 14x9
- Condensed characters — 7x9
- Proportionally-spaced dual pass — 21xn
- Proportionally-spaced high density — 13xn

Print Line

- P2
  —80 characters @ 10 cpi
  —96 characters @ 12 cpi
  —136 characters @ 17 cpi
- P3
  —136 characters @ 10 cpi
  —163 characters @ 12 cpi
  —233 characters @ 17 cpi

Dot Size

- 0.012-inch (0.3 mm)

Dot Spacing

- 1/240-inch horizontal and vertical

Vertical Line Spacing

- 6 or 8 lines per inch (lpi) or n/120 lpi

International Character Sets

- United States
- United Kingdom
- Germany
- Sweden
- France
- Italy
- Spain
- Denmark*
- Norway*
- Netherlands*
- Greece*
- Plus: download custom character sets

Paper Feed

- Friction Feed — standard
- Adjustable, snap-on, tractor — option (P2 & P3)
- Cut sheet guide — option (P2 & P3)
- Bidirectional tractor — option (P2 & P3)
- Automatic cut sheet feeder — option (P2 & P3)

Ribbon

- Endless loop, black fabric cassette, 2.2 million character life on P2
- Endless loop, black fabric cassette, 3.3 million character life on P3

Copies

- Original and 3 copies

Paper Size

- P2
  4-1/2 to 10 inches
- P3
  5 to 16 inches

Interface

- IBM PC
- RS 232C
- Industry-standard parallel
- 3.5K-character buffer

Environmental

- Operating temperature, humidity: 41° to 100 °F (5° to 38° C), 30 to 85% RH (noncondensing)
- Storage temperature, humidity: -13° to 140° F (-25° to 60° C), 0 to 90% RH (noncondensing)

Dimensions

- P2
  Width: 16.1 inches (410 mm)
  Depth: 13.1 inches (335 mm)
  Height: 4.0 inches (125 mm)
  Weight: 17.6 pounds (8.0 kg)
- P3
  Width: 22.4 inches (570 mm)
  Depth: 13.1 inches (335 mm)
  Height: 4.9 inches (125 mm)
  Weight: 24.3 pounds (11 kg)

Power Required

- 115 Vac ± 15%, 50/60 Hz
- 230 Vac ± 15%, 50/60 Hz

Acoustic Noise

- 62 dBA — high-speed mode
- 64 dBA — high-density mode

Reliability

- MTBF: 4000 hours
- MTTR: 20 minutes

Administrative Compliance

- UL 478
- CSA C22.2
- FCC Class B
- VDE 0806, 0871

* Depending on model.

This data sheet contains preliminary information and is subject to change without notice. For the latest information on the NEC Pinwriter, contact your nearest NEC Information Systems sales office.

NEC

NEC Information Systems, Inc.
1414 Mass. Ave., Boxborough, MA 01719

Pinwriter and Pin Mate are trademarks of NEC Corporation

Printed in U.S.A. Copyright 6-84 819-000130-2D01 Rev. 02

FIGURE 9.2 Specifications for the NEC Pinwriter™ Series Dot Matrix Printer P2/P3

Used with permission of NEC Information Systems, Inc.

When the standards are made more specific, so that actual measurements or quantities are stated, then you are listing specifications. In actuality, specifications are more narrowly defined or limited standards. In the example of the scientific calculator, for a standard the evaluator suggests that the calculator must be able to perform basic scientific functions, and the consumer adds the following specifications about the functions: "The scientific calculator must be able to perform logarithmic, trigonometric, statistical, and linear regression functions." The evaluator established the general principle for evaluating the calculator, and the consumer narrowed the standard to specifications.[1]

One way to establish standards and specifications if you are unsure about the consumer's needs is to examine the product literature of the items you are evaluating. You must establish criteria carefully to be both ethical and thorough. The criteria are the basis for your evaluation and final recommendation. If you have neglected certain criteria to make your case for a particular option stronger, then your reader will have reason to consider your report unethical. When you omit criteria rather than mention them and then dismiss them as irrelevant to the decision, the report will be incomplete. To avoid both charges, carefully consider all the criteria and then discuss the reasons for your choices. Writing to several manufacturers for their product brochures will secure you enough information to develop an informed standards and specifications list.

Figure 9.2 illustrates the standards and specifications that product literature supplies.

In the construction field, contractors must meet the electrical codes by using specific materials when they install outside conductors. These specifications are listed as articles in the latest edition (at the time of printing) of the National Electrical Code:[2]

> Article 310-11B CONDUCTORS FOR GENERAL WIRING
> B. Method of Marking
>   4. Optional Marking of Wire Size. For the following multiconductor
>   cables, the information required in (a) (4) above shall be permitted to
>   be marked on the surface of the individual insulated conductors.
>   a. Type MC (metal-clad) cable.
>   b. Tray cable.
>   c. Irrigation cable.
>   d. Power-limited tray cable

Often the needs include both general and specific features, so you may use the heading **Standards and Specifications** to list all the features. If the reader needs explanations to better understand the standards and specifications, then you should also include definitions, as the writer did in Figure 9.3.

Explaining the Method of Evaluation

You must explain your method for evaluating the items so that the consumer understands your rating system and your constraints. First you have to eval-

Standards and Specifications

In an evaluation of electric hand drills, workers suggested that the drill have the following characteristics:

1. versatility
2. convenience
3. durability
4. repairability.

Versatility: Because the drill would be used on a wide variety of jobs, it must be capable of being used in either 110 or 220 volt outlets. It must also operate at different speeds and accept bits with stems as large as ⅜ inches in diameter. Reversibility is considered a desirable feature.

Convenience: The drill should be appropriate for both right- and left-handed operators, and the trigger should have a stay-on mechanism.

Durability: The drill must be able to withstand considerable abuse, including falls from the top of 6-foot ladders to concrete floors. The electrical cord must also withstand abuse, particularly from bending, temperature extremes, and caustic substances.

Repairability: Spare parts must be available locally so that the workers themselves can repair the drill quickly.

Cost and safety must also be considered. The drill should conform to union and safety rules without being extravagant in cost. With the preceding criteria in mind, I established six standards and specifications for the drills under consideration.

1. For versatility, the drill must have
    a. a ⅜-inch chuck
    b. variable speed capability
    c. a two-prong plug for 110 or 220 volt outlets
    d. a reversible motor.
2. For convenience, the drill must have
    a. a reversible side handle
    b. a stay-on trigger, preferably adjustable.
3. For durability, the drill must have
    a. a shatterproof case
    b. a crack-resistant cord.
4. For repairability, the drill must have spare parts that are available locally.
5. For economy, the drill must cost between $30.00 and $50.00.
6. For safety, the drill must have UL approval.

FIGURE 9.3 Standards and specifications for an electric hand drill
Source: Adapted from a report by Carl Sauer, Technical Writing 421, Illinois Institute of Technology.

uate each item under consideration against every one of the standards and specifications. You can select a product and measure it against all the criteria before going on to the next product, or you can select one criterion first and measure each product/plan against it. When you organize by product, you are emphasizing the product rather than the criteria. In reports that are supposed to be objective, it is better to organize by criteria because the purpose of the report was to evaluate against criteria and the readers will judge the results on the basis of criteria.

Both organizational strategies use paragraphs of comparison to describe the products or plans. In the evaluation of electric hand drills, the writer selected a criterion first and then compared each product against the criterion. The paragraphs are organized around the criteria and not around the products. Module 3 on organizational strategies further describes paragraphs used in comparisons.

After the comparison, the products or plans all receive a rating on the basis of how well they meet the criteria. The reader will need an explanation of the rating scale. In the example of the electric hand drill, five drills were evaluated against 12 standards and specifications. The results of the evaluation are shown in Figure 9.4. A drill meeting the criterion received one point; if it did not meet the criterion, it received a zero. The maximum number of points possible was 12, and any drill with 12 points was considered excellent and the best for meeting the needs of the workers. Note how much more detail is given in the table compared to the prose description.

Method of Evaluation

To evaluate the drills, I constructed a table (see Table 1) divided into five main categories. Several of these categories were, in turn, subdivided. If the drill met the criterion specified, it received one (1) point; it was given a zero (0) if it did not. Any drill that did not receive at least one point in every main category was subsequently removed from consideration. I then totaled the points for each remaining drill. A maximum of 12 points was possible. The drills with points in each main category and totals closest to 12 were considered as meeting our minimum requirements and being the best for our needs.

Using Tables to Explain the Data

In evaluation and feasibility studies, tables are an integral part of the document. They present the data and the evaluation of the data. Because the consumer has become quite sophisticated in reading a multiple evaluation table, the tables can present a great deal of information. After reading an explanation of the standards and specifications, the consumer can glance at

Table 1 Comparison of Drills

Standards and Specifications	Sears Craftsman (31049)	Wards Powr-Kraft (6166)	Model and Number Black and Decker (7190)	Skil (1102)	Shop-Craft (3636)
Versatility					
Variable speed	1	1	1	1	1
⅜″ chuck	1	1	1	1	1
Two-prong plug	1	1	1	1	0
Reversing motor	1	1	1	0	0
Convenience					
Reversible handle	1	1	1	1	1
Stay-on trigger	1	1	1	1	1
Adjustable stay-on trigger	1	0	1	0	0
Durability					
Shatterproof casing	1	1	0	1	0
Crack-resistant cord	0	0	1	1	1
Repairableness					
Spare parts availability	1	1	1	0	0
Cost					
$30–$50	1	1	1	1	0
Safety					
UL approval	1	1	1	1	1
Total Points	11	10	11	9*	6*

*Eliminated for not meeting one or more of the 5 main criteria.

FIGURE 9.4 Method for evaluating the electric hand drills
Source: Carl Sauer, Technical Writing 421, Illinois Institute of Technology.

the table summarizing the evaluations and determine the ratings for each of the products.

You may wish to review the information on designing tables, explained in Module 5. The table number and brief title appear at the top of the table; a mnemonic device for remembering the position of the title is to think of a "tabletop." Also, if you consider the vertical and horizontal columns of a table, you will have to decide where to place the standards and the products being evaluated. The research on document design, published in *Guidelines for Document Designers,* indicates that the main comparisons (the criteria) should be given in rows rather than columns for easier addition and comparison of items in the columns.[3] But it is important to note here that *Consumer's Report,* a magazine that raises multiple evaluations to an art, places the products in rows and the criteria in columns.

In Table 9.1 the standards are on the vertical axis in rows and the products are on the horizontal axis in columns, so that the data for each product can be tallied at the bottom of the table, just as you would add a column of numbers.

Table 9.1 Hand Drills Evaluated in Columns

	Electric Hand Drills			
Standards	*Drill 1*	*Drill 2*	*Drill 3*	*Drill 4*
Standard A	+	+	+	+
Standard B	+	+	−	−
Standard C	−	+	−	−
Standard D	+	+	+	−
Total +'s	3	4	2	2

Source: Carl Sauer, Technical Writing 421, Illinois Institute of Technology.

On the other hand, Table 9.2 places the criteria in columns and the products in rows.

Designer Chair Evaluation
Table 9.2. Products Evaluated in Rows
Table 2 Data Evaluation

Chair	Cost	Comfort	Durability	Assembly	Notes
Barcelona	$1800	(fair)	(good)	(good)	1,2
Stressless	$ 650	(excellent)	(very good)	(good)	1,3,4
Ribbon	$ 125	(very good)	(very good)	(poor)	7,8
Eames	$ 900	(good)	(good)	(good)	1,3
Bruer	$ 80	(poor)	(poor)	(poor)	9
Herman Miller	$ 180	(fair)	(poor)	(poor)	5,6

Key	Symbol	Comfort/Durability	Assembly
	◑	excellent	simple
	⊖	very good	
	○	good	moderate
	⊖	fair	
	●	poor	difficult

Source: Steven Pyshos, Technical Writing 421, Illinois Institute of Technology.

The evaluation in Table 9.3 uses a design modeled visually after the evaluation tables in *Consumer's Report* but follows the advice from the Document Design Center.

You can also use a table to display the data. Table 9.4 allows the consumer to compare the actual data, but the table does not evaluate the items.

Table 9.3 DX Receivers Evaluated in Columns

Excellent ◐◒○◓● Poor	GE Superadio	Sony ICF-SSW	Realistic TRF
Purchase price	$55	$60	$30
Weight with batteries	8 lbs.	5 lbs.	3 lbs.
Sensitivity	◒	◒	●
Selectivity	◒	◐	○
Spurious signal resection	○	◐	◒
Directionality	◐	◐	◒
Audio quality	◐	◒	●
Dial calibration	◒	○	●
FM performance	◐	◒	—
Advantages	A	A,B,C	
Disadvantages	B,C	B,D	A

Key to Advantages:
   A Separate bass and treble controls
   B Zonal station chart on receiver
   C L.E.D. signal strength indicator

Key to Disadvantages:
   A Dial pointer too wide
   B Uses 6 "D" cells
   C Earphone jack inaccessible to normal earphone plug
   D Schematic diagram not included with receiver

All Receivers Have:
   Earphone jack
   External antenna terminal(s)
   Decimal logging scale
   Tone control(s)

Source: Michael Jeziorski, Technical Writing 421, Illinois Institute of Technology.

Table 9.4 Visual Display of Data

Unit	Power Rating (watts/channel)	Distortion (%)	Controls (#)	Weight (lbs)	Price ($)
1. Hafler DH-220	115	0.02	1	26	449.95
2. Hafler DH-500	225	0.025	1	45	749.95
3. Carver PM-1.5	450	0.1	5	21	700.00
4. Carver M-1.5t	350	0.1	0	16	775.00
5. Carver M-200t	120	0.15	1	10.25	495.00
6. Carver M-400t	201	0.05	0	9	770.00
7. Carver M-500t	251	0.05	0	22	900.00

Source: Michael Clemetsen, Technical Writing 421, Illinois Institute of Technology.

Explaining Your System

If you place your data in your first table, then you will need a second table to evaluate the items. On the other hand, if your standards and specifications are very specific, then you may begin evaluating the items in the first table, using a very simple rating scale such as a plus (+) for meeting the criteria and a zero (0) for not meeting the criteria. The more specific the standards and specifications, the less data you have to include within the columns. The more general the criteria, the more specific the data have to be. If you have to include the data in the first table, then you can evaluate the data with a simpler rating system in the second table.

The important points to remember about your *method of evaluation* are these:

- Explain your system.
- Measure each item or idea by every standard and specification.
- Present the data and results in tables.
- Describe the final evaluation:
  in qualitative terms such as **excellent, good, fair.**
  or
  in quantitative terms on an acceptability scale of 10 to 1, indicating whether a high score is more or less acceptable.

Discussing the Constraints and Choices

The discussion section of the evaluation report is the place for you to explain the rationale behind some of your choices and the constraints on your decision. You have the opportunity to explain the data and any special considerations not obvious from the data. In this discussion section, you can present two sides of an argument or the advantages and disadvantages of the criteria or the product/plan. You might also wish to explain some judgments you made in the final evaluation of the products. Besides giving the tally of the results in the discussion section, you can indicate which of the items has special features or takes priority over other features, thus offsetting the quantitative numbers alone. For example, in the multiple evaluation of electric hand drills in Figure 9.5, the evaluator writes in the discussion section:

Discussion
On the basis of the standards and specifications established prior to the evaluation, I eliminated the Skil and Shop Craft models because they did not meet the *repairability* and/or *cost* standards. The three remaining drills have scores of 10 (Powr-Kraft) or 11 (Craftsman and Black and Decker) out of a possible 12 points. Both the Craftsman and the Black and Decker models meet all the criteria of *versatility* and *convenience* whereas the Powr-Kraft meets those of *versatility* only. None of the

three drills meets the criteria for *durability*. The Craftsman has a shatterproof case whereas the Black and Decker drill has a crack-proof cord.
Drill cases are more difficult and expensive to repair. Should the Craftsman cord become cracked, it could easily and cheaply be replaced in a
matter of minutes. Furthermore, the replacement cord could be of the
crack-resistant type.

FIGURE 9.5 Special considerations in the discussion section
Source: Carl Sauer, Technical Writing 421, Illinois Institute of Technology.

Whether you plan to discuss advantages of products/plans or constraints
of criteria, you must use a persuasive organization of a fair, two-sided presentation because your reader is now knowledgeable on the subject. After all,
the reader has read your introduction as well as your explanation of criteria
and method of evaluation. The discussion section supplies the rationale for
your recommendation and assures the reader that you have been both ethical
and thorough. If you wish to read more about the two-sided presentation,
see Module 12.

Making the Recommendation

After you have analyzed the data and interpreted the information, the reader
expects you to explain the significance of the data and recommend the prod-
uct/plan or options to accomplish the goal of the evaluation. On the basis of
the standards established earlier in the report, you draw your conclusions
and make a recommendation. Of course, your recommendation is dependent
on the choice of your original standards and your ability to interpret and
judge the data. If you neglected an important standard or failed to weigh a
significant fact, then your reader may disagree with your recommendation.
Once again, the hand-drill example in Figure 9.6 demonstrates the final section of the evaluation.

Recommendation
The Craftsman and the Black and Decker drills, each with 11 points out
of 12, both merited serious consideration for purchase. The Craftsman,
however, is the brand I recommend. Although it and the Black and
Decker each has one point for durability, the fact that the Craftsman
has a shatterproof case, as opposed to the Black and Decker crack-
proof cord, was the deciding factor. In terms of cost, the Black and
Decker drill is $35.00, and the Craftsman is $39.00. The extra cost of
the Craftsman, however, is offset by its expected greater durability.

FIGURE 9.6 The recommendation
Source: Carl Sauer, Technical Writing 421, Illinois Institute of Technology.

Reexamining Multiple Evaluations

To conclude the discussion of multiple evaluations, let's consider some variations in the content. The evaluation of technical ink pens in Figure 9.7 exemplifies the standard model for this type of document, but it is missing a section on *standards and specifications*. On the other hand, Figure 9.8 provides an unconventional example of a multiple evaluation document. It measures the skill required to play a piece of music. The unique aspect of this study is that the goal—to measure the difficulty of a piece of music—is not easily measured. Music is not usually measured in an objective, quantifiable way, and yet the evaluator carefully establishes the section on *standards and specifications*. The question is, If the evaluator omits the standards and specifications (specs) or carefully explains them, is the writer's conclusion convincing to the reader? Your answer depends on your reexamining the importance of the evaluator's standards and specifications.

PROBLEM

The purpose of this report is to present the results of an evaluation to determine the best overall technical ink pen for use by designers. Designers use technical pens on a daily basis. The reason for choosing a particular brand of pen is often initial cost. However, less costly pens usually have to be replaced more often and in the long run can actually cost more to use. This study will determine which of the five most popular pens delivers the longest life, best line quality, and best economy.

METHOD OF EVALUATION

Six standards and specifications were selected for the purpose of evaluating five different pens: Faber-Castell, Rapidograph, Staedtler-Mars, Reform, and Keuffel-Esser. I evaluated each pen against the standards and specifications. Table 1 shows the results of the evaluation. A "YES" means the pen meets the standard, and a "NO" means it does not. Table 2 summarizes the ratings and explains the final evaluation.

DISCUSSION

Reform received the highest rating, six yeses out of six. Keuffel-Esser received a good rating, four out of six. However, its cost is much higher than the others tested. Faber-Castell had a poor rating, and Rapidograph and Staedtler-Mars each received a fair rating. This study indicates that Reform is superior to the other four because of its quality and outstanding value.

RECOMMENDATION

Although the Keuffel-Esser is excellent for drawing applications, it cannot be recommended because it is high-priced and difficult to clean. The Reform pen is recommended because of its superior overall value. Although its drawing quality is not quite as good as the Keuffel-Esser, the Reform pen meets all the criteria and is the best choice.

Table 1 Evaluation of Technical Pens

Standards and Specifications	Staedtler-Mars	Reform	Faber-Castell	Rapidograph	Keufell-Esser
Line quality: *The pen must deliver a consistent line width.*	Yes	Yes	No	No	Yes
Nonclogging: *The pen must not clog with normal use.*	No	Yes	No	Yes	Yes
Nonbreaking tip: *The pen's tip must not break with normal use.*	No	Yes	No	No	Yes
Cleanable: *The pen must clean easily.*	No	Yes	No	No	No
Airtight: *The pen must seal securely to prevent ink from drying inside.*	Yes	Yes	No	Yes	Yes
Cost: *The pen must not cost more than $75.00 for a standard five-pen set.*	Yes	Yes	Yes	Yes	No

Table 2 Basis of Evaluation

Number of Yeses	Rating
Below 2	Poor
2–3	Fair
4–5	Good
6	Excellent

FIGURE 9.7 Evaluation of technical pens
Source: Gordon Michaelson, Technical Writing 421, Illinois Institute of Technology.

Evaluating the Skill Required for a Piece of Music

Music is written for all levels of pianists—beginning, intermediate, and advanced. It is difficult for even the experienced pianist to distinguish between varying levels of complexity. I have evaluated the level of three pieces of sheet music for the piano and established a criteria system for use at home. This evaluation is based on eight standards and specifications. I applied these criteria to the sheet music. The report gives my evaluations.

Standards and Specifications
A. Length
The length of a piece of music gives a first, if sometimes incorrect, impression of difficulty. Generally, the longer a piece is, the harder it is to learn.

The measure according to length is as follows:

1–3 pages: a beginning level
3–5 pages: an intermediate level
5+ pages: an advanced level

B. Notes

Often the size of the notes will indicate the level of the music. The larger the note, the easier it is to read and play.

C. Time

Time is an expression used to explain how fast a piece is played. A slow-paced piece of music is considered the beginning level whereas a medium-to-fast-paced piece is at the intermediate level. A fast-to-very-fast piece is at the advanced level.

D. Synchronization

Synchronization involves the amount of interaction between the right and left hands. If the right and left hands play at the same time, the piece is easier in this regard. If, however, the right hand must play notes different from those played by the left hand, the piece becomes difficult.

If one hand plays alone or is very simply combined with the left hand, the piece is suitable for a beginner. If the piece requires both hands to play together, the piece is suitable for an intermediate pianist. If the piece requires intricate work between the right and left hands, the piece is for the advanced musician.

E. Chords

Two or more notes played at the same time with the same hand are called chords. The number of chords and the frequency with which they occur is very important in determining the difficulty of a piece of sheet music. If they are frequent and require odd shapes from the hand, the piece is hard. If they are simple or infrequent, the piece is considerably easier.

No chords or very few chords mean the piece is designed for a beginner. If there are few chords with three notes occurring with a moderate frequency, the piece is for the intermediate pianist. However, if there are many notes in the chords and they occur often, then the piece is probably meant for the advanced musician.

F. Reach

The number of piano keys the hand spans during a piece of music is called the reach. Reach plays a major role when determining the complexity of the music. It is much easier to span 5 or 6 notes than 30.

The measure according to reach is as follows:

1–10 notes: for the beginner
10–25 notes: for the intermediate person
25–88 notes: for the advanced person

G. Directions

Most pieces of music have directional words and symbols that are used to tell the pianist what kind of expression to play with or how loud to play the piece. The pianist usually finds it harder to change expressions frequently.

The evaluation according to directions is as follows:

1–3 directions: for the beginner
3–5 directions: for the intermediate person
5+ directions: for the advanced person

H. Feel

Each time a song is played, it sounds different. This change is due to the "feel" that each individual puts into the playing. Developing feel takes practice. Most often the songs that require a lot of feel from the pianist are the harder songs. When feel is necessary, frequently directions, such as slowly, softly, with liveliness, are omitted.

Method of Evaluation

Table 1 compares three pieces of music against the established criteria. A one (1) indicates the beginning level; a two (2), the intermediate level; and a three (3), the advanced level. The analysis of the total score is as follows:

1–10: Beginner
10–17: Intermediate
17–24: Advanced

Table 1 Music Comparison

Standards	*"Theme from Ordinary People"*	*"Für Elise"*	*"The Long and Winding Road"*
	Pieces of Music		
Length	1	2	1
Notes	1	2	2
Time	1	3	2
Synchronization	2	2	2
Chords	2	3	2
Reach	2	3	2
Directions	2	2	3
Feel	1	3	3
Score	12	20	17

Conclusion

1. The "Theme from Ordinary People" earned a rating of 12. It is two pages in length, has fairly large notes, and is played slowly. It requires some synchronization, but it is not very hard. The chords are at an intermediate level, and the hand does not have a hard reach. There are a few directions to follow, and the piece does not require a lot of feel.

2. "Für Elise" earned a score of 20. Written by Beethoven, it is six pages long and has fairly small notes. It is played very fast in some parts and requires a fair amount of synchronization. Its reach is for the intermediate pianist, and Beethoven does supply a lot of directions. For these reasons, the piece requires an advanced level of feel.

3. "The Long and Winding Road" scored 17. It is only two pages long, but its notes are small. The time is medium, the chords aren't hard,

and both the synchronization and the reach are for an intermediate student. There are a lot of directions, but it still requires an advanced pianist to give the feel of the piece.

4. From the information supplied in the standards and specifications section, a person can take a piece of music and apply the same criteria to the music. This process will provide the data to judge the difficulty of the piece for the musician.

Recommendations

From the ratings, the student can determine the level of the piece of music. The "Theme from Ordinary People" is on the lower end of the intermediate level. Therefore, an advanced beginner or an intermediate could play this piece. "Für Elise," on the other hand, earned a 20 rating, which falls in the middle of the advanced range. Considerable skill is needed to play this piece. "The Long and Winding Road" falls in the middle of these two pieces. With a score of 17, it is on the borderline between intermediate and advanced. An intermediate musician may find this piece difficult to learn but could be encouraged to attempt it.

FIGURE 9.8 Unique adaption of the evaluation report
Source: Theresa Pastore, Technical Writing 421, Illinois Institute of Technology.

Assembling Secondary Elements for a Formal Report

Although multiple evaluation/feasibility studies may be written in memo or letter format, they are frequently submitted as formal reports. Formal reports, like formal proposals in Module 8, require secondary materials that accompany the main sections of the report or proposal. Whenever you are submitting a formal report, you must make a checklist of accompanying secondary materials and begin to assemble these elements. This module describes secondary elements along with multiple evaluation/feasibility studies because it is not too soon to begin a checklist of secondary elements that will accompany the final technical report for your course in technical writing if you are asked to write a formal technical report. First draft the checklist:

Secondary Materials for a Formal Report
- cover
- title page
- letter of transmittal
- table of contents
- list of illustrations
- abstract (descriptive *or* informative)
- glossary
- appendixes

Then decide what elements will accompany your formal report.

Cover

The cover is a substantial folder that holds the pages of the report securely and allows the reader to read the document without obscuring any of the information. If you are using a cover that has a spine, a metal clasp, or fasteners that are threaded through punched pages, plan your left-hand margin to accommodate the spine or the fasteners. It is a good idea to allow three-quarters of an inch beyond the spine or the fasteners of the cover. Under no conditions should you use a plastic binder with a removable spine for a report of more than three pages. Over a period of time, these spines tend to pop off the plastic, and the pages spill out.

Title Page

If the cover is opaque, you should place a gummed label on the cover; usually, opaque covers will have a clearly demarcated space for this label. The label bears the title and subtitle (if appropriate), the author's name, the receiver (a company or a class), and the date. When the cover is clear plastic, you will not need the label because the title page, illustrated in Figure 9.9, contains the same information and is immediately visible to the reader.

AN EVALUATION OF LOGIC ANALYZERS

Prepared for

Dymatech, Inc.
Piscataway, New Jersey

by

Darryl Perrin, P.E.
Evaluation Engineering, Inc.

16 November 19XX

FIGURE 9.9 Title page

Title

The title of your report should be long enough to describe your topic in detail, but no longer than 15 words. As a rule of thumb, create a title that includes all the important nouns for indexing your report in a database of articles on the topic. The following titles provide enough indexing nouns:

Enhanced Oil Recovery by Alkaline Flooding—
Use of Microwave Attenuation Technique

Short-Term Investments for the Novice Investor

Instruction Manual for the Nuclear Magnetic Resonance Spectrometer

Engine Mount Design for the Austin Healey Sprite Mark I

Transmittal Letter

The letter of transmittal is a notice to the person who authorized the report that you are sending the document. Usually, the notice is in the full-block letter form. Within a company, the transmittal notice is usually a memo format. Module 12 provides more details on writing letters and memos. The first paragraph provides background about the report, including the date of the request for the report, the purpose of the report, and the title. The second paragraph summarizes the conclusion and adds a significant detail or two. The third paragraph briefly describes the methods used, and the fourth paragraph insures goodwill and offers future assistance. This letter, exemplified in Figure 9.10, accompanies the bound report as a separate page or may be inserted between the cover and the title page.

Evaluation Engineering, Inc.
906 Glenellen
Woodside, New Jersey 98011

December 12, 19XX

Dr. Samuel Golden
Dymatech, Inc.
Piscataway, New Jersey 98154

Dear Mr. Golden:

As we agreed in our correspondence dated September 25, 19XX, Evaluation Engineering has evaluated logic analyzers for developing and testing digital products. The results are included in the accompanying report entitled "An Evaluation of Logic Analyzers."

For this report, I evaluated the top six brands of logic analyzers and recommended the purchase of one—the Graham D105-F. None of the models met all the standards and specifications established for this evaluation.

FIGURE 9.10 Transmittal letter

Thus, it is important to select a logic analyzer on the basis of factors that are critical to your use.

I evaluated the six instruments first by examining the general characteristics of each model and then by taking a detailed look at the timing and state modes of each device. Because there are so many standards and specifications by which to evaluate these instruments, I tried to choose those criteria I felt to be the most critical. On the basis of those criteria, I believe my recommendation is fair and well substantiated.

Thank you for the opportunity to assist you in your decisions. We hope the information compiled in this report will aid you in your selection of a logic analyzer. If you have any questions about the findings presented in this report as they apply to present or future decisions, please let us know.

Sincerely,

Darryl H. Perrin, P.E.
Manager, Product Research

FIGURE 9.10 (cont.)

Table of Contents

The table of contents, shown in Figure 9.11, is simply labeled "CONTENTS" and is numbered with a *2* or *ii*, following the title page. You may use Arabic numbers throughout the report, or you may use lowercase Roman numerals for the pages preceding the introduction. From the introduction on, you must use Arabic numbers. The table of contents should include no more than first- and second-level captions. If you use tabs to separate the sections in your

FIGURE 9.11 Table of contents

```
┌─────────────────────────────────────────────────────────────────┐
│                          ILLUSTRATIONS                            │
│   TABLES                                                     page │
│       I. General Characteristics Data.......................   6  │
│      II. General Characteristics Evaluation................   7  │
│     III. Timing Analysis Data .............................   8  │
│      IV. Timing Analysis Evaluation........................   9  │
│       V. State Analysis Data...............................  10  │
│      VI. State Analysis Evaluation.........................  11  │
│                                                                   │
│   FIGURES                                                         │
│       1. Logic Analyzer Model MP 1340H ....................   4  │
│       2. Logic Analyzer Model Graham D105-F ...............   5  │
└─────────────────────────────────────────────────────────────────┘
```

FIGURE 9.12 List of illustrations

document, the tabs should indicate only the first-level captions. Divider pages with tabs help the reader locate contents quickly.

List of Illustrations

You need a separate list of illustrations only if you have more than three illustrations in your document. The list follows the table of contents and is headed "ILLUSTRATIONS." If you have only tables or only figures, then you may head the page "TABLES" or "FIGURES." Remember that the titles of tables and figures should be long enough to be self-explanatory. Figure 9.12 is an example of a page listing illustrations.

Abstracts

Abstracts are important because they help readers determine the appropriateness of the document to their needs. Good abstracts are self-contained and present the objectives, scope, and findings of a document concisely. The simplest abstract is a title only. A mini-abstract is one or two lines long and is used for bibliographies and symposia. Statistical or numerical abstracts use a tabular or numerical form to be concise and objective. Critical abstracts describe and condense the content as well as critically evaluate the work in relationship to other work in the field and its worth to the potential reader. The last two types of abstracts—descriptive and informative—frequently accompany technical documents.[4]

The title of the abstract announces the topic of the report, and the abstract discusses the content of the report. The descriptive abstract tells briefly what the document is about but does not give results or conclusions. This abstract entices the reader by perhaps giving the motive for the research and the scope of the investigation. Because it is written for the generalist rather than the specialist, the descriptive abstract, presented in Figure 9.13,

ABSTRACT

A *logic analyzer* is an electronic instrument that can be used to develop and test digital and microprocessor-based products. These devices help *digital system* designers debug hardware and software. In this report, the top six brands of logic analyzers are evaluated according to certain standards and specifications, including reliability, ease of use, memory depth, and cost. The results of this evaluation can be used to select the logic analyzer appropriate to the user's needs.

FIGURE 9.13 Descriptive abstract

is like the lead paragraph for a newspaper article; it is like a table of contents that allows readers to decide if they want to read the article.

The informative abstract summarizes the document's major arguments and presents principal data and conclusions. Often the abstract includes the objective of the research, the study design, the experimental methods, the material used, and the main findings. Information not stated in the paper should not be included in the abstract.

To prepare an informative abstract, you can choose or prepare a sentence that summarizes the main point of each major section of the document. These sentences should be prepared like topic sentences to describe the methods, results, and conclusions. Using the language of the paper itself is not only acceptable but preferable, as is stating the problem, the objective, and the scope of the document in the first sentence. Often the first sentence is the only sentence people have time to read. Whether an article or paper is read depends often on the strength of the abstract, so the abstract must have important information for the reader, as does the informative abstract in Figure 9.14.

In summary, descriptive abstracts imply the kind of information contained in the report or article but do not summarize the detail. The descriptive abstract often appears at the top of articles in professional journals, enticing the reader with seldom more than 15 lines. Informative abstracts are precise and maintain a proportion between the document and the abstract. The abstract should not be more than 10 percent of the original document and should give the outstanding facts from every section. Topic sentences or summarizing sentences are good sources of information for the abstract, which should be written in complete sentences, preferably in one paragraph, and single-spaced. An abstract of a research paper should be from 100 to 175 words; one for a review or theoretical article, between 75 and 100 words.

Glossary

The glossary is a list of words and meanings useful to the nontechnical reader who is reading the document. If the terms are defined within the text, you

ABSTRACT

Logic analyzers provide both timing and state analysis capabilities to solve hardware, software, or compounded faults. The timing analysis capabilities are used to troubleshoot hardware, and the state analysis mode is used to debug software. In the timing analysis mode, the number of data channels, the type of triggering available, and the ability to integrate to other modes are the most important factors. With state analysis, the factors of greatest interest are the number of data channels, the number of sequential triggering levels, and the ability to integrate to other modes of operation. General features include reliability, ease of use, memory depth, and cost. The greatest variety among models occurs in the criteria of data channels and cost. The Graham D105-F model is recommended because of its memory depth, data channels (16 channels for timing analysis and 32 data channels for state analysis), price ($14,985.00), reliability, and ease of use.

FIGURE 9.14 Informative abstract

do not need a glossary. When you need a glossary, it can precede the introduction or follow the references, but the words are listed alphabetically. The terms should be defined in a grammatically parallel structure. For example, if the term is a noun, then the definition should begin with a noun. In other words, the terms and the definitions should have a consistent grammatical structure, as they do in the example in Figure 9.15.

Appendixes

Finally, the appendix is a collection of supplementary material that further explains or supports the content in the document, but it is so specialized or ancillary that it would impede the reader's progress through the document. Such supplementary material might include the following:

1. lengthy tables
2. blueprints
3. lengthy and complex specifications
4. schematics
5. computer programs and printouts
6. questionnaires
7. manufacturers' brochures
8. equations
9. additional forms or correspondence relative to the subject of the document
10. lists with names and addresses

```
                            GLOSSARY
Acquisition memory  ........... The block of memory where the col-
depth                          lected data are stored. The depth of
                               the memory refers to the number of
                               locations in this block.

Glitch ........................... An undesirable voltage or current
                               spike on a data signal that causes a
                               false logic level transition.

IEEE-488 ....................... Electronic industry standard for par-
                               allel interface communication link.

Postacquisition  ................ Processing of data after they are col-
data processing                lected. Allows the user to view se-
                               lected portions of code and measure
                               time or occurrence distribution.

Parallel interface ............... A communication link that sends and
                               receives signals across many wires
                               connected in parallel.
```

FIGURE 9.15 Glossary

If you are appending just one exhibit, you can head it "Appendix." When you have two or more exhibits, you should insert an *Appendix* page after the last page of your report, label it "Appendixes," and list the appended items, as exemplified in Figure 9.16.

Summary

An evaluation or feasibility study requires several tasks: a **needs analysis,** relevant **criteria,** knowledge of possible plans or products, an evaluation, and a recommendation. A needs analysis surveys the buyers and users, reviews the options available, and assigns priorities to the list of needs. The needs analysis provides information for the introduction of the feasibility/evaluation report,

```
                            APPENDIXES
    1. Blueprint for Housing
    2. Specifications for Building Code
    3. Schematic of Electrical Wiring
    4. Questionnaire to Determine Residents' Needs
    5. List of Town Meeting Participants
```

FIGURE 9.16 Appendix page

including the background of the problem, the purpose of the evaluation, and an overview of options and criteria. Evaluation reports describe and evaluate products, and feasibility reports present optional plans.

Depending on the reader's preference, the organization of the report follows one of two **persuasive strategies:** conclusion followed by details (**deductive** strategy) or details and then conclusion (**inductive** strategy). Both strategies include sections on **standards** and **specifications,** method of evaluation, and a discussion. Standards and specifications are the criteria for describing and measuring products/plans. Standards are the general categories for scientific and technical measures, and specifications are the specific data. Criteria are usually enumerated in a list and must be presented in parallel structure. It is important to establish sound and accurate criteria because they are the basis for both the recommendation and the reader's decision to accept the recommendation.

The **method for evaluating** the products/plans is standard. Each product/plan must be evaluated against each standard and specification. **Tables** are an integral part of an evaluation because they display the data accurately and efficiently. The data are then evaluated as the products or plans are compared to the criteria, and the products/plans receive a **rating.** After the reader receives an explanation of the rating scale, a table can clearly present the ratings for the products/plans. Tables use rows and columns to display information on products and criteria. The products can be displayed in rows or in columns; if the products are displayed in columns, the results can be tallied at the end of each column.

The **discussion** section is the place to explain priorities, constraints, or judgments. A **two-sided presentation** of advantages and disadvantages provides the reader with an ethical, thorough report. The conclusion and **recommendation** follow from the discussion, the criteria, and the evaluation of the product/plan against the criteria. The recommendation may restate the limitations or the unique circumstances of the decision.

Multiple evaluations/feasibility studies are frequently submitted as formal reports and require secondary materials that accompany the main sections of the text. Not all reports require the same secondary materials, but it is a good idea to have a checklist of these elements: cover, title page, letter of transmittal, table of contents, list of illustrations, abstract, glossary, and appendixes. Of these elements, the abstract requires some summary comments.

Abstracts are self-contained and concisely present the objectives, scope, and content of a document. **Descriptive abstracts** are written for the generalist rather than the specialist and are like the table of contents, giving the scope rather than the results. The **informative abstract** summarizes the major arguments and presents both the principal data and the conclusions. The sentences for the informative abstract should use the language of the text itself when stating the problem, the objective, the scope, and the information in each section of the report. In all, the informative abstract should not be more than 10 percent of the original document.

Checklist for Multiple Evaluation/Feasibility Report

Have you considered the following sections for your evaluation or feasibility report? Check only those items to which you can give a positive response.

Yes

1. Does the introduction contain

_____ a purpose statement?

_____ background of the problem?

_____ overview of options and criteria?

2. Are the standards and specifications

_____ defined?

_____ compiled from consumers' and buyers' needs?

_____ compiled from review of the available options?

_____ listed in a style that has parallel construction?

3. Is the method of evaluation explained by

_____ evaluating each item against each specification and standard?

_____ presenting the rating of the product/plan in qualitative terms such as good or poor or in quantitative terms on an acceptability scale of 1 to 10?

4. Do the tables

_____ present the data?

_____ present the final evaluation?

_____ make appropriate use of rows and columns to tally product results?

_____ include simple, descriptive titles at the top of the table?

5. Does the discussion include

_____ a two-sided discussion of advantages and disadvantages?

———————   a rationale for judgments, such as priorities or constraints?

———————   6. Is there a clear recommendation with limitations or unique circumstances, such as where the product or plan exceeded or fell short of the standards?

                  7. Is the report clearly designed with

———————   headings and subheadings?

———————   the recommendation placed appropriately near the beginning of the report or at the end, depending on the reader?

Yes

                  8. Do you need secondary elements, including

———————   cover?

———————   title page?

———————   transmittal letter?

———————   table of contents?

———————   list of illustrations?

———————   descriptive abstract?

———————   informative abstract?

———————   glossary?

———————   appendixes?

Notes

1. John Robin, "Evaluation of Calculators," Technical Writing 421, Illinois Institute of Technology, 1985. This report provided the standards for the calculator.
2. Peter J. Schram, *1984 NFPA Handbook of the National Electrical Code*, 3d ed. (New York: McGraw-Hill, 1983): 248.
3. Daniel B. Felker et al., *Guidelines for Document Designers* (Washington, D.C.: American Institutes for Research, 1981): 96.

4. Dorothy J. Buchanan-Davidson, "The Abstract—A Powerful Communication Tool," in *Proceedings,* 29th International Technical Communication
Conference (Washington, D.C.: Society for Technical Communication,
1982): W-22–25. This article provided the information for the material
on abstracts. Used with permission.

References

Robert A. DeBeaugrande, "Communication in Technical Writing," *Journal of Technical
Writing and Communication* 8 (1978): 5–15.
Marilyn S. Samuels, "Scientific Logic: A Reader-Oriented Approach to Technical
Writing," *Journal of Technical Writing and Communication* 12 (1982): 307–328.
Mary John Smith, *Persuasion and Human Action* (Belmont, Calif.: Wadsworth Publish-
ing Company, 1982): 250–251.
Wayne N. Thompson, *The Process of Persuasion* (New York: Harper & Row Publishers,
1975): 120.

Applying Your Knowledge

EXERCISE 9.1

Write at least three standards for the following items.

an electric blanket
a toaster oven
a VCR
word processing software
a winter vacation

EXERCISE 9.2

In trade or popular magazines such as **PC World, Popular Mechanics, Modern
Photography, Stereo Review,** *and so on, find ads for three products that include
specifications. At a computer or typewriter, list these products and the specs
and then print out your specifications page for one of the products.*

For the next two exercises, work collaboratively.

EXERCISE 9.3

Look at the report on the technical ink pens in Figure 9.7.

1. Is the problem statement accurate and complete? Do you need to know
   more about technical ink pens and their use? Do you need to know more
   about designers?

2. Do you think the study needs a *Standards and Specifications* block, or is Table 1 adequate?

3. Is the rating system "YES" and "NO" appropriate? What would you use?

EXERCISE 9.4

Read the following information provided. Then reorganize it under the following sections: Purpose

               Background

               Standards and specifications

Finally, write each section, including an explanation of your method of evaluation and an accompanying table for data, and edit your standards and specifications for parallel construction.

    Multiple Evaluation of Three Backpacks for Use by a Boy Scout Troop

        The purpose of this report is to evaluate three different kinds of backpacks for use in hiking by a troop of Boy Scouts and to make a recommendation of the best one for the needs of the troop.

        Boy Scout Troop 14 of Denver, Colorado, has received a private donation of $1,000 for the purpose of camping equipment. The troop has been active in camping for many years and has acquired tents, buckets, Dutch ovens, and equipment storage boxes. The troop has decided to invest in backpacks for its members in order to go on more challenging hikes. If any money remains, they would like to buy cooking tarps and charcoal stoves, but backpacks are their highest priority.

        The troop has 11 Scouts at the time of the buying decision. Troop size varies from year to year between 10 and 15 members. The average number of Scouts on any one camp-out is 8. The troop's goal is to buy 10 backpacks to allow for increased membership.

        Members of the troop are between the ages of 11 and 15, so the packs must adjust to fit boys between 4'7" and 5'10" tall. The packs need to be lightweight, weighing no more than 3 pounds without gear. They also must be durable enough to withstand mildew, rust, tears, breaking, and abrasion. Finally, the backpacks must be within the budget of the troop.

        The Scouts need to have backpacks they can load and adjust themselves in a reasonable amount of time with required gear, sometimes under adverse weather conditions. In order to make this part of the buying decision, a local retailer is letting the Scouts borrow for a meeting the three backpacks under consideration. Patrol leaders will demonstrate how to load each pack and adjust it properly. The Scouts want to load and adjust the straps within 15 minutes, a reasonable time limit for anyone who has been taught how to load this gear and adjust the straps correctly. If gear cannot be loaded within that time, the pack is unacceptable for the troop's needs.

EXERCISE 9.5

Select a table from *Consumer's Report* or from any hobby magazine. Rearrange the table, and evaluate the effectiveness of both arrangements for presenting and evaluating the data.

WRITING ASSIGNMENT

Design and write a multiple evaluation paper presenting a conclusion and recommendation. Consider the following:

a piece of equipment (letter-quality printer)
a software program (spread sheet)
a device or mechanism (thermostats)
a plan or technique (health insurance plans).

MODULE | 10

Case/Assessment Studies and Design Reports

The purpose of some reports is to present a management plan or a design to accomplish an objective. Case or assessment studies review the history and current status of a company, a person, or a subject and then present a management plan for future action. In technical writing, the case study may be a study that assesses the relevant history and current market or situation to recommend a course of action. On the basis of the recommendation in the case/assessment study, the reader may want a design or a redesign of a product, a plan, or an action. When the writer specifies the methods and materials and produces a plan or a product, a blueprint, illustrations, or a prototype, then the writer has written a design report. Generally, case studies present concepts and abstract plans whereas design reports present concrete plans to produce a product. Frequently a case/assessment study will precede a design report.

For example, if you wanted to improve the environment around a housing project, you would have to study the background and objectives of the housing project and its surroundings in order to understand the original concept. Then you would have to determine the needs of the people living in the project and the limitations of the resources, both physically and economically. From your study of the history of the project and the current status—both its needs and constraints—you could draw conclusions and make recommendations. On the basis of this first study, the people then ask you to redesign the surroundings and present a long-term management plan for maintaining the surroundings. The second report presents the design and the long-term maintenance plan as well as a list of materials and a set of instructions for implementing the design and plan.

This module presents the strategies behind these two types of reports. With the addition of an organizational plan and visual techniques, you will be able to produce the case/assessment report and the design report.

Scope

In this module you will learn to

1. Review the history of a subject.
2. Conduct a needs assessment using surveys or interviews.
3. Organize the case/assessment report.
4. Prepare an executive summary or a conclusions section.
5. Use visual techniques to improve readability.
6. Organize the design report.

Introducing the Strategy for the Case/Assessment Study

Medical and research facilities keep files of case studies; companies frequently review and reassess their policies, products, and procedures:

- Bolinbrook Hospital records a fitness and nutrition plan for Mr. Thomas Pace.
- Northern Lumber Company has to reassess its timber stand in northern Vermont.

When you have to review a person's condition or assess a company's policy and recommend a course of action, you will eventually have to write a case/assessment study.

Before you write, you have to gather some information.

1. What is the purpose of the review?
2. What is the history of the subject?
3. Can you describe the present condition?
4. Based upon your review, what do you recommend as a future course of action?

These questions will ultimately contribute to the written report.

What Is the Purpose of the Review?

What is your purpose? Are you assessing the company's employee insurance plan? Are you assessing a person's physical fitness program? Are you reviewing your company's marketing strategy? Let's say your company wants you to study the status of home offices in order to design office furniture for the present and future home market.[1] You now know the subject of the study and the company's objectives. The company wants to design office furniture for the home office market. The company executives will want to read a report that analyzes the home office market and recommends a plan for designing this furniture.

What Is the History of the Subject?

A review of the subject includes both the past history and present situation. When you trace the history of the subject or product, you will want to focus on the factors relevant to designing the product or plan and not on the history of the subject for its own sake. The history of the home office may be interesting in its own right, but you want to study it in order to assess or design a product that will fit into the trends of the company and be functional over time. The purpose of the study determines the focus of the historical examination.

In the preceding example, if your company wants to design home office furniture, you have to trace the history of the home office and its users. The home office is more popular with white-collar workers who sit at desks than with blue-collar workers who work on assembly lines. Over the past 20 years, though, the work force has shifted from a predominantly blue-collar work force to a white-collar work force. Because the work force has shifted, the demand for home offices has increased. Along with the increased demand for home offices is a shift toward higher learning, the advancement of technology, and the increase of women in the white-collar work force. The past history and the present status of the market for the home office provide information that you can use later to make recommendations about the design of the home office and furniture.

What Is the Present Status?

The present status or situation is a crucial consideration. If management wants to establish a new line of office furniture for the home, then you have to describe the present home offices, the furniture, and the clients and users. Before you can recommend a plan, you have to analyze the needs of the users. A needs analysis or assessment

- Surveys and assesses the needs of buyers and users.
- Establishes criteria or objectives for future action.

Module 9 discusses needs assessment as a way of gathering information. This module elaborates on the advice.

Assessing the User's Needs

Many new products, plans, or documents depend on the data from surveys or questionnaires to establish the needs of the clients or consumers. The consumers supply feelings and opinions about a product by responding to an oral interview or a questionnaire or by participating in a focus group, a group devoted to discussing a single product. This measure of consumers' opinions and needs is called a needs assessment. Usually, you will be unable to gather a representative sample of consumers in a single room, so you have to ask the consumers to send their responses to you. Widely distributed questionnaires and surveys are another way to conduct a *needs assessment.* Questionnaire design is important if you want usable information from your consumers, and, as such, surveys and evaluation have become a field of specialization.

Every questionnaire and survey has a purpose, clear objectives for each question, and a plan for evaluating data. You should tell the readers the purpose of the questionnaire or survey so that they will know why it is important to respond. Figure 10.1 illustrates a survey with a clear purpose statement to the reader.

Make equally sure your questions will provide you with information that supports the reason for distributing the questionnaire. When designing a questionnaire, you should consider the following:

- Keep the questionnaire as brief as possible.
- Keep the questions clear.
- Provide enough space for the response.
- Know what the object of each question is.
- Minimize the complexity of the response by providing the reader with appropriate directions, for example:

EXAMPLE

The rating scale is based on the Likert scale of 5 points:

strongly agree (sa)	agree (a)	undecided (u)	disagree (d)	strongly disagree (sd)
5	4	3	2	1

Directions: Please use the rating scale and blacken the appropriate circle next to the question.

	sa	a	u	d	sd
Question 1. Engineers find writing to be an important part of their job.	o	o	o	o	o

---

Establishing Objectives for Future Action

Before asking questions, you must know your objectives. You will want to group your questions under your objectives and plan a way to evaluate the information you receive. For example, will the answers to some of your questions be worth more in points than others? Can you convert *yes* and *no* answers

Purpose of the survey: We are trying to determine the market for DX receivers and design a new receiver.

Directions: Please complete the following survey. Your name and address are not necessary and, if included, will be kept confidential.

SURVEY DISTRIBUTED TO DXERS

Age

Sex   M   F

Occupation

What area do you live in?
  United States
    Eastern time zone
    Central time zone
    Mountain time zone
    Pacific time zone
  Canada
  Other

Are you a registered amateur radio operator?

What bands are you interested in?
  Shortwave
  Medium wave
  FM
  TV
  Longwave
  Other (please specify)

Please list the brand name and model number of the receivers you have used for DXing, and indicate the band or bands they were used for.

Of the receivers just listed, which was (were) your favorite(s)? Why?

FIGURE 10.1 A survey with a purpose statement
Source: Adapted from a report by Michael Jeziorski, Technical Writing 421, Illinois Institute of Technology.

to a two-point scale? Are qualitative answers such as *strongly disagree* or *undecided* measured on a numerical scale? Modules 7 and 9 also discuss the need to establish a clear method of evaluation.

The survey in Figure 10.2 asks people about their preferences to determine the direction or the status of a situation. This type of survey would be appropriate for the case study. In the survey, the writer wanted to present the findings of a study to determine if a student drama club can exist at the university, and, if yes, under what conditions. Under the organizational plan,

Table 1 Theater Attendance

1. Have you ever attended a staged play?	87% Yes
	13% No
2. Approximately how often do you go to see a play on average?	69% Once a year or less
	23% 3 times a year
	5% 6 times a year
	3% 12 times a year
6. If you did not participate in the student drama club, would you support its productions?	69% Yes
	31% No

These questions were designed to determine the student's inclination to attend a play and the approximate future level of attendance.

Table 2 Past Theater Experience

3. Have you ever participated in a drama program at another university or in high school?	32% Yes
	68% No
3a. If yes, how many productions did you participate in?	35% 4 or more
	9% 3
	32% 2
	24% 1
3b. Also, in what area did you work?	41% Acting
	27% Production
	16% Acting and production
	8% Acting and advertising
	8% All areas

This information will show how much teaching of basic theater skills is necessary.

Table 3 Willingness to Participate

4. If there were a student drama club at the university, would you be willing to participate in it in any area?	37% Yes
	63% No
4a. If yes, in what area would you like to work?	40% Production
	18% Acting
	14% Acting and production
	12% All areas
	8% Advertising
	5% Production and advertising
	3% Acting and advertising
5. How many free hours do you have during the week (including weekends)?	54% 5 or less
	18% 10
	11% 15
	11% 20
	6% 25 or more

These questions determined how many students were willing to participate, in what areas they wished to work, and how much time they could devote.

FIGURE 10.2 The results of the survey
Source: Adapted from a report by Jim Branit, Technical Writing 421, Illinois Institute of Technology.

the report first discussed the history of the drama clubs at the university since 1949. Then it presented the findings of the survey of students at the university, and, finally, the writer evaluated the data and made appropriate recommendations about a drama club.

The population surveyed was 100 freshmen, and the questionnaire was designed to determine the following:

- The student's inclination to attend a play (questions 1, 2, and 6).
- The extent of the student's past theater experience (questions 3, 3a, and 3b).
- The student's willingness to participate in a drama club (questions 4, 4a, and 5).

Rather than recreate the questionnaire in the report, the writer illustrated the questionnaire by providing the results in three tables.

From these data the writer drew implications about the status of a student drama club at the university. And, from the implications, the writer recommended a course of action and established a management plan, a portion of which is given in Figure 10.3.

To return to the example of the users of the home office, experts indicate that "telecommuting" is going to become popular as more and more people, especially women, work out of their homes. Both the employees (women) and employers expect computers to play a large part in the home

---

RECOMMENDATIONS

Based on the data, I would recommend the following:

- The Student Union Board should attempt to form a student drama club at the university by fall 1987.
- A search for a qualified director should begin immediately. The director could also teach on a part-time basis (perhaps in speech or debate) and maintain the structure of the drama club.
- The standard club form of president, vice president, treasurer, and secretary should be used. The officers should be elected by the members, and members should not have to pay dues.
- The plays should be advertised in *University News* . . .
- A free preview performance should be given for the press.
- Advertising for the theater program should be solicited.
- Room 111, Wishert Hall, should be used for productions. It has a stage and is the appropriate size for the expected audience.

FIGURE 10.3 Evaluating the data and drawing conclusions
Source: Adapted from a report by Jim Branit, Technical Writing 421, Illinois Institute of Technology.

office as the women "telecommute," and an analysis of the present situation and future predictions indicate that technology will make the home office a convenient place for the business of telecommuting. So a needs assessment for the home office indicates three objectives. The home office

1. Accommodates women.
2. Accommodates computer equipment and other furniture.
3. Establishes a businesslike atmosphere.

To establish the standards and specifications for the office and the furniture, you have to interview some buyers and users. The buyers of telecommuting equipment want

- durable furniture
- secure offices

The users want

- comfort
- versatility
- practicality
- aesthetics

What Is the Implication or Recommendation for Future Action?

The implications or recommendation follow from the past and present status and the objectives or the needs of the users and buyers. The company may want a concrete management plan to market a product or establish a new procedure. The individual may want an exercise and nutrition plan to improve health. Finally, in the example of the home office, you conclude that any design for the home office must consider

Potential Users, Especially Women as
- Small businesses
- Executives
- Middle managers/private workers
- Clerical
- Others
    telecommuters
    salespeople
    insurance agents
    mail-order business
    service/repair personnel
    writers
    educators/instructors
    political representatives

Business Equipment
- Types
    computers and related equipment
    furniture
- Construction
- Size
- Flexibility

Business Factors
- Space
- Frequency of use
- Ownership of equipment
- Security of office

Writing the Case/Assessment Study

After you have gathered your information, you are ready to organize the report.[2] In the introduction you establish the context and the road map for the rest of the report. The report presents the answers to your strategic questions.

- Introduction
    What's the subject?
    Is there a problem?
    What's your objective or purpose?
    What's the organizational strategy?
- History
    What does a review of the subject's past reveal?
    Did you emphasize important points from the past?
- Present Status
    How would you describe the subject now?
    Did you emphasize important considerations?
- Analysis
    What are the objectives now for the subject? (the plan or person?)
    What are the needs or criteria?
- Implications/Recommendations
    What is your recommendation?
    Is there a plan for future action?

Does the Reader Want a Summary?

Often the case/assessment report is written for executives who want to know the implications or recommendation quickly without studying the entire report. You can summarize the report in an executive summary that precedes the introduction. Although the executive summary includes an overview of the document, it does not necessarily follow the organizational plan of the document because the summary emphasizes the results, conclusions, and recommendations. The executive summary is written for the decision maker who wants to read a thorough but brief review of the major points leading to the conclusion and recommendation and have enough information to make a decision. A concluding summary appears at the end of the document and follows the organizational plan of the document. Often you can restate the purpose of the document and then use sentences from each section, sentences that present the main point.

The executive summary for the home office study would focus on the following:

- The overview of the contents of the document, including the purpose of the study.
- The results of the needs assessment.
- The factors—users, equipment, business condition—influencing the design of the new home office.
- The course of action.

The concluding summary would include major points from each section in the following order:

- The purpose for designing a new home office.
- The historical rise of the white-collar worker.
- The present status of women in the work force and the advancement of technology.
- The results of the needs assessment.
- The factors influencing the design of the new home office furniture.
- The recommendation to the decision maker about the course of action.

What Visual Techniques Improve Case/Assessment Studies and Design Reports?

Your report will benefit from visual techniques appropriate for all reports:

- new page for each major section of the report
- heading and subheadings
- readable layout and typography
- lists (if appropriate)
- illustrations (referred to in text)

The status report in Figure 10.4 illustrates a study for a large company. The report begins with an executive summary and then presents the study of this large company with many branch stores. The report is incomplete, but it establishes an organizational strategy for a case report.

MANAGEMENT PLAN FOR SAFETY
IN THE GOURMET KITCHEN DEPARTMENTS

Prepared by
Gina Nan Visco

3 December 19XX

FIGURE 10.4 A case report with an executive summary
Source: Gina Nan Visco, Technical Writing 421, Illinois Institute of Technology.

CONTENTS

FIGURE 10.4 (cont.)

ILLUSTRATIONS (not included)

FIGURES

FIGURE 10.4 (cont.)

SUMMARY

This report presents a Management Plan for Safety in the Gourmet Kitchen departments. It is directed at improving the safety of the working conditions surrounding the use of the electric meat-slicers. Improving safety improves sales and service and, therefore, profits. Better conditions create good employee morale and lead to increased productivity. Safer conditions also lessen the financial, physical, and emotional costs by lessening the chance of on-the-job injury.

The report includes the following:

1. Management objectives for the Gourmet Kitchen departments.
2. Past operations.
3. A description of the problematic safety conditions involved with
   - the new service procedure
   - training and operating procedures
   - cleaning procedures
   - the poor performance of the guard on the electric slicer.
4. Recommendations for improving the safety conditions through
   - customized scheduling to handle the traffic flow
   - formal training and operating guidelines
   - adapting utensils
   - guard improvement.

Past operations in the Gourmet Kitchens departments called for preslicing products on automatic meat-slicers. Preslicing is safer than slicing-to-order because the employee takes less time to serve a customer, thereby reducing employee stress. Automatic meat-slicers reduce injury by limiting necessary contact with the machine during operation.

Preslicing, however, was eliminated and replaced by 100 percent slicing-to-order in order to provide fresher products sliced to the customer's order. This slicing-to-order takes more time when serving a customer. During heavy traffic periods, employees are pressured to work more quickly, a situation that creates a potential safety hazard. Customizing a schedule to accommodate the traffic flow can eliminate this problem.

Training in the Gourmet Kitchen departments is done mainly by the method of "watch and do, listen and learn." No standardized manual is used to train employees to operate and clean the slicers. For this reason, the training methods vary from employee to employee, and safety warnings may or may not be emphasized. Often an employee learns the importance of safety only after being injured. Training manuals will aid in the complete and standard training of new employees. Printed, brief guidelines for experienced employees will help employees concentrate on safety at all times.

To clean the slicers, employees should use inexpensive, long-handled utensils that can reduce hand contact with the slicers and increase safety. The present utensils do nothing to protect the employee from injury.

The guard on the slicers provides additional grip on products and reduces hand contact with the slicing blades. Although it works well on most meats, for some cheeses it does not hold the product sufficiently. This insufficient hold creates a hazard to safety. The guard must be redesigned to hold all products sufficiently.

FIGURE 10.4 (cont.)

Management Plan for Safety in the Gourmet Kitchen Departments

I. INTRODUCTION

Purpose

The purpose of this report is to present the findings of a study of the electric meat-slicers in the Gourmet Kitchen departments. The study focused on the safety conditions surrounding the use of the slicers. This report presents the description of the conditions, the implications, and the recommendations for improving these conditions.

Background

Work in the Gourmet Kitchen departments involves almost continuous use of the slicers. Throughout the day employees slice vegetables for party trays and sandwiches as well as meats and cheeses for customers. The closing procedures for the department require that the employees thoroughly clean the slicers at the end of each day. The extensive handling of the slicers creates a great potential for injury.

Until recently, the use of automatic electric slicers reduced the number of injuries. Now, with the change in procedure from preslicing most products on the automatic slicers to 100 percent slicing-to-order on the electric meat-slicer, Gourmet Kitchen departments must study the change in safety conditions due to this change in procedures. The electric meat-slicers present an increased hazard to employee safety.

Scope

This report discusses the present status of the safety conditions surrounding the use of the slicers and recommends improvements. The report is intended for readers who have a working knowledge of the general operations and use of the slicers in the Gourmet Kitchen departments. The appendix includes illustrations to support the findings of the study.

To aid in understanding the present status, the report first discusses the management objectives and the past operating procedures for the Gourmet Kitchen departments. Next it presents a description of potentially hazardous conditions in the department on the basis of the employee tasks, tasks that include service and training as well as operating the equipment, cleaning the area, and troubleshooting. Finally, the report offers specific recommendations for improving the safety conditions in the Gourmet Kitchens departments.

II. MANAGEMENT OBJECTIVES

The management objectives for operation of the Gourmet Kitchen departments are clear and receive top priority. Sales, service, and safety are interwoven in every Gourmet Kitchen operation. Good service as well as fresh products promote sales. Unsafe conditions hamper service and decrease sales. In addition, unsafe conditions increase the possibility of employee injury, and the costs to both the employee and the company are great. For this reason, safety is a major factor in the working conditions of the Gourmet Kitchen departments.

III. PAST OPERATIONS

Until recently, the majority of slicing was done on automatic meat slicers. These slicers require only minimal contact when slicing a product. The

FIGURE 10.4 (cont.)

operator loads the product onto the slicer, locks it into place, and turns on the slicer. The slicer than slices the product until the receiving tray is filled and automatically shuts off. The operator can remove the sliced product from the tray and turn the slicer on again to slice any remaining product. Never during the slicing process is the operator required to be in close proximity to the moving blade.

Preslicing on automatic slicers has some important advantages over hand-slicing the product to order. By limiting required contact with the slicer, preslicing on automatic slicers reduces injury. Preslicing also reduces the stress related with hurrying to serve a customer quickly and thus reduces another source of injury. Service to the customer is quicker because the items are presliced. Preslicing on automatic slicers is safer and quicker when serving customers.

However, preslicing does not provide the freshest product to the customer, nor does it provide the customer with the product sliced according to the customer's wishes. To give the customer a fresher product sliced as the customer desires, preslicing was eliminated; the automatic slicers were removed from the Gourmet Kitchen departments, and handheld electric slicers were installed.

IV. PRESENT STATUS: DESCRIPTION WITH IMPLICATIONS

The following descriptions of the conditions are based on my observation of the operations in the Gourmet Kitchen departments. I also interviewed the Gourmet Kitchen employees for additional insights into the problems of safety in the department.

A. New Slicing Procedures

Slicing-to-order is a plus for the customer who gets a fresher product sliced to his or her liking. However, it presents problems. Quick and efficient service is as important to the customer as is the quality of the product. Slicing-to-order takes more time than does preslicing. Employees must work more quickly during heavy traffic periods to keep service efficient. For this reason, they are under more pressure. This increased pressure can affect the employee's concentration on safety when slicing. During these heavy traffic periods, more employees should be scheduled to work these hours to reduce the pressure on any one employee and increase safety. At present, lack of appropriate scheduling increases the amount of rushing and stress to serve the customers efficiently. Gourmet Kitchen needs a better schedule to accommodate the traffic flow.

B. Training and Operating Procedures

1. Training

At present, training in the Gourmet Kitchen operates by a method of "watch and do, listen and learn." The employees learn the operation by trial and error. They must work hard to absorb what is shown to them and are expected to ask questions if anything is unclear. Many operations are a matter of common sense and depend on the individual employee's judgment. Employees are diverse. Some may find this way of learning very natural; others may have difficulty understanding and remembering all that is taught to them. Some feel embarrassed when they have to ask questions repeatedly about a complicated

FIGURE 10.4 (cont.)

operation. Managers and co-workers must have extra patience. Additionally, some operations are repeated daily; some, weekly; and others, perhaps only once a month. The learning operation is a lengthy one.

When the "watch and learn" method is applied to the operation of the electric meat-slicer, the person must handle equipment that requires warning statements, a list of instructions, and practical application. No formal training steps, no written instructions with warning or caution statements accompany the equipment. In addition, each co-worker teaches the operation of the slicers differently. Some may stress the importance of concentrating on the operation whenever dealing with the slicer. Others may mention safety and caution once or twice. Some may feel it is "common sense" to be careful; others may feel that overstating precautions to avoid injury may scare trainees. Even those who stress safety may forget some crucial point. Questions on the equipment are too late after an employee is injured. Employees should not have to injure themselves to learn the importance of safety. Gourmet Kitchens should have a written training manual.

2. Operating

Even for those employees who have experience, safety around the slicers should be a never-ending thought. Experience can work against the employee. Repeated action in any situation develops a routine and a lack of conscious effort. With repetition of some actions also comes speed. These factors work against the experienced employee's concentration on safety. An employee with experience operating the slicers may carry on conversations with customers and co-workers. Even experienced employees should follow some rules or guidelines to keep concentration on safety at a high level.

C. Cleaning Procedures

At present, cleaning procedures for the slicer are taught in the same manner as the operating procedures: without formal written instructions. Throughout the cleaning procedure the employee must exercise extreme caution. Often just a brush and rag are used with soapy water to clean the slicers. The removable parts—cover plate, guide tray, and sharpening cover—are removed to soak and wash in the sink. Doing so leaves the blade (usually sharpened before cleaning) completely exposed. Scrubbing the exposed blade and the rest of the slicer with a soapy brush requires caution so that the employee does not brush a hand against the blade's edge. Rinsing the slicer and wiping excess water with a rag requires even more caution. Slicing through a rag into a hand is an immediate concern. The hand should not be so vulnerable by being in such close proximity to the blade. To limit the chance of injury, the employee needs better utensils for cleaning.

D. Troubleshooting

The device to hold the product on the slicer is insufficient. The electric meat-slicers slice a large variety of products. Some products are soft, and some are hard, and there is a great range in between. Some products are slippery in texture and become more so as the products become smaller from slicing. Others are gummy and do not move well with the guide on the slicer. The variations in products create a problem of holding the item securely in place as it is sliced.

FIGURE 10.4 (cont.)

The securing devices—the guard and the hook—work best on hard or gummy products. But the slippery and soft products are difficult to hold and frustrate the employee. Employees will think of their responsibility to three people: the customer, the employer, and themselves. They are faced with a choice. One objective tells them to serve the customer quickly and efficiently, which includes a nicely packaged product. Another objective tells them to be cost-effective for the employer by utilizing as much of the product as possible. Finally, the third objective is to perform safely for their own sake and the sake of the company.

If the slicer cannot hold the product adequately, employees may either hold the product in their hand, or they may replace it with a new piece of the product. If they choose to hold the product because the piece is small, the hand is dangerously close to the moving blade. If they unwrap a new piece of the product, they avoid injury but increase the cost to the company, and they take longer to fill the order.

Neither choice is optimum. The costs of workers' compensation may outweigh the costs of not using all of a product, not to mention the physical and emotional costs to the injured employee. But those decisions are made in a matter of seconds, and the employee should not have to decide between injury or utilizing a product. The slicer should hold the product adequately to eliminate crucial decision making.

V. RECOMMENDATIONS

A. Traffic-flow Scheduling

I studied the traffic flow in a Gourmet Kitchen department for one month, recording the number of customers per hour. In the sample study, Thursday, Friday, and Saturday are the busiest days. This pattern may be the same for most Gourmet Kitchen departments, but the heaviest hours may vary from store to store, depending on the life-style of the customers who shop at the store. In the store studied, the hours of 4:00 to 6:00 P.M. were the heaviest.

For this study, the department manager adapted the employee work schedule to the flow of traffic. The employees tested the schedule for two weeks and discovered they worked better together, had less stress, and found the work more enjoyable. The duties were distributed more evenly, and the teamwork led to more efficient service during the peak periods and more productivity in all phases of the Gourmet Kitchen operations. The employees could concentrate on the task, providing less stress and promoting greater safety and skill.

This study can be adapted to each Gourmet Kitchen department. Each department should keep an hourly and daily schedule of traffic flow for one month. The department should then develop a customized schedule for the employees, taking into account employee availability and traffic flow. The district manager should explain to each department manager the simple, standardized method of developing a customized schedule and work with the manager for developing this customized schedule.

This simple process will yield better productivity, improve employee morale, and contribute to safety conditions.

FIGURE 10.4 (cont.)

B. Formal Training and Operating Guidelines

1. Formal Training

Although the scheduling for each Gourmet Kitchen department is customized, training and operating procedures are standard. For all employees,
new and old, as well as managers, a manual on equipment would be advanta-
geous. But this manual would not necessarily contribute to safety. During
training, the instructor should ask employees to repeat a procedure in their
own words. At this time, the instructor should try to make the employees feel
comfortable about asking questions.

For operating and cleaning the electric meat-slicer, employees wanted a
formal manual of instructions, with warnings and cautions emphasized. The
employee should be required to read and study the manual thoroughly before
visual instruction begins and before the employee attempts to use or clean
the slicer.

The manual would eliminate any variation in instruction and ensure that
all points are presented. An additional, simple "Do" and "Don't" checklist for
the experienced employee would retain the concentration on safety. The instructions from the manufacturers of the electric meat-slicers are inadequate
and should be adapted and customized for use in the Gourmet Kitchen departments. A bottom-line recommendation for safety in Gourmet Kitchen is a written Manual of Instruction for Operating and Cleaning the Electric Meat-Slicer.

2. Operating the Equipment

In addition to the manual, an experienced Gourmet Kitchen manager and
a writer should establish a general set of rules or guidelines for performing
safely. These guidelines should be posted in every department, and the employees should be encouraged to read and review them frequently. These guidelines
include the following:

- Do not hold conversations while operating or cleaning a slicer.
- Turn off slicer when not in use.
- Turn off slicer when loading or unloading product from guide tray.
- Never hold product with your hand when slicing.
- Always wait for blade to stop moving before taking anything off or putting
  anything on slicer.
- Use appropriate utensils to clean the slicer.

C. Adapting Utensils

Some household utensils can clean the slicers safely and inexpensively.
Steel mesh gloves are an ultimate safety aid, but they are expensive and not
absolutely necessary. Household utensils that keep the hands a safe distance
from the blade are recommended:

- Long-handled sturdy brush for scrubbing dried foods from slicer.
- Long-handled bottle brush for cleaning underneath the blade and between
  the blade and slicer body.
- Large rectangular sponge to rinse slicer and absorb excess water on the base
  of the slicer.

UNDER NO CIRCUMSTANCES SHOULD EMPLOYEES
USE RAGS TO CLEAN SLICERS.

D. Troubleshooting-Guard Improvement

Many products can be sliced without the aid of the guard. However, soft

FIGURE 10.4 (cont.)

or slippery products are not held adequately by the guard, and the employee's safety is at stake. The guard should be redesigned, or additional parts should be machined for a better grip. At present, the short, blunt stubs do not pierce the product sufficiently to keep it from slipping. The lack of proper hold on the product creates a hazardous situation when an employee uses the slicer. The guard needs additional hooks or needlelike prongs to improve the grip, or the guard should be totally redesigned for the electric meat-slicer.

VI. CONCLUSIONS

This Management Plan for Safety is directed at improving the safety of using the electric meat-slicer in the Gourmet Kitchen departments. Past operations in the departments involved preslicing products on automatic meat-slicers. To provide fresher products and greater customer satisfaction, 100 percent slicing-to-order was instituted. Slicing-to-order takes more time, creates pressure during customer rushes, and creates a potential safety hazard. A study of the traffic flow and customizing a work schedule can alleviate some of these potential safety hazards.

Another hazard to safety is training, presently accomplished by the "watch, do, listen, and learn" method. No standardized manual is used for training employees to operate and clean the slicers. Thus, training methods vary from instructor to instructor and differ from one Gourmet Kitchen to another. Often an employee learns the importance of safety only after being injured. Formalized training manuals ensure complete training. Guidelines keep experienced employees concentrating on safety.

Cleaning the slicer requires extreme care for safety, but inexpensive long-handled utensils can reduce the chance of injury. The utensils used presently do nothing to protect the employee from injury.

Finally, the guard on the slicers works well for most products but is inadequate for certain products. The guard should be redesigned or supplemented with additional gripping features. These recommendations for increased safety when using the electric meat-slicer will help the employee be more efficient, take fewer safety risks, and work more comfortably with co-workers and customers, all increasing profits for the company.

FIGURE 10.4 (cont.)

Introducing the Strategy for the Design Report

Like the case/assessment study, the design report identifies a problem. But the problem exists usually with a product.

- The Richard Advertising Company is opening a new office and wants to present its services in a visual display. What should this display look like?
- Western Airlines is remodeling its on-board kitchen and wants an efficient, practical design.

The design report provides a possible solution—either in an illustration of the product or as a prototype. Many design reports are actually redesigns of an existing product. For example, you might be asked to redesign an insurance form or a documentation manual. Redesigns involve the same steps as a completely new design. Both begin by your asking questions and gathering information.

- What does the client or consumer want or need?
  Conduct the needs assessment by questionnaire or interview to compile the information you have to use in designing or redesigning the product.
- What product standards and specifications will meet these needs?
  Establish the priorities, constraints, standards, and specifications to design the product.
- What is the new design or the redesign for the product?
  Draft the new design or revision based on the standards and specs.
- What parts or components do you need to produce the product?
  List the component parts, the materials, the cost (if appropriate).
- How will you produce or assemble the product?
  Describe the procedures to produce the product.
- How will you evaluate the success of the design?
  Plan a method of evaluation.

These questions become your steps for producing the design and organizing the report. Accompanying the design is a set of standards and specifications that the design meets, the components necessary to produce the product, the procedure for assembling the product, and, finally, an evaluation of the design or the product.

Writing the Design Report

The organizational strategy for the design report follows the plan in Figure 10.5.

Introduce the Report

Throughout this textbook you have been encouraged to incorporate four elements in the introduction: the purpose, the background, the significance or scope, and the organizational plan for the remainder of the document. For the design report, the *purpose* of the document is clear. If you are the designer, you will present a design for a new manual or a new car. Or you might present a design for an automobile turntable that can display the car of the future.

The *background* behind the design explains the problem with the prior art turntable. The previous turntables were heavy, cumbersome, and expensive and required large amounts of power to rotate the display stand. With the need to remain competitive, car dealers know the *significance* of portable, inexpensive display stands. So the rationale for the project is to produce a design that technicians can use to build an automobile turntable for the dealer's showroom. And the remainder of the document follows the *organizational plan* in Figure 10.5, with the standards and specs, an overview of the design, the components, the procedure for assembly, and an evaluation of the design.

INTRODUCTION with
- Purpose
- Background
- Report plan

STANDARDS and SPECIFICATIONS with
- priorities
- constraints
- data to design the product

DESIGN such as a(n)
- illustration of the product
- description
- overview

COMPONENTS such as
- materials
- equipment

METHODS OR PROCEDURES with
- theory
- instructions

EVALUATION to determine
- success of product
- satisfaction of user

FIGURE 10.5 Organizational strategy for a design report

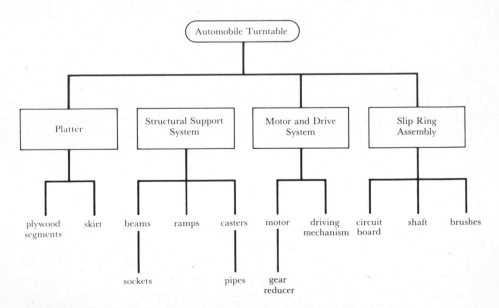

FIGURE 10.6 The parts of the automobile turntable
Source: Suzanne Glowiak, Technical Writing 421, Illinois Institute of Technology.

Establish Standards and Specifications

This section of the design report contains information similar to that in the multiple evaluation section of Module 9. The standards for the turntable are established in general terms because the list of components will specify the exact data and dollar amounts. The turntable will meet the following standards:

- low in cost
- lightweight
- portable
- dependable

Present the Design

The design section is usually a description of the product, divided into its main elements, and then each element is described separately. Figure 10.6 describes the automobile turntable and illustrates the parts of the turntable. Module 6 also has a description of a device, an adjustable wrench.

List the Component Parts

Components are, essentially, the specifications of the design. The technician who will build the product or replicate the design will read this section as if it were a shopping list. So if you are the designer and writer, you will try to be as accurate as possible in this section. To continue our example of the automobile turntable, you would itemize the components for each part of the turntable, illustrated in Figure 10.7.

Describe the Procedures

Like most reports, the design report presents the procedure for assembling the product and the theory or principle of operation on which the design is based. The methods section includes the following:

- theory behind the design
- instructions for assembly
- reference to illustrations
- warnings and troubleshooting.

Take our example of the automobile turntable. If you were the designer, you would include a reference to the stress analysis performed on the turntable structure using classical statics and strength of materials. The platter distributes the weight of the stand and the vehicle it is supporting over a number of casters surrounding the center of rotation. The center is bolted to four caster outriggers. The outriggers remain stationary while the platter, the support beams, and the ring rotate. The drive unit is affixed to the base of

List of Components and Costs

PLATTER

Plywood ¾ in. 4 ft. × 9 ft.
    8 sheets @ $20.00/sheet $ 160.00
Sheet aluminum 20 in. × 50 ft. and
    coil   .032 in.   87.08
Extruded neoprene 49.5 ft. @ $.30   15.00
Hardware   12.50

STRUCTURAL SUPPORT

Plywood ¾ in. 4 ft. × 9 ft.
    4 sheets @ $20.00/sheet   80.00
Casters 4 in. dia.
    12 casters @ 8.50/caster   102.00
Pipes 50 ft. @ .50/ft.   25.00
Miscellaneous hardware   11.00

MOTOR AND DRIVE

Winsmith 24 2.12 hp.   482.00

SLIP RING

Assembly   20.00
Tooling   300.00
TOTAL $1,294.00

FIGURE 10.7 Component parts for the automobile turntable
Source: Suzanne Glowiak, Technical Writing 421, Illinois Institute of Technology.

the stand, and power is supplied to the motor through a cord plugged into
a source of electrical power. This entire assembly is illustrated in figures
located in the appendix.

Finally, this section refers to any safety factors, such as the outrigger
casters to prevent the turntable from tipping and the placement of the electrical cord located in an outrigger so as not to interfere with the turning of
the platter. Because the platter and the vehicle are so heavy, none of the
weight is to be supported by the drive plate or the drive and motor assembly.

Evaluate the Design

In a design report, the evaluation usually involves testing the design against
the standards and specifications. If the design is a product, you may have to
construct a prototype and physically test the product. In the case of the
turntable, a prototype was designed, tested, and compared to prior art turntables. The casters were more troublefree and the plywood and electric motor
were more portable and less expensive that the prior art turntables. When
you design or revise a document, you can field-test the document by asking
people to read the document and follow the instructions or answer questions.
Modules 7 and 9 further explain methods of evaluation.

Draw Conclusions

The section of the report for drawing conclusions refers to previous information, briefly mentioning the purpose, the standards, the aspects of the design as well as the components, the methods and procedures, and the evaluation. This concluding summary differs from the executive summary in both organization and degree of specificity. Because the executive summary focuses on results, conclusions, and recommendations, it is more specific than the concluding summary. After all, to reach the concluding summary, the decision maker has read the entire document. In reading an executive summary that appears even before the introduction to the document, the decision maker may read no further; and, therefore, the executive summary has to focus on different sections with greater specificity.

Whether you use an executive summary or a concluding summary depends on the reader. When the reader wants to know the results of the study immediately, use the executive summary. When the technical aspects of the report are important to the reader, place the conclusion last. Figure 10.8 presents the conclusion of the automobile turntable report.

The automobile turntable meets the standards: portable, inexpensive, and troublefree. The components include the casters, the two-by-fours, the two-horsepower electric motor, and the drive system. The theory behind the design is to create a troublefree device that will operate over long periods of time. The casters are an improvement over the bearings used on the prior art turntables, and the weight of the platter and automobile is distributed over the casters and the base structure, not just on the bearings that required machining and critical, even distribution of the load. The entire turntable is designed to be lightweight, weighing 800 pounds, but capable of supporting a four-ton vehicle, and it rotates at one RPM for maximum cost-effectiveness.

FIGURE 10.8 Conclusion for the auto turntable report
Source: Suzanne Glowiak, Technical Writing 421, Illinois Institute of Technology.

Preparing a Document Design Report

The design document in Figure 10.9 uses a focus group to establish standards for redesigning a user manual accompanying an automatic blanket. A focus group is a group of people who gather to assess a product. They provide the information a designer needs to improve a product. In other words, a focus group is one method for conducting a needs analysis. The document also uses the executive summary because to the reader the product is more important than the technique. In the text, the writer provides the details and the data to support the recommendation about the revised user's manual for the automatic blanket.

USER MANUAL FOR THE
SIMS AUTOMATIC BLANKET

Design Project Report

Prepared by Linda M. Lee

for Humanities 421
Technical Writing

FIGURE 10.9 Redesigning a manual for an electric blanket
Source: Linda M. Lee, Technical Writing 421, Illinois Institute of Technology.

CONTENTS

FIGURE 10.9 (cont.)

ILLUSTRATIONS

FIGURE 10.9 (cont.)

SUMMARY

The objective of this project was to redesign the existing user's manual for the Sims Automatic Blanket.

Design criteria were developed first by analyzing the problems in the existing manual. Then the problems were partitioned into two categories: technical writing and graphic design. Technical writing comprises the overall organization of the text and the writing of the instructions. Graphic design includes type size, color, and layout. A focus group determined the users' needs and provided user comments when testing the manual. Finally, books on legibility studies and technical writing contributed to the final redesign of the manual.

The final design is an 8½ × 11-inch manual with a total of 10 pages. The manual has an index and 9 sections. Each section begins on a separate page, with the writing and the design of the manual closely following the established criteria.

The focus group judged the redesigned manual and the prior manual by the established criteria. The redesigned manual was rated superior to the existing manual. However, the focus group judged the new manual as lacking a certain "friendliness." For this reason, the manual needs additional attention: to increase the warmth of the manual, perhaps by color or illustration, and to re-evaluate the manual.

FIGURE 10.9 (cont.)

INTRODUCTION

This report presents a redesigned users' manual for the Sims Automatic Blanket. Consumers often purchase products that are accompanied by a badly written and poorly designed user manual. The manual may have confusing instructions, inadequate illustrations, and incomplete information. Sometimes the overall layout even hinders rather than helps reader comprehension. Such manuals can lead to customer frustration or even injury, product abuse or mishandling, and costly litigation.

The buyer is usually a nontechnical user who wants to use the product safely and efficiently. This report explains the criteria for redesigning the automatic blanket and presents the results of the evaluation—an evaluation performed by a focus group.

The report first presents the problems with the original Sims user manual. Then the focus group helps establish criteria for a redesigned manual, criteria aided by writing and design textbooks. Finally, the new manual is designed and evaluated against the criteria and the original manual.

FIGURE 10.9 (cont.)

I. DESIGN STEPS

Problem Statement
The existing Sims manual suffers from the following:

- poor text layout
- small type size
- poor choice of type color
- inadequate illustrations
- poorly written instructions
- inadequate emphasis of warnings/cautions.

Methods and Procedures

Analysis: The first step toward establishing criteria began with analyzing and partitioning the problems of the existing manual. The categories are (1) technical writing and (2) graphic design. The technical writing category includes the content and the organizational plan. The graphic design category includes the type size and color, the layout, and the illustrations.

Focus Group: The next step to establish criteria involved forming a focus group. A focus group is a group of people brought together to discuss and evaluate problems and issues about any topic.

The focus group consisted of five women and one man. Two people were between the ages of 20 and 25, and the others were from 30 to 35. Four of the people had undergraduate degrees; the other two were undergraduates. At the session the group discussed the advantages and disadvantages of user manuals in general and then focused on the Sims manual. The group also verified the problem found in the initial analysis of the manual and added other considerations at this session.

FIGURE 10.9 (cont.)

The focus group considered the size of the manual and recommended that it be 8½ × 11 for ease of filing. Furthermore, they discussed the "feeling" of the manual, a feeling of "friendliness" so that the user would not feel intimidated while reading the manual.

Library Research: A legibility book and a technical writing book provided the final criteria. The legibility book described optimum type size and color for reading. The technical writing textbook clarified sentence construction and organizational formats.

Design: The titles and body copy were typeset on a 7500 Compugraphic machine. All keylining and pasteup work was done at the Institute of Design, Illinois Institute of Technology.

FIGURE 10.9 (cont.)

II. DESIGN CRITERIA

The design criteria for the user's manual are summarized as follows.

TECHNICAL WRITING

<u>Content</u>: The content must be accurate, concise, and complete, with a clear set of instructions and appropriate warnings and cautions.

<u>Format</u>: The manual must include an index, a process description and a principle of operation section, instructions, and a warranty.

GRAPHIC DESIGN

<u>Type</u>: The type size must be between 9–12 pt. for legibility and of a color that enhances readability.

<u>Illustrations</u>. The illustrations must be clearly labeled and placed near the appropriate instructions.

FIGURE 10.9 (cont.)

III. FINAL DESIGN

The redesigned Sims manual is 8½ × 11 inches. The total of 10 pages includes the index and the warranty. A rule (a solid black line) is used at the heading line of the page to add visual continuity to the manual. Each informational/instruction section is placed on a separate page for the user's benefit. The instructions are written clearly and concisely, and the type size is 12 pt., with the type color black on a white background. Each illustration is clearly labeled and placed near the appropriate instruction, and warnings and cautions are *italicized* for emphasis.

A 38% reduction of the redesigned manual is shown on the next six pages. (The redesigned manual is omitted from this example; only one figure is included here.)

How Blanket Works

The blanket is composed of insulated wires covered by a washable polyester fabric. (See Fig. 1.)

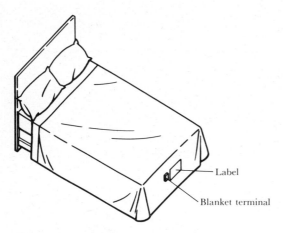

— Label

— Blanket terminal

Figure 1 Blanket

There is a terminal (near the label) at the foot end of the blanket. This terminal is the outlet for the wires in the blanket. The corresponding plug is at the end of the long extension cord that extends from the control unit.

The blanket will automatically warm up if the plug is plugged into the control unit and the control unit is turned on. Therefore, you should exercise caution when using this blanket.

FIGURE 10.9 (cont.)

IV. EVALUATION OF THE FINAL DESIGN

The focus group of six people evaluated the final design of the Sims manual on the basis of the criteria outlined in the design section. The manual is rated on each criterion using a three-scale rating: superior, acceptable, unacceptable. The numbers in Table 1 reflect the summaries of the results of the six evaluators.

| | Rating (based on number of people) | | |
Criterion	Superior	Acceptable	Unacceptable
Technical Writing			
+*Instructions*	2	4	
+*Organizational plan*	6		
+*Description*	2	4	
+*Warnings and cautions*	3	3	
Graphic Design			
+*Type size*	6		
+*Type color*	6		
+*Illustrations*	4	2	

Table 1 Evaluation of the Redesigned Sims Manual

Results
The final design is judged to be at least acceptable under all criteria. One judgment not measured by the criteria was the group's feeling of user manual friendliness. The redesigned manual felt less friendly than the original one, and the evaluators recommended using color or illustrations with people to provide more warmth to the manual.

All six evaluators rated the organization and legibility of the manual as superior. Overall, the redesigned manual is superior in communicating the necessary information to the user, who also finds the manual easy to use.

FIGURE 10.9 (cont.)

CONCLUSIONS AND RECOMMENDATIONS

The manual meets the following criteria:

- The text is well organized and easy to follow.
- The instructions are clear, concise, and complete.
- The illustrations are clearly labeled and appropriately placed.
- The warnings and cautions are properly emphasized.

The manual needs additional changes:

1. To increase the warmth of the manual.
2. To incorporate the suggestions of the focus group and reevaluate the manual.

FIGURE 10.9 (cont.)

E. REFERENCES

Juanita W. Dudley, *A Text-Workbook for English 421—Technical Writing: Engineering and Science Applications.* (West Lafayette, Ind.: Purdue Research Foundation, 1978).

Herbert Spencer, *The Visible Word.* (Hastings House, N.Y.: Visual Communications Books, 1969).

FIGURE 10.9 (cont.)

Summary

Case/assessment studies review a person's condition or assess a company's policy and *recommend* a course of action. These studies review a subject by looking at its past *history* and describing the *present status* of the situation. Often an *analysis* of the needs of the users, a needs assessment, will help determine the present status of the situation.

Needs assessments may take the form of questionnaires, surveys, or focus groups. *Focus groups* are people assembled to talk about and review a document. Questionnaires and surveys are usually distributed to consumers and should tell the respondent the purpose of the survey. Furthermore, each question should provide information that supports the reason for the survey, and, finally, the surveyor should have a plan for evaluating data before distributing the questionnaire. Well-designed *questionnaires* provide clear directions and enough space for a response, ask questions that support the writer's objectives, and minimize the length.

The written report includes an introduction with the necessary background information as well as an analysis of the history and present status and implications or a recommendation for future action. When the report is written for decision makers, an *executive summary* precedes the introduction and provides an overview of the document and a thorough but brief presentation of the results of the study as well as the conclusions and the recommendation or course of action.

When the technical aspects of the report are as important to the decision maker as the conclusion, the *concluding summary* is located at the end of the document and summarizes the major points from each section, following the organization of the document. The two summaries differ in the organization of the summary and the specificity of detail. The executive summary is more specific about results, conclusions, and course of action, but it omits reference to some sections of the document.

Visual techniques improve the readability of both status reports and design reports. Each major section of the reports should begin on a new page; headings and subheadings, layout and typography, as well as lists and illustrations, all contribute to the readability of the document.

The *design report* identifies a *problem,* usually with a *product,* and provides a possible *solution.* Solving design problems begins with asking questions and gathering information. After a needs analysis, the designer can establish *standards and specifications* and an overall *design* to solve the problem.

Writing the report includes an introduction, standards and specifications, the design, *component parts,* the *procedure for assembly,* and an *evaluation* of the design. Often the design report will have a concluding *summary.* When the technical aspects of the report are important to the reader, the conclusion is last.

Checklists for the Case/Assessment Studies and Design Reports

The information in this module covers the organizational strategies for two types of reports: the case report and the design report. The checklist for each of these reports asks you to consider or include the following items in your report and to indicate those items by checking them.

Include/
Consider IN YOUR *CASE/ASSESSMENT STUDY*, DID YOU

_____   Introduce the subject?

_____   purpose or objectives of the study?

_____   background of the problem?

_____   organizational strategy?

_____   Review the subject (history)?

_____   Describe the present situation (status)?

_____   Analyze and assess the situation?

_____   by survey/interview?

_____   by questionnaire?

_____   by focus group?

            Prepare for the assessment by
_____   stating the purpose/goal/significance of the measurement?

_____   planning the method of evaluation?

_____   giving the respondent appropriate directions?

_____   designing the measurement to be as brief as possible?

            Design the measurement to

_____   ask one question at a time?

_____   include a sample response, if appropriate?

——————— provide enough space for the response?

——————— Recommend an action?

IN YOUR *DESIGN REPORT*, DID YOU
Introduce

——————— the problem?

——————— the objective?

——————— the organizational plan?

——————— Establish standards and specifications?

——————— by needs analysis?

——————— by product review?

——————— Present the design?

——————— List the components?

——————— with data?

——————— with costs?

——————— Describe the assembly procedures, including

——————— theory?

——————— instructions?

——————— illustrations?

——————— warnings and troubleshooting?

——————— Evaluate the design?

——————— in a prototype?

——————— with users?

In both reports, did you
——————— summarize in an executive summary preceding the introduction?

                or
_____   summarize in a concluding summary in the last section?

               Use visual techniques with
_____   a new page for each major section?

_____   headings and subheadings?

_____   readable layout and typography?

_____   lists?

_____   illustrations?

Notes

1. Jonathan J. Dykstra, "Status of the Home Office," Technical Writing 421, Illinois Institute of Technology, 1982. This report provided the example of the home office for the case study.
2. Juanita W. Dudley, *A Text-Workbook for English 421—Technical Writing: Engineering and Science Applications* (West Lafayette, Ind.: Purdue Research Foundation, 1978): 233. The organizational patterns for status and design reports are adapted from this text.

References

Everett R. Rogers, *Diffusion of Innovations* (New York: Macmillan, 1983).

Thomas E. Pinelli et al., "Report Format Preferences of Technical Managers and Nonmanagers," *Technical Communication* 31 (Second Quarter 1984):6–7.

Helen E. Quinn, "Teaching Managerial Writing: Addressing Uncertainty in the Organization," in *Proceedings,* 33d International Technical Communication Conference (Washington, D.C.: Society for Technical Communication, 1986): 274–277.

Applying Your Knowledge

EXERCISE 10.1

Select a 4–6 page document to redesign. The document may be a

sales brochure
manual
technical description
informational or instructional booklet

trade publication
technical ad.

Then trace the history of the item or concept featured in the document you selected. For example, if you are redesigning the brochure that accompanies smoke detectors, first trace the history of smoke detectors. Draft a case study for the item.

EXERCISE 10.2

For this exercise, collaborate with three other people. Each person on the team of four people presents the document and the history of the item or concept. Then each person

- Conducts a needs assessment among team members to determine the needs of people who have to use the document.
- Establishes criteria to improve the document (also see Module 9 on standards and specifications).
- Schedules a time to have the team evaluate the redesigned document (also see Module 7 on evaluation techniques).

WRITING ASSIGNMENT

Write a design report that incorporates the redesigned document. Include

executive summary or concluding summary
history of the item or concept
assessment of users' needs
standards and specifications
design
components
assembly procedure (if appropriate)
evaluation of redesign
conclusion (unnecessary if already at the beginning)

M O D U L E 11

Scientific Reports: Experimental Research Reports, Laboratory Reports, and Field Reports

Scientific reports frequently involve experimental research and analysis of data compiled from laboratory and field tests. The content of these reports helps the reader arrive at the same conclusion as the writer. So the reports must present the data, the analysis, and the conclusions in an orderly way. Scientific reports may be submitted as formal or informal reports. Formal reports have secondary materials that accompany the primary information, making formal reports longer than informal technical reports. Module 9 has descriptions of this secondary material. Companies may have their own formats for formal and informal scientific reports. For example, many companies use a standard laboratory (lab) report format to assist the writer because the writer must always consider the same information when writing a lab report.

Experimental research reports present the results of experiments by including information and presenting it in a formal and organized way that is convincing to the scientific community. Laboratory reports present the results of a particular lab test or study and are generally shorter reports than the research report. Laboratory reports are often read by multiple readers, and, thus, the organizational plan has to be clear and flexible. The field report may be informal or formal, depending on the accompanying secondary materials. Like the laboratory report, the field report investigates a technical problem that frequently involves laboratory analysis. But in analyzing the sample and the data after the field trip, the investigator often includes some information supplied by other people at the field site. If you are the field investigator, you may have to summarize some of the discussion at the site, and presenting this information will involve a flexible organizational strategy.

As part of the support for your conclusions, you may want to present visual forms such as tables, graphs, figures, and illustrations. Of course, the design of the content and appearance of the document depend on the reader's expectations and the company's procedure. This module will discuss the content of scientific reports and present an experimental research report as well as examples from laboratory and field reports.

Scope

In this module you will

1. Identify the conventional content for an experimental research report.
2. Plan the document using visual techniques and secondary elements.
3. Write a clear purpose statement for the laboratory report.
4. Organize the sections for a field report.
5. Elaborate on interpretative statements of impact or findings.

Defining the Research Report

The experimental research report presents the results of experiments. This research begins either with an observation or experiment that moves toward a goal or with a theory that is tested by experiments. For example, if you ask the question, "Can food be cooked by microwave radiation?" then you begin with an experiment and move toward a goal—to answer your question. On the other hand, if you speculate that microwave radiation produces heat in food by agitating the bipolar water molecules in the food, then you test your theory by placing food in a microwave beam. After you measure the temperature rise, you determine, "Yes, microwave radiation does increase the temperature in food."

You may begin a research report with

• a practical question
  or
• a theoretical speculation

Both cases rely on laboratory observation or experiment. This type of research, also called physical research, is frequently conducted in the scientific and engineering communities. When writers in these fields present the results of their research, they have to include elements that convince the readers they have researched the field and know the scientific procedures. Some questions about the research project will help you plan the contents of your research report.

Questions About the Experimental Research Project

1. What's the purpose of your study or your experiment?
2. What is the problem that led to the study?
3. Do you know what other studies or experiments have been done on this topic?
4. Is there a standard procedure to follow when conducting these experiments, or did you originate your own?
5. What are your findings?
6. Are your results positive? negative? unique? statistically significant?
7. What are your conclusions and recommendations (if appropriate) as a result of your study or experiment?

Your answers to these questions become the content of your research report and convince the scientific and technical communities that you have done your research appropriately.

Using a Conventional Strategy

When you write your answers to these questions, you are following a conventional strategy for presenting scientific information. This strategy has frequently been adopted by researchers in disciplines other than science or engineering.

The conventional strategy for an experimental research report includes the following:

introduction
- purpose
- background
- scope
- plan of development
literature review
methods and materials (procedures)
results
discussion
summary/conclusions
recommendation (optional)

The longer, formal report may also include secondary elements:
cover letter
title page
table of contents
list of illustrations

abstract
glossary
appendixes

These secondary elements are described in Module 9. They are elements usually written after you write the primary sections because they depend on the content of the primary sections. Of course, some informal reports also include attachments that are often labeled as an appendix.

Writing the Experimental Research Report

The introduction includes the four elements that set the context for any report: the purpose, the background, the significance or scope, and the organizational plan. Modules 3 and 10 also discuss the context-setting introduction. In the research report, the introduction answers questions about the purpose of the study, the scientific problem that led to the study, and the general scope or procedure for the study. The organizational plan is a report-writing technique that tells the reader how the content of the report will be organized. In the longer, formal scientific reports, some writers use tabs as well as a table of contents to identify the sections of the report and to aid comprehension.

The section on the literature review documents the fact that you know about other research on the same subject. It references written material pertinent to your study, material that other researchers can examine to advance their own knowledge of the subject. The procedures section tells readers about the materials and the steps necessary to conduct the experiment or study. This section should be so clear that the reader could replicate the experiment if the reader wished to do so.

The most important section of the report for a technical reader is the results section. In this section you present your laboratory data and findings. Whether the findings indicate the experiment was a success or a failure, your study has contributed information to the scientific community. For writing the report as efficiently as possible, the rule of thumb is to place your data into tables or graphs immediately following the experiment. In other words, you should prepare the results section first. Once you present the results visually, you have a clear picture, literally, of what you have to describe and explain in the report.

Your discussion section provides a rationale for your findings, and the conclusions section summarizes the facts from the main sections of the report. Module 10 explains in detail how to summarize. Finally, some research reports include a recommendations section because the writer has to suggest the future action or direction of the research or the study.

Figure 11.1 presents a formal report on experimental research. The report is condensed but still illustrates the primary and secondary elements of a formal report. After reading this version of the report, read the analysis of the primary sections of the report.

CENTER FOR ENGINEERING ANALYSIS
Northbrook, Illinois

RESEARCH AND DEVELOPMENT

TITLE: The Testing of Hyperbaric Oxygen Therapy
                      on Normal Wounds in the Rat Tail
                                    by
                      Barry N. Feinberg, Ph.D., P.E.

REPORT DATE: June 29, 19XX

PROJECT NUMBER: 428.RD

DISTRIBUTION: K. Hobmer
                      L. Lasiter
                      S. Thomas
                      C. Demoplaus

FIGURE 11.1 Research report
Source: Barry N. Feinberg, Ph.D., P.E. Used with permission.

TABLE OF CONTENTS

ii

LIST OF TABLES (This section is not included.)

iii

LIST OF FIGURES (This section is not included.)

iv

FIGURE 11.1 (cont.)

1.0 INTRODUCTION

This report presents the results of an animal study done under test protocol 569-001-84, on the effects of hyperbaric oxygen (HBO) on surgically induced wounds located on the tail of a rat. The purpose of the study was to determine the time course of cellular events, under hyperbaric oxygen conditions, as compared with normal healing conditions for the rat.

The problem of slow or nonhealing wounds has been a frustration to medical practitioners. The exact reasons for the retarded rate of healing or, in some cases, the lack of healing, depend on the type of wounds. In almost all cases of lack of healing, a common feature is the hypoxic condition of the central wound cells. Cellular hypoxia is brought about by a lack of vascularization or injury to the wound cells.

Oxygen plays an active role in the metabolism required for cell repair and reproduction. The literature indicates that hyperbaric oxygen therapy (HBO) has had great success as an adjunct to other methods of wound healing whereas the other methods alone did not produce healing. For example, HBO therapy was useful in the healing of a 40-year-old venous stasis ulcer when other methods failed.

The scope of this experiment is limited to determining the time course of cellular events as determined by gross visual observation and by pathology in the wound healing of the rat tail. The condition of the wound is needed to determine if the local application of hyperbaric oxygen affects the rate of wound healing. This experiment will contain modifications of current procedures; that is, the hyperbaric chambers and associated seals are removed after a day's treatment to eliminate the conditions that promote infection of the rat tail.

FIGURE 11.1 (cont.)

2.0 LITERATURE REVIEW

Medical use of hyperbaric chambers for oxygen therapy has been in the literature since early 1956 [8] when Dr. I. Boerma, at the University of Amsterdam Medical School, began the clinical application of hyperbaric oxygen. A few hospitals in this country and abroad have experimented with the use of hyperbaric chambers. The School of Aerospace Medicine, San Antonio, Texas, has conducted extensive research in the medical use of multiplace hyperbaric chambers [11], and manufacturers of monoplace hyperbaric chambers are beginning to advertise their devices for use in hospitals.

Oxygen plays an active, often controlling, role in the reparative process. It is probably the most sensitive nutrient of the wound [38]. An actively healing wound has a higher oxygen demand than healthy connective tissue. Injury to tissue has a detrimental effect on local circulation, making local circulation least able to supply oxygen when the demand is the greatest.

During this time the wound becomes moderately hypoxic. In the initial stages of wound healing, moderate hypoxia may stimulate the replication of fibroblasts and the production of collagen. A problem exists when the wound area is chronically hypoxic, that is, PO_2 less than 10mmHg. The fibroblasts can no longer divide, synthesize collagen, or migrate. These inabilities may account for the fact that some wounds, like venous stasis ulcers, do not heal and why treatment in a hyperbaric chamber has produced good results in causing these wounds to close [3, 5].

FIGURE 11.1 (cont.)

3.0 <u>TEST METHODS</u>
    3.1 <u>Materials</u>
        The experiments on the local application of hyperbaric oxygen were carried out in the Safety Assessment Facility of the Bennet Research Laboratory. The following materials were used.
        3.10 Hyperbaric test fixtures to accommodate 200–250 g rats. Cleaned and cold disinfected. (See Figure 1).
        3.11 Albino female rats 200–250 g.
        3.12 1% Povidone iodine surgical scrub.
        3.13 70% Isopropyl alcohol.
        3.14 Template to produce uniform wounds. (See Figure 2).
        3.15 Lidocaine HCl 1%.
        3.16 Ether
        3.17 Tetracycline
    3.2 <u>Procedure</u>
        The rat's cage and location in the hyperbaric test apparatus were numbered for identification purposes. Twenty-seven Sprague-Dawley rats weighing between 230 and 270 grams were used in the experiment; 22 were used to send specimens to the pathologist, and the rest were reserve. The rats were anesthetized with ether, weighed, and placed into the hyperbaric test apparatus with their tails in the hyperbaric chamber opening and their hips restrained with the "saddle." (See Figure 3.)

        The tail was then injected with 0.1 cc of Lidocaine HCl, 1 percent to numb the area where the wound would be made. (See Figure 4.) Once there was no feeling in the root area of the tail, a full thickness wound was produced 2 cm. below the base of the tail using a sterile scalpel and metal template to produce a uniform wound. Eleven of the rat tails were placed in the hyperbaric chambers and subjected to a 12 psi (620.52 mmHg) of a 100 percent oxygen atmosphere.

FIGURE 11.1 (cont.)

A second group of 11 animals was placed in the test apparatus with their tails in the chambers in the same manner as those receiving hyperbaric therapy. These animals had their tails exposed to filtered room air at approximately 0 psi. The air was pumped into their chambers for the same length of time that the other 10 animals received their hyperbaric oxygen therapy. Each group of animals received this form of treatment for one hour in the morning and one hour in the afternoon.

At the end of days 3, 6, 9, 11, 14, 17, 18, and 20, animals from the hyperbaric group and from the untreated group were sacrificed and the wound sections of the tail harvested for pathological examination. The wounded area of the tail was saved in a specimen jar with 10% neutral formalin solution and sent out of the lab for histopathological evaluation by an animal pathologist.

FIGURE 11.1 (cont.)

4.0 <u>RESULTS</u>
    4.1 <u>Visual Data</u>
        Each rat tail was visually inspected daily by Dr. Kenneth Shaker, DVM.
        He inspected the wounds with respect to the following visual character-
        istics:
        1. Epithelialization at wound margin
        2. Periwound condition
        3. Wound Quality
           a. serous
           b. serosanguineous
           c. purulent
        A typical data sheet containing visual observations is shown in
        Table I.

        In performing all the localized HBO experiments where there is high-
        pressure gas applied to an open wound, we realized that the potential
        existed for the hyperbaric apparatus to produce a gas embolus in the ex-
        perimental animal. The observational data indicates no physical evi-
        dence of a gas embolism in any of the test animals. If emboli were
        present in the experimental animal, their effect would cause the greatest
        problem in the heart, lungs, and brain.
    4.2 <u>Pathology Data</u>
        On designated days, animals from both the treated and untreated groups
        were sacrificed, and the section of the animal tail containing the wound
        was taken and preserved in a labeled jar containing 10% formalin solu-
        tion for preservation. At the end of the experiment, all the jars contain-
        ing wound tissue samples were sent to Biology Associates, Inc., Chicago,
        IL, for microscope slide preparation, staining (hematoxylin and eosin,
        trichrome stains), and histopathological evaluation. Figure 4 is a micro-
        photograph illustrating stained tissue from the pathology assessment of
        the tail.

FIGURE 11.1 (cont.)

5.0 DISCUSSION

The results of this experiment have shown the following:

5.1 Visual

Based on these preliminary experiments, we conclude that localized hyperbaric oxygen therapy appears to be a safe mode of wound treatment. There was no evidence of stroke, myocardial infarction, or cardiac arrest in the rats that would be produced by oxygen gas bubbles in the blood system.

5.2 Pathology

From the comments of the consulting pathologist, Richard McNamarra, DVM (Exhibit 1) and an analysis of the data in Table II, we conclude that there was no significant difference in the progress of the wounds between treated and untreated animals in this experiment.

Table II indicates that there is very little difference between specimens that received air at 0 psi and those treated with hyperbaric oxygen at 12 psi. In both cases only the normal progression of healing wounds is observed from day 3 to day 20. In almost all categories dealing with the epithelium and subcutaneous tissue, the comparison day by day between normal and HBO-treated tissue indicates that the changes taking place in the wound are doing so at the same rate. As a typical example of this, we see in Table II that in category hypertrophy/hyperplasis of cells, the scoring between the normals and HBO is almost the same as we examine the table from day 3 to day 20.

Since the wounds produced in the tail of the rat were done surgically, without any change induced in the vascular system of the tail, then the wounds were of normal type and were of normal vascularization. What emerges from interpreting the pathology data is that when a wound is normal and has normal vascularization, using hyperbaric oxygen therapy does not accelerate or stimulate wound healing. Similar results were obtained by Hunt et al. in the book by Davis [13], using rats with normal wounds in a hyperbaric chamber.

FIGURE 11.1 (cont.)

The majority of the hyperbaric literature deals with abnormal wounds and benefits of hyperbaric therapy for these wounds. To see the effects of localized hyperbaric oxygen, the experiment would have to be elevated to human clinical experiments where abnormal wounds are available.

6.0 CONCLUSIONS

This experiment has proved the following:

1. Based on these preliminary experiments, localized hyperbaric oxygen therapy appears to be a safe mode of wound treatment. Even subjecting the wounded rat tail to pressures as high as 30 psi did not produce any physical symptoms that could be associated with gas embolism. Though more testing for safety needs to be done, we draw a preliminary conclusion that the use of localized hyperbaric oxygen therapy appears to be safely used on the animals.

2. Since the pathology indicates that no significant difference exists between treated and untreated specimens, we conclude that hyperbaric oxygen therapy does not have a stimulating or accelerating effect on the healing of well-vascularized, full thickness wounds at pressures of 12 psi.

FIGURE 11.1 (cont.)

REFERENCES

1. Balin, Arthur K., et al., "The Effect of Oxygen Tension on the Growth and Metabolism of W1-38 Cells," *J. Cell Physiol.* (1978) 89: 235–250, 1978.
2. Bass, B. H., M.D., MRCP, "The Treatment of Varicose Leg Ulcers by Hyperbaric Oxygen," *Postgraduate Medical Journal* 46: 407–408, July 1970.
3. Besznyak, I. et al., "The Use of Hyperbaric Oxygen in Treatment of Experimental Hypoxaemic Skin Ulcers of the Limb," *Acta Chirurgica Academiae Scientiarum Hungaricae* 11, 1970.
4. Boerema, I., "High Tension Oxygen Therapy," *Arch. Chir. Necrl.* [Den Haag], 8:193, 1956.
5. Bradley, Mark E., "Hyperbaric Oxygen Therapy," Naval Medical Research Institute, Bethesda, Md., Report NMAI 82–80, 1982.
6. Burgess, Ernest M., M.D., "Wound Healing After Amputation," *The Journal of Bone and Joint Surgery*, Vol. 60-A, No. 1, pp. 245–246, March 1978.
7. Davis, Jefferson C., M.D., et al., *Hyperbaric Oxygen Therapy*, Undersea Medical Society, Inc., Bethesda, Md., 1977.
8. Deneke, Susan M., Ph.D., et al., "Normobaric Oxygen Toxicity of the Lung," *The New England Journal of Medicine*, 303, No. 2: 76–78, July 10, 1980.
9. Ehrlich, H. Paul, Ph.D., et al., "Metabolic and Circulatory Contributions to Oxygen Gradients in Wounds," *Surgery*, Vol.72, No.4, October 1972.
10. Feinberg, Barry, "A Comparison of the Effects of Hyperbaric Oxygen Therapy in Wound Healing to Normobaric Oxygen and Room Air," Protocol 569-0284, September 1984.

Note: The references have been edited to conserve space.

8

FIGURE 11.1 (cont.) (end of report)

The analysis provides a brief explanation as well as an illustrative excerpt for each section of the report.

1. The *INTRODUCTION*—the *purpose* of the report and study
"This report presents the results of an animal study. . . . The purpose of the study was to determine the time course of cellular events, under hyperbaric oxygen conditions, as compared with normal healing conditions for the rat."

—the *background* for the study
"The problem of slow or nonhealing wounds has been a frustration to medical practitioners. The exact reasons for the retarded rate of healing, or in some cases the lack of healing, depend on the type of wounds. In almost all cases of lack of healing, a common feature is the hypoxic condition of the central wound cells."

—the *scope* of the study
"The scope of this experiment is limited to determining the time course of cellular events as determined by gross visual observation and by pathology in the wound healing of the rat tail."

—the *plan of development* for the study
In the research report, the writer gives no plan of development, probably because the report is formal and uses other techniques in report writing to help the reader discover the organizational strategy. The table of contents, the tabs for the sections in the original report, and the readability of the headings all clearly indicate the organization of the report.

2. *LITERATURE REVIEW*—the references relevant to the specific project under investigation
You should avoid including all the references to your subject because some will be only tangentially related and you will bore the reader. Note also that the following reference is numbered and refers to the citation in the List of References attached to the report.
"Medical use of hyperbaric chambers for oxygen therapy has been in the literature since early 1956 [8] when Dr. I. Boerma, at the University of Amsterdam Medical School, began the clinical application of hyperbaric oxygen (HBO)."

3. *METHODS AND MATERIALS*—the *apparatus and materials* used
The writer details the apparatus, the test subjects, and the other materials.

3.1 Hyperbaric test fixtures to accommodate 200–250 g rats. Cleaned and cold disinfected.
3.2 Albino female rats 200–250 g.
3.3 1% Povidone iodine surgical scrub.
3.4 70% Isopropyl alcohol.
3.5 Template to produce uniform wounds.

—the *procedure* for conducting the experiment
The writer explains the steps of the experiment so that other researchers could replicate the steps if they wished.

"Twenty-seven Sprague-Dawley rats weighing between 230 and 270 grams were used in the experiment; 22 were used to send specimens to the pathologist and the rest were reserve. The rats were anesthetized with ether, weighed, and placed into the hyperbaric test apparatus. . . ."

4. *RESULTS*—the findings of the experiment

Although this section is not necessarily the longest in a research report, it is the most important. The writer usually supports the results with tables, charts, or graphs, which are referred to in the text but included in the appendix.

"The wounds were inspected with respect to the following characteristics: . . . A typical data sheet containing visual observations is shown in Table I. . . .

At no time throughout the experiment did our observation indicate the animals suffered from a myocardial infarction. There was no observed stress on the animals during the pressure cycles applied to them and no death of the animals."

DISCUSSION—a frank explanation of the findings. This section provides the writer with an opportunity to select, highlight, and draw relationships between demonstrated findings and phenomena, including

- success, failure, conclusiveness
- significance of the study
- reference to original purpose and scope

"What emerges from interpreting the pathology data is that when a wound is normal and has normal vascularization, hyperbaric oxygen therapy does not accelerate or stimulate wound healing. . . . The majority of the successful hyperbaric therapy deals with abnormal wounds."

SUMMARY/CONCLUSIONS—a concise restatement of the discussion section and condensed facts and details from the main sections of the report.

Some technical writers suggest that writing the summary is similar to writing the abstract. You should try to include facts or details or topic sentences from each major section in proportion to the number of words in that section. Rather than counting the number of words in a section, remember that the summary gives the crux of the experiment, with its methodology, findings, and significance.

"This experiment has proven the following:
1. Localized hyperbaric oxygen therapy appears to be a safe mode of wound treatment based on these preliminary experiments. Subjecting the wounded rat tail to pressures as high as 30 psi did not produce any physical symptoms that could be associated with gas embolism."

RECOMMENDATIONS (Optional)—the judgment of the researcher based on the findings and indicating the reader's options or next action.

". . . we are left with two avenues of pursuit. The first is to try and develop an avascular preparation. . . . The second option is that we design and build a human version of our current test apparatus system for use of human limbs in the clinical setting. A clinical experiment is necessary because . . . we must work with abnormal wounds to observe the benefits of local hyperbaric oxygen therapy."

Designing the Visual Forms

The long, formal report benefits from visual and design techniques common to all technical reports:

- New page for each major section of the report.
- Headings and subheadings.
- Illustrations (referred to in text):
  - tables
  - photographs
  - drawings
  - graphs
  - report forms
  - maps
  - flowcharts
  - schematics
- Numerical sequencing of sections and subsections.
- Readable layout and typography.

Some secondary elements also add to the readability of the long report. The visual designs for the secondary elements are listed here and described in Module 9:

- Appropriate binder.
- Tabs identifying major sections.
- Separate pages for:
  - title page
  - abstract
  - table of contents
  - list of illustrations
  - glossary
  - appendixes

Writing the Laboratory Report

Laboratory reports, often referred to as lab reports, are usually short reports that present the purpose for the lab test, the lab procedure, the data, an analysis, and the conclusions. This content is so familiar to the scientific community that many companies establish a style sheet for lab reports. General Motors Research Laboratories uses a format for a lab report that is a standard for many industries. The organization of the report is appropriate for the executive reader as well as for lab experts, and the format encourages the use of headings to make the organization clear to the reader. You can vary the layout to permit tables or figures either within the text of the document or attached to the document in an appendix. This flexible layout permits you to consider the needs of the multiple reader, needs discussed more thor-

```
                                                          Page 1 of _____ .

                          LABORATORY REPORT

    Subject

    Prepared By

    Date                                   Approved

    Purpose

    Conclusions and Recommendations

    Methodology (optional, if project warrants)

    Results and Discussion of Analytical Data

    Appendix (includes charts, graphs, tables, and so on)

    Bibliography (optional, if project warrants)
```

FIGURE 11.2 Conventional format for a laboratory report
Used with the permission of General Motors Research Laboratories.

oughly in Modules 2, 7, and 10. Figure 11.2 shows an example of the General Motors format for a laboratory report.

Stating the Purpose

The *purpose statement* in a laboratory report tells the reader what the objective of the lab work is, what the lab technician's task is. Some writers confuse the task with the conclusion. Because the laboratory report distinguishes clearly between the task and the conclusion, you can clearly express the purpose as the technician's task.

> *A Faulty Purpose Statement for a Laboratory Report*
> The purpose of this study is to suggest that the Auto-sampler AS-50 is imprecise in its measurements because of its age and to recommend that a new auto-sampler be purchased.

The writer confuses the conclusion and recommendation with the objective or the technician's task.

> *The Revised Purpose Statement*
> The purpose of this study is to evaluate the accuracy of the Auto-sampler AS-50 and to make a recommendation.

Organizing the Report

The remainder of the laboratory report presents the material in an orderly way, using an organizational design that is effective for both content and readability. The organizational strategy is similar to the one for experimental research, but in the shorter laboratory report the conclusions are presented early to provide information quickly to the executive reader.

- *Conclusion*—what is observable or what the data indicates.
- *Recommendation*—the writer's judgment based on the data.
- *Methodology*—the procedure used to compile the data.
- *Discussion*—the connection between the data and the writer's interpretation of the data.
- *Bibliography*—references used in major sections (optional).

Figure 11.3 presents a laboratory report that follows the conventional General Motors format. The writer incorporated the table into the text rather than placing it in an appendix.

Page 1 of 1
LABORATORY REPORT

Subject Monoethylene Glycol Analysis at Jaycord Laboratory

Prepared By

Date

Purpose:
> To review the current procedures employed in the analysis of monoethylene glycol (MEG) samples and, where necessary, recommend adjustments or improvements to expedite dispatching a formal report.

Recommendations:
> As new methods are developed on recently acquired instrumentation, several improvements can be made in the Jaycord Laboratory analysis regime. The suggestions outlined in the following report should be given consideration.

Conclusion:
> MEG samples can be analyzed and reported without delay if they receive the same priority as waste waters and corrosivity samples and if the laboratory personnel follow the new procedures.

Procedures:
> Possible procedures for individual analyses include:

pH	Ionics or pH meter
T. Alk	Ionics, A-Z indicator, pH meter
Phosphate	50X Dilution—Dionex
	Current Method—Spectrophotometer
	Ionics? UV?

| Reserve Alk | Current Method—Titrimeter Ionics? |
| Ash, Sp. Gravity, Color | Current Method Current Method |

Discussion:

1. pH determined by pH meter or Ionics requires no preparation other than sample distribution to proper containers. The Ionics method, however, would be more efficient since one sample preparation would suffice for several analyses.
2. XXXXX
3. XXXXXX
4. Reserve alkalinity analyzed by the current procedure involving the titrimeter requires approximately 10–15 minutes, including sample preparation. Results are consistent and reproducible. The potential of the Ionics for this analysis is undetermined.
5. Ash, specific gravity, and sample color can continue to be analyzed in the current manner.

FIGURE 11.3 Laboratory report using the General Motors Research Laboratory format

In the laboratory report shown in Figure 11.4, the writer includes accompanying graphs as attachments to the text. The graphs are referred to as Exhibits I and II, not as figures or appendixes. Using the term *exhibits* emphasizes the support for the writer's conclusion.

For content and readability the writer uses

- Headings
    purpose
    conclusion
    methodology
    discussion
- Reference to Attachments (Exhibits) within the text
- Reference to Attachments and Distribution (cc:) at the end of the document
- Illustrations.

Writing the Field Report

Field reports require greater flexibility in their organization than laboratory reports because several people may have to investigate and evaluate the site. The field report begins with a trip to evaluate a site. Module 13 describes the trip report, a report that often involves completing a form. You may have to take notes at the site or complete a standard form at the site and write the field report later, after you have made some laboratory measurements. Often

SUBJECT   Effect of Kontol KG-2 on Total Acidity and Total Alkalinity of
           Aqueous Samples

PREPARED BY

DATE   March 30, 1982   APPROVED   Ref. No.

Purpose:
    To determine the effect of Kontol KG-2 corrosion inhibitor on the total
    acidity and total alkalinity of aqueous samples.

Conclusion:
    Total alkalinity and total acidity are proportional to the concentration of
    Kontol KG-2 as indicated in Exhibits I and II. The information from this
    investigation can be used as a blank for aqueous samples containing sig-
    nificant levels of this corrosion inhibitor.

Methodology:
    Standard solutions of Kontol KG-2 were prepared for analyses of total al-
    kalinity and total acidity. The total alkalinity and total acidity were ana-
    lyzed using standard titrimetric methods. The total alkalinity test was
    performed on duplicate samples to a pH endpoint of 4.5 and the total ac-
    idity test on duplicate samples to 8.2.

Discussion:
    Kontol KG-2 chemically contains acylated amines. Acylated amines are
    formulated by the amination of carboxylic acids. The resulting functional
    group can display properties characteristic of either an acid or a base
    (amphoteric). This condition can analytically impact alkalinity and acid-
    ity determinations.

    It appears aqueous samples containing significant quantities of KG-2 can
    be stoichiometrically adjusted or compensated for the amount of KG-2
    present. This correction will more closely reflect the true alkalinity and/
    or acidity of the sample.

Attachments:

cc:

FIGURE 11.4 Laboratory report with attachments

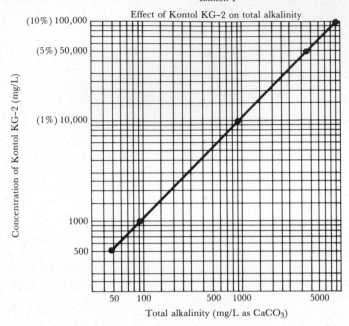

Exhibit I

Effect of Kontol KG-2 on total alkalinity

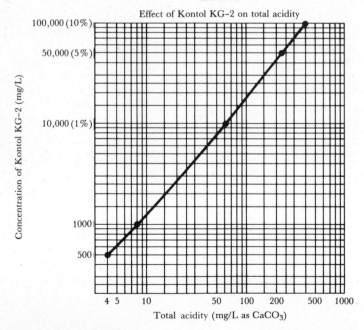

Exhibit II

Effect of Kontol KG-2 on total acidity

FIGURE 11.4 (cont.)

both the trip report and the laboratory report provide the organizational plan for reporting an on-site inspection, as it does in Figure 11.5.

SUBJECT   Boiler Inspection at Station 111

PREPARED BY

DATE 6/8/   APPROVED   Ref. No.

PURPOSE:
   To inspect the boiler at Station 111 and to recommend remedial action as required.

CONCLUSION:
   The boiler appears to be slightly cleaner than last year. However, scale still exits on the waterside of the steam drum, mud drum, and boiler water tubes. In addition, there appear to be silicalike deposits on the boiler tubes.

RECOMMENDATIONS:
   1. Install new softeners as soon after acquisition as possible.
   2. Make the dealkalizer system operational as soon as possible.
   3. Replace the manually set continuous blowdown valve with an automatic blowdown valve.
   4. Establish a schedule to daily blowdown the boiler mud drum.
   5. Replace contact meter that triggers the boiler chemical feed pump.
   6. Continue to follow the testing schedule recommended by the company.

DISCUSSION:
   On May 17, 19XX, E. Bridel, L. Said, M. McMahon, and B. Philos inspected the boiler at Station 111.

   Deposits included the following:

FIGURE 11.5 Field report about boiler inspection

Organizing the Report

When you have to organize a field report, you can use some of the strategies and headings from the trip report and the laboratory report as did the writer who used the headings and plan in Figure 11.6. The content, the organization, and the layout of the field report contribute to its readability.

1. Identification (of the facility inspected)
       address (of the site)
       permit number (to operate the facility)
       responsible official (of the facility)
2. Date of inspection
3. Participants

4. Objectives (of the inspection/evaluation—the objectives are itemized and organize the remainder of the document)
5. Summary of findings and conclusions
6. Discussion of operations
7. Sample collection (for later analysis)
8. List of attachments

FIELD REPORT

1. Site Identification
   Address
   Wesley Water Control Center
   142 Ontario Street
   Wesley, DE 50928

   Permit Number
   DE0045179   Effective: 9/01/82–9/30/85

   Responsible Official
   Dr. Stephen Elcott, Director
   City of Wesley
   2473 Lake Road
   Wesley, DE 50928

2. Date of Inspection
   June 19, 19XX

3. Participants
   Water Control Board
   David Lock, Environmental Engineer
   Samuel Adams, Laboratory Personnel

   Delaware Control Board
   Larry Kawalski, Environmental Engineer

   Site Personnel
   Melvin Daniels, Supervisor
   Lucille Richards, Laboratory Director

4. Objectives
   The objectives were to inspect and evaluate the facility's water-monitoring practices, including flow measurement, sampling techniques, analytic procedures, and data reporting.

5. Summary of Findings and Conclusions
   a. Flow Measurement
      An oversized flow measurement meter may be providing questionable flow data. The facility is also experiencing problems with the totalizer.
   b. Sampling Techniques
      At the time of inspection, 24-hour samples were not refrigerated during the monitoring period. The improper preservation could affect laboratory results for parameters including turbidity, suspended solids, and ammonia.

FIGURE 11.6 Organization and design of a field report

c. Analytical Procedures
   Our detailed laboratory inspection revealed that the plant's staff and facilities are very capable of generating high-quality water-monitoring data.

d. Data Reporting
   Our review of the reporting code found the analytical data valid. In the future, the laboratory should explain any deviations from the reporting code.

6. Discussion of Operations
   The facility is designed to measure water flow for a population of 68,000 and is located in the area _____ presented in Attachment 1. (See List of Attachments following.)

a. Flow Measurement
   Flow is measured in a 48-inch pipe with a 35 Pentell meter. _____

---

b. Sampling Techniques
   The plant samples at the following locations:

Sampling Location	Description of Location
A204	Site effluent prior to combining with bypass stream
A205	Raw influent
A206	Facility bypass
A207	Sludge deposits prior to land disposal

Effluence at the facility is measured downstream of chlorination for ____

---

c. Analytical Procedures
   A detailed report of laboratory procedures is presented in Attachment 3. The findings of the report are summarized further on. The staff, facility, and laboratory equipment were judged more than adequate to yield high-quality data. The laboratory evaluation is acceptable.

d. Data Reporting
   A completed Water Control Board inspection form is found in Attachment 4.

7. Water Control Board Sample Collection
   During the inspection, one sample, SA5090, was taken of ferrous chloride. The Control Board will analyze the sample and report the results to Wesley Water Control Center.

LIST OF ATTACHMENTS
(Attachments are not included in this example of a field report.)

Attachment No.	Description
1	Area Location Map
2	Wesley Water Flow Schematic
3	Facility Operation Design
4	Water Control Board Inspection Form

FIGURE 11.6 (cont.)

Interpreting the Findings

Field reports usually include the evaluator's judgment of the site, the product, or the procedure examined. This judgment may be placed at the beginning or the end of the document, depending on the company's preference for reporting information. In Figure 11.6 the writer's objectives were to evaluate

- flow measurement
- sampling techniques
- staff's analytical procedures
- data reporting.

The writer supported the evaluations with descriptions of the facility and equipment, the sampling techniques of the staff, and data from the laboratory analyses.

The writer makes these judgments after observing or measuring the data, the product, or the situation. Although the writer tries to base these decisions on logical thinking, the decision is still only an inference; and the judgment can only be as accurate as the data collected or the logic, knowledge, or experience of the person making the judgment. Module 3 on organization discusses inference, as well as inductive and deductive reasoning. Judgments frequently appear under the headings

findings/results
recommendation.

Other headings for judgment statements are

impact
consequences
significance
implications.

The following impact statement makes an observation and an assumption that the writer infers from the data but cannot know for certain.

IMPACT: The ACME Waste Removal Co. removed 90 drums of phenol-contaminated oil, 80 cubic yards of contaminated soil and empty drums, and approximately 900 gallons of sulfur monochloride. This action prevented these materials from contaminating a tributary of the Wesley River and alleviated a potential fire and air pollution hazard.

The field report uses the same organizational strategy as the trip report, but because the field report usually involves some laboratory testing, the content for both laboratory and field reports is similar.

Summary

The technical reports in this module require data from laboratory and field tests and experimental research. *Experimental research* begins with a practical question or a theoretical speculation that is tested in the laboratory. When writers present the results of their experimental research, they have to include information that is convincing to the community of scientific readers. The strategy for presenting this information is fairly standard and includes sections on

introduction
literature review
methodology
results
discussion
conclusion
recommendations (optional)
references (optional)

Longer, formal reports also include secondary material such as a transmittal letter, title page, table of contents, abstract, list of illustrations, glossary, and appendixes. These materials are also described in Module 9.

The *introduction* establishes the purpose of the study, the background of the problem, and the scope or overview of the procedure. The *literature review* documents the other research on the subject, and the *procedures section* describes the equipment, materials, and steps to perform the experiment. The *results* section presents the laboratory data, and the *discussion* section provides a rationale for the findings. The *conclusion* section is a summary of the main sections; the *recommendation* and *reference* sections are optional depending on the reader's needs.

Visual aids for scientific reports include headings, numerical sequencing, illustrations as well as report binders, tabs identifying major sections, lists, and separate pages for all major headings and secondary elements.

Laboratory reports are usually short reports that present the purpose for the laboratory study, the procedure, the data, an analysis, and conclusions. The conclusions frequently appear early in the laboratory report, after the purpose, because the executive reader needs to know the results of the study first. The purpose statement avoids mentioning the conclusion, the organizational plan uses clear headings, and the design is flexible to permit tables or figures within the text or attached in an appendix to the document.

Field reports have a flexible organization because several people may contribute to the field study. The strategy for the trip report in Module 13 is useful for the field report. Both reports identify the *site* and the *participants* and often use a report form. Because the site inspection may involve some lab measurements, the laboratory report also provides an organizational plan for the field report. The organization also includes purpose or objectives, findings, procedures, discussion, and attachments. In a field report, the *find-*

ings reveal the writer's judgment after observing or measuring the product or the situation. Although the writer bases a judgment on data or logical thinking, the judgment is still only an inference and frequently appears under such headings as impact, consequences, significance, or implications. Field reports, laboratory reports, and reports on experimental research share similar organizational strategies and involve research and analysis of data compiled in a laboratory.

Checklist for Scientific Reports

This module covers the major content for three types of reports: the experimental research report, the laboratory report, and the field report. In addition, this module itemizes the secondary elements that accompany long, formal reports. The checklists for the reports and the secondary elements ask you to consider the items and to check only those items to which you give a positive response.

Yes

IN YOUR *EXPERIMENTAL RESEARCH REPORT*, DID YOU

Introduce the subject with
_____   purpose of the study or experiment?

_____   problem that led to the study?

_____   scope or overview of the experiment?

_____ Document the literature review?

_____ Describe the materials?

_____ Explain the methods or list the steps in the procedure?

_____ Present the results in visual forms such as tables or photographs?

_____ Provide a rationale for your findings in the discussion section?

_____ Summarize the facts from the main sections of the report?

_____ Recommend future action or further direction of the research?

_____ List the relevant references in a bibliography?

ARE YOU SUBMITTING A REPORT THAT NEEDS ANY OF THE *SECONDARY ELEMENTS*?
_____ transmittal letter?

_____   title page?

_____   abstract?

_____   table of contents?

_____   list of illustrations?

_____   glossary?

_____   appendixes?

**DO YOUR REPORTS USE THE *VISUAL AND DESIGN
TECHNIQUES*, SUCH AS**

_____   New page for each major section?

_____   Separate pages for the secondary elements of the report?

_____   Numerical sequencing of sections and subsections (optional)?

_____   Appropriate binder (optional)?

Readable layout and typography with
_____   tabs identifying sections?

_____   headings and subheadings?

_____   appropriate indenting and lists?

_____   illustrations (referred to in text)?

IN YOUR *LABORATORY REPORT*, DID YOU

_____   Separate the purpose from the conclusion?

_____   Place the conclusion early in the report?

_____   Provide the recommendation, if appropriate, early in the report?

_____   Explain the procedures?

_____   Present the results or data, either in an appendix or within the
            text?

_____   Interpret the results in the discussion?

Include
_____   attachments (referenced in text)?

_____   distribution list?

_____   headings?

IN YOUR *FIELD REPORT,* **DID YOU**
_____   Use some organizational headings such as

_____   site identification?

_____   date of inspection?

_____   participants?

_____   purpose or objectives?

_____   lab analysis?

_____   discussion?

_____   summary of findings, judgment, or impact?

_____   Refer to and attach supporting documents?

References

Lester Faigley and Thomas P. Miller, "What We Learn from Writing on the Job,"
    College Composition and Communication 44 (1982): 557–569.
Paul D. Leedy, *Practical Research,* 3d ed. (New York: Macmillan, 1985).
Janet H. Potvin and Robert L. Woods, "Teaching Technical Communication at the
    Graduate Level: An Interdisciplinary Approach," *Journal of Technical Writing
    and Communication* 13 (1983): 235–246.
Jack Selzer, "The Composing Processes of an Engineer," *College Composition and Com-
    munication* 34 (1983): 178–187.
Freda F. Stohrer and Thomas E. Pinelli, "Marketing Information: The Technical
    Report as a Product," *Technical Writing: Past, Present, Future,* NASA Technical
    Memorandum 81966 (March 1981).
Thomas Warren, "Teaching Formal Technical Reports," *Teaching English in the Two-
    Year College* 8 (1982): 137–142.

Applying Your Knowledge

EXERCISE 11.1

*Draft a lab report from the paragraphs provided. You will have to reorganize
paragraphs, provide headings, and incorporate a table.*

LABORATORY REPORT Page 1 of ——— SUBJECT Station 124—Liquids in
The Wyoming Extension
Prepared by
Date   Approved   Ref. No.

The API gravities were determined according to ASTM method D-287
and distillations according to ASTM method D-285. Water content determi-
nations were accomplished by Karl Fischer; titrimetry and carbon number
distribution analyses were done by flame ionization detector gas chromatog-
raphy.

Fluid samples submitted from the Station 124 Drip Tank (Lab. No. 82-
258) and Unit No. 1 Fuel Filter (Lab No. 82-259) are composed primarily of
hydrocarbons. The sample from the fuel filter is "heavier" in consistency than
the drip sample as indicated by the API gravities, distillation profiles, and the
carbon number distribution analyses. Water was not present in either sample.

To characterize liquids passing beyond slug catcher, through the inlet
separator, and fouling the fuel filters at Station 124.

Jaycord Laboratory was asked to characterize fluids coming into Station
124 from the Wyoming Extension. Composition was essentially hydrocarbon
in both cases. Here is the data from routine hydrocarbon assays.

Pipeline Fluid Analysis Report

Apparent Color:	Light Brown
API Gravity (60 Deg.F/60 Deg.F):	50.8
Water Content (Weight percent)	0

Approximate Carbon Number Distribution Analysis by FID Chromatography

Constituent	Weight
Methane	0.00
Ethane	0.01
Propane	0.12
Isobutane	0.13
Normal butane	0.42
Isopentane	0.66
Hexanes	3.15
Heptanes	8.45
Octanes	16.34
Nonanes	18.02
Decanes	16.90

EXERCISE 11.2

CASE: You are a field engineer for your company. On December 3, 19XX, Ray
Bolster of the Rathod Field in Shreveport, Louisiana, discovers a leak in gas
pipeline segment No. 3. He notifies the home office and begins procedures to
replace the segment. You will have to inspect the site as soon as the repairs
are completed.

By December 15, the pipe is replaced with a 4½ × 0.337 piping. Leaving
the home office on December 16, you visit the site on December 17. Tom
Jackson, director of the Shreveport Field, accompanies you. You inspect both
the repair and the leaky pipe and learn that the size of the leak was a pinhole;

the cause of the leak was internal corrosion from static liquids and deposits. You fill out the company's standard leak report while you are there, sketch a drawing of the corroded pipe as a segment of the pipeline, and take the corroded pipe back with you to the laboratory for analysis of the deposit.

The repair seems to be holding, and the pipeline is losing no more gas. Repair crews will continue to investigate the pipeline near the corrosion. This segment of the pipeline was originally installed in 1977. The cost of the repair is $6,882.57 for labor, $1862.30 for equipment, and $517.75 for X ray.

When you return to the home office on December 18, you send the pipe to the lab for analysis of the deposits and begin to draft the field report. What items will you include in your report? Write the headings and a sentence or two under each section to indicate what the sections will include. Remember to identify supporting documents.

EXERCISE 11.3

For this exercise, collaborate with two other people to work on an experimental research project. First, draft an outline of a report on one of the research projects listed or on a subject of the team's choice:

Effect of different concentrations of alcohol on bacteria.
Effect of radiation on plant growth.
Effect of carbon concentration on hard steel.
Effect of light on eye pupil size.
Effect of eye scanning on reading comprehension.
How alcohol affects reaction time.
How people stabilize themselves as they rise from a chair.
How any specific medication affects the illness.

Next, each member selects a task:

Task 1. Briefly review some literature on the subject, and draft one or two paragraphs for the literature review section.

Task 2. Gather (or simulate) some data, and write a paragraph or two each on the methods and materials used to collect data.

Task 3. Write a brief introduction indicating the purpose of the report and the research, the scope of the study, and the organizational plan for the report.

Finally, the team compiles the sections, revises the drafts, and collaborates to produce a condensed experimental research report.

UNIT 3

The Components of Professional Communication

M O D U L E 12

Letters and Memos

With letters you correspond with people either inside or outside your company. Memos, on the other hand, are usually in-house documents used to update a file or inform the staff about company business—anything from new procedures to important visits. Letters and memos are both more informal than reports and hasten communication even in a technical environment. Many more documents are written as letters or memos than as formal technical reports. So this module stresses the importance of the letter and memo.

In essence, letters and memos about professional and technical subjects contain the same content as well as most of the same sections as those that appear in technical reports. When you write a clear letter or memo, you are applying the same principles of technical writing that you have applied to other types of reports and documents.

Technical and professional letters and memos incorporate the basic elements of technical writing, including writer's purpose, reader's needs, organization, readability in both style and visual techniques, and revision. Unless you initiate the correspondence, you will be responding to a reader's letter that indicates the reader has certain needs. The readers and their needs determine your purpose for writing. Once you have determined the reason for writing your letter, you can gather the information you need to respond and begin to organize your response. This module will help you analyze the audience and purpose, select an appropriate organizational strategy, and write an effective letter or memo.

A good letter or memo communicates information accurately and briefly, but the information must also be complete so that the reader knows how to respond to the message. When the reader understands what is expected of him or her, then the letter or memo accomplishes the main goal of the communication—clarity. Some additional factors relevant to letters and memos include these:

• Opening and closing paragraphs and the layout of letters.
• Subject and distribution lines and the layout of memos.

This module explains these factors and illustrates their use.

Scope

In this module you will learn to

1. Consider your audience and tone.
2. Determine the purpose.
3. Organize so that the reader has a clear idea of the purpose.
4. Clarify the message by using unambiguous language, accurate terms, concise words, and complete information.
5. Use appropriate openings and closings.
6. Design the format of the letter.
7. Write the formal letter of application and résumé.
8. Apply the components of technical writing to the memo.

Analyzing the Audience

Consider the letter in Figure 12.1 to Mr. Wiggins. It's an example of an inappropriate response to a citizen who has corresponded with people in the Urban Development Administration.[1]

The letter is written by someone whose idea of government style is to sound quasi-legal, overbearing, and obscure. When you respond to a client's or customer's letter, you have to imagine the reader's ability to understand the response and attempt to respond with a message the reader can understand. You can even use the writer's correspondence as insight into how to respond. If the writer is emotional and disorganized, as the portion of the letter in Figure 12.2 illustrates, you will have to determine the main issues and organize your response.

When the writer is knowledgeable and purposive, you can respond by providing the information or answering the question in a straightforward

Mr. Donald Wiggins
123 Main Street
Cicero, New York 12546

Dear Mr. Wiggins:

In order to facilitate the early and expeditious transmittal of the said prospectus more easily, it is hereby requested that your current total space requirements be submitted on the format, UBA Form 342, which is attached herewith. Each and every change that you deem significant and that you can anticipate for and during the period of the next five years should also be furnished.

For the purpose of lending us assistance in connection with the discharge of our responsibilities in reference to the development of this project, it will be appreciated if this information can be submitted as expeditiously as possible and with a minimum of delay.

Sincerely yours,

D. H. Green

FIGURE 12.1 Inappropriate letter for the audience
Source: *Writing Effective Letters* (U.S. Office of Personnel Management: U. S. Government Printing Office, 1985).

July 23, 19XX

Clinical Engineer
Anthony Hospital
137 Elton Circle
Baltimore, Maryland 21299

Dear Sir:

All you people care about is making money. But when it comes to making the patient comfortable, you're unconcerned. I'm referring to your refusal to let me bring my new TV set to the hospital. I'm told I can't have my perfectly good TV brought to the hospital because the clinical engineer has a policy. Well, your policy is costing me $1.00 rental/day. Don't the hospitals make enough money without gouging the patient for something he can supply himself?

Peter T. Loames
Room 341
Anthony Hospital

FIGURE 12.2 An emotional letter

way. For example, if the writer used numbered questions, you can respond by numbering your answers to correspond with the writer's questions. Figure 12.3 illustrates a letter of inquiry with numbered items.

1305 Elm St.
Toledo, Ohio 43606
August 19, 19XX

FREEDOM OF INFORMATION OFFICER
U.S. Congressional Record
230 S. DuPont, N.W.
Washington, D.C. 20001

Greetings:

Under the provision of the Freedom of Information Act, 5 U.S.C. §552, I am requesting access to certain information available from your agency.

I am extremely concerned about the potential health hazards associated with consumption of trace level toxic organic chemicals in drinking water. Consequently, I am requesting that a summary of available information detailing the quality of my drinking water be sent to me immediately. In particular, please provide the following information:

1. What toxic organic chemicals have been identified in my water supply and in what concentrations.
2. When those tests were conducted and by whom.
3. When further monitoring will begin.
4. What analytical techniques and instruments were utilized.
5. What was the supply's compliance record for attaining U.S. Public Health standards for water purity during the last year.

Also, please inform me of all the studies that exist on the subject of toxic contamination of my water supply system, as well as how I may obtain copies of them or review them in person.

In addition, please inform me of all hazardous waste or sanitary landfills and industrial discharges of toxic heavy metals and organic chemicals located within a 25-mile radius of my home. I would also like to know what documents and internal studies on these subjects exist, as well as how I obtain copies of them or review them in person.

If there are any fees imposed for searching or copying the materials I have requested, please inform me of that fact before filling this request.

I would appreciate your handling this request as quickly as possible.

Thank you for your courteous attention. I await your reply.

Sincerely yours,

FIGURE 12.3 Letter of inquiry

You also have to decide whether your writer is making a routine complaint or request or whether the complaint or request requires special care. Routine requests and complaints are those you can easily fill or resolve—or at least offer alternative suggestions. The more problematic complaints and requests are those that require persuasive organizational strategies and responses that suit the specific case. Especially in problematic complaint and request letters, you have to avoid anger and assume your reader will respond reasonably. In other words, you have to be mindful of your tone.

Achieving the Appropriate Tone

Tone is difficult to define. The feeling you have for the reader and the words you choose to express this feeling create the tone in your correspondence. Tone is mainly the choice of words, words that attract readers rather than antagonize them. If you are insensitive to words that accuse others of making a mistake, of being dishonest or stupid, of being nonhuman, then you are repelling others with your tone. With tone, what you think your words say and what readers think your words say produce two different meanings. For example, if you say, "You misunderstood," the reader feels blamed for the mistake. Many professional writers are sensitive to a list of words that create a negative tone.[2]

Words that blame the reader for a mistake include the following:

failed	standstill	ruin	neglected
waste	deadlock	misunderstood	
wrong	unfortunate	liable	

Words that accuse readers of being dishonest include these:

allege	complaint	impossible	despite
deny	alibi	prejudiced	
discredit	exaggerate	claim	

Words that accuse readers of being stupid or nonhuman include these:

hardship	it stands to reason	administrative action
insolvent	obviously	undoubtedly
infer	as you were previously informed	attention to the fact that
claimant	reject	

The idea to remember is that messages should be written as positively as possible, and a Yale University study mentions some words that are immediately negative: *despite, reject, regret, if, but, however, fail, nevertheless.* Avoid words that arouse this negative feeling and select words people like:

ability	benefit	easy	guarantee
achieve	comprehensive	economy	health
advantage	determined	free	helpful

industrious	money	reliable	useful
judgment	new	save	you
liberal	please	service	
love	reasonable	truth	

Rewrite letters that have this tone:

> *Not this:* We are herewith returning your application because you neglected to submit with it the necessary information that we requested. We cannot process your claim unless this is done as required.
>
> *But this:* Please return the attached form, along with the information requested, to us by December 15 so that we may process your claim promptly.

Determining Your Purpose for Writing

Not only do you have to consider your reader and tone, but you must clearly state your message. Why are you writing this letter? Are you writing an expository letter, that is, a letter that provides information in answer to an inquiry?

> *Neutral information:* You will have to submit your total space requirements on UBA Form 342.

Do you wish to praise the reader or announce good news?

> *Positive news:* The Sampson Insurance Company is now providing additional coverage for dental care.

Will you have to complain or deny the reader's request?

> *Negative news:* You are ineligible to receive benefits from the Social Security Administration.

Or are you writing a persuasive letter? Do you have to persuade the reader to accept your views or take appropriate action?

> *Persuasive message:* We find that you owe us $228.60.

Your purpose for writing most letters and memos will fall into these four categories, correspondence that provides

- neutral information
- positive news
- negative news
- persuasive messages.

Organizing Around the Purpose

Generally, when the letters can be routine, the first paragraph includes the purpose for the letter or memo. The next paragraphs provide the details to support the purpose, and the last paragraph closes the message either by restating the purpose or ending on a positive note. Figure 12.4 summarizes

ORGANIZATIONAL STRATEGIES FOR ROUTINE MESSAGES

TYPES OF MESSAGE	-- -- -- Dear --:
Neutral	1. Precise subject and purpose. Present the reader with the main information—what he or she most wants to know. 2. Necessary details in order of importance or natural sequence. 3. Short positive statement, *only* if the letter requires one.
Positive	1. Main idea—preferably in the first sentence. 2. Necessary details in order of importance or natural sequence. 3. Short statement (punch line) recalling the benefits of the good news.
Negative	1. Buffer statement; then state the bad news carefully and concisely. USE POSITIVE LANGUAGE as much as possible. 2. State reasons why you cannot do what the reader wants OR write a sentence or two SUPPORTING your actions. Again, remember to use POSITIVE LANGUAGE as much as possible. 3. Suggest possible alternatives. 4. End on a positive note; show helpfulness and understanding. Be TACTFUL *but* don't get carried away with overdoing any apologies you might have.
Persuasive	1. Put the reader in the picture ("you" attitude). Catch his or her interest. 2. Make your request. (This is the best place psychologically to do this. Make it short and simple.) 3. Supply any fact and figures or evidence to persuade the reader to act. 4. Restate your request; give a deadline for action.

FIGURE 12.4 Organizational strategies for four types of routine messages
Source: *Writing Effective Letters* (U.S. Office of Personnel Management: U.S. Government Printing Office, 1985).

Routine Message: Routine Neutral Information

Mrs. J. Simmons
1234 Main Street
Your Town, USA 00000

Dear Mrs. Simmons:

Subject   →   Funding for extra income benefits has recently become available for people in your income bracket living in this community.

Main   →
information   Because you may be eligible to receive these funds, we are enclosing a brochure describing the program and an application blank. Please note especially the criteria set forth on page two of the brochure. These criteria give you the condi-

Details   →   tions you must meet to qualify under this program.

Positive   →
close   We will send you additional information as it becomes available.

Sincerely,

FIGURE 12.5 A letter organized to give a neutral message
Source: *Writing Effective Letters* (U.S. Office of Personnel Management: U.S. Government
Printing Office, 1985).

the organizational strategies for the four types of routine messages. Remember that these strategies, especially the strategies for negative and persuasive messages, apply only to routine complaints and requests and *not* to problematic requests and complaints that require you to plan your organizational strategy with special care. The letters in Figure 12.5 through 12.8 exemplify the strategies for routine messages.

Often these organizational strategies are inappropriate because many letters are complicated, and the organizational strategies for letters depends on audience and purpose. Readers are complex people, and you may have a couple of reasons for writing. When you have to write a letter with negative news and still persuade the reader to take some action, when you have to convince a hostile reader that your viewpoint has some merit, when you have

Routine Message: Routine Positive News

Mrs. J. Simmons
1234 Main Street
Your Town, USA 00000

Dear Mrs. Simmons:

Main idea →	Your application for extra income benefits has been approved.
Necessary details →	You will begin receiving monthly checks on June 1 for $243.50. If you fail to receive your initial check by June 5, please call Mr. Johnson at (123) 456-7890.
Punch line →	Extra income benefits have assisted many people in the past; we hope that this added income will help you in meeting the high cost of living.

Sincerely,

FIGURE 12.6 A letter organized to give a positive message
Source: *Writing Effective Letters* (U.S. Office of Personnel Management: U.S. Government Printing Office, 1985).

to write a long, technical letter or a cover letter for a technical or business report, then you have to plan your organizational strategy to suit the specific case.

To Write a Long Letter with Technical Information

You have at least two options when you have to write a letter with extensive technical or business information. You can place the information in a report and attach a cover letter that tells the reader about the report; or you can write the letter like a report, using headings, subheadings, lists, and illustrations. In either case, you need an introduction that provides the context and

Routine Message: Routine Negative News

Mrs. J. Simmons
1234 Main Street
Your Town, USA 00000

Dear Mrs. Simmons:

**Buffer
statement →
bad news**

     We have reviewed your application for extra income benefits; however, our office is unable to approve it.

Reasons →

     You are ineligible for extra income benefits because your application states that you are currently employed part-time and are also receiving veteran's pension income. This total income exceeds the maximum allowed for individuals to receive extra income benefits.

Alternatives →

     Although you are ineligible for extra income benefits, you may possibly be eligible for pension-plus income. Please contact Ms. Jane Adams at the Pension Office (phone: 333-4545) to find out more information on this.

**Positive
note →**

     If your income status changes in such a way that you find you may be eligible for extra income benefits, please call us at 456-8765, and we will be happy to work with you on this.

Sincerely,

FIGURE 12.7 A letter organized to give a negative message
Source: *Writing Effective Letters* (U.S. Office of Personnel Management: U. S. Government Printing Office, 1985).

the organization for the rest of the letter or for the report that will follow the cover letter. In Module 3 and here in Figure 12.9 the Document Design Center and the American Institutes for Research suggest considering five items in the introduction. The purpose for the document, the topic, and the organizational strategy are always incorporated in the introductory section of any technical document.

To Complain or Answer a Complaint

To complain or answer a complaint when the complaint is not routine requires special skills. As always, you must consider the reader and establish rapport. Before you begin, carefully consider the reason for the letter; then complain or respond to a complaint by selecting relevant information and omitting extraneous details.

Routine request for action

Mrs. J. Simmons
1234 Main Street
Your Town, USA 00000

Dear Mrs. Simmons:

Put
reader →
in picture

We are currently processing your application for extra in-come benefits; however, we still need further information from you to complete our work.

State →
request

Please send us the following:

1. A copy of your tax returns for the years 19XX, 19YY, and 19ZZ.
2. Your current employer's name and address.
3. A copy of your (a) phone, (b) gas, and (c) electric bills for the past three months.

Reasons →
why

This information will complete our records on your appli-cation, and we should be able to give you a decision within 10 days after we receive these papers.

Restate
request →
deadline

Please send this information to me no later than June 10. I am enclosing an addressed, stamped envelope for your use.

Thank you.

Sincerely,

FIGURE 12.8 A letter organized to give a persuasive message
Source: *Writing Effective Letters* (U.S. Office of Personnel Management: U.S. Government Printing Office, 1985).

ORGANIZING

- Introduce the topic.
- Explain the purpose of the document.
- Clarify the audience.
- Briefly state the thesis (the major point, the result or conclusion, if any).
- Lay out road map for the document or through the document.

FIGURE 12.9 Introduction for a technical or professional letter
Source: Dixie Goswami, Janice C. Redish, Daniel B. Felker, and Alan Siegal, *Writing in the Professions* (Washington, D.C.: American Institutes for Research, 1981): 77. Copyright owned by the American Institutes for Research and the Document Design Center, and this material is used with permission.

In writing a complaint, you usually want to move your reader to action. Unlike the routine complaint letter, the persuasive complaint letter uses a different organizational strategy. Figure 12.10 illustrates a complaint letter that asks a company to replace a faulty piece of equipment with another, more expensive piece of equipment, free of charge.

Writing a persuasive complaint letter to move your reader to action requires persuasive writing that moves from detailed support to your final

October 29, 19XX

Dear Mr. Steele:

On October 19, 19XX, our company purchased from you a Holter seismograph (Cat. No. 786-1243-01, Purchase Order No. 92-1473, October 9, 19XX). After spending three days assembling it and evaluating its performance under various geological conditions, we determined that the instrument's sensitivity is well below specs; in fact, it is completely erratic.

Writer builds details.

On October 20 and 21, I received the setup and operating procedures by telephone from Ms. Moranda Feat, your technical representative. After determining that we had, in fact, set up and operated the machine properly, she suggested that we might need a service representative, who could not be available for at least a week.

Requests action.

After consulting with our colleagues, we have determined that a different instrument would better suit our needs. We wish to exchange the Holter seismograph for a McKuen seismograph. We realize that the purchase price of the monitor is higher by $150.00 but feel that your company should absorb the cost. We believe that the Holter seismograph is defective and would be exchanged anyway; the extra cost of the McKuen seismograph will offset our lost time.

Sincerely yours,

Suzanne Meister
Chief Geologist

SM/sfg

cc: F. O. Martin

FIGURE 12.10 A complaint letter with persuasive writing
Source: Adapted from an anonymous student response.

request. When writing the complaint letter, decide whether the complaint is routine or unique, avoid anger in your tone, assume the reader will wish to respond reasonably, and then choose your organizational strategy.

Writing a complaint letter involves organizational decisions, but responding to the complaint letter is even more difficult. When you respond to a complaint, the rule of thumb is to deal with the writer's complaint and not to answer some emotional or implied question that is irrelevant to the main issue. In other words, as the respondent, answer the writer's major question, avoid emotional issues, and do not ask another question of your own. Do not put words in the writer's letter, words the writer never used. The models in Figure 12.11 and 12.12 present a complaint and a response. The response avoids being pulled into other controversies.

March 23, 19XX

Midwest Chemical Corporation
137 Elton Circle
Chicago, Illinois 60614

Dear Sirs:

It would appear that your company cares more about profits than about human health—as evidenced by your production of ethylene dibromide (EDB). Both the National Institute for Occupational Safety and Health and the Environmental Defense Fund have asked EPA to impose restrictions on the use of EDB. The production and use of EDB are hazardous to the public at large. Don't the chemical companies make enough money without having to endanger the health of the public?

Sincerely,

Peter T. Loames

FIGURE 12.11 Letter with an emotional question

Questions to Ask Yourself When You Write a Complaint Letter:

1. Have I stated the problem?
2. Is the complaint routine or persuasive?
3. If the complaint is routine, did I first state the request for action?

4. If the complaint is persuasive, did I state the details before the request for action?
5. Have I selected information to support my claim?
6. Did I avoid irrelevant issues?
7. Did I clearly state the action I think the reader ought to take?
8. Did I avoid anger and assume reader rationality?

March 30, 19XX

Mr. Peter T. Loames
63 Elm Drive
Potsdam, New York 13676

Dear Mr. Loames:

Thank you for your letter of March 23 regarding the production of ethylene dibromide. Your concern for human health is of utmost importance, and it is Midwest Chemical's primary concern as well. The public has a right to know of chemicals that could be dangerous to the environment or to human health.

EDB has been manufactured in the U.S. for 52 years without serious hazard to those who produce or use it. Unfortunately, the primary study cited against EDB employed excessively high doses and a route of exposure that is virtually impossible to replicate in the real world. Health surveys of workers exposed to EDB show no significant adverse health effects, and crops grown in soil fumigated with EDB contained no EDB residues. The importance of EDB in gasoline, as a fumigant and as a manufacturing intermediate, is so great that, although data indicate no potential problem with EDB in the workplace, we at Midwest Chemical will further increase the safety factor regarding the production of EDB.

Midwest Chemical Corporation has prepared a report on EDB for the Environmental Protection Agency, a copy of which will be sent to you if you so wish. We are eager to comply with EPA restrictions when they are imposed on chemical production, and we appreciate your concern on behalf of the people of our country.

Thank you for your letter and for the opportunity to explain our position on ethylene dibromide.

Very truly yours,

James T. Williams
Vice President
Corporate Technology

FIGURE 12.12 Letter avoiding an emotional question

Questions to Ask Yourself When You Respond to a Complaint Letter:

1. Did I identify the main issues?
2. Is the response routine or persuasive?
3. Have I gathered information to support my response?
4. Have I organized the response
   - to persuade the reader?
   - to answer the issues one by one?
5. Did I encourage the reader to consider my viewpoint by establishing rapport or suggesting positive action?

To Sell a Service or Persuade to Your Viewpoint

The **technical sales letter** responds to a request for information about the product or solicits new business by informing people about the service. Like the accompanying letter for a **résumé** that essentially sells the candidate, the technical sales letter should be courteous and accurate, providing complete information so that the reader can make a decision but selecting only the appropriate information so as to respect the reader's time. If you are selling a service, you should provide your reader with

- features
- benefits to the customer
- cost

The design of the sales letter will contribute to the sale of the product. Most sales letters typically follow this outline:

1. attention-getter
2. introduction of product/service and presentation of evidence
3. mention of price
4. call for action

Using headings in the technical sales letter will help the reader find the information and make a decision. The format for the sales letter in Figure 12.13 presents the information in such a way as to answer the customer's questions and persuade the reader to become a customer.

Module 8 also prepared you to write the technical sales letter—a type of **proposal.** For now, remember that the reader wants information on a course of action, so the principle of writing in the plain style of agent, action, goal, discussed in Module 4, is appropriate here. Inflated language and wordiness interfere with the message and may confuse the reader, thus negating the entire purpose for writing the letter.

Letterhead

October 19, 19XX

Inside Address

Dear Ms. Lombard:

Subject: Unique Features of the Alpha Printer

The Alpha Printer xxxxxxxxxxxxxxxxxxxxxxxxxxxxxxxxxxxxxxxxxxxxxxxxxxx
xxxxxxxxxxxxxxxxxxxxxxxxxxxxxxxxxxxxxxxxxxxxxxxxxxxxxxxxxxxxxxxxx

Unique Features

xxxxxxxxxxxxxxxxxxxxxxxxxxxxxxxxxxxxxxxxxxxxxxxxxxxxxxxxxxxxxxxxxx
xxxxxxxxxxxxxxxxxxxxxxxxxxxxxxxxxxxxxxxxxxxxxxxxxxxxxxxxxxxxxxxxxx

Specifications of the Printer

| xxxxxxxxxxxxxxxx | xxxxxxxxxxxxxxxx | xxxxxxxxxxxxxxxx |
| xxxxxxxxxxxxxxxx | xxxxxxxxxxxxxxxx | xxxxxxxxxxxxxxxx |

Costs

xxxxxxxxxxxxxxxxxxxxxxxxxxxxxxxxxxxxxxxxxxxxxxxxxxxxxxxxxxxxxxxxxx
                    xxxxxxxxxxxxxxxxxxxxxxxxxx
                    xxxxxxxxxxxxxxxxxxxxxxxxxx
                    xxxxxxxxxxxxxxxxxxxxxxxxxx

Options

xxxxxxxxxxxxxxxxxxxxxxxxxxxxxxxxxxxxxxxxxxxxxxxxxxxxxxxxxxxxxxxxxx
xxxxxxxxxxxxxxxxxxxxxxxxxxxxxxxxxxxxxxxxxxxxxxxxxxxxxxxxxxxxxxxxxx

For further information xxxxxxxxxxxxxxxxxxxxxxxxxxxxxxxxxxxxxxxxxx
xxxxxxxxxxxxxxxxxxxxxxxxxxxxxxxxxxxxxxxxxxxxxxxxxxxxxxxxxxxxxxxxxx

Sincerely yours,

Seller
Mail Stop S-23
ext. 435

enc.

bc: R. A. Richardson (does not appear on original;
           copy stamped COPY)

FIGURE 12.13 Technical sales letter

Sometimes presenting your ideas systematically may not be enough when you are trying to influence a reader's opinion or persuade a hostile reader to consider your viewpoint. When you want to influence a neutral reader's opinion, state the most important or the most positive information first. Organizing your letter with the most positive information first places that information in the **primary** position.[3] Research indicates that initial material influences how people react to later material.

In an experiment with the use of adjectives in introducing someone, the researcher first described the person as "intelligent, industrious, impulsive, critical, stubborn, and envious."[4] Under another condition, the researcher reversed the order of adjectives. The findings indicate that the people encountering the positive adjectives first formed a significantly higher opinion of the introduced person than those who encountered the negative adjectives first.

You can affect the influence of the primacy position by warning people against the influence of first impressions. In fact, you can promote the opposite influence, the power of placing important information in the last or **recency** position, when you tell people to consider all the information and suspend judgment until the end of the information.

When you have to write to a **hostile reader** or write about a **controversial issue,** you face the decision of how to organize your information and what information to include. First, what information should you include when discussing a controversial issue? Should you present a one-sided argument (only ideas that support your position) or a two-sided argument (ideas both for and against your position)? One expert in persuasion summarizes five findings.[5]

- If your readers are hostile, use a two-sided presentation.
- If your readers are fairly well educated and you have strong evidence on your side, use a two-sided presentation.
- If your readers have limited knowledge or education, use a one-sided presentation to influence them.
- If your readers mildly support your position, use a one-sided presentation to encourage them.
- If your readers are likely to hear the other side, use a two-sided approach to immunize them against the influence of the other side.

Then, when you organize your points under your one-sided or two-sided presentation, follow the rules of primacy or recency.

Finally, when you have to write a letter that requires both a negative response and a persuasive request for the reader to take action, combine some organizational strategies, but apply them one at a time. To write negative news, first establish rapport and then give the negative news, providing your reasons and details. Next you can move into the persuasive task of presenting your viewpoint or making your request and organizing your details to persuade the reader to act. Figure 12.14 illustrates this organizational strategy.

ARCHEOLOGICAL SURVEY COMMISSION
1 Lincoln Center
Washington, D. C. 20023

March 14, 19XX

Dr. Scott Thompson
Director of Geological Surveys
Minerals Analysis, Inc.
6007 North Pine Road
Lincoln, Nebraska 80023

Dear Dr. Thompson:

Subject: Compliance Reporting of Archeological Surveys

On November 2, 19XX, the Archeological Survey Commission (ASC) requested
the documentation of environmental compliance for the West Plains Project.
This documentation included archeological surveys necessary to continue with
your construction activities. You were to submit the documentation by January 3, 19XX. We have not yet received that report. In accordance with the
Archeological and Preservation Act (Law 52:153), we must withdraw your
permit for construction activities until we receive your compliance documentation. As of March 15, 19XX, you may not proceed with construction activities
until you have taken the following actions:

1. Provide the ASC with a schedule for completion of surveys and compliance reports.
2. Submit the completed surveys and reports on the forms enclosed.
3. In the future, submit the remainder of the documentation on the
    scheduled dates approved by the ASC.

Schedule of Compliance Reports

xxxxxxxxxxxxxxxxxxxxxxxxxxxxxxxxxxxxxxxxxxxxxxxxxxxxxxxxxxxxxxxxxxx
xxxxxxxxxxxxxxxx necessary information xxxxxxxxxxxxxxxxxxxxxxxxxxxxx

Forms for Surveys and Reports

xxxxxxxxxxxxxxxxxxxxxxxxxxxxxxxxxxxxxxxxxxxxxxxxxxxxxxxxxxxxxxxxxxxx
xxxxxxxxxxxxxxxx description of forms xxxxxxxxxxxxxxxxxxxxxxxxxxxxxxx

ASC Approval of Future Compliance Reports

xxxxxxxxxxxxxxxxxxxxxxxxxxxxxxxxxxxxxxxxxxxxxx
xxxxxxxxx details for future approvals xxxxxxxxx

If you have any questions, please contact Dr. Richard Mielsen at 212/652-2200,
extension 256.

Sincerely,

FIGURE 12.14 Letter with multiple purposes

Clarifying the Message

The concept of clarity is closely allied with readability and writing for the reader. Module 4 is devoted to clear writing, and some of the advice from that module is reviewed in this section. Clear letter writing makes the reader's task easier by using accurate information instead of imprecise terms and by using detail instead of ambiguous or inflated language. Clarity comes from completeness, but not from long-windedness. On the other hand, excessive brevity may also confuse the reader.

Executives have made the following observation about day-to-day correspondence:[6]

EXCESSIVE BREVITY—The writer fails to explain the subject matter adequately. He is very familiar with the problem . . . and unconsciously assumes others are, too. Result—reader is left confused or misinformed. —Product Engineering

Avoid Ambiguity

An ambiguous sentence contains more than one possible meaning, as in the phrase *temporary suggestion box*. Is the box temporary or the suggestion temporary? In Module 4 on style, the advice to clarify ambiguity is to change the word order and add small words. The clarified phrase is: *The suggestion box is temporary.*

Give Accurate Details

Accuracy is precise language that supplies the reader with necessary information. If the reader knows that the price of a dot matrix printer must remain within the department's budget, the reader knows very little about how to evaluate the purchase of a printer. On the other hand, if the cost of the dot matrix printer must remain below $1,000.00, then the reader has a clear idea of the price range for possible printers.

Accurate information supplies limits for the reader to use as standards on which to make a decision. When a client wants to hire a consultant for the day, the consultant to be paid by the hour, then it is important for both the client and consultant to know whether the day begins at 9:00 A.M. and ends at 5:00, for a total of eight hours or whether the morning hours are 9:00 A.M. to 12:00 and 1:00 P.M. to 4:00 P.M., for a total of six hours. Accurate information helps the reader fill an order for half a dozen screws when the reader knows the size of screw and the model number of the instrument or piece of equipment. Inaccurate or incomplete information invites the reader's frustration. When you write, include facts and figures; in other words, give accurate details.

Be Brief

Brevity encourages us to use straightforward language rather than inflated language to impress the reader. We are all tempted to demonstrate our facility with words by using wordy expressions when declarative statements will suffice. But by the time a person reads the following statement on a wall, the message may be too late:

Not this: In the event of fire, evacuation of the building should be implemented.
But this: IN CASE OF FIRE, LEAVE THE BUILDING. USE THE STAIRS. DO NOT USE THE ELEVATORS.

Many sentences are clearer when they are shortened, especially when you remember that the direct, active style is more effective than sentences with nominalizations and weak verbs.

Not this: Improved manpower utilization can affect the modification of the building in an elapsed time period of three working days.
But this: We can modify the building in three working days if we use the personnel effectively.

Module 4 discusses brevity and inflated language in sentences. In this module, wordiness in diction also defeats the conciseness of letters and memos. The following list reminds you to be more concise with connecting words, phrases, and clauses.

Increase Brevity in Letters and Memos
Use one connecting word instead of three or four:

What We Write	**What We Mean**
until such time as	until
with regard to	about
with reference to	about
in view of the fact that	because, although
in the amount of	for
on the occasion of	when
for the purpose of	for
prior to	before
subsequent to	after
in the event that	if
at the present time	now
along the lines of	like
during such time as	while

Use a strong verb instead of a phrase:

make inquiry concerning	ask about
he is of the opinion	he believes
it is our understanding that	we understand
give consideration to	consider
in compliance with your request	as you requested
afford an opportunity	let, permit
appreciate it if you would furnish	appreciate your furnishing

Use one or two words instead of a clause:

the question as to whether: **whether**	the fact that I had arrived: **my arrival**
there is no doubt but that: **no doubt**	
used for fuel purposes: **used for fuel**	in the case of: **if**
	in the event that: **if**
he is a man who: **he**	in the nature of: **like**
in a hasty manner: **hastily**	in the neighborhood of: **about**
this is a subject that: **this subject**	in terms of: **in, for (or leave out)**
owing to the fact that: **since, because**	on the basis of: **by**
	on the grounds that: **since, because**
in spite of the fact that: **though, although**	prior to: **before**
	with a view to: **to**
call your attention to the fact that: **remind you**	with reference to: **about (or leave out)**
I was unaware of the fact that: **I was unaware**	with regard to: **about (or leave out)**
	with the result that: **so that**

Source: *Professional Writing Techniques* (U.S. Office of Personnel Management: U.S. Government Printing Office, 1985).

Give Complete Information

Do not confuse completeness with long-windedness. The reader needs details but not irrelevant information. You should include all the necessary information and important ideas, but they should be accurate and brief. One of the problems, of course, is knowing when the information is necessary and when it is irrelevant. When in doubt, it is better to include the information for accuracy or to repeat the key word for clarity. In its final definition, completeness means including all the necessary details but avoiding excess information. The following examples clarify the distinction between complete information and information that is excessive or too concise:

Excessive Information
The Wankel engine is an engine that was developed by Wankel and introduced into the American car industry by German-born Franz Wankel.

Complete Information
German born Franz Wankel introduced the Wankel engine into the American car industry.

Incomplete Information
The Marmon Group is a complex of companies.

Complete Information
The Marmon Group is a rapidly growing multinational complex of companies whose principal activities include manufacturing and marketing of capital goods, equipment, and products.

Opening and Closing the Correspondence

Many writers say that writing the first and last paragraphs of the correspondence is the most difficult.[7]

Use the beginning to

Introduce the subject or purpose.	We are glad to give you the information asked for in your letter of November 14.
Make a direct statement about your purpose or subject.	We have decided to accept your recommendation for changes in office procedures.
Ask a question or make a request.	Will you please send us your hiring request by June 13 so that we may process it quickly?
Focus on your reader.	Your request for publications on hazardous waste has been transferred to this office.

Rewrite openings to be brief, clear, and responsive.

Not this:
Re your letter of August 10, please be informed that this office does not keep statistical data on the number of people in federal employment.

But this:
Replying to your August 10 letter, we are sorry to inform you that this agency does not keep the statistical data you requested.

Use the closing to

Make a courteous request.	Will you please notify us of any developments in the energy conservation policy?
Make a courteous command.	Please sign and return the enclosed form by May 3.
Ask a pertinent question.	May we have your answer before June 15?

Instead of closing with a timeworn and, therefore, meaningless expression, express yourself sincerely and accurately.

Not this:
Please contact us if we can be of further service to you.

But this:
We appreciate helping you and hope we can assist you again in the future.

Not this:
Your prompt attention to this matter would be appreciated by this office.

But this:
Please call me sometime before June 10 so that we can resolve the fuel emission problems.

Designing the Letter

Both the public and private sectors usually have a design for the layout of letters. You will have to examine the files or the style guide of the company or agency to determine the acceptable format. Because letter formats are determined by the company's preference, this section will consider the two most popular letter styles: *full block* and *modified block*.

Full-Block Letter

The *full-block* style uses *single-spacing* between lines and starts or *aligns* each line with the left margin, leaving a blank line between each paragraph and each section of the letter. Aligning the last word in each line with the right margin is called *justifying* the right margin. With word processors or computers it is easy to justify the right margin, but remember that justifying the right and left margins may create a river of white spaces in the text. Module 5 discusses the problem of justifying both margins. The letter in Figure 12.15 uses the full block style and a *ragged* or uneven right margin, a style popular in business because it is easy to produce at the computer or typewriter. The main caution is to remember the blank line between paragraphs in the full-block letter because the reader no longer has the indented words that indicate a new paragraph.

Printed Letterhead
or

(Format Instructions)
1 inch down from top of page
Radiographics, Inc.   **maximum number of lines/page = 60**
2072 West Greenland Lane   **single-space**
                                              double-space
June 21, 1983   **left justify; left margin = 1 inch**

                                              4 spaces

Theracon, Inc.
104 South Ashland Avenue   **single-space**
La Grange, Illinois 60525   **inside address**
                                              double-space
Dear Ms. Colbson: **salutation**
                                              double-space
Subject: Exchange of radiographic   **subject line (optional)**
equipment   **double-space**

The body of the letter, Paragraph 1
xxxxxxxxxxxxxxxxxxxxxxxxxxxxxxxxxxxxxx   **single-space, line length = 65**
xxxxxxxxxxxxxxxxxxxxxxxxxxxxxxxxxxxxxx

                                              double-space between paragraphs
The body of the letter, Paragraph 2
xxxxxxxxxxxxxxxxxxxxxxxxxxxxxxxxxxxxxx
xxxxxxxxxxxxxxxxxxxxxxxxxxxxxxxxxxxxxx

                                              double-space
Sincerely yours,   **complimentary close**

                                              written signature
                                              (4 spaces)
Henry Franklin   **typed signature**
Manager   **title single-space**
                                              double-space
HF:wp   **writer, typist (word processor)**
                                              double-space
cc: C. L. Close   **carbon copy notation**
    A. Lawson

                                              double-space
bc: OM   **blind copy (does not appear on origi-**
                                              nal; copy stamped COPY)

FIGURE 12.15 Full-block letter

Modified Block Letter

Hundreds of companies modify the full-block style to suit their message, to make their letters more readable, and to take advantage of the options now

Letterhead or   (Format Instructions)
Minerals Analysis, Inc.
6007 North Pine Road   **align first letters**
Lincoln, Nebraska   **or center**

                                                double-space
November 20, 1986   **align or center date**

                                                4 spaces

Mr. Sheldon Decker   **inside address**
Decker Consulting Inc.   **single-space**
4047 Lake Bluff Drive
New York, New York 30667

                                                double-space
Dear Mr. Decker: **salutation**
                                                double-space
Subject: Compliance Report for Archaeologi-   **(optional)**
cal Commission
                                                double-space
Paragraph 1 xxxxxxxxxxxxxxxxxxxxxxxxx   **maximum line length = 65**
xxxxxxxxxxxxxxxxxxxxxxxxxxxxxxxxxxxxxx   **characters**
                                                double-space
Paragraph 2 xxxxxxxxxxxxxxxxxxxxxxxx   **single-space**
xxxxxxxxxxxxxxxxxxxxxxxxxxxxxxxxxxxxx

                                                double-space
          Sincerely yours,   **complimentary close**
                                                first letter starts
                                                at center

          Scott Thompson, Ph.D.   **single-space**
          Director of Geological Surveys   **title**
                                                double-space
ST:cal   **identifying initials**
enc. (or Encl.)   **enclosure**
                                                double-space
c: R. O. Nelson   **copy notation**
                                                double-space
bc: R. T. Howells   **blind copy (does not appear on**
                                                original; copy stamped COPY)

                                                maximum lines/page = 60

FIGURE 12.16 Modified block letter

available for computers and printers as well as for typewriters. A popular
modified block letter centers the date and the closing line under the letterhead,
either indents the first word of each paragraph or aligns it with the left
margin, and aligns all other lines. Figure 12.16 illustrates the modified block
style.

Subsequent Pages of the Letter

When the letter exceeds one page, you must head all subsequent pages with the receiver's last name, the page number, and the date.

Example

Dr. Thompson   March 14, 19XX   Page 2

Lines with Precise Information

In both styles, many letters now include a **subject line** before the salutation, following the salutation, or instead of the salutation. The subject line helps the reader focus on the message; for this reason the subject line must include precise information:

> *Not this:* SUBJECT: Richardson Investment Inc.
> *But this:* SUBJECT: Request from Richardson Investment Inc. for land lease at Los Alamos

Some additional lines in letters also present precise information:

attention line   —following the inside address and relating the precise information to the reader
writer's title   —following the signature
writer's mail stop —following the title of the writer

These lines of precise information appear in the example.

Example

                                        Myra Simpson
                                        Sales Representative
                                        Mail Stop S-23

Notation Lines

Finally, both letter styles have notations, when necessary, at the left margin below the signature:

Example

- **identifying initials**—the initials of the letter writer and the person who made the copy
  SG:ec (Susan Gordon, the writer; Evelyn Criles, the secretary)

- **enclosure notation**—an abbreviated note indicating another document is attached or enclosed
      Encl(s).
      Attachment(s).

- **copy notation**—an abbreviated note indicating the names of people who received copies of the letter. When it is inappropriate (for whatever reasons) for the receiver to know copies have been sent to others, the copy notation does not appear on the original letter, but the word *COPY* appears on the *blind copies.*
      c: J. Sutpen
         R. Irving

Visual Design and Readability

In a letter, using visual techniques to help a reader find information is as important as the visual techniques in a manual or a report. Whereas most visual aids such as figures accompany the letter as an attachment, some letters incorporate tables in the body of the letter, and most letters can benefit from

- headings and subheadings:
- underlining, bold type, or italics
- enumerated lists or bulleted items
- white space

Headings and subheadings organize the information and forecast the content. Figure 12.17 uses headings, incorporates a table in the letter, and makes effective use of white space around the precise information. Like most documents, letters benefit from visual planning; they need not be solid paragraphs of print, always aligned along the left margin. Remember some of the design and readability techniques when writing letters.

Writing the Letter of Application

The content, the style, and the visual design of the letter depend on the purpose and the receiver. You will probably write many letters during your career, *expository* letters that provide information, such as

- neutral information
- positive news
- negative news

and *persuasive* letters that present

- controversial issues
- requests for action
- sales messages.

October 13, 19XX

Geraline Chapman
Indiana Pollution Control Board
224 South Dakota Street
Indianapolis, Indiana 44077

Dear Ms. Chapman:

In your letter of October 3, 19XX, you requested information on levels of air emissions from Wastewater Treatment Plants.

Background
Emission values are rough estimates from simplified, preliminary studies. Our database is narrow, and evaporation affects our calculations. We can provide you only with potential emission data. We are also enclosing a report by our professional staff on methods of estimating emissions from treatment plants.

Potential Emissions

Facility	Flow Rate (million gallons/day)	Emissions (tons/yr)
Philadelphia	160 mgd	98–148 t/y
Indianapolis	145 mgd	94 t/y
Dayton	54 mgd	56 t/y
Rockford	39 mgd	16 t/y

We emphasize the fact that the emission values are only rough estimates. We will keep your office apprised of any further developments on this subject.

Sincerely yours,

Victor M. Jones
District Administrator

Enclosures

cc: ODA
    L. Kanara

FIGURE 12.17 Letter with embedded table

But no letter will be more important to the beginning of your career than the letter of application.

Essentially, the letter of application is a sales letter, a letter selling yourself. It accompanies the résumé as a cover letter and often makes a bid for an interview. Whereas cover letters should express the individuality of the writer, they should also include certain information that tells the reader you are the appropriate candidate for the job.

First the Résumé

Write your résumé first because it has the data and details you will need to write a strong, clear letter of application.

The résumé includes information about your

- education
- previous work experiences
- special interests, skills, and honors
- publications and projects record
- availability

Because there are as many designs for a résumé as there are writers, the important advice is that the résumé should appeal to the reader. A neat, uncluttered résumé with clear headings to help the reader find the important information is crucial to the success of the résumé. Look at the clarity of the résumé in Figure 12.18.

MICHAEL J. CLEMETSEN
4162 Apple Lane
Glenview, Illinois 60025
(312) 555-2453

CAREER OBJECTIVES	Employment as a <u>fire protection engineer</u> with emphasis on fire investigation, construction review, and extinguishing systems. Hope to obtain a higher degree in a management-related field.
EDUCATION	<u>Illinois Institute of Technology.</u> Chicago, Illinois. B.S. Fire Protection and Safety Engineering Graduation Date: December 1984. Co-op student with Rolf Jensen and Associates.
ENGINEERING EXPERIENCE	<u>Illinois Institute of Technology.</u> Laboratory Instructor. Taught practical laboratory in sprinkler design to senior class of 1985. August 1984 to present.
	<u>Rolf Jensen and Associates.</u> Deerfield, Illinois. Co-op Student/Technician. Responsible for providing technical support for fire protection consulting engineering firm. Specifically: Design review, construction inspection, hotel and industrial fire investigation, hydraulic calculations, literature research, and light drafting. August 1981 to August 1982 and March 1984 to present.
Note idea of coursework as experience.	<u>Illinois Institute of Technology.</u> Independent study classwork. Built and calibrated the "Ohio Rate of Heat

FIGURE 12.18 Clear résumé
Source: Michael J. Clemetsen, Technical Writing 421, Illinois Institute of Technology.

	Release" test apparatus. Installed and implemented a computer for use in the academic department office. Included writing and using Fire Protection Applications programs. August 1983 to May 1984.
OTHER EXPERIENCE	McClurg Court Sports Center. Chicago, Illinois. Lifeguard; part-time while attending school. September 1982 to May 1984.
HONORS AND ACTIVITIES	Dean's List; Grendahl Scholarship recipient; Student Chapter of the SFPE—secretary, treasurer; Clinton Stryker Distinguished Service Award; IIT Varsity Swim Team—team captain, National Championship qualifier, Varsity record holder; Beta Omega Nu Fraternity—president, vice president; Sigma Phi Epsilon Fraternity—sports and social chairperson Enjoy sailing, racquetball, and reading.
PERSONAL	Born 7/12/61. Single. Excellent health. Willing to travel and relocate.
REFERENCES	Available on request.

FIGURE 12.18 (cont.)

Also the purpose of the résumé may affect the information in the résumé and the order in which this information is presented. In some situations you will wish to stress your education first; at other times your experience may be more important. You may write the straight list-of-data résumé or, as you do in a persuasive letter, you may wish to organize your data to make a persuasive presentation or emphasize a major point about yourself. The persuasive résumé is sometimes called the "talking" résumé.

The résumé you practice here has one main purpose—to get a job, or at least an interview. But the type of job and the level of the candidate's credentials influence the résumé. So, as the résumé writer, you have some design decisions to make. The visual layout is as important as the content and style. You have to design the résumé with knowledge of the custom in your field and an eye toward the position of the information.[8] This section illustrates traditional résumé formats, as in Figure 12.19, but some nontraditional approaches are becoming more and more acceptable. You might want to examine some nontraditional approaches in the books referenced at the end of this module.

Most résumés include standard information:

- objectives
- education
- experience.

STEPHEN H. SMITH

HOME ADDRESS
928 Western Ave.
Claredon Hills, IL 60514

SCHOOL ADDRESS
1323 Hoyle, Apt. 3F
Chicago, IL 60616
(312) 326-5970

OBJECTIVE: Employment in a DIGITAL-oriented environment with an emphasis on computer applications.

EDUCATION: Illinois Institute of Technology, Chicago, IL
8/80 to present Bachelor of Science, expected December 1984
Major: electrical engineering
Minor: computer engineering
GPA: 2.7 / 4.0
Honors: Dean's List (Fall 1983, Spring 1984)

Major Subjects	Minor Subjects
digital systems	logic design
solid-state circuits	microcomputers
circuit analysis	switching circuit theory
energy conversion	operating systems
transmission lines	computer programming using
signals and systems	Pascal, Fortran, Basic, M6800
electrodynamics	assembler

Related Subjects: engineering economics, technical writing

Special
Project:

E.E. Department Research Project: Designed, constructed, and tested an X—Y Positioning System for precise, digital control of an ultrasonic transducer.

EXPERIENCE: Electronic Technician.
Summer 1984 Total Control Products, Berkley, IL.
Constructed prototype printed circuit boards for new product line. Assisted design engineers with initial testing. Tested and inspected final product as quality control. Involved with reading schematic diagrams. Gained considerable insight into design techniques, problem areas, and trade-offs.

Assistant Manager.
1977 to 1983 Convenient Food Mart, Bellwood, IL
(summers) Gained insight into retailing and management. Involved interacting with the public.

ACTIVITIES: IEEE, publicity chairperson for Student Branch of IEEE, student aide for American Power Conference (1983, 1984), Alpha Epsilon Pi Fraternity—held offices of president, steward, social chairperson.

INTERESTS: Microcomputer design, racquetball, bowling, golf.

FIGURE 12.19 Traditional résumé

RÉSUMÉ

Kathryn Youder

1255 W. Logan Drive   EXCELLENT HEALTH
Portland, Oregon   SINGLE
(949) 555-2076   5'2", 120 pounds

EDUCATION

Currently enrolled in a Medical Technology program
at McCormick University, affiliated with Rush-University (St. Luke's Presbyterian Hospital). Curriculum includes:

Too much of a list.

GENERAL BIOLOGY........................5 credits
MICROBIOLOGY...........................6 credits
ANATOMY AND PHYSIOLOGY.............4 credits

**Use more discussion of
courses.**

STRUCTURAL INORGANIC CHEMISTRY .. 4 credits
ORGANIC CHEMISTRY....................4 credits
ANALYTIC CHEMISTRY ....4 credits

AFFILIATIONS

You've never worked?

NATIONAL HONOR SOCIETY
SOCIETY OF DISTINGUISHED STUDENTS
UNION OF CONCERNED BLACK STUDENTS
WOOTEN CHORAL ENSEMBLE

HOBBIES

TENNIS
CHESS
BACKGAMMON
ORGANIST

REFERENCES AVAILABLE ON REQUEST

FALL 19XX

RED FLAG PROBLEMS:
1. No dates for education   Candidate didn't take
2. No job objectives   time to write an accepta-
3. Any work experience?   ble résumé—just a list of
4. Any accomplishments?   items.

FIGURE 12.20 Résumé that raises questions

The best résumés are

- brief—one page for individuals with a B.A. or B.S. and five years of experience; two pages for everyone else; three pages for a Ph.D. with a long history of publications.
- organized.

- neat and appropriately formatted—no fancy type or cute format.

Be sure to

- Spell out *acronyms* (letters that stand for words) and technical terms.
- Explain what you did instead of just providing the job title.
- List jobs in reverse chronological order.
- Edit for typographical errors and *red flags*.

A red flag is information in the résumé that raises more questions than it answers. The model in Figure 12.20 is an example of a résumé that raises questions.

The model in Figures 12.21 illustrates the résumé of a candidate with related job experience.

PERSUASIVE, OR TALKING, RÉSUMÉ

BARBARA JONES-SMYTHE   PREFER MASS., N.H., CT.
3784 14th Street
Wayland, Massachusetts 01872   CURRENT SALARY: $38,000/yr.
(617) 388-7686 (Residence)   ① ASKING SALARY: $38,000/min.
(617) 465-6868 (Work—Discreetly)
CANDID INFORMATION

PERSONAL: Married, No Children U.S. Citizen
     D.O.B. 10/12/57 5'7" 135 lbs. Homeowner

EDUCATION:
6/78   BOSTON UNIVERSITY, Boston, Massachusetts
     B.S. Mathematics   G.P.A. 2.9 of 4.0

MISC.:   Alpha Gamma Gamma Sorority President
     28 weeks total schooling on Digital Equipment
     Corporation Computers (VAX/VMS operating system,
     Decnet, etc.). Significant college experience
     programming on Data General Eclipse Series
     computers, AOS operating system, mainly in Fortran.
     Worked as student programmer on school
     administration applications.

OBJECTIVE: ②   Seeking an applications programming position with
     project leader responsibility. Prefer D.E.C./VAX
     Computer installation running either VMS or UNIX
     operating systems. Prefer commercial applications
     (not accounting) with substantial user/customer
     involvement for the lead programmer. I have enjoyed

FIGURE 12.21 Résumé of person with job experience
(Source: Scientific Placement, Inc., Houston, Tex. 77224).
Used with permission.

my systems programming experience and feel that it has given me excellent technical skills. However, I miss the people involvement and the day-to-day real-world problems that applications programming can provide. Long-term, I would like to know as much about business as I do about programming so that I would feel competent to design really good programs that are user oriented.

BUSINESS
EXPERIENCE:

10/80 to
Present

CAMBRIDGE HOUSE, INC., Cambridge, Mass. Software Engineer developing system software to run on Digital Equipment Corp. Computers (VAX and PDPII).

Currently functioning as lead programmer on a team charged with implementing a new database management system (DBMS-BESTO) for VAX that would run on the VMS operating system. This software product is a full relational DBMS that includes shared files, transaction processing, logging, etc. The initial release is aimed at vendors of turn key systems (technical OEM's) and is limited to VAX, but the product is ultimately to have much wider application. Serve as the primary interface between the system designer (outside consultant and university professor) and a team of 3 working systems programmers.

During my first year at Cambridge, I worked on a series of utility programs that were designed to help D.E.C. PDP11 users migrate commercial applications programs from the PDP11 to the VAX computer. These utilities were aimed specifically at converting from the RSTS/E interactive multiuser PDPII operating system to VAX/VMS. User programs were to be converted from Basic Plus 2 (RSTS) to the VAX native mode Basic language. This assignment gave me a good understanding of language compilers and of the problems faced by users having many programs to migrate to a different system.

③ Skills summary: DEC PDP11 & VAX Computers, RSTS/E & VMS operating systems, Languages: Fortran, "C," Basic Plus 2, VAX Basic, Macro-II, Assembler.

6/78 to
10/80

ATLAS AUTO PARTS COMPANY, Worcester, Mass. Applications Programmer for large multilocation wholesale auto parts distributor. Wrote new

FIGURE 12.21 (cont.)

programs, debugged and enhanced existing programs, for order entry, inventory, and warehousing applications. These were on-line interactive programs written to be very user friendly (fill-in-the-blank screen formats, numerous data entry edits, help messages, etc.). The computer environment was distributed processing with 4 Digital Equipment Corporation (D.E.C.) PDP11/70 computers each running the RSTS/E operating system and interconnected with DECNET network software. My major projects were: (1) An inventory program for small parts and incidentals designed to cut down on paperwork; (2) A formal study evaluating the problems of converting our applications software from the PDP11 to VAX; and (3) Becoming the DECNET expert.

Skills summary: DEC PDP11 computer, RSTS/E operating system, DECNET communications and networking software, Basic Plus 2 language.

A very impressive résumé aimed at a limited market but likely to draw quite a bit of interest. It succeeds in giving the reader a clear picture of Barbara's interests and qualifications without getting lost in D.E.C. technical verbage.

① Barbara fears that her salary is on the high side, so she included asking salary to indicate flexibility.

② The objectives are up front because she is seeking to change the direction of her career.

③ A skills summary is included after each job because the skills are crucial to her vocation.

FIGURE 12.21 (cont.)

Again, the important advice is to avoid "red flags" and to consider the reader who must find the information quickly.

. . . Then the Application Letter

The cover letter highlights and interprets the résumé, perhaps expanding on a detail or adding an anecdote of a project. The letter does not repeat the résumé; rather the letter argues, sells, interprets, and selects the mere data of the résumé. In the first paragraph the reader may want to know what you know about the company, the people working for the company, or the job in the company. In the following paragraphs you may emphasize certain aspects of your experience that are applicable to a particular employer. You may also use the cover letter to overcome any questions the résumé raises and to make the employer aware of important attitudes. For example, if you interrupted your education to work and earn tuition, in your cover letter you should explain the lapse in dates on the résumé.

The last paragraph requests the interview for the job and provides the reader with your telephone number and available dates and times. Figure 12.22 shows how the application letter does much more than summarize the résumé; the letter

- Introduces the candidate.
- Exhibits interest in the company.
- Applies for a specific job.
- Lists relevant coursework.
- Mentions previous jobs.
- Requests an interview.

1283 S. Plaza Ave., Apt. 3F,
Chicago, IL 60616
November 26, 1984

Sharon Jackson
Personnel Director
Telecommunications Techniques Corporation
444 North Frederick Avenue
Gaithersburg, Maryland 20877

Dear Ms. Jackson:

Personal interest.   While reading the September 6th issue of <u>EDN</u> magazine, I came across your company's job listing in the career opportunities section. I noticed that your company is currently involved in some very interesting projects that are similar to my interests. I would very much like to become a member of TTC's engineering department. I am applying for the position of *electronic engineer.*

Relevant coursework.
Specific project.   In December I will be graduating from the Illinois Institute of Technology with a bachelor of science in Electrical Engineering. I have taken a number of courses in digital electronics and computer design. In addition, for a senior project, I designed and built a digitally controlled X–Y positioning system, which my instructor was very pleased with.

Previous job.   This past summer I assembled prototype circuit boards at an engineering firm. After inserting and soldering components onto the boards, I assisted the engineers in testing them. From this experience I learned quite a bit about how a product goes from a

FIGURE 12.22 Application letter with important information

design on paper to a working product. Because of this practical experience and the knowledge gained from my project and coursework, I feel that I would be a worthy addition to your design engineering team. You will find more information about my education and work experience in the enclosed résumé. I can supply personal references and a report on my positioning system.

Interviewing request.   I would appreciate an opportunity to visit with you and discuss how I might best meet your needs. Would it be possible to arrange an interview for the middle of next week? You can contact me at (312) 555-5970 any weekday morning before noon or any evening after 5:30 P.M. I would be happy to elaborate on my educational credentials and work experience at your convenience.

Sincerely yours,

Stephen H. Smith

FIGURE 12.22 (cont.)

Remember to stress the concept of the *you* attitude in your application letter. This attitude simply means that you should consider the reader more often in the letter than yourself. In other words, the letter should use *you* more frequently than it uses *I*. These words of advice are summarized thus:

- Be courteous, but state your strengths with accurate detail.
- Be unique, but avoid bravado.
- State your job objectives, but wait for the company to begin salary and benefit discussions.

> *Not this:* I believe my academic record reflects my ability to understand the concepts involved in this field.
>
> *But this:* The work I have done in electrical engineering to achieve a 3.8 average out of 4.0, along with my project, "Satellite Communication Systems," will help me understand the engineering projects at TeleCommunications, Inc.
>
> *Not this:* If you want to corner the market on computers in the Southwest region, then I am the employee for you.
>
> *But this:* While employed at Chicken Little's, I suggested a campaign to organize marching bands of youngsters in all 50 states. The Chicken Little Corporation acted on this suggestion, and the parents of these musicians began to partronize our restaurants in 50 states. At Delton International, I would also try to suggest ways to sell more Delton products.

Not this: Because of the cost of living in California, I must have a minimum of $25,000.00 a year and health insurance that includes dental and optical benefits.

But this: I would like an entry-level job in clinical engineering that would enable me to work with the equipment and the personnel in the hospital. Ultimately, I hope to move into hospital administration.

Figure 12.23 is a model of an application letter that enhances the mere data of the résumé with personal, selective, and interpretive statements while avoiding the error of bravado or false humility. It also demonstrates the "you" attitude and the final bid for the interview.

247 LaPorte Drive
Addison, WI 60101
September 19, 19XX

Mr. Robert Hines
Chief Engineer, Research and Development
Werner Brothers, Inc.
222 Hartrey Avenue
Milwaukee, WI 55521

Dear Mr. Hines:

It is my understanding that Shure Brothers, Inc., is presently seeking recent graduates to fill positions in its Engineering Research and Development group. In May 19XX I will be graduating from State Institute of Technology with a B.S. in electrical engineering, with several additional graduate courses to my credit. I am quite interested in applying for a position in your group.

Previous experience.

I have entertained professionally with a musical group for the past eight years. It was through music and my contact with electronic sound equipment that I first became interested in electronics. I enrolled in three years of electronics courses in high school,

Personal interest.

which led me to pursue electrical engineering as a career. My interest in Werner Brothers dates back several years. In October 19XX, I requested a special interview with Cheryl Richardson, who was conducting on-campus interviews for full-time positions with your company. At that time I was seeking a Co-op position with Werner Brothers. Ms. Richardson felt that my background was exceptional, but owing to the state of the economy, your company was not seeking any new Co-op students.

FIGURE 12.23 Application letter with enhancements
Source: Frank Trimble, Technical Writing 421, Illinois Institute of Technology.

Select detail and interpretive statement.	Over the past several years and hundreds of playing dates, I have learned that the microphone and sound system is the performer's link with the audience. I have long admired the genuine quality of Shure equipment and have been impressed by the many innovations your company has introduced over the past several years. I would welcome the opportunity to work for a company that is respected by entertainers and sound equipment manufacturers alike.
Relevant coursework.	As you will see by my résumé, my senior electives included audio and electroacoustics, R.F. design, and logic design and implementation. In addition, my experiences as a Co-op student taught me the importance of communication in any organization and prompted me to take courses in technical writing and visual and verbal communication. I have also made an attempt to keep abreast of developments in the sound equipment field by attending the past four NAMM shows held at McCormick Place, as well as the 1981 Conference held at State Institute of Technology.
Interview request.	I would very much appreciate the opportunity to meet and talk with you sometime in October. Would it be convenient to arrange an interview? My telephone number is (618) 555-2134.
	Very truly yours,
	Frank Trimble

FIGURE 12.23 (cont.)

Writing the Memo

Memorandums may constitute as much as four-fifths of the writing you have to do on the job. You will have to write memos to your colleagues about tasks and equipment as well as to technicians about improvements on products and to supervisors about suggestions for research and sales. But you will probably have little time for extensive rewrites, and knowing how to write a brief yet informative memo will save you and the reader considerable time.

Unlike the letter that goes to a reader outside your company, a letter that you revise carefully because it represents your company, the memo remains inside the company. But the memo and letter share drafting techniques similar to those of the other documents discussed in detail in this book. Although this section on memos is brief, the advice on drafting memos builds on the advice already presented in other modules.

One of the first ways to think of drafting a memo is to consider the reader's tasks. Is the reader to take action based on the memo, or is the memo for the reader's information only? The memo also

- Employs a precise subject line.
- Provides a context and road map.
- Uses a direct style.
- Applies visual aids of headings, underlining, lists, white space.

When you write a memo, consider the five *w's* plus the *h* that journalists consider: *who, what, when, where, why,* and *how.* Because a memo should be short, these six questions may constitute the entire message in the memo. Fortunately, the conventional format for a memo requires some immediate answers to these six questions.

To:	(Who)
From:	(Who)
Distribution:	(Who)
Subject:	(What)
Date:	(When)

The text of the memo continues to answer the questions the reader has. Like all technical documents, the first section of the memo provides the reader with the context. This introduction tells the reader the background of the problem and the purpose of the memo, answering the questions . . . *what* and *why?* If the memo exceeds one page, you should also provide the reader with the organizational plan or the road map. The plan of organization suggests headings, and headings are appropriate for memos as well as letters. Organized under the headings are the details that answer the questions . . . *when? where? how?* The memo in Figure 12.24 illustrates the introduction and the headings.

To Initiate Action

The action memo provides the reader with a course of action. Usually, the reader has to act on information in the memo, so the memo may provide instructions or a procedure. Memos that require the reader to take action fall basically into two categories:

- instructions
- policy

An instruction memo tells the reader how to place a long-distance call or how to access database information. It lists the steps logically and clearly so that the reader can follow the set of instructions. As the writer, you should include a list or a clear statement of what the reader must do. If the reader has to write or call someone, then use the principles of readability and design and provide the address and phone number in a conspicuous place in the memo. Figure 12.25 illustrates the clear action memo.

ANTHONY HOSPITAL

Unit: Administration:	Location: B2739	Date: June 9, 1980
To: Bio-Medical Staff		
From: Ralph Tomes, Bio-Medical Engineer		

PURPOSE:

On July 15 Anthony Hospital will have a Joint Commission on Accreditation of Hospitals inspection. Our primary concern is to achieve a two-year rather than a one-year accreditation. We are to meet the following requirements, most of which are ongoing tasks. These procedures are to be completed by July 15.

      problem

      purpose

      task

PROCEDURES:

1. Complete the Preventive Maintenance Schedule through July 15.
2. Clean the shop and put equipment in order.
3. Update the records and work orders through June 30. Record all repairs on the status of each piece of broken or repaired equipment.

CONCLUSION:

Our ongoing procedures were established with the help of the Joint Commission on Accreditation of Hospitals. I foresee no problem with accreditation provided we meet the above-mentioned requirements.

FIGURE 12.24 Memo with headings

A policy memo is a directive with further explanations so that the reader can take appropriate action. The memo in Figure 12.26 is a directive that sets policy for both technicians and managers. Both the TO: and DISTRIBUTION: lines alert the appropriate readers. The technicians who specify chip transistors must read and follow the procedures; the project engineer, production manager, quality control manager, and engineering manager must read and approve the procedure because all future specifications will be written according to this procedure.

To Share Information

The *information-only* memo follows the format for the standard memo. The organizational plan for the information-only memo is very important because it tells the reader what items the memo is discussing and in what order. Often

To: All Departments Receiving Financial Awards

From: Ronda E. Graham, Program Administrator

Date:

Subject: FINANCIAL AWARD NUMBER _____ .

The enclosed Financial Status Report (FSR) and/or request for Advance or Reimbursement (SF-270) is/are forwarded to you for the reasons noted below.

Please return the request/report with the appropriate documentation or action within 10 days from the date of this memo. If you have any questions, call Dena Miller at extension 4792.

1. ☐ Our office needs an original signed copy of the FSR.

2. ☐ The FSR or SF-270 does not indicate whether this is an interim or final report/payment.

3. ☐ The FSR/SF-270 has been *revised* by _____ at ext. 948 and should be retained for your records.

4. ☐ Amounts shown do not balance. Please recheck:
   a. FSR
      ☐ Line number(s) _____
         Pages(s) _____

   b. SF-270
      ☐ Line number(s) _____
         Page(s) _____

5. ☐ The name of the department on the SF-270 does not agree with the Notice of Financial Award.

6. ☐ The SF-270 does not clearly indicate if this is a request for an advance or a reimbursement of costs incurred.

7. ☐ Your report received on _____ requires the additional enclosed forms to be completed:
   ☐ Original FSR (Form SF 269)
   ☐ Project Status Report Form (PSR-459A)
   ☐ Technical Assistance Final Report Form (ICP-F-TA)
   ☐ Energy Conservation Measures Final Report Form (ICP-F-ECM)

8. ☐ The final reports appear to have the following missing or incorrect data.
   ☐ Did not use actual costs.
   ☐ Did not include TA credit as part of total outlays.
   ☐ Did not include ECM credit as part of total outlays.
   ☐ Did not use original base energy cost savings for payback calculations.

FIGURE 12.25 Memo with instructions

CTS CORPORATION

Title:	Date:
Procedure for Preparing Chip-Transistor Specifications	June 13, 19XX

Distribution/Approval:		Drawing No.:
Project Engineer	Quality Control	61600010-01-08A
Production	Engineering Manager	

Purpose:

The purpose of this memo is to provide a standard procedure for specifying chip transistors.

Procedure:

When you specify chip transistors, you will need the following information:

1. materials needed
2. mechanical detail
3. electrical data
4. list of vendors
5. approvals
   a. project engineer
   b. chip and wire production manager
   c. manager of quality assurance
   d. chief electronic engineering manager

FIGURE 12.26 Directive memo

a memo that indicates what sort of memo it is—information or action—is the most efficient way to communicate with the reader. Again, headings in the memo aid the reader in locating important information quickly. Figure 12.27 illustrates the information-only memo. The content of this memo, notes from a meeting, is discussed in detail in Module 13.

A *telephone memo* is a good example of an information memo that documents a telephone message to be distributed to others or filed for future use if necessary. Figure 12.28 illustrates the telephone memo.

September 9, 19XX

TO: Board of Directors   cc: Gunther Marx
              Assistants to the President   Helen Caird
              Executive Director   Susan Feinberg

FROM: Ken Cook, Jr.

SUBJECT: Report of the Strategic Planning Committee

This is an INFORMATION-ONLY report

Abstract

The committee met in Houston during the ITCC to discuss the member questionnaire results, Board workshop results, STC functions and processes, task analysis versus society guidelines, and outside consultant selection. Tasks assigned to committee members included integration of the member questionnaire responses with the Board Workshop results and creation of a five-year STC Strategic Plan based on a Public Relations Society of America (PRSA) Strategic Planning Model. Board approval is requested for $6,000 for committee travel and outside consultant service. A preliminary strategic plan will be submitted to the board in January 19XX.

Report

Action items from the Houston meeting are described in Attachment A. Bill Stolgitis will distribute results of the member questionnaire to the Board at the September meeting. Strategic planning addresses only those responses to Part I of the questionnaire.

Board workshop (September 19XX) results were integrated with the member questionnaire results. Areas of mutual concern include improving chapter activities, conducting regional workshops, and defining the profession. Attachment B describes the integrated results. (Attachment C is for your reference—Board Workshop)

Using the integrated results, a five-year strategic plan will be created that relates society goals to specific objectives and assigns operating responsibilities. We consider the PRSA Strategic Plan an excellent model and will use it to guide the development of the STC Strategic Plan.

There appear to be several objectives evolving from the workshop and questionnaire results that do not relate directly to society goals. We intend to seek Gunther Marx's opinion as manager, Goals Committee.

FIGURE 12.27 Information memo
Source: Kenneth J. Cook, Jr., Ken Cook Co., Milwaukee, Wis. Used with permission.

      Memos are versatile documents that benefit from the basic components of technical writing: audience, clear purpose, organization, readable style, and visual design.

CONVERSATION RECORD	TIME 2:45	DATE 10/11/xx

TYPE

☐ VISIT   ☐ CONFERENCE   ☑ TELEPHONE

☑ INCOMING
☐ OUTGOING

Location of Visit/Conference

ROUTING

NAME

miller
Lee
nebs
Winchell
Sash

NAME OF PERSON(S) CONTACTED OR IN CONTACT WITH YOU	ORGANIZATION (dept. office)	TELEPHONE
Peter Thames	*State Dept.*	8-555 372-4400

SUBJECT

STATUS OF STATE ACTIVITIES

SUMMARY

The governor declared the emergency with little fanfare and filed the Emergency Rules on October 9, 19XX. With this action the state now has all the legal authority it needs to implement the program. The emergency rules basically contain the analyzer specifications.

The state sent notice of the filing of the emergency rules to numerous manufacturers as well as to 5,000 repair shops in the seven county Lincoln area. In the notice that went to the 5,000 repair shops, the state included a questionnaire on prospective involvement in the program as well as the announcement of three evening seminars to be held in early December. At the seminars both state personnel and equipment manufacturers will discuss the program and the equipment.

FUTURE ACTION:
1. The state will hold hearings in March to turn the emergency rules into permanent rules.
2. Garage licensing will begin in January.

ACTION REQUIRED/TAKEN:
Continue to track progress of activities.

NAME OF PERSON DOCUMENTING CONVERSATION	SIGNATURE	DATE
M. Bolton	*M. Bolton*	10/11/xx

FIGURE 12.28 Telephone memo

Summary

In both the public and private sectors many more documents are written as memos or letters than as formal technical reports. However, this type of correspondence incorporates the components of technical writing: writer's purpose, reader's needs, organization, readability in both style and visual techniques, and revision.

When you write to a client or customer, you have to imagine the reader's ability to understand your message. If you are responding to the writer's letter, then you can use the correspondence to gain some insight into your reader and decide how to respond. In all your correspondence, you have to be *sensitive to tone.* Tone is both empathy for the reader and an appreciation for words to express this feeling. Words such as *allege* or *regret* create a negative tone. Besides using positive words like *benefit* and *reliable,* you can create a positive effect by putting the reader in the picture with the *you* attitude.

Your purpose for writing most correspondence falls into two categories: *expository* and *persuasive.* Sometimes you have to provide neutral, positive, or negative information and persuade the reader to accept your view or take appropriate action. Your purpose for writing determines your *organizational strategy.* To write a long, detailed letter or a cover letter for a technical report, you need an *introduction* that provides the *context* and the *road map* or scope for the rest of the document. To respond to a complaint, you have to establish rapport, identify the main issue, organize the response, and suggest a positive action, if possible. To persuade the reader, you have to organize the letter by placing the most positive information in either the *primacy* or *recency position,* depending on the attitude and knowledge of your reader.

Clear correspondence makes the reader's task easier. First, avoid *ambiguity* by changing word order and adding small words. Second, provide *accurate* and precise *details.* Third, be *brief:* use one connecting word instead of three; a strong verb instead of a phrase; one or two words instead of a clause. Fourth, give *complete* information.

Opening and *closing paragraphs* give you the opportunity to introduce the purpose, focus on the reader, and make a courteous request. Designing the *format* of the letter uses *visual* techniques. *Full-block* style aligns all lines with the left margin. *Modified block* style centers the date and closing line, either indents the first word of each paragraph or aligns it with the left margin, and aligns all other lines. The styles share similarities: head all *subsequent* pages of the correspondence; include (if appropriate) a precise *subject line;* note *identifying initials, enclosures,* and *copies;* use *headings, underlining,* and items with *bullets.*

The *letter of application* helps you seek a job and often makes a bid for an interview. The application letter accompanies your *résumé* that has information about your education, work experience, interests, projects, and availability. Remember to avoid *red flags,* raising questions in the résumé. Stress the *you* attitude in the application letter.

Memos are *in-house* correspondence whereas letters are correspondence with people outside the company. But letters and memos share drafting techniques of purpose and reader's tasks, context and road map, direct style, subject line, visual techniques, page headings, and notations. The memo, with its emphasis on brevity, usually follows a company style and presents *information,* requests *action,* or combines both purposes using the journalists' *five w's plus h.*

Checklist for Correspondence

Check only the items to which you can give a positive response!

Check here

BEFORE YOU BEGIN TO CORRESPOND, DID YOU
_____ Imagine the reader?

Determine your message to be
_____ neutral information (technical information or cover letters)?

_____ positive news?

_____ negative news (such as complaints or denials)?

_____ persuasive messages (sales letters or controversial issues)?

DID YOU APPLY THE PRINCIPLES FOR CLEAR, EFFECTIVE CORRESPONDENCE BY USING
_____ A positive tone?

_____ The *you* attitude?

One of the organizational strategies, such as
_____ direct statement of purpose, courteous request?

_____ purpose, details, closing with rapport?

_____ background, road map for remainder of document?

_____ problem or main issue or issues, support following primacy or recency position, rapport, or positive action?

_____ who, what, when, where, why, how?

Words that
_____ avoid ambiguity?

_____ give accurate, precise details?

_____ are concise?

_____ give complete information?

WHAT FORMAT AND VISUAL TECHNIQUES DID YOU USE IN YOUR CORRESPONDENCE?
_____ Full-block?

_____ Modified block?

_____ Conventional memo format of *To: From: Subject: Date:?*

_____ Justified right margin?

_____ Headings for subsequent pages?

Lines with precise information, such as
_____ subject line?

_____ attention line?

_____ title?

_____ extension or mail stop?

_____ identifying initials?

_____ enclosure notation?

_____ copy notation?

_____ distribution?

Visual techniques, such as
_____ headings?

_____ underlining?

_____ bulleted list?

_____ white space?

DO YOU HAVE A SPECIAL PURPOSE?
_____ Did you ask for an interview at the end of your letter of
     application?

Does your résumé
_____ place important information in a strategic position on the page?

_____ avoid raising red flags or problems?

_____ Did you clearly indicate the action the reader must take?

_____ Did you document the telephone message?

Notes

1. *Writing Effective Letters* (U.S. Office of Personnel Management, Chicago Regional Training Center: U.S. Government Printing Office, 1985). This booklet provided background material and examples for the letters section.
2. *Professional Writing Techniques* (U.S. Office of Personnel Management, Chicago Regional Training Center: U.S. Government Printing Office, 1985):23–25.
3. *Professional Writing Techniques*, pp. 33–35.
4. From *Professional Writing Techniques*, pp. 23–25.
5. Wayne N. Thompson, *The Process of Persuasion* (New York: Harper & Row, 1975): 120.
6. Susan Feinberg and Irene Pritzker, "An MBA Communications Course Designed by Business Executives," *The Journal of Business Communication* 22 (Fall 1985): 75.
7. *Writing Effective Letters*, pp. 37–40.
8. *Résumé Workbook and Career Planner* (Houston, Tex. 77224: Scientific Placement, Inc. P.O. Box 19949, 1985). This workbook provided background material for the résumé section.

References

Richard Nelson Bolles, *What Color Is Your Parachute?* (Berkeley, Calif.: Ten Speed Press, 1986).

Myra Kogen, "The Role of Audience in Business and Technical Writing," *The ABCA Bulletin* 46: 4 (1983): 2–4.

C. H. Knoblauch, "Intentionality in the Writing Process: A Case Study," *College Composition and Communication* 31 (1980): 153–159.

Richard Lathrop, *Who's Hiring Who?* (Berkeley, Calif.: Ten Speed Press, 1977).

Earl E. McDowell and Thomas E. Pearsall, "Perceptions of the Ideal Cover Letter and Résumé," in *Proceedings*, 32d International Technical Communication Conference (Washington, D.C.: Society for Technical Communication, 1985): RET 45–48.

B. Wells, N. Spinks, and J. Hargrave, "A Survey of the Chief Officers in the 500 Largest Corporations in the United States to Determine Their Preferences in Job Application Letters and Personnel Résumés," *The ABCA Bulletin* 44 (1981): 3–7.

Merrill D. Whitburn, Marijane Davis, Sharon Higgins, Linsey Oates, and Kristene Spurgeon, "The Plain Style in Scientific and Technical Writing," *Journal of Technical Writing and Communication* 8 (1978): 349–358.

Applying Your Knowledge

Group Editing

Edit or rewrite the following exercises, paying attention to accurate information, openings and closings, tone, rapport, and ambiguity.

EXERCISE 12.1

These sentences are lacking accurate information. Rewrite them, adding precise details.

1. In a memo requesting the purchase of an EKG Monitor/Defibrillator, Dr. Peppard suggested evaluating some of the devices on the market.
2. If our company wants to sell a personal computer to the home market, the cost cannot be prohibitive.
3. When selecting stereo speakers for your home, you have to consider several factors.
4. You must be able to see the lights on an oncoming car at an acceptable distance.
5. In our letter to the Hoover Vacuum Cleaner Company we requested replacement bags for our Hoover upright cleaner.

EXERCISE 12.2

Rewrite the following openings:

1. Reference is made to your letter of January 2, 19XX, transmitting copies of correspondence prepared in your Examining Division, which you are desirous of having reviewed by our correspondence experts. We will have them make this review.
2. This is in reply to your letter of May 2, 19XX, in connection with your interest in a position with our company. As you know, the letter was originally sent to Mr. Adams, who, in turn, forwarded it to this office for reply.
3. In response to your letter, this is to advise that information on payroll deductions can only be answered on an individual basis.
4. Reference is made to your letter of April 7, 19XX, enclosing the receipt for $123.00, which was requested by a letter from this office dated April 4, 19XX.
5. This responds to your recent letter concerning your request for an extension of your deadline date.

EXERCISE 12.3

Rewrite the closings:

1. If we can be of further service to you, please do not hesitate to contact us.
2. Complete the attached form, and return it to us as soon as possible.
3. We hope to hear from you at your earliest convenience.
4. Your prompt response to our request will be greatly appreciated.
5. If additional information is required, please do not hesitate to either call or write S. Robinson at the address shown above or contact by telephone at 216/543-6789.

EXERCISE 12.4 ══════════════════════════════

Revise the following letter to retain rapport.

I recommend disapproval of the supervisor's technology transfer request for two hearing examiners to attend "Conference 90's" in New Hampshire on September 22–24, 19XX. Training related to hearings is not among the technology transfer priorities this year, and the agency's particular interest in public utilities hearings is not relevant to our liabilities program. In addition, participation in conferences is not a priority area.

A copy of the supervisor's letter requesting technology transfer funds is attached. If you have any questions, please contact Ms. Susan Smith, program specialist, at (618) 555-2134.

Sincerely,

Jack Norris
Business Manager

Attachment:

JN:mvr

EXERCISE 12.5 ══════════════════════════════

Revise the following sentences to incorporate a more positive tone.

1. We are herewith returning your application because you neglected to submit with it the necessary information that we requested. We cannot process your claim unless this is done as requested.
2. Because you failed to understand our policy, the only course left open to us is to return your proposal.
3. Our records disagree with your claim that you were overcharged.
4. We cannot be expected to take care of routine requests such as yours; send your inquiry to our local office.
5. Undoubtedly, you are ignorant of the facts in this case.
6. Please try to understand our position in this matter.
7. We hereby request that you return the enclosed form, complete with your signature, to this office.
8. The responsibility for administering the Ohio State law belongs to the state of Ohio. This agency is interested only when the matter affects federal laws.
9. Your statement about the treatment you received from one of our employees is indeed surprising because we instruct all our employees to be civil, kindly, and thoughtful—even under the most trying circumstances.

Source of Exercise 12.5: *Writing Effective Letters* (U.S. Office of Personnel Management: U.S. Government Printing Office, 1985).

EXERCISE 12.6 ═══

Rewrite the items to eliminate ambiguity:

1. *Purpose.* To define procedures for the reporting of nuclear materials trans-
   actions, inventories, and material balances and to define procedures for
   submission of nuclear materials transaction, inventory, and material balance data to the nuclear materials management and safeguards system
   (NMMSS).
   (As Edwin Newman once said, "The Russians will never crack the code.")

**And for fun (from Professional Writing Techniques (U.S. Office of Personnel
and Management): U.S. Government Printing Office, 1985).**

2. Woman Disappears in Bathing Suit
3. Man Needed for Spare Parts
4. Temporary Suggestion Box
5. John Likes Entertaining Women
7. Boy Critical After Being Hit by Truck
8. Police Grill Suspect over Big Blaze
9. Hoosier Father-Son Team Tops Hog Show

Collaborative Planning and Writing

*For the following exercises, work in teams of three to analyze the problems,
reorganize the drafts, and write either new or better solutions to the problems.*

EXERCISE 12.7 ═══

For the Pandora collision, reorganize, design, and rewrite the memo.

Subject: *Pandora* collision

Date:
In Reply Refer To:

From: A. Hab, Transport Service Officer

Your Reference:

To: S. D. Orichalcum, Transport Service Operations Officer,
       Buzzards Inlet

Our ship, *Pandora*, will arrive at Buzzards Inlet on the day after tomorrow. So
far, we are not sure what caused the collision or who was responsible for it.
We are fortunate that there were no injuries or loss of life. For a while, until
temporary repairs were made, water came in faster than the ship's pumps
could take care of it. You should keep an accurate and detailed record of the
damage done to the ship's cargo as a result. Damage to the vessel was just
forward of midships on the starboard side. Plates were ruptured.

Since the Phoenix Salvage Company is the only concern of its kind in the area,
we have contacted them, asking for their advice and assistance in unloading
the cargo. They will help salvage as much of the cargo as possible. Keep a
detailed record on the costs of unloading cargo.

If there are any questions as to whether any parts of the cargo are salvageable and materials need to be tested, send samples to the Reliable Testing Company. No one knows just how much damage was done before the ship's pumps got ahead of the leaks.

Remember to keep a close record of what cargo was saved. Since unloading the vessel so as to salvage cargo will cost more than a normal unloading, let me know your estimate of the difference between the two.

As I said, damage to the *Pandora* was just forward of amidships. Naturally, we want to know the extent of the damage. The Phoenix Salvage Company will assess the damage. Make sure they take a good look at more than just the area surrounding the ruptured plates. A bid on repairs to the vessel should be obtained from Buzzards Inlet Shipbuilding Corporation as they provide the only available repair facilities in the area.

Go to Buzzards Inlet and report on all the above-mentioned matters as soon as possible.

Source of memo: *Professional Writing Techniques* (U.S. Office of Personnel Management: U. S. Government Printing Office, 1985).

EXERCISE 12.8

Reorganize, edit, and rewrite the letter from the Department of Social Services.

DEPARTMENT OF SOCIAL SERVICES

Dear

Your letter of May 12, 19XX, requested approval of a delay in implementing one of the provisions of the Income and Eligibility Verification System (IEVS), Section 1137 of the Social Security Act (the Act). The IEVS provisions were added to the Act by Section 2651 of Public Law 98-369, the Deficit Reduction Act of 1984. They require matching of public assistance files with federal data maintained by the Social Security Administration and the Internal Revenue Service (IRS), as well as state files on wages and unemployment compensation. A delay in implementing certain IEVS provisions may be granted under the statute and federal regulations at 45 CFR 205.62(a), provided the state can demonstrate a good faith effort to comply. However, the implementation date of May 29, 19XX, cannot be delayed beyond September 30, 19XX.

You have requested a delay until September 30, 19XX, in implementing the provision at 45 CFR 205.55(a)(4). This provision requires that the state request unearned income information from IRS for all Aid to Families with Dependent Children applicants and recipients. The reasons for the delay are that the IRS identification number has not been received and that you lack the integrated database required to complete the match. Although receipt of the IRS number is expected by July, the database will not be ready until September.

You have demonstrated a good faith effort to comply and your plan is on target for the mandatory implementation date. I approve your plan and grant a delay of the effective date for the provision at 45 CFR 205.55(a)(4) until September 30, 19XX.

If you have any questions, please contact Matthew Rok, state program specialist, at (513)555-8282.

Sincerely,

Source of letter: U.S. Office of Personnel Management.

EXERCISE 12.9

What is wrong with the cover letter, and how would you revise and improve it?

Richard Kater
4329 S. Wilcox Drive
Glenview, Georgia 47203
September 21, 19XX
(715) 555-9272

Theresa Barr
Telden Technology
432 Torrey Avenue
San Diego, Calif. 90732

Dear Theresa Barr:

I am interested in Telden Technology and believe that my training and experience can be beneficial to your company. My specific goals are to receive a professional position performing one or more of the following tasks: designing and implementing computer logic, hardware and software interfaces, or audio and communication systems.

I will be completing my education at Central University in December, 19XX, and receive a Bachelor of Science in Electrical Engineering. I have a broad background in engineering and have specialized in microcomputer architecture and interfacing and also audio and communications systems design.

Finally, I would like to mention again, that my knowledge and qualifications could be a great attribute to a company like Telden Technology. You would be receiving a young, dedicated, and persistent electrical engineer with futuristic ideas. I am available weekdays after 5 P.M. at (712) 555-7292.

Sincerely yours,

Richard Kater

Individual Writing

The following exercises all involve situations that require analysis, planning, organization, and design of the document. After reading and thinking about the problem, design and write an appropriate response.

EXERCISE 12.10

Mr. Michael Reardon of McLean School System writes to ask if the vocational education class of 30 students can visit the Clinical Engineering Laboratory at Anthony Hospital. Unfortunately, the answer is no! Write a response that explains the policy and attempts to retain his goodwill.

EXERCISE 12.11

Write a memo to discourage your staff from making nonbusiness telephone calls.

EXERCISE 12.12

Write a memo to praise a report completed by a select committee of your staff.

EXERCISE 12.13

Analyze the following problem; then reorganize and rewrite the Social Security letter to Mrs. Sullivan. Finally, send a memo to your department's account clerk, explaining the financial situation and asking the account clerk to prepare a billing.

Social Security Letter

SITUATION: Mrs. Sullivan has, during the past few years, received too much money in benefits from the Social Security Administration (SSA) and now SSA is requesting a refund of this money that was overpaid to her. She had asked to be relieved from the responsibility of paying this money back, and this rough draft is the response to her request.

Dear Mrs. Sullivan:

This letter refers to your request to be relieved from the responsibility for repayment of $1,345.50 in Social Security benefits. Based on your work earnings of $3,645.00 in 1980, we should have withheld $322.00 from your benefits. Since we did not withhold any benefits, you received $322.00 more than you should have for 1980. We used $139.80 that was due you for 1981, based on your estimate of $6520.00, to reduce your 1980 overpayment to $182.20.

However, you reported on your annual report for 1981 that you earned $9,625.00 in that year. Based on these earnings, you should not have received any benefits for 1981. Since you received a total of $753.90 for the year, including the $139.80 that we used to reduce your 1980 overpayment, you were overpaid an additional $753.90.

You were also overpaid $204.70 per month for 2/82 through 3/82 because Kevin was age 18 in 2/82. The total overpayment is $1,345.50.

Under Social Security law, any overpayment must be withheld from benefits or paid back unless *both* of the following are true: (1) The overpayment was not your fault in any way and you accepted the payment or payments because you thought they were correctly paid to you, *and* (2) You could not meet necessary living expenses if you had to pay back the overpayment or have it withheld from your Social Security benefits; or it would be unfair for some other reason.

After careful consideration of your statements regarding the overpayment, we find that you may not be relieved from the responsibility for repayment.

In your letter dated 6/19/82 you made the following statement: "In 1980 I received Social Security benefits because I wasn't working full-time. In December 1980 I received a full-time position at Smith County Rehab as a job developer and counselor. I notified the Social Security Office in Blanksville, Illinois, as soon as I was accepted for the job—around December 20—immediately after I finished my B.A. studies at Johnson University. I told Mrs. Harris, who always helps me, that I had a job and did not need any more help. Six or eight months or so later, around October 18, I received a letter from the Chicago Social Security office that I'd been paid over $182. But a week or so later I was sent another letter stating that I'd receive $182 or $186 plus another $26. I presume that whatever the Social Security office says is correct. However, I told Mrs. Harris about it. Around the first of 1982—or maybe in December 1981—I received a check for $204, and I received one in January and February. I called the Blanksville office and told them that I was working for District 3 School District as a reading teacher aide and also a couple other part-time jobs and was able to support myself—and didn't believe I should be receiving any benefits, nor did I want any. I then went into the Blanksville office and talked to a man (in February). He wouldn't write a letter for me but said that I should send in my annual wage report—which he did for me. He said I might be entitled to the benefits. Then I began getting letters about returning the money. Why did I receive this money anyway? I had reported working in December 1980."

When you filed for benefits on 4/14/66, you signed an application for Survivors Insurance Benefits. This form included an explanation of the effect that work and earnings would have on your benefits. It also informed you that you would no longer be entitled after the last child attained age 18.

The same information was included in the booklet "Your Social Security Rights and Responsibilities," which was sent to you along with your award certificate. You also received stuffers with your checks wherever there was a change in the Social Security law that could possibly affect you. In addition, you agreed on your application to return any checks you received if you were not entitled to them.

. Our records show that in 10/80, you reported that you were working in 1980, but that you estimated you would earn $3,000.00. Since this estimate would not require the withholding of any benefits, we paid you a check of $939.60, which represented all benefits previously withheld in 1980.

You also reported an estimate of $8,000.00 for 1981 in 12/81, as you indicated in your letter. However, when you filed your annual report for 1980, in 9/81, you reduced your estimate for 1981 to $6,520.00, and we paid benefits to you based on that estimate.

Because of the information you received, you should have known that you could be overpaid if the estimate you submitted later turned out to be too low. You should also have known that you were not due benefits for 2/82 and 3/82. Your low estimates for 1980 and 1981 and your failure to return the check for 2/82 and 3/82 were the causes of the overpayment. Therefore, we cannot find that you were without fault. Since you do not meet both of the above requirements for waiver, you are required by law to repay the money.

If you believe that this determination is not correct, you may request that your case be reexamined. If you want this reconsideration, you must request it not later than 60 days from the date you receive this notice. You may make any such request through any Social Security office. If additional evidence is available, you should submit it with your request.

Please refund $1,345.50 within 30 days from the date of this letter. If you cannot pay the full amount now, you should submit a partial payment along with a definite plan for regular installments of at least $29.00 per month. Please make your check or money order payable to the "Social Security Administration, Claim Number 12345," and send it to us in the enclosed envelope.

We recently notified Kevin that your overpayment would be withheld from his benefits, beginning with his check for 8/82. This action will not be taken at this time because of your protest. However, if you do not start refunding the overpayment as instructed above, it may be necessary to withhold it from future benefits due Kevin.

If you have any questions about your claim, you may get in touch with any Social Security office. Most questions can be handled by telephone or mail. If you visit an office, however, please take this letter with you.

Sincerely,

I. M. YOUR
Claims Examiner

Source of letter: *Effective Letter Writing* (U.S. Office of Personnel Management: U.S. Government Printing Office, 1985.)

EXERCISE 12.14

Rewrite the telephone message to include the information provided:

Date: January 27, 19XX
Subject: Chromate Spillage—Station 310
To: P.G. Woden, Lab Director   From: J. Kilgren

In phone conversation with Kay Lob, district superintendent, Station 310, the following information concerning the chromate spillage of January 10–12, 19XX, was obtained.

Three of the Lube Oil Cooling Water Fin Fan Coolers froze on January 10. During thawing operations and repairs of January 10, 11, and 12, approximately 1,300 gallons of LOCW containing 700 mg/L sodium chromate (225 mg/L hexavalent chromium) were spilled into the ditch between the coolers and the No. 1 building.

The spillage froze before progressing very far down the drainage ditch.

The contaminated ice has been removed from the ditch and is temporarily stored in a plastic-lined pit.

A vacuum was used to collect any liquid, including a trace of rain. This liquid was put in a waste tank.

Approximately 1¼ inches of rain have fallen since the cleanup. No visual evidence of contamination remains in the ditch.

I have requested soil samples from the concerned areas and samples of the liquid or contaminated ice.

WRITING ASSIGNMENT

Select an ad appropriate to your field from the employment listings in your area newspaper. Apply for the job by

- *Preparing your résumé.*
- *Writing a cover letter to accompany your résumé.*

If necessary,

- *Visit your library to find information about the company.*
- *Access a database for information about the company.*
- *Phone the company and request (1) its annual report and (2) name of supervisor of department appropriate to your interests.*

MODULE 13

Trip Notes, Minutes, and Meeting Notes

This module prepares you to take notes and write them up after a trip you have taken or a meeting you attended. As a part of your job, you may be sent to sites to examine a product or a process. Or you may have to make a visit to obtain information on a specific subject or to find answers to a problem. Frequently, you may have to attend meetings and report on them. Less typically, you may even be the recording secretary and have to take minutes at a meeting. Organization is the primary rule for writing up these notes or minutes. You must use an organizational strategy for your trip notes and meeting notes, and the strategy begins before you make your visit or attend the meeting. Brainstorming, anticipating information, reviewing the agenda are the keys to clear and orderly trip notes, minutes, and meeting notes.

Planning prior to the trip aids you in gathering the appropriate information when you make a site visit or attend a meeting. The purpose of the trip or the meeting will determine both the content and the organization of the trip notes or meeting notes. This module begins with some ideas about planning for the trip and moves to a variety of organizational strategies for trip and meeting notes.

Scope

In this module you will practice

1. Brainstorming that can help you gather information.
2. Anticipating and collecting additional information while at the site or meeting.
3. Identifying the purpose of the visit or meeting.
4. Organizing your material prior to the trip or meeting to respond to the purpose of the occasion and the information your reader needs to know.
5. Using visual and stylistic techniques for readability.
6. Reviewing the agenda and *Robert's Rules of Order* for content and form.

Planning for the Trip

- Anthony Jarzevich has to evaluate the new bottling equipment at the Carefree Hair factory.
- Barbara Thompsen has to examine the groundwater at the Richard Walter farm in Jasper County, Indiana, and recommend a course of action.
- Michael Lee is gathering information about on-the-job communications for a report he has to submit.
- Indira Jane is attending a meeting to discuss the future policies for X-ray spectroscopy.

These people have to make a trip. Usually, the purpose of the trip is inherent in the reason for making the trip. When you have to evaluate a product or a process, obtain information on a particular subject, or solve a problem, the purpose of the trip is clear. But trips are time-consuming and costly, so you will want to prepare for the trip and plan to ask the right questions while you are at the site. This front-end planning will make your final report easier and faster to write. The trip with the most ambiguous purpose is the trip to gain information. If you are making a trip to obtain information on a subject, you may want to brainstorm with your colleagues to consider all the points you could investigate.

Brainstorming

Brainstorming helps you discover items you might not otherwise consider. It is better to think about an item and dismiss it as irrelevant to the purpose of the trip than to return from a trip and discover another question you should have asked. Whether you brainstorm by yourself or with others, you should record all ideas first and judge them later. Brainstorming works on the principle of quantity rather than quality. Because of the freedom of brainstorming, you must later organize and assess the ideas to use this technique to its best advantage. Module 2 presents a technique for brainstorming. The Nominal Group Technique has five steps that are useful for solving problems or generating ideas. You might want to review that technique now.

Students in a technical writing class had to interview people about the communications tasks the respondents performed in their fields. Most of the students selected people who were working in the field the students hoped to enter; the objective was to find out something about communication tasks in the student's field. The objective is so broad as to be unfocused, so the class brainstormed to provide some questions for the upcoming interview. Following are some of the questions the students brainstormed; obviously, many questions overlapped.

List of Questions to Ask About Communication on the Job

1. Do you write memos, proposals, evaluations, progress reports, and so on, and do they follow any formats?
2. How much time does an electrical engineer spend on communication tasks?
3. Do you make oral presentations, how often, and what sort of presentation is it?
4. What support do you have to produce your written communication?
5. Do you use word processing or computers when you write?
6. Do you spend more time on oral or on written communication?
7. What methods of communication do you use with your clients?
8. How do you communicate information: Phone? Memo? Oral presentation? Written report?
9. What types of communication projects do you undertake in a normal week?
10. Which communication skill is the most important to you?
11. Do you establish your own communication deadlines?
12. What takes more time and effort for you, planning or writing the document?
13. Do you spend more time on internal or external communication?
14. What projects does your technical writing staff work on?
15. How much time per week do you spend in oral communication?

After brainstorming, the students organized the questions under major categories:

- Oral communication for your job.
- Written communication for your job.

To focus the questions they used subheadings:

amount of time
types of writing
assistance available
problem areas
external/internal audience

Now they were ready to select categories and questions to focus their interview. After the interview, they wrote up their trip notes based on the information obtained during the meeting.

Anticipating Information

To save yourself time after the trip you must be prepared to obtain information usually associated with any job-related trip.

- Lists of attendees/participants
  - correct spelling of names
  - titles
  - complete addresses
  - phone numbers
- Samples
  - for testing or evaluation
  - for study
- Handouts or questionnaires/inspection forms
  - for additional data
  - in support of primary information

Anticipating your need for this information when you write your report, you should make a list of this information before you leave the site. Having to phone, send, or return for this information will delay your report and inconvenience other people. Save yourself and others some time and frustration by creating a checklist of information or items you will need for your report.

Organizing the Trip Notes

Before the trip, you have to focus on the sort of information you hope to obtain and ask questions appropriate to your purpose or objective. When you write your trip notes, writing the purpose statement in a sentence or two will help the reader focus on the subject of the trip or the meeting. The information on the subject has to be selected and organized so that the reader can follow the information. One such organizational strategy supplies answers for questions.

Trip Notes
Purpose, subject, objective of the trip?
People attending? (Use an appendix if the list is extensive.)
Organizational plan or procedure followed in the report?
Results of the trip, sequenced in order of the plan or procedure?
Recommendations of the writer (if appropriate)?

State the Purpose

The purpose statements for some of the student *trip notes* following an interview are these:

- *Purpose:* To determine the communications needs of a physicist working in industry.
- *Purpose:* The purpose of this interview was to determine the amount of time a typical electrical engineer spends on communication tasks at the Zenith Radio Corporation.
- *Purpose:* The purpose of the interview was to obtain information from a director about the types of internal communication he performs.

List the Participants

If you request the names, telephone numbers, and addresses of other people at your meeting while you are still at the meeting, you will save yourself time later on. The list you collect will help you if you have to do the following:

- Verify information from another participant.
- Contact the list of participants.
- Distribute the notes to others who may need to know how to contact the participants.

Plan to collect a list of people with their titles, complete addresses, and telephone numbers before you attend the meeting; that way you will arrive with the appropriate legal pad to pass around the room or to record the necessary information, and you will avoid saving names and addresses on little slips of paper.

When you begin to write your report, depending on the number of participants, you can place the names and addresses in the appendix. Simply state the location of this information in your report.

> For example: *ATTENDEES:*
> See Attachment A

State the Plan

In trip notes as well as in other documents, the road map or organizational plan provides the reader with the order of the notes. Trip notes may be written in the form of a memo or a brief report. Whatever form you use, the organizational plan, sometimes called the scope in trip notes, provides an overview of the items in the report. The body or main part of the trip notes elaborates on the items in individual sections. Figure 13.1 illustrates two different scope statements, each providing an overview of the report and referring to attachments.

- *Scope*
      This interview was limited to written and oral communication within the Zenith Corporation. Neither professional communication (to journals or books) nor external communication (to consumers, suppliers, or salespeople) was discussed. Examples of the type of communication we discussed are attached to this trip report.
- *Scope:* The interview covered three areas: (1) personal background, (2) communication problems encountered in that area of design, and (3) recommendations for obtaining good communications skills. A copy of Mr. Grant's publication, *City Reader*, is attached.

FIGURE 13.1 Scope or overview of items in the report

Use Visual Techniques

Trip reports and meeting notes both benefit from visual techniques. Because of the separate sections in the notes, you will want to consider layout, readability, and illustrations. For most notes you must consider

- format (memo as well as report formats are appropriate for notes)
- headings and subheadings
- white space
- columns and lists
- attachments
- illustrations, if available

      The use of illustrations in trip notes is uncommon, but if you have additional materials you collected during your trip, including illustrations, you can attach them to the trip notes, with a reference in the document to the attachment. Figure 13.2 is a diagram accompanying a site evaluation.

Applying the Strategies

People in business and industry frequently make trips to accomplish at least three common objectives:

- to obtain information
- to solve problems
- to evaluate sites.

Sometimes companies will establish a format for trip notes, such as a memo format. Often companies will call trip notes by a different name. For example, one chemical company calls trip notes "Reports of Call." The important principle to remember is that similar documents by any other name still require similar sections of information. If you use the checklists at the end of this module, you will be encouraged to consider sections that you may include or

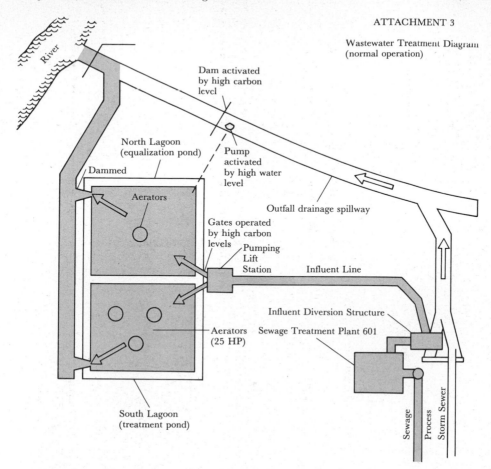

ATTACHMENT 3

Wastewater Treatment Diagram
(normal operation)

FIGURE 13.2 Attachment: diagram of a site

discard, as appropriate. At the very least, you will be reminded about your
options.

To Obtain Information

People who can tell you about a subject are often the objects of your visit.
They provide you with information, and that is the purpose of your visit.
The writer of the document in Figure 13.3 interviewed a colleague in her
field to find out about communication on the job. To write the trip notes,
she uses a memo format and a layout that has an uncluttered appearance
because of the use of white space.

To Solve Problems

In industry and government agencies, employees make trips to solve problems by talking to people. Whether they write their trip notes in memo format

TRIP NOTES

Date:	October 27, 19XX
Person Interviewed:	Mr. Edward Grant Art Director *City Reader* Grant Advertising and Design 473 West Lee Avenue Minneapolis, Minnesota 612/555-2405
Purpose:	The purpose of this interview was to obtain information about the kinds of communication skills necessary for a design career and what paths are recommended to obtain them.
Scope:	The interview covered three areas: (1) personal background, (2) communication problems encountered in that area of design, and (3) recommendations for obtaining good communication skills.
Personal Background:	_____ _____
Communication Problems:	_____ _____
Recommendations:	_____ _____

FIGURE 13.3 Memo format with layout for white space
Source: Linda M. Lee, Technical Writing 421, Illinois Institute of Technology.

or in a short report format, the purpose of the trip, as well as a statement of the problem and the organization of the notes, must be apparent to the reader. In the following trip report, the writer provides the names of the participants, the purpose of the trip, and the order for the report, all in the introductory paragraph.

Each item then follows in an orderly manner, and the writer uses

- numbers
- headings
- bullets
- dashes

to make the document clear and readable. Notice the clear statement of purpose and problem, the organizational plan (scope), and the design of the trip report in Figure 13.4.

SUBJECT: Trip Report for Water Survey Department
FROM: Michelle S. Freedman
TO: David N. Harrigan
            Chief, Water Compliance Commission (WCC)
DATE: November 18, 19XX

On November 14, 19XX, Donald Egers and I met with Stacey Fleming, director of the Water Survey Department (WSD) and Terry
Kelter of WSD. WCC has had a problem with receiving WDS's reports on time. The primary purpose of the meeting was to discuss
these reporting problems for the following activities: the previously funded water survey strategy, future funding of water survey
related activities, and participation in consolidated water survey
plans.

1. Water Survey Strategy
   • Stacey Fleming reaffirmed WDS's commitment to complete the
     strategy report.
   • WSD would address the deficiencies articulated in WCC's Au-
     gust 23, 19XX, letter. The response would provide both WSD
     and WCC with a comprehensible and usable document.
       Note: Terry Kelter originally intended to respond to the Au-
       gust 23, 19XX, letter under separate cover and not integrate
       the response into the strategy report.
   • WSD will complete the strategy report and submit it to WCC
     no later than February 28, 19XX.
2. Future Funding of Water Survey Related Activities
   • We will consider WSD's funding of water survey activities for
     the 19XX year after the strategy report is submitted.
3. Consolidated Water Survey Plans
   • Stacey Fleming will submit a consolidated plan by December
     15, 19XX.
   • We will process the WSD submission concurrent with WSD's
     efforts to complete the strategy report. We explained that the
     review takes approximately three months. A December 15
     submission translated into a mid-March decision.

Analysis and Recommendations
Stacey Fleming appears to be sincerely concerned and committed
to submitting the water strategy report on time. Terry Kelter has
been assigned the tasks of completing the strategy report and developing the consolidated water survey plan.

I suggest that WCC send a letter to WSD, detailing our November
14, 19XX, meeting and reminding WSD that it is in their interest
to finish the water strategy report and submit the consolidated
plan on time. Postponing the report could delay processing the
plan to a time when all funding has been exhausted.

MSF:ems
cc: D. Egers
     L. Horn

FIGURE 13.4 Trip notes to solve a problem

The multiple copies notation at the end of the document indicates the distribution list, and the writer has a record of all the informed readers. The distribution list

- Assures the writer that all the people who need to know are informed.
- Records the writer's activities on the job.
- Provides visibility for the writer within the workplace.

To highlight the results of a conference where shared information led to a decision, you could use an organization similar to the trip notes in Figure 13.5. The document has the general design of a memo.

To Examine a Site

Many companies conducting routine site inspections will provide forms to report on these visits, probably because site inspections can become quite technical and may require additional laboratory work. Some of these forms require data that can simply be written in the blank spaces provided. However, after the trip, the inspector usually has to use the forms to write up a discussion of the facts, the results, and the recommendations, if any. Figure 13.6 illustrates a completed site inspection report.

If you are making a site visit to inspect a specific problem, determine in advance if an inspection form exists. An inspection form will prompt you to examine the appropriate items. Whether or not you have an inspection

DATE: August 16, 19XX
SUBJECT: Trip Report, August 10, 19XX
FROM: Jack Smith, Director, Environmental Control Commission
TO: Files

PURPOSE
    To discuss coordination of water survey activities with representatives from the Water Quality Divisions of the Department of Environmental Control (DEC) and discuss tasks.

    The DEC is about to be reorganized into six divisions:
        Air Quality Division
        Ground Water Division
        Surface Water Division
        Hazardous Waste Division
        External Services Division
        Internal Services Division

    Two immediate areas of concern are services and compliance Inspections.

ATTENDEES:
    See Attachment A

FIGURE 13.5 Trip notes with highlighted solution

A. Services

The department will decentralize functions to two regional offices and nine district offices. The reorganization is scheduled to be effective October 1, 19XX.

Action:

1. The Internal Services Division will be responsible for providing laboratory services.
2. The External Services Division will have responsibility for all grants including construction grants.

B. Compliance Inspections

All the candidates were recently inspected by DEC

_____

_____

Action:

1. Mr. Jones will provide me with the updated list of completed inspections, as well as those in progress.
2. I will convey DEC's concerns pertaining to review of the candidates and arrange a conference call between DEC and the Environmental Control Commission to resolve remaining differences.

cc: S. Routhers
   D. Bennet
   E. Nisen
   D. Paters
   P. Kaad

FIGURE 13.5 (cont.)

form, you will have to organize your information on your return from the site.

Writing Formal Minutes

According to *Robert's Rules of Order,* minutes record the proceedings of what was done at the meeting rather than what was said.[1] If you are the recording secretary of an organization, you should review *Robert's Rules of Order* for recording minutes. The rules indicate the content of the minutes as well as the rules and practices for relating the proceedings of the meeting. For example, the first paragraph of the minutes includes

1. the kind of meeting
2. the name of the society

MIDWEST PAINT COMPANY

DATE: October 20, 19XX

SUBJECT: Trip Report—Plant 15
Louisville, Kentucky

FROM: Allen Moore
Plant Examiner

TO: Files

Date of Inspection:

September 6, 19XX

Personnel Participating:

Sherwin Pasten, Supervisor, Plant 15
Arthur Grice, Plant 15

Plant Description:

Plant 15 coats and cleans some parts of turbine engines with a surface coating of metal products and solvent metal degreaser. Although the coating and cleaning is done in a booth for spray paint, the surface coating releases metal emissions into the air. These emissions have to be avoided.

Findings:

1. Plant 15 will change its surface coating to water-based paints. All of the paints used at this plant will be changed to water-based paints.

2. All cleaning will be performed in cold cleaners that use mineral spirits as the solvent. These cleaners are equipped with covers, and the waste is sent off-site to a solvent claim specialist.

Recommendations:

Plant 15 has solved its emissions problems. I recommend no further action.

bcc: Gerry Tampolina
Larry Grenelik

FIGURE 13.6 Report of a site inspection

3. the date, time, and place of the meeting
4. the names of the presiding person and secretary
5. the reading and approval of the minutes.

The body of the minutes contains separate paragraphs for motions, points of order, and appeals as well as other content from the meeting. The last paragraph states the hour of adjournment, and the secretary then signs the minutes. Figure 13.7 illustrates a model form for minutes:

MINUTES OF THE FACULTY SENATE SPECIAL MEETING
OF OCTOBER 23, 1987

Having determined that a quorum was present, Professor Roth, chairperson of the Senate, called the meeting to order at 12:39 P.M. Upon a motion, the minutes of the special meeting of October 15 were approved as distributed.

Professor Zia Hassan moved to adopt the report of the Undergraduate Task Force of UFPC, including the summary of research. Professor Barrett presented an overview of the material contained therein.

Professor Root called the question, which was passed by a hand vote. The motion of Professor Hassan was then passed without dissent by a hand vote.

Professor Roth indicated that the Coordinating Committee would develop a strategy for implementation of the recommendations of the Undergraduate Task Force.

Professor Brubaker presented a summary of his proposal for novel postbaccalaureate programs, contained in a previous mailing. Professor Knepler moved that the Brubaker proposal be accepted for implementation by the Coordinating Committee.

Professor Barrett moved to substitute for Professor Knepler's motion, which was accepted by Professor Knepler: "It is the sense of the Senate that development and promotion of postbaccalaureate programs using the Brubaker report as a basis be a high priority of the institution and that appropriate actions be taken by university officials."

The Knepler motion, thus amended, was adopted by a hand vote.

Professor Roth presented an overview of the responses to the faculty questionnaire on the draft COMFIIT report. About 70 responses have already been received, and all faculty were urged to return the questionnaires.

Professor Lavan moved that the Senate suggest that a COMFIIT report will not be accepted at this time pending a change in the administration. Professor Knepler moved to table the motion, and by a vote of 18–4 the motion was tabled.

Professor Kumar presented highlights of a report on the Board of Higher Education Faculty Advisory Committee, which will be distributed in written form to the faculty.

There being no further business, the meeting was adjourned at 1:37 P.M.

Respectfully submitted,

Charles N. Haas, Recording Secretary

FIGURE 13.7 Formal minutes
Source: Charles N. Haas, Illinois Institute of Technology. Used with permission.

Writing Informal Notes from a Meeting

Unless you are the secretary, you will seldom have to submit formal minutes to your company. But, frequently, your company will ask you to submit notes from a meeting. The notes from a meeting record the information relevant to a company and also

- verify a participant's attendance at a meeting,
- inform a company of action that may involve the company,

and may be distributed around the company or simply filed to record attendance at the meeting.

Reviewing the Agenda

Meeting notes differ from trip notes in that meetings usually follow an agenda. Trip notes are more exploratory and allow a greater range of discussion. Because of the difference between the two, meeting notes are easier to organize; they simply follow the order of the agenda, and any new business discussed beyond the established agenda is itemized and summarized in order.

When the meeting is going to be fairly technical in content, the organizer often distributes the agenda prior to the meeting so that participants can prepare their information. In a published agenda

- The introduction reiterates date, place, and participants.
- The items are numbered to establish the order and subjects for the meeting.
- The closing suggests an additional item for the agenda and offers a phone number if other participants wish to comment on the agenda.

Figure 13.8 illustrates the agenda for a technical meeting.

TECHNICAL ADVISORY BOARD

1223 W. 55th Street
New York, New York 11250
(212) 439-2300

December 8, 19XX

Engineering Consulting Service
Attn: Jane Wensel
4700 Timberlane Road
Seattle, Washington 94807

Dear Ms. Wensel:

As agreed, the meeting between Technical Advisory Board, Engineering Con-

FIGURE 13.8 Agenda for a technical meeting

sulting Service, and Belden Engineering will be held in our New York office on Wednesday, December 15, 19XX. We will discuss the items listed as follows:

1. Forensic Testing—advances in technology.

2. Photographic Admissions—specifications in equipment.

3. Liability Insurance—options in insurance plans.

4. Contract Standards—Technical Advisory and Belden Engineering balance standards whereas Engineering Consulting standardizes depending on agreement.

5. Incorporation Techniques—varies state by state.

We have enclosed a form for New York State Incorporation for your review prior to our meeting. If you have any questions or comments, please call Helen Prid at (212) 439-2324.

Sincerely,

Gus Forsen
Manager
Legal Services Department

bc: R. Totenham
    B. N. Brigone

FIGURE 13.8 (cont.)

Organizing the Meeting Notes

When you have to write up and distribute the notes from a meeting, keep the agenda near you as a reference tool. Based on your reader's needs, select an organizational pattern for straight summary of the agenda, modified agenda summary, or meeting highlights:

1. Straight summary of the agenda list.
   If you use a memo format, as the writer does in Figure 13.9, include the background information in the beginning. Then an AGENDA SUMMARY indicates the organization of the following notes. The reader knows what topics this meeting covered and in what order they will be discussed.

2. Modified agenda summary (less formal than straight summary).
   Figure 13.10 apparently follows the agenda without repeating it. The notes, in a memo format, follow a standard outline with Roman numerals and summarize the action taken at the meeting. These notes are distributed to those present to remind them of their tasks, and the notes may be more widely distributed to keep the members-at-large fully informed.

ENVIRONMENTAL CONTROL COMMISSION

DATE: December 21, 19XX

SUBJECT: Notes from the 15th meeting of the Regional Coordinating
         Committee (RCC)

FROM: Janet Megolis
         Director, Compliance Division

TO: RCC members and Environmental Control Commission attendees

The 15th meeting of the RCC was held on Thursday, December 12,
19XX, at 1:30 P.M.

Agenda Summary

   I. Grants for 19XX

  II. Briefing on the GUST Implementation

 III. Status report on the National Task Force

  IV. Annual agenda for the Coordinating Committee

   I. Grants for 19XX

Walter Philton summarized the status of the grants for each
state.

Minnesota:

Wisconsin:

Indiana:

Illinois:

Michigan:

Ohio:

  II. Briefing on the GUST Implementation

Ellen Herbinger explained how the Environmental Control
Commission is implementing the GUST program. Some issues
and questions being considered during this policy development
process are these:

- Should tank owners be subjected to the same requirements
  as owners of waste facilities?
- What should trigger corrective action?
- Is a permit program necessary?
- What type of time schedule and resources are needed?

 III. Status Report on the National Task Force

Phillip Louder summarized the proposed changes for the National Task Force. The proposed changes were

FIGURE 13.9 Using visual techniques in meeting notes

A. To determine the remaining criteria.

B. To make site specific decisions.

IV. <u>Annual Agenda</u>

The purpose of the agenda is to give committee members ample time to provide thoughtful opinions on GUST issues. The committee members are requested to give annotated copies of the annual agenda to Mr. Philton by the close of the business day, December 30, 19XX.

V. The next RCC meeting will be January 25, 19XX, at 1:30 P.M. in the director's conference room.

Distribution Attached:

FIGURE 13.9 (cont.)

August 13, 1985

TO: Strategic Planning Committee   cc: Gunther Marx

FROM: Ken Cook, Jr.

SUBJECT: Action items from Houston Committee meeting Tuesday, May 21, 1985

ATTENDEES:

Jeff Hibbard	Helen Caird
Paul Blakely	Bill Stolgitis
Janis Hocker	Ken Cook, Jr.
Dick Wiegand	

I. Member Questionnaire—Results

A. Distribute copies of the results to the Board.
B. Prepare article for *Technical Communication,* describing the questionnaire, methods, results, and application to strategic planning.—Cook
C. *Intercom* to provide "snapshots" of results in future issues.—Stolgitis
D. Members of the committee will review the results this summer and request *any* additional correlation studies (for example, computer industry and English majors).

II. Board Workshop Results

A. Integrate with member questionnaire results.—Cook
B. Develop an action plan from the above combination of expressed needs.—Cook

III. STC Functions and Processes

Functions and processes will be analyzed later in the governance planning process. A structure audit is needed.

FIGURE 13.10 Informal notes from a meeting
Source: Kenneth J. Cook, Ken Cook Co., Milwaukee, Wis. Used with permission.

IV. Task Analysis Versus Society Guidelines

Jeff Hibbard reported major differences in many cases. He will request current administration members to review their respective guidelines and task descriptions and modify each to make it accurately reflect the position.

V. PRSA Strategic Planning Model
Dick Wiegand will prepare a five-year plan for STC based on the PRSA model. This will be accomplished by the September Board meeting.

VI. Future Actions

A. It appears that Robert Smit's fees are unreasonable for value received. Bill Stolgitis will investigate the credentials of Perry Holt by contacting organizations he has consulted with recently. We may want to meet with Mr. Holt in November.

B. Strategic planning will maintain close liaison with the Goals Committee (Gunther Marx). Jeff Hibbard believes the Goals Committee is the "conscience" of strategic planning. A business model will be constructed (why do we exist?).

FIGURE 13.10 (cont.)

3. Selected highlights of the meeting.
These notes, also in memo format, select highlights of interest to the company in order of importance, as illustrated in Figure 13.11. The notes summarize the numbered items, maintaining short paragraphs and accurate information about names, projects, and expenses. Note that the active style of agent (subject), action (verb), and goal (object) shares a place with the passive style of goal and action, often with the agent unknown.

The organization of the notes is the key to understanding the content of the document. These notes are organized

• To help the reader follow the information.
• To present the information clearly and concisely in brief paragraphs.
• To use the active style.
• To provide accurate information about dates, finances, and regulations.

Using Visual Techniques

The visual techniques contribute to the overall readability of the meeting notes. Some techniques include

• numbered text (standard outline with Roman numerals or Arabic numbers)
• underlined headings
• indented text
• short paragraphs
• bullets.

METRO ENERGY   Interoffice Correspondence
Date: June 28, 19XX
Subject: ASTM Committee D-3—June 1982 meeting
From: Denise Wharton
To: Henry A. Kopple
                   Director

Among the items discussed at the ASTM D-3 meeting in Toronto on June 22 and 23, 19XX, were several of interest to Metro Energy.

1. Proposed Standard D-4087 "Standard Specification for Pipeline Quality Natural Gas" received favorable subcommittee and main committee ballots, but received one negative at society ballot. This negative was held to be persuasive at both subcommittee and main committee, but is subject to confirmation by letter ballot of the main committee. The net effect of this action is to return the method to subcommittee level for future action.

2. Ivanhoe Gas Energy has proposed a commercial round-robin reference program. They propose sending reference samples to each participating laboratory four times per year. Analytical results would be statistically compared and reports sent to all participants. Laboratories would be identified by name or number as desired. Cost is estimated at $800.00.

3. Many companies are finding that so-called certified standards are not accurately prepared or analyzed. The Research Center for Gases is investigating production of a certified gas standard in cooperation with the National Bureau of Standards.

4. The proposed standard for calorific value of gases by stoichiometric combustion will be subjected to a round-robin test in the next few months. Two instruments will be used: Precision Measurement's Thermtitrator and Honeywell's Gas BTU Transmitter.

5. The Energy Association's Liaison to Committee D-3 presented their report (see attached).

Attachments:
c: I. Penney
    M. Hodges

FIGURE 13.11 Informal notes from a meeting: highlights

Summary

In both private industry and public agencies, employees take business trips to obtain information, solve a problem, or evaluate a product or process. Trips are time-consuming and costly, so preplanning will aid in writing the final report.

Front-end planning includes *brainstorming* to discover ideas relevant to the objectives of the trip. Whether a group or an individual brainstorms, all ideas should be recorded first and judged later. Anticipating information is also important to preplanning. A *checklist* of data necessary for report writing—data such as names of other participants, samples, handouts, forms to complete—reminds writers to obtain information before leaving the site.

Writing the purpose statement is the first step in organizing trip notes. After the *purpose* or objective of the trip, the list of *attendees,* the organizational *plan,* the *results,* and the *conclusion* or *recommendation* follow. The purpose helps the reader focus on the subject of the trip. The list of attendees helps to verify the information in the report. The organizational plan, often called the *scope* in trip notes, provides the reader with a road map of the items in the report. A memo format as well as visual aids including headings and subheadings, columns and lists, white space, attachments, and illustrations, contribute to readability. Some trip notes require a distribution list and completed questionnaires or inspection forms.

Minutes follow a general procedure established in *Robert's Rules of Order,* a procedure that recording secretaries must be familiar with. Instead of formal minutes, most companies request meeting notes with information relevant to the company. These notes may be organized around the formal agenda, a modified agenda summary, or highlighted items of interest to the company. Most meeting notes are distributed in memo format to inform the company of action or simply filed to verify a participant's attendance at a meeting. Following the order of the agenda helps to organize meeting notes.

Informal meeting notes use visual and stylistic techniques to contribute to the readability of the notes, techniques that include numbered items, indented text, short paragraphs, active style, precise information, headings, and bullets.

Checklist for Trip Notes

This checklist asks you to consider these options for your notes. Check only those items to which you give a positive response.

Yes   **FOR YOUR TRIP NOTES, DID YOU**
        Gather information by
_____   brainstorming?

_____   collecting samples?

_____   completing questionnaires/inspection forms?

_____   Use a memo format?

        State the purpose
_____   to obtain information?

_____   to solve a problem?

_____ to evaluate a product or process?

_____ List the people attending by title, affiliation, phone number?

_____ in an appendix, if appropriate?

_____ State the organizational plan or scope?

_____ Discuss the results?

_____ Draw conclusions or make recommendations?

_____ Use style and visual techniques to increase readability with headings and subheadings?

_____ indented text?

_____ bullets?

_____ brief paragraphs?

_____ accurate information?

_____ active style?

Checklist for Minutes and Meeting Notes

Have you considered the following items for your minutes or notes? Check those items to which you can give a positive response.

Yes

_____ If _you_ are writing formal minues, are you using the form in _Robert's Rules of Order?_

FOR YOUR MEETING NOTES,
_____ Are you using a memo format?

_____ with a subject line, including name of organization, date and place of meeting?

_____ with a list of attendees, including phone numbers and affiliations, if appropriate?

_____ with an agenda summary, if the agenda is long?

_____ with selected highlights in order of importance to the company?

Is the content
_____ written in an active style?

_____ accurate in terms of correct names, figures, titles?

Do the visual techniques include
_____ indented text?

_____ numbered text?

_____ headings and subheadings?

_____ bulleted items?

_____ Can the reader quickly find the action the participants took at the meeting?

_____ Is there a distribution list?

_____ Are attachments referenced in the notes?

Notes

1. General Henry M. Robert, *Robert's Rules of Order* (Glenview, Ill.: Scott Foresman, 1981): 389–391.

References

Richard M. Davis, "Presenting Courses in Government and Industry," *The Technical Writing Teacher* 9 (1982):65–74.

Robert W. Kelton, "The Internal Report in Complex Organizations," in *Proceedings, 31st International Technical Communication Conference* (Washington, D.C.: Society for Technical Communication, 1984): RET 54–57.

Applying Your Knowledge

EXERCISE 13.1

As a group, brainstorm the kinds of communication problems people handle on the job. Use the nominal group technique described in Module 2. At the end of the brainstorming session, try to establish major categories and subcategories.

COLLABORATIVE EXERCISES ===

For the next two exercises, in teams of two or three people, collaborate on producing drafts of the two trip reports from the notes provided. Select your own format (memo or report), and organize the material. Remember to design and write the content for readability.

EXERCISE 13.2 ===

MEMORANDUM

TO:	J. I. Kilgren, Director	DATE: 6/12/XX
FROM:	P. Milring	Information only
SUBJECT:	Inspection of the Madison Landfill	Response requested

On 6-4-XX a cover inspection was conducted at the above-named facility. The area involved the old landfill located in the northern section. The new landfill located in the southern section was covered and checked on 10-24-XX and 11-06-XX.

Final cover requirements were determined by setting up a grid system with a 100-foot interval (see diagram). After the grid system was established, a tractor with a rear-mounted auger would drill holes at each marked interval. The above writer accompanied the owner, Mr. King, and the tractor while making a visual and manual inspection at each boring. The visual inspection consisted of looking for refuse being brought up by the auger while the manual involved precise measurement with a yardstick to ensure the required 2 feet of cover. In reference to the attached diagram, several inadequately covered areas were discovered. Three out of the four areas were rather small in size, but area A covered an extensive area. The perimeters of the inadequate areas were determined by the use of auxiliary holes. Once an area was found to be inadequate by utilizing augured holes, several additional holes were drilled to determine the extent of the area. Once the perimeters were established, grid stakes were set indicating the additional amount of cover needed. As previously stated, four inadequate areas were found, with the largest area measuring 244' × 50' (see A on diagram). Areas B and C were small in dimensions and were receiving additional cover at the end of my inspection. The final area D, according to Mr. King, would receive additional cover simultaneously with the back filling of the haul road. Mr. King was questioned on the dredging of the drainage way on the southern portion of the fill. Mr. King responded by stating that the dredging would be completed in the next four weeks. At this time the entire landfill would be graded and seeded with a variety of grasses. I then advised Mr. King to notify me when the seeding was to take place. At this time, a secondary check would be conducted on the delinquent areas referenced above.

EXERCISE 13.3 ===

INTEROFFICE CORRESPONDENCE

DATE:	February 22, 19XX	
SUBJECT:	Short Course	
TO:	Matthew Landeau	FROM: Jennifer Klyzinsky
	Laboratory Director	

On Friday, February 19, 19XX, Francis Thomas and I attended a short course in atomic absorption spectroscopy at the Conference Center. The course was given by the Scientific Instruments Corporation (SIC). The purpose of the course was to make potential customers aware of the company's latest advances in graphite furnace and hydride systems.

One of their least expensive advances is entitled a microflame sampling system. It is simply a teflon cup that acts as a sampler. This cup fits on the end of the nebulizer. The system is designed to be used with a recorder or microprocessor to measure the peaks produced from the sample injection. This system is designed for samples of high, dissolved, solid concentrations. It uses standard flame techniques, requires only a small sample size, and allows for a high sample throughput rate. Some disadvantages of this system are poorer precision than with standard solution aspiration. The sensitivity is poorer than with most furnace or boat techniques. Basically, it is designed to do some of the same types of analysis as the furnace where the cost of a graphite furnace cannot be justified.

Graphite furnaces are designed for samples of low concentrations where trace analyses are important. They require only a small amount of sample and are capable of analyzing for some elements not possible to analyze for by conventional flame AA.

Similar statements can be made regarding the hydride system. The hydride system works only for the following elements: As, Se, Te, Sb, Bi, Sn, Ge. The hydride system reduces matrix interferences, improves precision, and is highly sensitive.

SIC researches not only to update their current instrumentation but also to determine the instrumentation of the future. Recently, they have been looking into the field of the inductively coupled plasma (ICP). It has been found that flame AA is faster for small numbers of elements to be analyzed; the ICP, however, overtakes the flame whenever more than five to eight elements are being analyzed. This is because the ICP has multielement capabilities not possessed by conventional AA. The ICP has fairly good detection limits for refractory elements and is hampered by few chemical or ionizational interferences. The range of analytical linearity is extended by the use of the ICP. The flame, on the other hand, has better precision than the ICP, and the graphite furnace has better detection limits. One of the greatest differences is that conventional AA is much cheaper to obtain than the ICP.

During the lunch break, several people from SIC were available for questions. At this time, Francis and I received a demonstration on the use of the graphite furnace. This served to give me a better understanding of the operation of the furnace and some of the techniques involved in furnace work.

In my opinion, the meeting proved to be a good learning experience. I am now more aware of some of the advances in the field of atomic absorption spectroscopy. The lecture was presented in such a way that it was fairly easy to follow, even with only limited knowledge of the equipment.

cc: F. Thomas

EXERCISE 13.4 ══

Using the diary provided, reorganize the information as trip notes under appropriate headings, revise the content, and design and write the report.

TO: John Right, Manager
FROM: Paul Bastion
DATE: March 23, 19XX
SUBJECT: Trip to Fabrication Plant, March 13–16, 19XX
PERSONNEL: Mark Young, Ron Niles, Alice Pearson, and several plant technicians

The trip began with a visit to the fabrication plant on Monday, March 13, 19XX. On arrival at the airport, I telephoned Mr. Young, who had to delay meeting with me until after 5:00 P.M. owing to his attending another meeting. On several occasions during this four-day visit, Mr. Young was unavailable owing to other assignments. His attention is clearly not 100 percent on this project.

I witnessed a special test of the hydraulic expansion tubes, which had suddenly been scheduled by the engineers from Ron Niles' group, who are studying the problems encountered on hydraulic tube expansion. The test was followed by a discussion between Alice Pearson and me, along with several other plant technicians. I quizzed Alice on the implementation of her recommendations in the report submitted in late 19XX. She could not show me evidence that these recommendations have been effectively put into practice although she was able to describe in detail how these corrective actions can be implemented on the project. Many of them properly belong in the scope of either welding activities or the maintenance program, both of which are still being revised, so it is reasonable to expect the corrective actions will be implemented in the shop once these two tasks have been fully revised. Alice still evidently endorses the corrective actions she recommended earlier but is not in a position to implement them herself. I made it clear to her—and later to Mark Young—that we want those recommendations implemented.

On Monday evening, I met with Mark Young and briefly discussed all major tasks, together with a schedule for detailed discussions of each task the next day. However, he told me that a specialist would be at the plant on Tuesday to discuss X-ray films, which were receiving inconsistent readings.

The full day of Tuesday, March 16, 19XX, was devoted to the X-ray problem, with only a brief discussion on the hydraulic tube expansion problem. Initially, the X-ray inconsistencies were attributed to a difference in the rod-anode method and the isotope-source method, but after I heard a description of the data, it became clear that the inconsistency was due to human error made by the film reader. It was determined that future film readings should be done independently by two experienced film interpreters. Arrangements to have the main plant read films after they have been read first by the fabrication plant should be made, if possible. We also need to follow up on the welding and maintenance tasks as part of the hydraulic tube expansion problem. The plans will be needed within two weeks.

EXERCISE 13.5 ══

In a memo, draft the following notes from a meeting. The notes should go to the director of your laboratory and then to the files. Remember to organize, write, and design for readability.

Acme International, Inc.   Interoffice correspondence

September 2, 19XX
—Northern Water Analysts (NWA) bimonthly meeting 08/17/XX
—Director, Roger Podiatric
—Writer, George Cracken
—New business covered by President Barbara Leland included
—Would there be interest in a round-robin analysis of ATP-Bacteria samples
    using Spectrophotometer 20? Yes
—(I did not feel this analysis was appropriate for Acme International.)
—Discussion of a future group tour of the ECC (Energy Control Commission)
    Laboratories in Maywood, Kentucky.
—Environmental Pollution Control Board revised water quality standards for
    ammonia nitrogen and un-ionized ammonia discharge levels. (See
    attached.)
—October, 19XX, NWA Meeting will be held in Joliet.
—Meeting adjourned.
—Guest speaker, John Siddleman from Fisher Scientific, discussed "Computer
    Use in the Lab" and explained features of the "Commodore International"
    computer.

WRITING ASSIGNMENT:

Interview an appropriate person in either the private or the public sector about communication problems in your field. Establish your questions before you go to the interview. Then

• Draft, design, and write your trip notes from this interview.
• Send a thank-you note to your interviewee. Enclose a copy of your trip note
  report as an attachment.

MODULE 14

Oral Presentations and Interviews

This module introduces you to oral presentations and interviews. Both depend on the self and the receiver, and both can be successful if you have knowledge and experience. In fact, your previous work gives rise to these communication projects. You probably wouldn't be making an oral presentation unless you were knowledgeable on the subject, nor would you be an interviewee or an interviewer unless you had the appropriate background and expertise.

But each of these areas requires special skills, and knowing some of the tools will help you avoid common mistakes and arm you with the basic techniques for success. Both require careful preparation; this planning stage, sometimes called *front-end preparation,* is important for any project. With oral presentations and interviews, the situation includes the physical presence of other people, a situation that simply isn't true of written documents even when the writer keeps the reader continually in mind.

Oral presentations and interviews involve a physical, immediate, and continuous interpersonal interaction. Perhaps, after reading that last line, you felt an undefined fear. It's the fear many people feel when they have to communicate orally. The speaker has to control so many factors, factors that interact in a dynamic synthesis that underlies all effective oral communications.

One way to conquer the fear is to analyze the situation and arm yourself with successful techniques, a list of do's and don'ts that guide you through the process of planning, writing, critiquing, and delivering your message. Here, then, is a technique to analyze the oral presentation and interview, presented in discrete categories. Remember, though, that communication is dynamic and the components flow into each other.

Scope

This module will help you

1. Analyze the nature of the audience.
2. Organize your presentation.
3. Plan your timing and your notes.
4. Practice the presentation.
5. Plan your visuals, equipment, handouts, space.
6. Deliver your talk.
7. Interview for a job or for information.

Oral Presentations for Technical Talks

You have been asked to talk about your research on blood pressure devices at the company's annual technical colloquium. Or you agree to speak to a group of educators about the software available for interactive writing using computers. Both talks acknowledge your expertise on the subject, and you have adequate time, called *lead time*, to prepare your presentation. In your job, you will soon be involved in one of two types of speaking opportunities: impromptu and prepared oral communication. Impromptu, or spontaneous, speaking is unrehearsed. This module will discuss only the prepared speech because technical presentations as well as informative talks must include facts presented in a logical pattern. But the dynamics of any oral presentation includes the interaction of the five elements in Figure 14.1.[1]

Audience—Who Is Listening?

In all the communication situations so far, you have been advised to consider your audience. Now you can ask your contact person about the expected audience. How large a group is it? Is it small enough to respond as a group of individuals or so large it can respond only in the mass? Even more important, what is the nature of the audience? Are they business people and at what level—chief executive officers (CEOs), technical people? How knowledgeable are they on the subject of your talk, and what type of companies are they from? What do they know about blood pressure devices or software for writing at the computer?

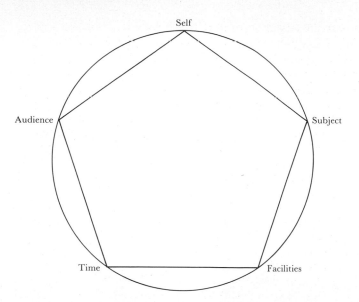

FIGURE 14.1 **The interaction of elements in oral presentations**
Source: Robert Irving, Verbal and Visual Communication 427,
Illinois Institute of Technology.

Other aspects about the audience include age, sex, level of education, and interest. Assuming that you can discover a general level, pitch the talk's technical level slightly above what appears to be the middle level in the audience. You should consider the audience's reason for being at the talk. Are they required to attend your presentation because it is a job-related activity? And if so, what can the audience expect to gain from the presentation? Are they to be informed about the software programs available or persuaded to buy a blood pressure device? Is this a training session or a sales session? Is the audience expected to participate? Or has the audience come voluntarily because they have an interest in this subject? Interaction between the speaker and the audience is an important factor in successful speaking.

Summary of Hints to Increase the Dynamics Between You and the Audience

1. Learn all you can about the nature of the audience in advance of your talk.
2. Remember to observe your audience while you are speaking so that you can notice their shifting in seats or shrugging shoulders.
3. Don't be disturbed about a smaller audience than you expected. They are likely to be embarrassed that the turnout is small and view you more charitably as a result.
4. Better to talk slightly above your audience's heads than to condescend—but not too far above.
5. Consider any likelihood that the audience may have prejudices or irrational attitudes toward your subject apart from their knowledge of it.

6. Be sure you set up the space properly if you want the audience to participate.
7. If you plan a question and answer session, plant a friend in the audience with a prepared question to begin the question period.

Time—How Long Should You Take?

Most program planners will tell you how long you may take to speak. Twenty minutes is enough time for any speaker, but if your contact suggests a longer presentation, say that no professional speaker ever inflicts more than 20 minutes of wisdom on any audience, but that you would entertain questions and answers for another 10 minutes.[2] You might even suggest a panel discussion if your contact wants a longer program.

If you have a poor time slot for your talk, such as after lunch when the audience is drowsy, consider involving the audience by posing questions or creating a workshop type of situation. Ask the audience to consider a scenario in which they have to solve a problem associated with the topic for discussion. Changing your format can solve some time slot problems. Whatever your time slot and format, it is important to adhere to a time schedule. The time schedule gives point and shape to the presentation. For the purpose of preparing the talk, consider three types of timing.

Loose timing is the timing of most presentations that are not being recorded or broadcast. You are bound largely by courtesy to the group and to other speakers, but you should establish a cursory time line that permits you to check your time at major points in your talk so that you adhere to a time schedule.

Tight timing is the timing for a program where other presentations must be fitted in, where other discussants or a moderator or a rebuttal have time slots. Under these circumstances, timing must be careful. For a 15-minute speech you should hold yourself to 15 minutes plus or minus 2 minutes. In your time line for your talk, you can indicate where you could lengthen or shorten your piece.

Critical time is the timing of the radio or television studio. Timing here is absolutely precise. To be broadcast, any presentation exceeding five minutes in total length must have an exact time line. An exact copy of the talk, called scripting, must have notes indicating where expansions and contractions can be introduced to remain within the critical time limits.

Closely related to timing, as well as to the technical difficulty of the material, are the notes for oral presentations. Here are the types of notes with some hints and problems for each.

1. *Cue cards* (cards with simple words to cue the speaker).

Cue cards are usually 3 × 5 cards containing no more information than a word or phrase each. They serve as a help to your memory, but they are not suitable for a technical talk with complex information or for a talk lasting more than 10 minutes. Figure 14.2 illustrates a cue card outline to the basic elements of oral presentations.

A CUE CARD OUTLINE
TO THE BASIC ELEMENTS OF
ORAL PRESENTATIONS

CUE CARDS

#1

   I SELF—Who am I?

      A. The speech *persona*
      B. My articulateness
      C. My knowledge

#2

   II AUDIENCE—Who are they?

      A. Their physical makeup
      B. Their knowledge
      C. Their motivation

#3

   III SUBJECT—What am I presenting?

      A. Its depth and scope
      B. Its mode—informational, persuasive,
         and so on
      C. Its nature—visual vs. auditory

#4

   IV TIME—How long may I take?

      A. Loose timing
      B. Tight timing
      C. Critical timing

#5

   V FACILITIES—Where will I speak?

      A. Scale
      B. Atmosphere
      C. Aids and assistants

FIGURE 14.2 Cue card outline
Source: Robert Irving, Verbal and Visual Communication 427,
Illinois Institute of Technology.

2. *Topical outlines.*

      Topics are arranged on separate cards or on script sheets in outline form with far greater detail than cue cards. Separate cards allow reediting and necessary additions and contractions. On a script sheet you should indent so that you can find your place easily when you look down at your notes. Also, you should mark off the elapsed time at each major head of the outline. This time line will assist you in determining whether you are running on, ahead, or behind schedule.

3. *Scripting.*

      When you prepare the complete text of your talk, you are scripting. Scripting is essential for long or complex talks with critical timing. But what you gain in security, you may lose in spontaneity. The script is also the least flexible for lengthening or shortening talks, and it is the hardest on you as speaker because you must read and yet keep eye contact with the listeners and remain lively and spontaneous.

Some Final Hints on Timing and Notes
- Practice to verify time.
- Type or write your outline or talk in large type or triple space, with room to mark up pauses, smiles, eye contact, and where to use visual aids.
- Number your pages in case you drop them and have to reorder them, but leave pages unstapled so that you can shift them on the rostrum.

Subject—What Are You Presenting?

Of course, you must consider the nature of the audience and the timing of the presentation when preparing the content for your talk. It is better to cover a smaller area fully than to sweep vaguely across an area too large for the time.

      1. Begin to **structure your remarks under a tentative working title,** such as "An Evaluation of Blood Pressure Monitors." If the purpose of the talk is mainly informational, then remember that informational subjects tend to be both factual and dry. Collect concrete examples, case studies, anecdotes to support your general points and to give the subject greater appeal. A talk whose purpose is persuasive, "Noninvasive Blood Pressure Monitors—Why Use Them?" lends itself to more emotional treatment, but it must still be factual and include concrete examples. If you need additional material, interview colleagues and experts on the subject to stimulate your own thinking.

      2. After you have collected your examples, data, case histories, quotes, and visuals, **consider the essential nature of your subject.** Is your subject essentially visual or almost purely nonvisual? Do the visuals supplement the talk, or do your comments supplement the visuals? Obviously, a presentation on graphic techniques is almost purely visual, but do not automatically assume that the ideal condition for every presentation is to be as visual as possible.

When deciding on the number of your visuals, remember that most presentations fall somewhere between two extremes:

- You and your speech are the essential and continuing point of the focus, and your visuals simply explicate your speech.
- You are an assistant to the main action that dominates center stage—your visuals—and you reveal the significance of the visuals to the audience, perhaps in a darkened room where you are no more than a voice.

Decide where you want your presentation to fall and then

- Use the simplest visual effects that will serve your needs.
- Limit the number and variety of visuals because presentations swamped in special effects can lose their impact and become gimmicky.

3. **Write your first draft.** Remember the purpose and objectives of your presentation, and then boil them down to three or four main points. Put together an outline linking these main points to your purpose. Like the introduction for a written report, your opening remarks can provide your listeners with a road map for the rest of the presentation. Throughout the talk, remember to link your subordinate ideas to your main points. If you write a script, plan on 250 words taking about 2 minutes to read; a 20-minute speech requires approximately 10 double-spaced pages. But remember the advice on notes for a speech. A script increases security but reduces spontaneity whereas a topical outline permits spontaneity and your more immediate response to the audience. For example, you can elaborate on a point if the audience looks confused.

4. **Practice and Rewrite.** Look at the rough draft after a few days, and check for logical flow and transition. You may discover some missing logical links that can be solved by adding *however* or *in fact*. Finally, rehearse out loud for friends and colleagues, speak in front of a mirror, or talk into a tape recorder. You should weed out words you stumble over and mark your notes with pauses, eye contact, and places where you plan to use visuals. In fact, as you practice, this is a good time to consider yourself as a part of the dynamics of the presentation. The following hints combine both content and delivery.

Hints That Combine Both Content and Delivery[3]
1. Keep your opening simple: Thank the host; greet the audience; state the topic. You do not need an opening joke. Try a rhetorical question or two to capture the audience's attention and create drama: "Do you know what executives say their technical professionals need?" Or establish rapport by using an anecdote. "One technical writer seeking an entry-level position carried her portfolio with her to her first interview. When the interviewer asked her if she could write instructions, she took out her instruction sheet on how to use a wrench. This example landed her the job."
2. Use conventional style: Keep sentences short and use active voice and vivid verbs (see Module 4 on style).
3. Avoid clichés but use dramatic language: "This device could revolutionize the health care industry."

4. Follow all general statements with specifics: "This blood pressure device is noninvasive and can be used with newborns as well as adults."
5. Repeat your main points. Most people retain little of what a speaker said. Conclude with your main points even if you say, "The three points I want to stress are. . . ."
6. If you must include statistics, round off numbers and humanize them, "Fifty percent of the entry-level technical professionals, or one out of two. . . ." Keep the numbers to a minimum, or use charts or handouts so that listeners can study them after you stop talking.
7. Don't strain for humor; if in doubt, leave it out. And of course, don't put yourself or anyone else down.
8. Continue the rapport with the audience by sharing problems and solutions: "Our problem to solve; our goal to reach." Remind the listeners about how the topic relates to their concerns, "An interviewer may ask you to comment on your communication skills. Mention your portfolio and the types of documents you wrote, the visuals, the speeches, the collaborative work."

When you have finished speaking, know how you plan to end your presentation. If time permits, you could ask, "Are there any questions?" By opening the discussion, you take the audience' eyes off yourself for a few moments. When there are no [more] questions, you can simply say, "Thank you."

Self—Who Are You?

It is much easier to think of giving a talk if you plan to use your own style. Are you naturally flamboyant, reserved, friendly, assertive? When people compliment you on your personality, what qualities do they focus on? Be that personality, but you are also about to give a performance, and you want to rise to it. So a middle ground as a speaker is to think of choosing a speech **persona** (Latin for mask). You want to choose a persona like your best self, but different enough so that you can judge the persona objectively. You want to feel comfortable but not entirely exposed.

Dress in keeping with the occasion and your personality. The general advice about clothes is to wear loose enough clothing to allow ease of motion. It is all right to stand out somewhat as long as you remain approachable. Flashing jewelry is distracting and may prevent sharp videotaping or good sound reproduction if these are a part of your presentation.

Nonverbal communication such as eye contact and body movement greatly influences the audience. In oral communication 55 percent of the message is communicated through body language.[4] Your movement and gestures should be relaxed, easy, appropriate to your personality, the space, and the nature of the material. Here are some specific hints about motion:

• Remember that too motionless a stance is mesmerizing whereas excessive movement is distracting, particularly if you are close to the audience.

- Don't bounce, sway, or make sudden changes in direction. If you are being taped, these motions become more exaggerated.
- Keep gestures small if you are close to your audience. Up close they can see the expression on your face, which is much easier to follow. Use broader gestures when a large part of your audience is distant from you. Remember that modern speakers use fewer rhetorical gestures than those speakers in the grand old films you've seen.
- If you are nervous, place yourself behind a desk or lectern; put your hands firmly on the lectern (not in your pockets); put your notes on the lectern rather than holding them in your hands.
- Watch for distracting mannerisms, such as playing with notes or chalk or fingering garments.
- Above all, *look* at your audience; maintain eye contact with different listeners in various parts of the audience.

Finally, you want to control the level of your voice. If you can be heard comfortably by all the people in the room, speak without a sound system. You should check your audibility by stepping away from the mike and asking your listeners directly whether or not they can hear you.[5] If they can hear you, dismiss the sound system, but be watchful of your audience. When you see people begin to look puzzled and turn ears toward you, it may be time to turn up the volume on your voice. If you must use a microphone, find out what type it is:

1. Unidirectional—eliminates outside distracting sounds but restricts your head movement.
2. Bidirectional—good for question-and-answer session because it picks up audience questions but bad because it picks up distracting audience noise during your talk.
3. Omnidirectional—used frequently because it allows free movement but picks up stray noises from any direction, including the rumble of the competing air-conditioning system.

Whatever microphone you use,

- Adjust the mike to your mouth level; aim it at your mouth about six to eight inches away from you.
- Talk into it normally and breathe slowly and fully.
- Repeat any question from the audience over the sound system (this procedure gives you an extra moment to frame an answer).

Whether or not you use a mike,

- Check all unfamiliar terms for proper pronunciation in advance. If you stumble, repeat correctly.
- Watch for slurring or clipping (dropping final syllables) and linking words together. But avoid overly precise diction that can sound affected.
- Watch your audience for feedback about voice volume and pace. If you drop your eye contact, you will almost certainly begin to speak more quickly

and at a lower volume. *Remember:* Most people speak too fast when nervous. *Slow down* to emphasize a point or give statistics.

- Vary your pace, your tone, and your pitch (within limits).
- Use pauses to shape your next major point and to scan your audience for feedback.
- If you are nervous, breathe slowly, and make sure you're provided with water for a dry throat—and *use* it!

Space—What Are the Facilities Like?

The physical environment of the presentation plays a large role in determining how it should be presented. A small room dictates an informal low-keyed quality that focuses on the audience as individuals. The closer the distance between you and the listeners, the more intimate the atmosphere. If you want the presentation to be speaker-dominated, you must place yourself at the head of a long table or in front of the audience, perhaps behind a lectern or podium. If you wish to act as a guide or discussion leader, you must be on the same level as the audience to allow them to see both you *and* each other. A group around a round table is psychologically equal. As the speaker, what do you want, and what is available to you?

If you need visual aids to support and clarify your message, then you will need materials and equipment. First, determine your aids and your equipment needs. Will you use

1. Flipcharts—large notepads that are good for spontaneity and returning to a previous visual but bad for ease of movement because the stand is often awkward to move.
2. Slides—good for accuracy of product but bad for audience rapport because the listeners cannot see you in the darkened room. Preparing slides can also be time-consuming and expensive.
3. Chalkboard—good for spontaneity but bad for audience rapport because your back is often to the audience. Furthermore, what you write is often erased and cannot be referred to later.
4. Posters—good for clear messages because you prepare them in advance but bad because they are often awkward to transport or handle easily. You can control the size of the poster to make it more manageable for one person.
5. Overhead transparencies—good for clear messages because you can prepare them in advance. They are also easy to transport, reusable later in the talk, complementary with audience rapport because you do not have to turn your back or darken the room, and inexpensive to prepare. You even have spontaneity with transparencies if you bring blank ones with you and use markers to draw and write on them during your talk.
6. Hardware—good for authenticity but bad for a large audience unless the object is quite large, and then it may be too heavy or bulky to transport easily.

7. Handouts—good for visual accessibility but bad for distraction they offer to audience. Handouts may be best to give out at end of talk for the audience to take with them.

Whatever visual aid you decide to use, remember to tell your audience why you are using it. Consider the nature of your presentation first, and unless your presentation is primarily visually oriented, your visuals should supplement, not dominate, your talk. Audiovisual professionals make the following recommendations for overheads, but the principles apply equally to any visuals.[6]

- Don't cram too much information on a visual (six or seven lines of six words each on a single theme is plenty, as illustrated in Figure 14.3).
- Use type or print large enough to be readable throughout the room.
- Use colored transparency-marking pens or colored adhesive film to liven up visuals. Computer plotters print overheads in four or more colors, and photographic transparency-maker equipment produces full-color copies of photographs and artwork.
- Look at your screen, just as your audience does, rather than looking down at your transparency.

If you create a checklist of materials and equipment before the day of your presentation, you will reduce your anxiety on the day of your presentation.

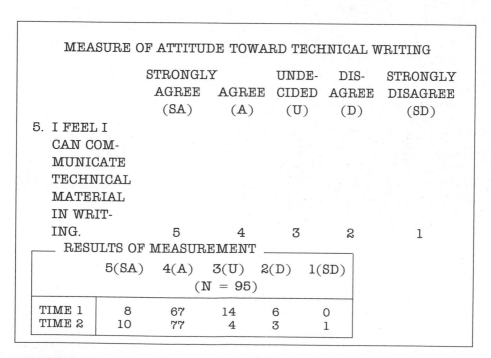

FIGURE 14.3 Transparency using white space to provide complex information

It is always a good idea to arrive early to try out the equipment and familiarize yourself with its operation.

Checklist for Audiovisual Aids

Did you bring
_____ handouts, including brochures and fact sheets with data?

_____ a biography or written introduction (providing one allows you to shape your image to your advantage)?

_____ reprints of the speech?

_____ transparencies, slides, posters, or hardware (object)?

Will the organizer provide you with
_____ lectern or podium?

_____ microphone?

_____ overhead or slide projector, flipchart, personal computer/terminal?

_____ chalk, marking pens?

_____ assistants who may be filming or taping (if possible, control your own slides)?

In Conclusion—Be Prepared!

After you consider the five interactive elements that make up an oral presentation—audience, time, subject, yourself, facilities—something may still go wrong. If you drop your note cards on the way to the podium, take the audience into your predicament. They will empathize with you if you smile and say, "It will take me a few seconds to reorganize my notes." If the AV equipment malfunctions, remind them and yourself of Murphy's law: "Anything that can go wrong will, and it will go wrong at the time it can do the most harm." Be sure, however, that you have examined the AV equipment before you begin to speak. And, finally, remember the words of an excellent speaker, Mark Twain: "It takes three weeks to prepare a good impromptu speech."

Interviews

An interview is an important factor in a communication process. You will certainly have the opportunity to interview in two situations:

- To gather information.
- To apply for a job.

Whether you are interviewing for a job or to gather information for a writing project, you must be aware of the dynamics of the interviewing process. The three interactive elements of the interview are shown in Figure 14.4.

Purpose—What Do You Seek to Accomplish?

If you are **interviewing for information,** make the personal interview your last step. You want to elicit information from someone who can help you, and therefore, you don't want to ruin your chances by asking foolish questions or stepping on someone's toes. If you plan to interview the owner or author, that person's ego is involved, so, like the job interview, your purpose is to create a good impression to get the cooperation and information you need. Christine Browning, author of *Guide to Effective Software Technical Writing,* suggests you do the following before you interview:[7]

- Find specifics on the subject from external sources. For example, if you were going to write a software reference manual, do not track down the programmer and start asking questions. First, look around for the design specifications. Why was the program created, what does it do, and how does it work? Write down any questions you have after examining external sources.
- Examine other reference manuals to help you define components and duplicate material that is common to all reference manuals. Write down any questions you still have after examining similar material.
- Collect any programming notes from the programmer. Ask only for the notes. Do not hang around and ask questions—yet. Write down any questions you have after examining these notes.

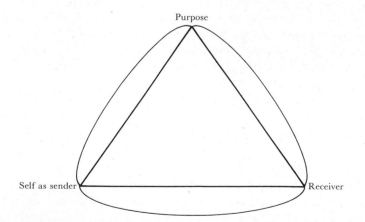

FIGURE 14.4 The interactive elements of the interview

- Ask programmers for any other documentation they can spare. Again, do not ask questions yet. Add your questions to your list, which should be changing constantly as you find the answers to many of your questions. If you think you may have overlooked some questions, brainstorm with your colleagues. Module 2 offers some brainstorming techniques.

When you are finally ready to interview, go to the interview with a list of precisely honed questions that will give you the information you still need.

If you are **interviewing for a job,** your purpose is to make a good impression on the interviewer (receiver). Before you go on the interview, you can advance your purpose by arming yourself with information and questions about the company and the job. A national outplacement firm offers some advice on interviewing:[8]

- Find out about the company by checking their references in Dun & Bradstreet, trade associations, and other sources. Read their annual report.
- Look at an organizational chart to see where the job you are applying for falls. This chart will tell you about the top people and the people you will be working with.
- Prepare questions to ask. Good bosses want to hire someone who wants to know as much about them and the job as they want to know about you.

Self and the Receiver—Can You Separate *You* from *They?*

If you are **interviewing to gain information,** you are inextricably linked to the receiver. You have done your homework; you have all available information and knowledge about the subject. Now organize the remaining questions, and ask them one at a time. If you are prepared, interested, and enthusiastic, you will create a good impression. The receiver (owner) will be pleased to talk about the project; after all, the owner's ego is tied up with the project.

When the owner takes over the interview and begins to tell you more about the product than you ever cared to know, keep a normal sense of humor, don't step on toes, and return to your questions as soon as you can. As you take notes, verify them with the owner immediately. And either offer to send the write-up to the owner or verify the manual with the owner *If* it is necessary. Do not promise to verify if you are meeting a tight deadline.

If you are **interviewing for a job,** separate the *you* from *they* and remember:[9]

- They are "screening out" candidates, eliminating those candidates who **in their estimation** are unqualified or don't fit.
- They are usually a member of the human resources staff, especially at the initial interview, without any hiring authority. But they do submit to the hiring manager the names of candidates who they believe can do the job.
- They have personalities. How do your personalities match?
- They are interviewing because they have a position to fill.

If they hire you, they will hire you because

- Your personal chemistry complements that of the receiver.
- You can satisfy a specific need.
- You can make or save some dollars (impact the bottom line).
- You can provide something the receiver doesn't have—you don't pose a threat.

For entry-level jobs, they are looking for

verbal skills that indicate you are a logical and analytic thinker
education
skills
experience
creativity/initiative
honesty/principles
maturity
loyalty

Questions They Are Likely to Ask You

1. Tell me about you!
2. What do you know about our company?
3. Why do you want to work for us?
4. What can you do for us?
5. What about our position do you find most attractive? Least attractive?
6. What important trends do you see in our industry?
7. In any previous position, what features did you like the most? Least?

Prepare to answer their questions by doing your homework on their company and knowing your strengths and weaknesses.

- Establish realistic objectives.
- Be enthusiastic and interested; plan to listen as well as talk.
- Keep a normal sense of humor.
- Present yourself in a straightforward and honest manner.
  If you do not know the answer to a question, admit it.
- Be prepared for salary discussions.
  Try to generalize, particularly in the initial stages.

Questions You Should Ask Them

1. Who are the people I will work with?
2. What did the previous incumbent do in the job?
3. Where is the organization going? Plans? Products? Projects?
4. What are the lines of communication?
5. What problems do you anticipate in the future? Are they new?

After the interview, do a personal critique. Think it through question by question. What didn't you handle well? Where could you have elaborated? Did you ask pertinent questions? What did you learn that will help you in the next interview? Bolster any weak points for subsequent interviews. And, finally, drop a note to your interviewer and express appreciation. Keep it simple, as exemplified in Figure 14.5. Module 13 illustrates the formats for letters.

Summary

Oral presentations may be impromptu or prepared, but technical presentations are always prepared. The dynamics of oral presentations includes the interaction of audience, time, subject, speaker, and facilities. The contact person should provide information about the audience, including size, professional interests, reason for attending talk, and prejudices regarding the subject. It is better to pitch the talk's technical level slightly above the middle level in the audience than to condescend.

Most program planners will suggest a time limit; 20 minutes is usually adequate for any presentation. A question-and-answer period or a panel presentation will extend the length of a program. When the program is not being recorded or broadcast, most speakers observe *loose timing*. *Tight timing* is timing for a program that includes other discussants or rebuttals. *Critical timing* is the timing for a radio or TV broadcast.

Closely related to timing and the technical difficulty of the subject are the notes for oral presentations. *Cue cards* are index cards containing a word

HEADING

November 24, 19XX

Reginald Potsdam
Director, Deer Park Laboratory
Lander Technologies, Inc.
423 Greenleaf Drive
Trenton, New Jersey 08648

Dear Dr. Potsdam:

I appreciated the opportunity to meet with you on Wednesday afternoon to discuss your engineering position. I was impressed with what I heard and would be very interested in exploring it further. You can contact me at (414) 786-9438.

Sincerely,

FIGURE 14.5 Thank-you letter following an interview

or phrase each to jog the memory, but they are not suitable for a long, technical talk. *Topical outlines* are separate cards or script sheets in outline form, complete with elapsed time at each major heading to help the speaker locate the place in the talk and keep track of time. *Scripting* is the complete text of the talk and is essential for long talks with critical timing. Scripting offers the speaker security but hinders spontaneity and eye contact. It is a good idea to number the pages of notes, to type the notes in large type or triple-space, and to practice the talk to verify time.

When you prepare the content, it is better to narrow the subject than to cover a large area vaguely. Titles help structure the content and purpose of the talk. The first draft narrows the subject to three or four main points, points supported with concrete examples and anecdotes. The talk may also need visuals to *supplement* the subject, but the visuals should be simple and limited in *variety* and *number* unless, of course, the presentation is primarily visual. *Rehearse* the talk out loud to check the logical flow of the content as well as the timing and the delivery.

Use a style that *complements* your personality, and dress in clothing that allows ease of motion without distracting the listener. Nonverbal communication such as *eye contact* and *body movement* are as important as the words. Too motionless a stance is *mesmerizing,* but too much movement is distracting. *Grand rhetorical gestures* are outdated, but eye contact with *members* of the audience is essential. Use a sound system only if the people cannot hear you without it.

The physical environment plays a large role in the presentation. Plan the room *arrangement* to control the formality of the presentation, provide the program organizer with a list of needed equipment, and create a checklist to help you remember your visual aids—all before the day of the presentation.

Like the oral presentation, the interview is also a dynamic, interactive process. The *interview for information* is the last step in the process after examining written material. After having all available information on the subject, organize the questions and schedule the interview, then ask the questions one at a time. The *job interview* begins with knowing something about the company before going to the interview. Prepare to answer and ask questions by doing research on the company and knowing your strengths and weaknesses. After the job interview, do a personal critique to improve future interviews, and drop a brief thank-you note to your interviewer.

Checklist for Oral Presentations and Interviews

Check only those items you have considered for your presentation or interview.

Yes   **BEFORE DELIVERING THE PRESENTATION,**
_____   1. Did you consider the size of the group?

_____   their reason for attending?

_____   their experience with the subject?

_____   their general level to pitch the talk slightly above it?

_____   their prejudices regarding the subject?

_____   2. Are you covering the appropriate amount of material for the time slot?

_____   with a descriptive title?

_____   with three or four main points?

_____   with concrete examples, anecdotes, case histories?

_____   with visuals that are appropriate both in number and simplicity?

_____   3. Have you timed your talk or arranged your presentation to fit your time slot?

_____   using a script (the complete text of your talk) for complex talks with critical timing (for broadcasts)?

_____   using a topical outline on separate cards or script sheets for technical talks with tight timing (to accommodate other presentations)?

_____   using cue cards with no more than a word or phrase for short, general talks?

_____   4. Did you number your pages/cards and type your outline/script in triple-space or large type?

_____   with marked-up pauses and eye contact?

_____   with comments about where to use visual aids?

            5. Is your delivery
_____   dramatic, opening with a question or anecdote?

_____   direct, with short sentences, active voice, vivid verbs?

_____   repetitive, so that listeners remember your main points?

_____ audience-directed, humanizing statistics and establishing rapport by sharing problems and solutions?

_____ loud and clear, so that listeners are not twisting in their seats?

6. Are you comfortable with
_____ your clothes?

_____ your persona?

_____ your body movement?

_____ your eye contact?

7. In advance of your talk, have you prepared for
_____ microphone (to be used only if necessary for the audience)?

_____ water?

_____ podium, chalk, marking pens?

_____ visual equipment, such as flipcharts, projectors, computers?

_____ assistant to run equipment, if necessary?

_____ arrangement of room for type of presentation (round table and so on)?

_____ materials such as handouts, reprints, transparencies, slides, biography for introduction?

_____ friend in audience to begin question-and-answer period with a prepared question?

Yes **BEFORE INTERVIEWING FOR INFORMATION,**
_____ 1. Did you examine available written sources first, such as reference manuals, notes?

_____ 2. Have you organized your remaining questions, planning

_____ to ask the questions one at a time?

_____ to verify the answers one at a time?

BEFORE INTERVIEWING FOR A JOB,
1. Did you do your homework by
_____ checking the company's references?

_____   looking at an organizational chart to locate your job position?

_____   reading an annual report for future plans, products, projects?

    2. Are you prepared to

_____   answer questions about yourself, your objectives, your contributions to the company, your general salary requirements?

_____   admit to not knowing the answer to a question?

_____   listen to descriptions of the job, the other employees, the company?

_____   ask questions about the previous incumbent in the job, the organization, the problems?

AFTER INTERVIEWING, DID YOU

_____   1. critique the interview, question by question?

_____   2. drop a simple, appreciative note to your interviewer?

Notes

1. Professor Robert Irving, Humanities Department, Illinois Institute of Technology, provided his class notes for English 427—Verbal and Visual Communication as background material for this module.
2. Eleanor Foa Dienstag, "The Fine Art of Speaking in Public," *Working Woman* (February 1986): 78–80 and 106. This excellent article provided material for both the content and delivery sections of this module. Used with permission.
3. E. F. Dienstag, "The Fine Art of Speaking in Public." These hints summarize the advice in Dienstag's article. Used with permission.
4. Jan Petty, manager, U.S. Operations for Training in Writing, Ltd.
5. John Stoltenberg, "How to Use a Microphone Well," *Working Woman* (February 1986): 79.
6. Gini Johnson, Audio Visual Division/3M, St. Paul, Minn., provided this information in a letter to the editors, *Working Woman* (January 1986).
7. Christine Browning, *Guide to Effective Software Technical Writing* (Englewood Cliffs, N.J.: Prentice-Hall, 1984): 28–30. Used with permission.
8. Costello, Erdlen & Co., Inc., *Job Hunting Guide*, 1982. This guide provided the advice in this module on interviewing for a job. Used with permission.
9. Costello, Erdlen & Co., Inc., *Job Hunting Guide*. These hints summarize the advice on interviewing for a job. Used with permission.

References

David I.. Carson and Craig Harkins, "A Technical Communication Course in Graphics and Audiovisuals," *The Technical Writing Teacher* 7 (1980): 56–59.

C. C. Dennison, in *Proceedings,* 33d International Technical Communication Conference (Washington, D.C.: Society for Technical Communication, May 1986): 381–386.

M. W. Holcombe and J. K. Stein, *Presentations for Decision Makers* (Belmont, Calif.: Lifelong Learning Publications, 1983).

L. Levine, "Interviewing for the Information," *Technical Writing and Communication* 14:1 (1984): 55–57.

E. E. McDowell and B. A. Mrozla, in *Proceedings,* 33d International Technical Communication Conference (Washington, D.C.: Society for Technical Communication, May 1986):285–288.

Applying Your Knowledge

EXERCISE 14.1

Prepare the cue cards and one visual aid for the proposal you wrote for Module 8. Include the background of the problem, your proposal, and your procedures. Then make your presentation to your class audience. If you end your presentation with "Are there any questions?" prepare to answer questions about the cost of the project, the time it will take, and your qualifications to accomplish the project.

EXERCISE 14.2

Scenario: An inventor/creator in your company has just
   designed or redesigned a product *or*
   formulated an innovative strategy *or*
   written an instructional or informational document *or*
   conducted a successful experiment.
You are the marketing writer who has to sell the product or the idea that the creator/inventor produced. You decide to interview the creator to learn more about the product.

The class participates in the interview as both audience and brainstorming group. Before the interview, the creator/inventor steps outside. You as the interviewer and the class brainstorm some questions and agree on a number of questions that time will permit. Then you conduct the interview while the class audience takes notes.

After the interview, the entire group establishes standards to evaluate the interview.

EXERCISE 14.3

CASE: Freddy Snow has not taken a communication class and is apprehensive about an upcoming job interview. He has asked you to help him, and you have devised a plan to help him prepare for the interview. Provide Freddy with a written copy of your plan.

EXERCISE 14.4 ===

If you have written a final technical report for your technical writing class, in a group discussion prepare to discuss the subject of your document. As an expert on the subject, how will you deliver your talk?

How do you characterize your audience?
What is the title of your presentation?
How long is your talk?
What are your three or four main points?
Are you using cue cards or an outline?
What equipment, materials, room arrangements, visuals will you need?
What else will you consider

- *before you speak?*
- *during your presentation?*
- *after your presentation?*

APPENDIXES

Style Manual

APPENDIX A

Documentation and Citations

In general, you will have to cite sources in one or two sections at the end of your document, sections entitled

- Bibliography
- Notes

Bibliography

The bibliography is the list of references you used to prepare your document whether or not these references are cited within your text. The list is arranged in one of three ways; the first is the most common:

1. Alphabetically, by author's **last name** or by the first letter of the title if there is no author (excluding **A, An** or **The**).
2. Chronologically, with the date preceding the author's name.
3. By categories or order of importance.

   Each entry follows a bibliographic form that is designed for clarity and economy. Bibliographic forms differ depending on the subject and the style guide of the publication. The two bibliographic forms presented here, one for the arts and the other for the sciences, follow *The Chicago Manual of Style,* 13th edition. *The Chicago Manual* advises the use of Arabic, not Roman, numbers for volume numbers, a minimal use of punctuation, and the use of periods after each main entry:

author's name
title
publication date

Before you prepare your bibliography, you should examine the citation style of the publisher, paying particular attention to punctuation and capitalization because the forms can differ.

Most bibliographic forms will include a list of the following facts:

For a Book
1. Name of author (last name first), editor, or institution responsible for writing book.
2. Full title of book, including subtitle (sometimes omitted).
3. Title of series, and number in series.
4. Volume number or total number of volumes.
5. Edition, if not the original.
6. City of publication.
7. Publisher's name (sometimes omitted).
8. Date of publication.

For an Article
1. Name of Author (last name first).
2. Title of the article.
3. Name of periodical.
4. Volume number (sometimes issue number).
5. Date.
6. Pages.

The bibliographic forms are illustrated for various sources:

Books	**A** (Form favored by the arts, literature, history)	**B** (Form favored by the natural and social sciences)
One author		
	Ginzberg, Eli. *Life Styles of Educated Women.* New York: Columbia University Press, 1966.	
		Hebb, D. O. 1949. *The organization of*

behavior. New
York: Wiley.

Two or more authors

Lundberg, Ferdinand,
and Farnham,
Marynia. *Modern
Woman: The Lost
Sex.* New York:
Harper Brothers,
1947.

Meadows, D., Mead-
ows, D. L., Ran-
ders, J., and Beh-
rens, W. 1972. *The
limits to growth.*
New York: Uni-
verse Books.

Subsequent reference
(When more than one
work by the same
author is cited, give
a short title in addi-
tion to the author's
last name.)

Lundberg and Farn-
ham, *Modern
Woman,* 108.

Meadows et al., *The
limits to growth.*
273.

Editor

Borko, Harold, ed.
*Automated Lan-
guage Processing:
The State of the Art.*
New York: Wiley,
1967.

Harlow, H. F., and
C. N. Woolsey, eds.
1958. *Biological
and biochemical
bases of behavior.*
Madison: Univer-
sity of Wisconsin
Press.

Books

	A	B
	(Form favored by the arts, literature, history)	(Form favored by the natural and social sciences)

Organization

A: American Telephone and Telegraph Company. *Engineering Economy.* 2d ed. New York, 1963.

B: American National Standards Institute. 1970. *Vocabulary for information processing.* New York: ANSI.

Volume

A: Byrne, Muriel St. Clare, ed. *The Lisle Letters.* 6 vols. Chicago: University of Chicago Press, 1981.

B: Bigelow, R. P. 1972. *Computer law service.* 12 vols. Wilmette, Ill.: Callaghan & Co.

Edition

A: Thuesen, H. G., Fabrycky, W. J., and Thuesen, G. J. *Engineering Economy.* 4th ed. Englewood Cliffs, N.J.: Prentice-Hall, 1971.

B: Date, C. J. 1981. *An Introduction to database systems.* 3d ed. The systems programming series. Reading, Mass. Addison-Wesley.

Chapters or parts of a
 book

> Hayes, J. R., and
> Flower, L. "Uncov-
> ering Cognitive
> Proccsses in Writ-
> ing: An Introduc-
> tion to Protocol
> Analysis." In *Cogni-*
> *tive Processes in*
> *Writing,* edited by
> L. Gregg and E. R.
> Steinberg. Hills-
> dale, N.J.: Law-
> rence Erlbaum,
> 1983.

> > Knuth, D. E., and
> > Pardo, L.T. 1980.
> > The early develop-
> > ment of program-
> > ming languages. In
> > *The history of com-*
> > *puting in the twen-*
> > *tieth century.* ed.
> > Metropolis, N. et al.
> > New York: Aca-
> > demic Press.

Microform

> U.S. Congress. House of Representatives. *Hear-*
> *ings and Reports of the House Committee on*
> *Un-American Activities, 1945–54.* Washington,
> D.C.: Brookhaven Press, 1977. Microfilm.

Journal Articles	**A**	**B**
	(Form favored by the arts, literature, history)	(Form favored by the natural and social sciences)

Authors—same as for
 book authors; See
 the following exam-
 ples:

> Applewhite, Lottie B.
> "The Author's Edi-
> tor." *Medical Com-*
> *munication* 1
> (1973): 16–19.

Journal Articles

	A	B
	(Form favored by the arts, literature, history)	(Form favored by the natural and social sciences)

Catano, J. 1979. Poetry and computers: Experimenting with the communal text. *Computers and the Humanities* 13:269–75.

Fred, H. L., and Robie, Patricia. "Dizzy Medical Writing." *Southern Medical Journal* 77 (1983): 1165–66.

Embley, D. W., and Nagy, G. 1984. Behavioral aspects of text editors. *Computing Surveys* 13:1 (March): 33–70.

Jordan, Michael P. "If Not And Or But: Conjunctions in Sentential and Deductive Logic." *Journal of Technical Writing and Communication* 5:1 (1975): 25–26.

Ossanna J. F., and Saltzer, J. H. 1970. Technical and human engineering problems connecting terminals to a time-sharing system. *American Federation of Information Processing Societies (AFIPS) Conference Proceedings* 35:355–62.

Jong, Steven F. "Documenting the New Computers." *Proceedings of the 31st International Technical Communication Conference* (1984): RET 45–47.

Sonnenblick, E. H. 1962. *Amer. J. Physiol.* 202:931–39.

Popular magazines

Cosmopolitan Love Guide. New York: Cosmopolitan Magazine, 1972.

Prufar, Olaf. 1964. The Hopewell Cult. *Scientific American,* Dec. 90–102.

Unpublished Material

Doheny-Farina, Stephen. "Writing in an Emergent Business Organization: An Ethnographic Study." Ph.D. diss. Rensselaer Polytechnic Institute, 1984.

Feinberg, B. N. 1969. A simple model of pulmonary mechanical dynamics and its use as a diagnostic aid for obstructive pulmonary lung disease. Ph.D. diss. School of Engineering, Case Western Reserve University, Cleveland.

Journal Articles	**A**	**B**
	(Form favored by the arts, literature, history)	(Form favored by the natural and social sciences)
Public Documents		
	National Academy of Sciences. 1968. *The Mathematical Sciences: A Report.* Publication 1681. Washington, D.C.	
		DISPAC. House Science and Technology Subcommittee on Domestic and International Science Planning, Analysis and Cooperation. 1975. *Hearings on Computers and the Learning Society.* Washington: GPO.

Computer Programs
Statistical Package for the Social Sciences Level M Ver.8.1 (SPSS Lev. M 8.1). Chicago: SPSS.

Interviews
Irving, Dr. Robert A. Interview with author. Chicago, 15 May 1987.

Personal Communications
Katz, Sumner P. Telephone conversation with author. 30 August 1987.

Notes

If you have quoted directly, used data or illustrations, or paraphrased sources within your text, you will have to document these sources in one of three ways:

- author—date system
- endnotes
- footnotes

This appendix will illustrate only the first two methods because, even with a computer, footnotes are a time-consuming luxury.

Author–date system

In this system, the author's last name and the date of publication are placed in parentheses within the text and near the reference, just before a mark of punctuation, if possible (Ginsberg 1966, 121). The page number is optional. The full reference to the source appears in alphabetical order in the bibliography.

Endnotes

With endnotes the references are numbered consecutively throughout the text, and the numbers are placed in parentheses at the end of the referenced sentence following punctuation marks. (1) The full reference to the source appears at the end of your document, after the appendix and before the bibliography, in a section entitled **Notes.** The general rules for citing references in notes are the same as for bibliographic entries, with three major exceptions:

- The author's first name precedes the last name.
- Punctuation between author's name, title of the work, and facts of publication consists of commas and parentheses.
- The note carries a specific page number.

Notes for Books	A (Form favored by the arts, literature, history)	B (Form favored by the natural and social sciences)
One author	2. Eli Ginzberg, *Life Styles of Educated Women* (New York: Columbia University Press, 1966), 113–15.	
Two or more authors	3. Ferdinand Lundberg and Marynia Farnham, *Modern Woman: The Lost Sex* (New York: Harper Brothers, 1947), 205–6	7. D. Meadows et al., *The limits to growth* (New York: Universe Books, 1972), 529–31.

Notes for Books   **A**   **B**
                                        (Form favored by the   (Form favored by the
                                            arts, literature,   natural and social
                                              history)   sciences)

Subsequent reference
(When citing more than one work by the same author, give a short title in
addition to the author's last name.)

                                          9. Lundberg and
                                                Farnham, *Modern
                                                Woman,* 210.

(When the source has more than three authors, use **et al.**

                                                                          8. Meadows et al.,
                                                                                *The limits to
                                                                                growth,* 273.

Editor

                                        10. Harold Barko,
                                                ed., *Automated
                                                Language Process-
                                                ing: The State of
                                                the Art* (New
                                                York: Wiley,
                                                1967), 421.

Organization

                                        11. American Tele-
                                                phone and Tele-
                                                graph Company,
                                                *Engineering Econ-
                                                omy,* 2d ed. (New
                                                York, 1963), 105.

Volume

                                                                        17. R. P. Bigelow,
                                                                                *Computer law
                                                                                service* (Wilmette,
                                                                                IL: Callaghan &
                                                                                Co., 1972), 12:
                                                                                111–313.

Edition

                                        20. H. G. Thuesen,
                                                W. J. Fabrycky,
                                                and G. J. Thue-
                                                sen, *Engineering
                                                Economy.* 4th ed.
                                                (Englewood Cliffs,
                                                N.J.: Prentice-
                                                Hall, 1971),
                                                206–10.

Chapters or parts of a
book

              12. J. R. Hayes and
                  L. Flower, "Un-
                  covering Cogni-
                  tive Processcs in
                  Writing: An
                  Introduction to
                  Protocol Analy-
                  sis," in ***Cognitive***
                  Processes in Writ-
                  ing, ed. L. Gregg
                  and E. R. Stein-
                  berg (Hillsdale,
                  N.J.: Lawrence
                  Erlbaum, 1983),
                  351–62.

**Notes for Journal
Articles**
Authors—same as for book authors;
See the following examples:

              1. Lottie B. Apple-
                white, "The Au-
                thor's Editor,"
                Medical Communi-
                cation 1 (1973):
                16–19.

                                5. D. W. Embley and
                                  G. Nagy, "Behav-
                                ioral Aspects of
                                Text Editors,"
                                Computing Surveys
                                13:1 (March 1975):
                                33–70.

**Notes for
Unpublished Material**

              4. Stephen Doheny-
                Farina, "Writing
                in an Emergent
                Business
                Organization: An
                Ethnographic
                Study." (Ph.D
                diss. Rensselaer

Notes for Unpublished Material	**A** (Form favored by the arts, literature, history)	**B** (Form favored by the natural and social sciences)
	Polytechnic Institute, 1984), 102–4.	
Notes for Public Documents		6. House Science and Technology Subcommittee on Domestic and International Science Planning, Analysis and Cooperation, *Hearings on Computers and the Learning Society,* DISPAC (Washington, D.C.: GPO, 1975), 134.
Notes for Interviews and Personal Communications		17. Dr. Robert A. Irving, interview with author. Chicago, 15 May 1987.

Practice in Documentation

Using the following Checklist for Documentation and Citations, select three sources in your field and complete the checklist. You will have to examine the method for citing sources within the text and the sections on bibliography and notes.

- Select a book, an edited book, and a professional journal in your field.
- In the checklist, write a bibliographic entry and a note entry (if appropriate) *in the documentation style* of the book, edited book, and professional journal.

Checklist for Documentation and Citations

Source	Bibliography	Notes	Method for Citing Source Within Text
Book with single author or multiple authors			
Edited book			
Include an entry for a book with several volumes			
Include an entry for a book in its latest edition			
Include an entry for a book produced by an organization (without an author's name)			
professional journal article with volume and issue number			

APPENDIX B

Grammar

Grammar is the study of the way the language is used. In the English language the verb is the most important part of the language structure because it is the action word of the sentence. The subject and verb of the sentence must always be in agreement both in person and in number. When the subject and verb do not agree, the sentence has a grammatical error. Another common grammatical error occurs when a modifier is misplaced within a sentence. This section of the appendix explains agreement and modifiers.

Agreement

Make the Subject and Verb Agree

The subject must agree with the verb: A singular subject takes a singular verb; a plural subject takes a plural verb.

Example

A **manual** *provides* clear, comprehensive sections that include explanations and instructions.

Job aids *provide* a clear, brief set of instructions.

When the subject is a person, then the verb must agree with the person and follow the same rule: a singular subject takes a singular verb, and a plural subject takes a plural verb.

Example

Singular subject	**Plural subject**
I am awake.	We don't know.
You are awake.	Are you working?
It is working.	What do they want?

When two singular subjects are joined by **and,** the number of subjects is plural, and the verb must be plural.

Example
The director and his staff *are* in conference.

Determine the Number of the Subject

Sometimes determining the number of the subject is difficult. The following guidelines will help you determine the number of the subject:

1. The number of the subject is not changed by a phrase between it and the verb.

   Example
   The **assistance** of three attorneys, two economists, and a scientist *was* not necessary to prepare the case.

   The **secretary,** together with her assistant secretaries, *is* expected shortly.

2. Even though two single subjects are connected by **and,** they may present a single idea and require a singular verb.

   Example
   Bread and jam *is* the child's favorite food.
   Ham and eggs *was* a popular breakfast before the study on cholesterol.
   Playing the piano **and singing** *is* popular with the Gilbert and Sullivan crew.
   A large **home and** a sizable bank **account** *is* the professional's aim.
   Hawkins and Thurston *is* a law firm.

3. When two or more subjects are connected by **or, either . . . or, neither . . . nor,** the verb agrees with the nearest subject.

   Example
   Neither the pacemaker nor the leads were implanted properly.
   Either the leads or the pacemaker was implanted improperly.

4. Words stating time, money, fractions, weight, and amount are usually considered singular and take a singular verb.

   Example
   Twenty **minutes** *is* not long enough for the test.
   Fifty **cents** *buys* a fruit drink.
   Two-**thirds** of three *is* two.
   Three **tons** *is* too much gravel.
   Five **yards** *is* enough cloth.

BUT *data* and *statistics* *are* still considered plural and take plural verbs.
The **data** *require* confirmation by an external agency.
Are the **statistics** valid and reliable?

5. Don't be fooled by sentences beginning with **there, here, where.** These words are not the subjects of sentences. Determine the correct subject, and select a verb to agree with it.

Example
There *are* three **courses** of action we can take.
Here *are* the defective **leads and pacemaker.**
Where *are* the defective **pacemaker and leads?**

6. The English language has special situations.
   - The phrase **the number** is singular; **a number** is plural.

   Example
   The number of exceptions to the rule *is* astonishing.
   A number of exceptions to the rule *were* illogical.

   - The words **every** and **many a** before a word or a series of words take a singular verb.

   Example
   Every man, woman, and child *was* asked to follow the same instructions.
   Many an engineer *has* contributed significantly to the progress of medicine.

   - Book titles, plays, and works of art express a single idea and are singular.

   Example
   The Chicago Manual of Style is a handy reference book.
   Henry Moore's "Family Group" illustrates the nuclear family.

Recognize Indefinite Pronouns

Indefinite pronouns do not stand for a specific person, place, thing, or idea. Some indefinite pronouns take a singular verb; others, a plural verb; and still a third category takes singular or plural verbs depending on the antecedent.

Example

Category 1 (singular verb)	Category 2 (plural verb)	Category 3 (verb depends on antecedent)
each	several	some
someone	few	any
either	both	none
neither	many	all
somebody		most
nobody		
everybody		
anyone		
nothing		

Each of the manuals *has*
a troubleshooting
section.

Few of the manuals
have a glossary.

Some of the **work** *was*
done.
Some of the **jobs** *have*
been done.
(The number of the
noun in the
prepositional
phrase controls the
verb.)

Identify Collective Nouns

Collective nouns take a singular or plural verb depending on whether the noun refers to the group as a whole or to each member as an individual.

Example
A trio of boys *was* scheduled to sing.
Our soccer team *is* popular.

Our group of dancers *were* fitted by the seamstresses.
The crowd *were* fighting for their lives.

PRACTICE IN AGREEMENT

Select the appropriate verb to agree with the subject.

1. Every planet, including the Earth, (revolves, revolve) around the sun.
2. The cost of his explorations (was, were) paid by scientists.
3. One-third of the boats (was equipped, were equipped).
4. The number of accidents (is, are) great.
5. The data on air pollution (receives, receive) media attention every year.
6. Fifteen minutes (is, are) enough time to make a decision.
7. Every one of her daughters (have, has) gone to college.
8. Both the funds appropriated by the legislature and the income from the sales tax (was exhausted, were exhausted).
9. Macaroni and cheese (is, are) the cafeteria special on Friday.
10. *Mortal Lessons* (is, are) worth reading.
11. The vessel, with its entire crew and cargo, (was lost, were lost).
12. The village as well as the association (provides, provide) services.
13. Either one or two more examples (is, are) needed.
14. The men or Russ (needs, need) those data.
15. A box of screws (is, are) on the table.
16. There (is, are) a group ready to enter now.
17. Here (comes, come) the president and his advisers now.
18. Neither Cathy nor Regina (wants, want) (her, their) office moved now.
19. The monkey or the mice (arrives, arrive) today for the testing.
20. Nancy or I (is, am) responsible for the laboratory experiments.
21. A number of men (was hurt, were hurt).

22. The new model, as well as several older models, (is included, are included) in the sale.
23. The purpose of such fantastic claims (is, are) to create panic among investors.
24. Three quarts of antifreeze (is, are) not enough.
25. The slum districts of any large city (breeds, breed) crime and disease.

Modifiers

Modifiers are words, phrases, or clauses that elaborate on words in the sentence. Frequently, modifiers are incorrectly placed in a sentence and modify the wrong words. This guide recognizes three problems with modifiers:

1. *Squinting modifiers*. A squinting modifier is a word that could modify more than one of the words in the sentence.

   Example
   Incorrect
   The physician told him frequently to exercise.

   Should the patient exercise frequently? *or*
   Did the physician frequently mention exercise?

   Correct
   The physician told him to exercise frequently.
   The physician frequently told him to exercise.

2. *Misplaced Modifier*. A misplaced modifier is a word, phrase, or clause that is placed next to the wrong word in the sentence.

   Example
   Incorrect
   No security regulations shall be distributed to personnel who are out-of-date.

   Correct
   No security regulations that are out-of-date shall be issued to personnel.

3. *Dangling Modifier*. A dangling modifier is a phrase that cannot refer logically to the subject of the main clause.

   Example
   Incorrect
   To apply for a job, a Form 57 must be completed.

   (A form cannot apply for a job.)

   Correct
   To apply for a job, the applicant must complete Form 57.
   or
   When the applicant applied for a job, he (or she) must complete Form 57.

   Incorrect
   Rushing to meet the deadline for the project, many errors were made.

   (Errors can't rush to meet a deadline.)

Correct
Rushing to meet the deadline for the project, we made many errors.

or

When we rushed to meet the deadline for the project, errors were made.

PRACTICE IN MODIFIERS

Correct the problems with modifiers in the following sentences.

1. Following the supervisor's instructions, the work was soon finished.
2. After sitting in the outer office for an hour, the interviewer arrived.
3. To get the most out of the course, a definite time should be set aside.
4. I talked to the agent who is sitting at the desk without a coat.
5. The boss asked for a report of the number of computers in the offices that are over a month old.
6. When boiled for hours, four people can feast on the corned beef.
7. He said today that the game would be played.
8. Automobiles will not be auctioned to the participants unless they are dented first.

APPENDIX C

Punctuation

In general, punctuation marks make documents easier to read. But good sentences usually need few punctuation marks. This section summarizes information on punctuation from the *U.S. Government Printing Office Style Manual, 1984.*

Apostrophe

Use the apostrophe:

- To indicate contractions or omitted letters.

    I've   It's   TV'ers

- To indicate the coined plurals of letters, figures, and symbols.

    three *R*'s   5's and 7's   +'s

- To show possession.
  —with nouns already ending with an *s* sound, just add an apostrophe.

    Mars'   Schmitz'   hostess'   Jones'   officer's

—with nouns not ending with an *s* sound.

> Co.'s   officer's

—with compound nouns, add the apostrophe or *'s* to the last noun.

> brother-in-law's   secretary-treasurer's

—with nouns in a series to show joint possession, add the apostrophe or *'s* to the last noun.

> soldiers and sailor's home

—with nouns in a series to show separate possession, add the apostrophe or *'s* to each noun

> John's, Thomas', and Susan's ratings

—with indefinite pronouns, add the apostrophe or *'s* to the last component of the pronoun

> someone's desk   somebody else's books   others' homes

Do not use the apostrophe:

- To form the possessive of personal pronouns.

> hers   theirs   ours

- To form the plural of spelled-out numbers or words already containing an apostrophe. Do add *'s* if it makes the plural easier to read.

> twos and threes   do's and don'ts   ifs, ands, and buts   which's and that's

- To follow names of countries and other organized bodies ending in *s*.

> United States control   United Nations meeting   merchants exchange

Brackets

Use brackets in pairs:

- To enclose a correction.

> The documents contained 29 [27] errors.

- To supply something omitted.

> Ms. Clarke walked [around] the lake.

- To explain or identify.

> The regional director [Roberts] spoke briefly.

- To instruct or add comment.

> The computer responds with NAME> [type your name].

- To enclose **sic** when it is used to show that an error has been recognized but not changed.

  The journal technical communication [sic] should appear in caps.

Use a single bracket:

- At the beginning of each paragraph when several paragraphs must be bracketed, but only at the close of the last paragraph.

Colon

Use the colon:

- To separate an introductory statement from descriptive material that follows.

  The competition has three divisions: technical art, technical publications, and interactive software.

  Enter your data; save your data; back up your disks: These commands are crucial when using the computer.

- To introduce formal statements, questions, or quotations.

  The company stated its policy thus: When in doubt about your reader, it is better to repeat information than hope the reader remembers it.

  The following question came up for discussion: Does the computer contribute to breach of privacy?

  She said: [If the quotation is only one sentence, use a comma instead of a colon.]

- To follow a formal salutation.

  Dear Dr. Plarha: Colleagues: To whom it may concern:

- To separate the hours and minutes.

  12:15 A.M.   8:00 P.M.   11:30 A.M.

- To separate parts of citations [leave a space after the colon].

  Journal of Education 3: 342–359   Ecclesiastes 12: 9

- To indicate proportion [use double colon as a ratio sign].

  1:2::3:6   [read one is to two as three is to six].

Comma

Use the comma:

- To set off words, phrases, or clauses.
  —that introduce, break, or follow a short direct quote. The comma is not

needed if a question mark or an exclamation point is part of the quoted matter.

> I said, "Don't you understand the question?"
> "I understand it," he replied, "but I disagree with the answer."
> "Why?" she queried.
> "It's unproved!" he exclaimed.

—that are parenthetical and thus not essential to the sentence.

> The atom bomb, developed by the Manhattan Project, was first used in World War II.
>
> The situation in the Middle East, we now know, is always explosive.
>
> *But* The person who started the fire is an arsonist. (The clause "who started the fire" is essential information and is not set off by commas).

—that are in apposition or in contrast.

> Ms. Kay, the prosecutor, asked for a delay. The motion was denied, not sustained.

—that directly address a person or persons.

> Jury, the court is in session.

- To separate.
—words, written figures, or numbers that create misunderstanding or misreading.

> Instead of hundreds, thousands came.   Out of 99, 9 are acceptable.
> To Henry, Smith was helpful.   If it's that, that is absurd.

—a series of modifiers.

> The document is organized, readable, and practical. But he is a clever young man. (No comma when the final modifier is considered part of the noun modified.)

—introductory phrase from the subject it modifies.

> Beset by problems, the engineers canceled the launch.

—titles, organizations, academic degrees, and names of states preceded by names of cities.

> Henry Smith, Jr., chairperson   Smith, Henry, Sr.   chief, Insurance Branch
> Howard Strauss, Ph.D.   Washington, D.C., schools

—clauses of a compound sentence joined by a simple conjunction such as *and, but, or, nor, for.*

> You can enter information, but you will need a security clearance.

—numbers of four or more digits.

> 5,500   4,000,000 $25,491.00

—year following day of the month.

> The reported dates of January 4, 19XX, to December 24, 19XX, were incorrect.

- To indicate the omission of an understood word or words.

> At first the system worked well; then, erratically.

- To follow a series of three or more words, when the last two are joined by *and, or,* or *nor.*

> by the foot, by the yard, or by the bolt   by ones, tens, or hundreds   neither rain, snow, nor heat of day

Do not use the comma:

- To separate the month and year in a date.

> Production for July 19XX   On 7 August 19XX DOD investigated the site. (Military date)

- To separate numbers in fractions, decimals, page numbers, serial numbers (except patent numbers), telephone numbers, and street addresses.

> 1/2500   Motor No. 437028
> 2.90877   303/967-5604
> page 1087   4077 Russell Lane
> 1100 meters   1450 kilocycles (for radio, use comma if more than four
>   digits)

- To precede an ampersand (&) or a dash.

> Smith, Lynch & Barney (except in indexes: Lynch, M.L., & Co.)

> There are other factors—time, cost, and color—but quality is the most important.

- To separate the name and the number of an organization.

> Retail Clerks Union No. 748

Dash

Use the dash (two hyphens and no spaces):

- To mark a sudden break or abrupt change in thought.

> If the bill passes—which I doubt—all contracts will be canceled.

- To indicate an interruption or unfinished word or sentence.

> Did you stop in the mid—?

- To clarify a meaning when the comma or parentheses won't serve.

> Waste deposits—chemicals, paint, fuel—will have to be buried.

- To introduce a final clause that summarizes a series (instead of using a colon).

    To enter, to save, to back up—these are the crucial functions in computing.

- To precede a credit line or signature.

    And gladly would he teach, and gladly learn.
                                                —Chaucer

    At this point in time.—A. Politician

Exclamation Point

Use the exclamation point to mark surprise, appeal, admiration, or other strong emotion.

    "Let her rip!" he shouted.
    Three, two, one. Lift off!
    Who shouted, "Next!" (question mark omitted)

Hyphen

The current trend is to use the hyphen sparingly.
    Use the hyphen:

- To connect the elements of certain compound words (see also Compound Words).

    pre-Civil War   ex-president   user-defined   8-hour shift   single-letter code

- To divide a word at the end of a line.
- To emphasize the letters of a word.

    Win M-O-N-E-Y

Parentheses

Use Parentheses:

- To set off information not part of the main sentence but important enough to be included.

    The data (see Figure 2) support this theory.

- To enclose a parenthetic clause where the interruption is too great to be indicated by commas.
- To enclose an explanatory word that is not part of the statement.

    The Chicago (IL) Regional Office *but* the Regional Office of Chicago, IL.

- To enclose letters or numbers indicating items in a series (in a paragraph).

With this program you can (1) enter personnel data, (2) update data, (3) display data, (4) print data.

- To enclose a reference at the end of a sentence.

    The site is indicated on the map (Appendix).

    —If the reference is a complete sentence, place the period inside the parenthesis.

    The lever can be reset to the starting position. (See Figure 3.)

Use a single parenthesis:

- At the beginning of each paragraph when several paragraphs must be enclosed, but only at the close of the last paragraph.

Period

Use the period:

- To end declarative and imperative sentences.

    NASA will launch the missile on June 25, 19XX.
    Copy your disks before turning off the computer.

- To end an indirect question or a question requiring no answer.

    Tell me how the rocket will be launched.
    May we hear from you soon.

- To indicate omission within a sentence, use three periods with spaces between; at the end of a sentence, use four.

    He called . . . and left. . . . He returned the next day.

    —Use spaced periods on a separate line to indicate omission of paragraphs.
- To follow abbreviations unless by usage the period is omitted.

    U.S. DOE USDA NW. km. cm.

    —In abbreviations made up of single letters, use no space between the period and the following letter *except*: Use one space after the period following the initial in a proper name.

    A. J. Punkhauser

Question Mark

Use the question mark:

- To indicate a direct query, even if not in the form of a question.

    What did he do? He did what? Can the money be raised? is the question.
    Who asked, "Why?" (Use only one question mark inside the quotation marks.)

- To express more than one question in the same sentence.

  Can we do it? on time? within the budget?

- To express doubt.

  We said we can do it for $25.00 (?), including time and materials.

Quotation Marks

Use quotation marks:

- To enclose a direct quotation.

  "Have you received our order?" they wrote. The answer is "Yes." "In May 19XX," said Jody Poker, "we will ship the order."

- To enclose words following the terms *entitled, the word, the term, marked, endorsed, signed.*

  The report entitled "The Effects . . ." After the word "theory," insert a comma. Sign the transmittal letter "Sarah Wendell."

  —*Use quotation marks around expressions sparingly.* Do not use them to enclose expressions following the terms *known as, so-called,* and so on, unless the expressions are slang, coined, or used in an arbitrary way.

  the so-called investigating body

  —*and,* as a rule of thumb, avoid coining words and using slang expressions.

Limit quotation marks:

- Limit quotation marks to three sets (double, single, double).

  "The question is, 'Can we conduct a "bona fide" experiment?' "

Place comma and final period inside quotation marks:

  "The company," he said, "will ship the order today."

Place question mark and exclamation point inside ONLY if they are part of the quote.

  Is this the correct use of the word "Telex"? "Have you filed your return?" The programmer said, "No smoking!" Did the programmer say, "No smoking"?

Semicolon

Use the semicolon:

- To separate independent clauses or to join them by a conjunctive adverb such as *hence, thus, therefore, however, moreover,* and so on.

The order will be ready this afternoon; you may pick it up at 4:40.
You may not charge the purchase; however, we will accept a check.

- To separate two or more phrases or clauses with internal punctuation.

    When this screen appears, the cursor is positioned at NAME; type your last name, followed by a space; then type your first name, space, and middle initial.

- To separate statements that are closely related.

    I typed START; the computer responded with CONTINUE OR END?>
    To continue, press <ENTER>; to terminate, <ESC>.

- To precede explanatory or summary phrases or abbreviations such as *for example, namely, that is, i.e.*

    We plan to use a variety of aids; for example, slides, transparencies, flipcharts, films, handouts, and props.

    You can add more categories; i.e., library research and progress reports.

PRACTICE IN PUNCTUATION

Provide the punctuation for the following sentences.

1. Some engineers are objective critical analytical and thorough.
2. He knew that he was going to win the case therefore he was relaxed and happy.
3. The scientists waited for the results of the experiment but the data were unconvincing so they decided to wait until the next day.
4. We must be sure therefore that he understands the serious nature of the charges.
5. Exhausted from a long day of meetings he stuffed the report into his briefcase and he left for the airport.
6. Mr. Green our technical sales representative will arrive in time for your staff meeting.
7. Because the investigator was unfamiliar with the case he needed more time to assemble the statistics.
8. The solution to this fiscal problem will not be solved with this one plan nor can we expect to solve it unless everyone cooperates.

APPENDIX D

Compound Words

Compound words combine two or more words, with or without a hyphen, to convey a single idea.

<u>**Use a hyphen:**</u>

- To <u>form certain compound words.</u>

    —compound words expressing an idea that would not be clearly expressed in separate words

        right-of-way   mother-in-law   up-to-date   Johnny-come-lately

    —compound words that are improvised or used as verb forms.

        know-how   know-it-all   do-it-yourselfer   blue-pencil   cold-shoulder

- To <u>combine a capital letter with a word.</u>

        X-ray   Y-shaped   U-turn

- To <u>give compass directions consisting of three points</u>.

        north-northwest   *but* northwest (two points)

- To <u>combine compound adjectives that precede the word they modify</u>.

long-term loan	law-abiding citizen	well-kept farm
lump-sum payment	well-known politician	still-new car
twenty-first century	Spanish-American descent	well-designed keyboard
income-tax payer	Israeli-owned factory	solid-state circuit

- To relay the basic elements common to a series of words.

| 8-, 10-, and 16-foot boards | small-, middle-sized-, and giant companies |
| moss- and ivy-covered walls | first-, second-, and third-class tickets |

- To refer to compound numbers.
  —from twenty-one to ninety-nine and in compounds with a number for the first element.

| 7-hour day | 10-minute delay | 24-inch ruler |
| 3-week vacation | 90-cent transfer | 8-day cruise |

  —between fractions.

  three-fourths   two-fifths   two four-hundredths

- To avoid doubling a vowel or tripling a consonant and to join prefixes and suffixes.

  semi-independent   shell-like   anti-inflation

  —prefixes *all*, *ex*, *self*, *vice*, and *quasi* and suffix *-elect* take a hyphen.

  ex-governor   self-control   quasi-argument   president-elect

  —prefixes preceding a capital word.

  un-American   pro-British   post-World War II

  —prefixes that permit ambiguity.

  un-ionized   co-op   re-treat

Do not use the hyphen:

- To separate compound words.
  —when the initial word of the compound ends in *-ly*.

  eagerly awaited moment   newly formed company   wildly anticipated moment

  —where meaning is clear and readability is not aided.

| atomic energy power | child welfare plan | civil service examination |
| real estate tax | social security loan | special delivery mail |

  —where the words appear in regular order and the omission causes no confusion.

blood pressure	living costs	patent right	training course
afterglow	bookkeeping	footnote	newsprint
whitewash	praiseworthiness	airline	chairperson

—where the foreign phrase conveys a single idea.

>   per capita tax   ex officio member   per diem expenses   prima facie evidence

—where the letter or number is the second element of the compound words

>   Ward D patients   strontium 80 effects   point 4 program   item 3 factor

- To combine personal pronouns.
—combine as one word.

>   herself   oneself   itself   ourselves   yourselves

—also combine as one word **any, every, no,** and **some** with **body, thing,** and **where**

anybody	anywhere	everywhere	nowhere	something
anyone	everybody	nobody	somebody	
anything	everything	nothing	someone	

—combine as two words **some one** and **every one** when the combination refers to a particular person or thing.

—*always* separate **no one** and **any one thing**

APPENDIX E

Capitalization

Three rules govern the use of capitals: (1) Capitalize proper nouns, titles and first words; (2) do not capitalize common nouns, and (3) be consistent. If you capitalize a word for emphasis, consistently capitalize it throughout the document.

Nouns

Capitalize proper names.

Sara Owens   Owens family
Paris   Parisian
Italy   Italian
Federal Express
Versailles Treaty
British Commonwealth

Capitalize full names and shortened names of federal agencies, organizations, divisions, departments, and so on.

Do not capitalize names that have general meanings.

whitewashed
plaster of paris
italics
the express to New York
the treaty of 1919
a commonwealth of nations

Do not capitalize unless used as the name of the specific unit.

the Federal Government	a federal union a city government
88th Congress	a congress of citizens
Department of Energy	any of the government departments
the Census Bureau	taking a census
Justice Dept.	traffic court
U.S. Navy	naval shipyard
Div. of Grants	a division in the organization
Internatl. Security Council	an international assembly of people

Capitalize names of members of organized bodies.	**Do not capitalize when used to describe the general position.**
a Representative (Member of Congress)	a representative of the group
a Catholic	catholic interests
a Democrat	democratic form of government
Capitalize names of regions, geographic locations, and so on.	**Do not capitalize terms that suggest direction.**
the Province of Quebec	mining provinces of Quebec
the North the Midwest	Go north until . . . midwest region
Chicago's North Shore	the shore north of Chicago
Capitalize names of calendar terms, holidays, historic events, and periods of time.	**Do not capitalize seasons, the words year and century, the terms A.M. and P.M., or events and holidays unless used as the specific event.**
January Wednesday	spring fall autumn winter summer
Fourth of July	on July the fourth the 20th century
Battle of Bunker Hill	the battle fought at Bunker Hill
Feast of the Passover	a religious feast

Titles

Capitalize titles preceding proper names, used alone for preeminence, or following names (optional).	**Do not capitalize titles when the name follows the title or when a name is omitted.**
Queen Elizabeth	a queen of clubs
Ambassador Lodge	ambassador at large
Mr. President	the president of the club
Your Excellency	the executive's suite
John Long, Executive Director of the Foundation	John Long, executive director of the foundation
Capitalize all words in titles of publications and documents, including articles, prepositions, and conjunctions that begin or	**Do not capitalize the following words in the titles unless they begin or end the title or they follow a verb.**

**end titles; that are more than
three letters; or that follow verbs.**

Of Mice and Men   a, an, the, at, by, for,
Mastering DisplayWrite 3   in, of, on, to, up, and,
Planes Delayed By Gunmen   as, but, if, or, nor
Warsaw Pact   the pact signed at Warsaw

First Words

**Capitalize the first word of a
sentence, of a direct quote, of a
line of poetry, of a series, or a
statement after the colon.**

**Do not capitalize a brief remark
after the colon.**

The question is, Shall we have a closed
vote?
And Ahab said, "No!" in thunder.
They had the whole world before them
Where to choose
In summary: The candidate was elected:
24, for; 11, against.

We heard the admonishment: be brief.

Additional Capitalizations

**Capitalize races, ethnic groups, and
political parties.**

**Do not capitalize slang words for
races or the word party.**

Negro   Caucasian   Republican party

blacks   whites   Communist bloc

**Capitalize scientific names for
genus.**

Do not capitalize species.

Homo

sapiens

**Capitalize abbreviations when they
stand for capitalized words.**

J.D.   Ph.D.   M.D.

PRACTICE IN CAPITALS ═══════════════════════════

*In each of the following sentences, decide whether the underlined word or
words should be capitalized or not.*

1. Should the term <u>plaster of paris</u> be capitalized and <u>italicized</u>?
2. The <u>Mississippi river</u> runs between Illinois and Missouri. This portion of
   the <u>river</u> flows <u>east</u>.
3. The <u>delegates</u> were chosen from <u>counties</u> in the <u>pacific northwest</u>.
4. The fiscal year ends next <u>spring</u>.
5. He is from the <u>new england states</u>, but his accent sounds as if he is from
   the <u>midwest</u>.

6. He made a <u>Xerox</u> copy of the article on <u>lasers</u>, an article appearing recently in <u>scientific american magazine</u>.
7. How are they renovating the paintings done during the <u>renaissance</u>?
8. Ms. Vanick is a <u>member</u> of the U.S. <u>house of representatives</u>.
9. Have any <u>nations</u> signed the <u>nuclear test ban treaty</u>?
10. The Illinois <u>constitution</u> contains a <u>law</u> on cats that was called the <u>cat provision</u>.

In the following sentences, add or delete punctuation and capitalization as necessary.

1. The president supported further negotiations as was to be expected the nation watched critically.
2. He stated firmly and none of us dared argue the case is hopeless.
3. We will explain that this equipment is 1 state of the art 2 portable 3 compatible with other pc's 4 moderately priced
4. To buy or sell futures options you must know the meaning of put and get both terms are discussed in chapter 5.
5. The question is can a person who has not filed Tax Records for five years and is known locally as a hustler be seriously considered as a candidate?

APPENDIX F

Numbers

In general, you should spell out numbers at the beginning of a sentence and spell out numbers under 10. To express time, money, measurement, and numbers over 10, use figures for numbers.

Spell out numbers:

- Single numbers of less than 10 within a sentence.

    five times as large   four factors

- Numbers less than 100 preceding a unit modifier containing a figure.

    two 6-foot standards   twelve ¾-inch chips   250 ⅛-inch screws

- Round numbers and indefinite numbers.

    students in the eighties (or 1980's **but not** '80's)
    less than a thousand dollars
    fewer than twenty-five people

- Large numbers in legal work.

    One hundred and ninety-nine thousand and sixty

- Fractions standing alone or followed by **of a** or **of an.**

  one-half of a page **but** 1½ pages
  three-quarters of the committee

Use figures to express time, money, measurement, figures over 10 and the following:

- Numbers in a series when 1 of the numbers is 10 or over.

  We ordered 25 books, 12 notepads, and 9 documents in one week's time. (NOTE: *One week's time* is not part of the series.)

- Numbers expressing age and date.

  6 years old   March 3 to March 9, 19XX

- Numbers referring to documents.

  Appendix 2 (prefer Arabic to Roman numerals).
  page 6   Chapter 4   Article 1   Figure 7

- Decimals, percentages, proportion, market quotations, mathematical expressions.

  0.25 inch (If there is no unit before the decimal, add a zero except in market quotations.)
  15.5 percent or 15.5%
  1 to 5   1:5
  Dow-Jones was up by .07.   7¾-percent bonds
  factor of 4   divided by 2

PRACTICE IN NUMBERS

Decide whether to spell out or use numbers in the following sentences.

1. Fifty or sixty miles away is the Wisconsin border.
2. She will have to buy one hundred twenty two-cent stamps.
3. He chose sixteen-inch boards for the ceiling.
4. The market price of sixteen dollars ($16.00) is subject to change without notice.
5. Form 1045 lists 3 cannibalized refrigerators, 8 repaired ranges, and 18 renovated air conditioners.
6. The domestic price was five percent lower than the price of wheat on the floor of the Board of Trade.
7. In April your staff numbered 97, bringing the monthly average of staff members to 105.
8. The village board of trustees authorized the 8.5 million dollar construction of the hospital.

A P P E N D I X   G

Proofreading

Proofreading for errors is an important part of producing a completed document. When proofreading your own text, you might try reading from right to left to help you concentrate on each word. Familiarize yourself with the standard proofreading marks.

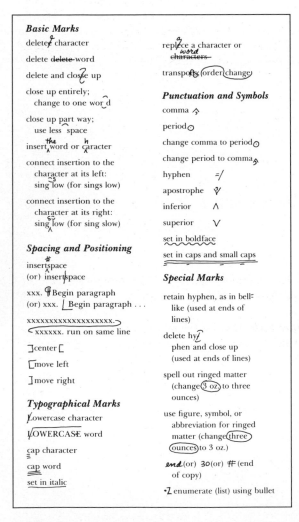

Basic Marks

delete a character

delete ~~delete~~ word

delete and close up

close up entirely;
   change to one wor‿d

close up part way;
   use less space

insert_the_ word or c_h_aracter

connect insertion to the
   character at its left:
   sing low (for sings low)

connect insertion to the
   character at its right:
   sing low (for sing slow)

Spacing and Positioning

insert space
(or) insert space

xxx. ¶ Begin paragraph
(or) xxx. ⌊ Begin paragraph . . .

xxxxxxxxxxxxxxxxxxx.
   xxxxxx. run on same line

] center [

[move left

] move right

Typographical Marks

/owercase character

/OWERCASE word

cap character

cap word

set in italic

replace a character or
   ~~characters~~

transpose (order) change

Punctuation and Symbols

comma ⋀

period ⊙

change comma to period ⊙

change period to comma ⋀

hyphen   =/

apostrophe   ᵛ⁄

inferior   ⋀

superior   ⋁

set in boldface

set in caps and small caps

Special Marks

retain hyphen, as in bell=
   like (used at ends of
   lines)

delete hy‿
   phen and close up
   (used at ends of lines)

spell out ringed matter
   (change 3 oz. to three
   ounces)

use figure, symbol, or
   abbreviation for ringed
   matter (change three
   ounces to 3 oz.)

end (or) 30 (or) # (end
   of copy)

•Z enumerate (list) using bullet

PRACTICE PROOFREADING

Read the following letter and use the standard proofreading marks to make changes, add missing items, and delete unnecessary information.

Your facility has received 9 quality deficiency reports to date. Of these 9 reports over 60 violations have been noted. 10 of these deficiencies
there have were issued since september 1987. Because some of the quality assurance procedures were not approved not submitted prior to production, as required by this contract this ofice finds you in non compliance with Quality Assurance procedures 1-02467.
Owing to the these excesive number quality deficiency reports, for repetative deficiencies, and evidence of of general deterioration in your program inspection, this office will institute method c to correct over sixty violations.

our investigating team willtake immediate action against your compnay and submit a report for evaluation and followup to assure implementation. You will have thirty days to correct the deficiencies according to method c. Failure to comply will result in loss of contracts. And awards to Houston TX and and Atalnta Georgia. If you have any questions please contact the undersigned or ROBERT HARMS at the above mentioned address

Sincerely

B>J> HArmony
Quality assurance representative

Notes

1. *The Chicago Manual of Style,* 13th edition (Chicago: The University of Chicago Press, 1982). This book provided the information for the section on documentation and citations.
2. *U.S. Government Printing Office Style Manual* (Washington, D.C.: U.S. Government Printing Office, 1984). This manual provided the sections on punctuation, compound words, capitalization, and numbers.
3. *Effective English Workshop* (U.S. Office of Personnel Management, Great Lakes Region: U.S. Government Printing Office, 1985). This booklet provided some of the information and exercises on grammar, punctuation, capitalization, and numbers.

Index

Index

539

Technical reports, 351–76. *See also* Research
  reports
Technicians, 12–13
Telephone memos, 427–29. *See also* Memos
Terminology, 72. *See also* Diction
  in instructions, 198–99
Testing, exercises in, 241
  thinking-aloud method, 228–29
  types of, 227–30
  usability, 220–25
  See also Evaluating documents
Text analysis programs, 108–9
The Chicago Manual of Style, 494
Tight timing, 472. *See also* Oral presentation
Timing, 472. *See also* Oral presentations
Title page, 296
Titles, first words, 526
  of documents, 525–26
  oral presentation, 474
  of preeminence, 525
  for reports, 297
  See also Capitalizing
Tone, exercise in, 435
  in letters, 389–90
Transmittal letter, 297–98. *See also* Letters
Transparencies, 478–79
Tree charts, 68–70. *See also* Charts; Design;
  Visual aids
Trip notes, 443–53
  anticipating information for, 446
  attachments for, 448–49
  brainstorming for, 444–45
  collecting samples for, 446
  examining sites for, 452–54
  examples of, 451–53
  front-end planning, 444
  for information, 449–50
  inspection forms for, 446
  organizational strategy for, 446–48
  participants in, 446–47
  purpose for, 447
  readable, 450
  reports of call, 448
  scope statement in, 447–48
  to solve problems, 449–51
  visuals aids for, 448–49
Troubleshooting, 189
Type size, 122

Typeface, 121
  sans serif, 121
  scrif, 121
Typography, 120
  exercise in, 151

Usability testing, 220. *See also* Evaluating
  documents
Usage, 506–11
User, advanced, 188
  novice, 185–88
  See also Audience
User friendly, 218

Validation methods, 229. *See also* Evaluating
  documents
Verb, action, 84
  in a sentence, 84
  See also Readability; Style
Visual aids, 55–56, 115–46. *See also*
  Illustration; Design
  audience, 115–16
  effectiveness, 126–28
  enlarging, 119
  exercises in, 152–53
  exploded view, 147
  hints for transparencies, 479
  letters, 411
  meeting notes, 460
  research reports, 367
  trip notes, 448–49
  oral presentations, 478–80
  readability, 117
Voice level for, 477

Warnings, 191–92. *See also* Instructions
White space, 124. *See also* Readability
Word processing, 217–19
Work statements, 59–60
Writer's Workbench, 109
Writing process, 11
  computer assisted, 37–38
  drafting the document, 37
  model of a, 5–6
Writing tasks, logs, 7, 9. *See also* Tasks

"You" scenario, in letters, 391
  reader in the, 17